# INTERNATIONAL FINANCE AND MONETARY POLICY

# International Finance and Monetary Policy

## Gleb P. Severov
### Editor

**Nova Science Publishers, Inc.**
*New York*

**Library of Congress Cataloging-in-Publication Data**

ISBN 1-60021-103-8

*Published by Nova Science Publishers, Inc.* ✢*New York*

# CONTENTS

**Preface**                                                                    **vii**

**Chapter 1**  Interest Groups and Monetary Policy Management                     **1**
             *Giovanni Di Bartolomeo*

**Chapter 2**  Global Divergence                                                 **29**
             *David-Mayer Foulkes*

**Chapter 3**  Learning to Live with the Float: Turkey's Experience 2001-2003    **61**
             *Faruk Selcuk and Oya Pinar Ardic*

**Chapter 4**  Managing External Volatility: Central Bank Options in Low-        **87**
             Income Countries
             *Stephen O'Connell, Christopher Adam, Edward Buffie and*
             *Catherine Pattillo*

**Chapter 5**  The Choice of Exchange Rate Regimes in Transition Economies:      **117**
             Evolution and Determination
             *Jizhong Zhou and Jürgen von Hagen*

**Chapter 6**  STAR-GARCH Models for Stock Market Interactions in the            **135**
             Pacific Basin Region, Japan and US
             *Giorgio Busetti and Matteo Manera*

**Chapter 7**  Nonlinear Tools for Analyzing and Forecasting Financial Time      **157**
             Series: An Application to US Interest Rates
             *Nicolas Wesner*

**Chapter 8**  The Macroeconomy and the Yield Curve: The Search for a            **187**
             Unified Approach
             *Zeno Rotondi*

**Chapter 9**  The Effect of Government Ownership on Bank Profitability and      **209**
             Risk: The Spanish Experiment
             *Ana Isabel Fernández, Ana Rosa Fonseca and Francisco*
             *González*

**Chapter 10**    Liquidity Consequences of Lockup Expirations                    **229**
                *Charles Cao, Laura Casares Field and Gordon Hanka*

**Index**                                                                         **261**

# PREFACE

International finance is the branch of economics that studies the dynamics of exchange rates, foreign investment, and how these affect international trade. In a globalizing world, the policies of various central banks and similar institutions impact large and small players alike. This new book presents new and important research on issues of interest in international finance and monetary policy.

Chapter 1 studies the efficacy of monetary policy management by considering society as the arena of the cooperative and non-cooperative interplay of different social groups, i.e. associations of people created to support particular interests. Our approach is clearly distant from the traditional one of the benevolent social planner or that of the representative agent. In our setup, government, worker associations, and monetary policy have preferences that mainly depend on those of the lobbies and groups supporting them. Hence policymakers' preferences may be or may be not in opposition and their interplay generally does not lead to a Pareto efficient outcome. In particular, our aim is to link the partisan approach with the macroeconomic theory of labor unions and to study their mutual effects on monetary policy. By using a simple setup, we are interested in comparing the efficacy of monetary policy under left and right wing governments and under different structures of the labor markets. Clearly we aim to show how much relevant social, economic and political differences are in explaining the monetary policy efficacy and that there is not a policy good for all seasons since efficacy of monetary policy strictly depends on the institutional context where it is managed.

In Chapter 2, the author shows that the evolution of cross-country incomes during the period 1960-1997 is characterized by global divergence. To do this, the sample of non-mainly-petroleum-exporting countries having market economies during this period is divided into five clusters of countries by a regression clustering algorithm according to the levels and rates of change of income and life expectancy. The five clusters correspond to advanced countries, especially fast growing countries, and three tiers of less developed countries with qualitatively different development paths. The following properties hold for these clusters. 1) Growth rates across groups of countries are globally divergent; some successive groups converge while most diverge. 2) Income inequality *between* these groups of countries has *increased* while income inequality *within* the groups has remained almost *unchanged*. 3) The five groups of countries exhibit $\beta$ and $\sigma$ income *divergence between groups* and *convergence within groups*. Besides, the implied steady state growth rates across groups of countries are globally divergent, the five-club convergence model is much more significant than the one-club model, and the *distributions* of country-specific convergence regression *coefficients* are significantly different across groups of countries. The convergence found within groups is consistent with the relative convergence (to steady state trajectories) found in the literature. However, relative convergence only means that there are a series of perhaps distinct, local equilibrium processes going on. Indeed, these may themselves be due to economic forces that *prevent* global convergence. The empirical facts are consistent only with theories of economic growth *explaining divergence and proposing multiple steady states* or other explanations for prolonged transitions Such models usually reflect advantages of the rich and disadvantages of the poor. A descriptive study of the five groups of countries suggests, as a stylized fact, that there are three large-scale steady states or convergence clubs, *semi-stagnation* (low income and life expectancy), *semi-development* (middle income and high life expectancy) and *development* (high income and life expectancy), according to whether countries have overcome barriers to human development and to technological innovation. Three of the five groups lie in each of these steady states and the other two transit between them.

The conduct of policy under floating exchange rates is becoming an increasingly important concern for developing countries. The challenge facing the central banks is to contain the volatility of the exchange rate while achieving low inflation and stimulating output growth. As a complement, the governments must implement sound policies to bring the fiscal and legal environments close to those of the advanced economies so as to enhance long-term economic growth. One recent example of an emerging economy that confronts this challenge is Turkey with a history of high inflation and a collapse of a fixed exchange rate based stabilization program that resulted in a marketforced devaluation. After a review of the literature, Chapter 3 analyzes the developments in the foreign exchange market in Turkey in light of the Central Bank's policies during the floating exchange rate system between February 2001 - November 2003. The results indicate that the Central Bank had been successful in containing volatility and reducing the average inflation rate. However, the accumulated risks in the economy, such as the extreme appreciation of the currency and high real interest rates make the system vulnerable to adverse shocks.

Low-income countries have participated in the worldwide move towards greater *de jure* flexibility of exchange rates since the late 1980s. In practice, however, the move to exchange rate flexibility has been fairly cautious, both by comparison with public pronouncements and by the standards of the more decisive legacy of the period, the abandonment of tight exchange controls and disequilibrium exchange rates. Our own interpretation of the African experience since the early 1990s places a heavier emphasis on the desire to reconcile low inflation with a competitive and stable real exchange rate. In Buffie *et al* (2004) we focused on the large increases in aid received by a number of African countries starting in the late 1990s. Using a calibrated general equilibrium model, we showed that a persistent surge in aid can produce distinctly unpleasant macroeconomic outcomes under floating exchange rates, given structural conditions typical of low-income economies. We showed that a strategy of substantial and non-sterilized foreign exchange intervention is warranted in this situation. Section 1 of the paper introduces the core model. In Section 2 we specify policy behavior, including the response of government spending to aid and the intervention and sterilization behavior of the central bank. In Section 3 we linearize the model and calibrate it to Uganda, Tanzania and Mozambique in the later 1990s. Section 4 contains a set of simulation results for an aid-only version of the model, and in Section 5 we expand the analysis to include commodity price shocks. Section 6 concludes.

In Chapter 5 we provide an empirical analysis for the evolution and determination of the choice of exchange rate regimes in 25 transition economies. We apply the IMF's new regime classification scheme backwards to classify exchange rate regimes in these countries during the 1990s. We estimate transition matrices to study the evolution of exchange rate regimes. We also run tests for various implications of the "hollowing-out" hypothesis, but do not find supporting evidences. We develop a multinomial logit model to analyze the choice of exchange rate regimes and estimate both static and dynamic version of the model. We find that past regime choices have strong influences on current choices. Both versions of the model provide some support for the relevance of the traditional OCA guidelines for the choice of exchange rate regimes. The variables related to macroeconomic stabilization and the risks of currency crises are also found playing some role in the determination of exchange rate regimes. There are evidences, however, that these influences may not be monotonic, since in some cases intermediate regimes are preferred to both fixed and flexible regimes.

In Chapter 6 we investigate the financial interactions between countries in the Pacific Basin region (Korea, Singapore, Malaysia, Hong Kong and Taiwan), Japan and US. The originality of the paper is the use of STAR-GARCH models, instead of standard correlation-cointegration techniques. For each country in the Pacific Basin region we find statistically adequate STAR-GARCH models for the series of stock market daily returns, using Nikkei225 and S&P500 as alternative threshold variables. We provide evidence for the leading role of Japan in the period 1988-1990 (pre-Japanese crisis years), whereas our results suggest that the Pacific Basin region countries are more closely linked with US during the period 1995-1999 (post-Japanese crisis years).

Chapter 7 aims to present qualitative and quantitative techniques which stem from the theory of deterministic chaos and to apply them to the study of US interest rates dynamics. The first part of the article provides theoretical backgrounds concerning the detection of nonlinear determinism in a time series and the use of this property for prediction. Methods for estimating the dimension of a time series, visual recurrence analysis, local prediction methods and surrogate data analysis are described. Then, those methods are applied to weekly variations of yields on US 3 month and 1 year Treasury bill and 5 year and 10 year Treasury bonds. Dimension estimation does not provide evidence in favour of low dimensional chaos but visual recurrence analysis permits us to detect several regime changes in the time series. In order to explore the possibility to exploit nonlinearities for prediction, out of sample forecasts from a local predictor are compared with those from a linear model. Finally surrogate data analysis is performed to assess the statistical significance of the results. In particular the method permits us to reject the hypotheses that nonlinear mean predictability is spurious and that it comes from linear dependencies.

Chapter 8 focuses on the recent literature - started by the seminal article of Ang and Piazzesi (2003) - aimed at developing macro-finance models that combine finance specifications of the term structure of interest rates with standard macroeconomic aggregate relationships for output and inflation. We review the alternative models proposed in this new literature and discuss their main features. An alternative analysis based on the theory of cointegrated vector autoregressive models is developed and tested with the data available for the US.

Chapter 9 analyzes the effects on Spanish savings banks' performance and risk when they shed their mutual structure to become government-owned banks. Such a situation arose in 1985 when Spain's central government allowed regional parliaments to modify savings bank ownership regulations. Regional regulations increased government participation at the expense of depositors' ownership. This regulatory change constitutes a natural experiment to study the consequences of government ownership on bank behavior. The results of our study suggest that enhanced government ownership leads to an increase in risk. This is particularly marked amongst those savings banks that most increased the weight of local and regional governments on their governance bodies. However, no variation in savings bank performance has occurred. The net result, therefore, is an increase in performance-adjusted risk.

A principal purpose of an IPO is to gain access to a liquid market. However, post-IPO liquidity may be impaired by the information asymmetry between outsiders and the firm's founders and early investors. Consequently most IPOs feature "lockups" that prohibit insider share sales for six months. In Chapter 10 we present the first detailed analysis of the liquidity consequences of lockups, by examining liquidity changes around the expirations of 1,497 IPO lockups in the period 1995-1999. We find substantial increases in market depth as measured by quote depth, average trade size, and number of trades. As predicted by asymmetric information models, we find a statistically significant increase in trading costs as measured by effective bid-ask spreads. However, this effect has small magnitude and dissipates within a week. We find no material increase in the asymmetric information component of the spread, nor do we find other expected signatures of information asymmetry. Overall, these data show that a large body of well informed, block-holding insider traders can enter a market from which they had previously been absent, and substantially change trading volume and share price, without reducing market depth or causing more than a small, temporary widening of bid-ask spreads. A practical implication is that market liquidity probably cannot be enhanced by strengthening the current legal restrictions on trading by insiders, even in young, growth firms with potentially high information asymmetry.

In: International Finance and Monetary Policy
Editor: Gleb P. Severov, pp. 1-27

ISBN: 1-60021-103-8
© 2006 Nova Science Publishers, Inc.

**Chapter 1**

# INTEREST GROUPS AND MONETARY POLICY MANAGEMENT

## *Giovanni Di Bartolomeo*[*]
Department of Media Studies, University of Teramo

## Abstract

This chapter studies the efficacy of monetary policy management by considering society as the arena of the cooperative and non-cooperative interplay of different social groups, i.e. associations of people created to support particular interests. Our approach is clearly distant from the traditional one of the benevolent social planner or that of the representative agent. In our setup, government, worker associations, and monetary policy have preferences that mainly depend on those of the lobbies and groups supporting them. Hence policymakers' preferences may be or may be not in opposition and their interplay generally does not lead to a Pareto efficient outcome. In particular, our aim is to link the partisan approach with the macroeconomic theory of labor unions and to study their mutual effects on monetary policy. By using a simple setup, we are interested in comparing the efficacy of monetary policy under left and right wing governments and under different structures of the labor markets. Clearly we aim to show how much relevant social, economic and political differences are in explaining the monetary policy efficacy and that there is not a policy good for all seasons since efficacy of monetary policy strictly depends on the institutional context where it is managed.

## 1   Introduction

The objective of this chapter is to investigate the mid-run effects of monetary policy management on employment and inflation in different context where monetary authorities may face different *kinds* of private or public agents. Our main sources of inspiration are two books published in the mid-eighties: "The Economy of Worldwide Stagflation" (written by Michael Bruno and Jeffrey Sachs) and "Economia Politica del Lavoro" (written by Ezio Tarantelli). In accordance with the former, we consider that the effects of monetary

---

[*] E-mail address: gdibartolomeo@unite.it

management cannot be properly understood without taking into account their interrelation with the supply side of the economy and its institutions. In line with the latter, we consider the economic system as complex and differentiated. Therefore, the need arises of making use of flexible tools—which also capture some social aspects of the society—to represent it.

After fifteen years from the studies of Bruno, Sachs, and Tarantelli, economic theory has gone, however, several steps further. In particular, after the Lucas rational expectation revolution it is clear that interrelations among agents have to always be taken into account when the policymaking process is investigated. Furthermore, empirical evidence has highlighted some specific regular empirical evidences and many theoretical models have been suggested to interpret it. In revisiting the approach proposed by the above-mentioned economists, the new state of the theory cannot be neglected.

1.  Empirical evidence emphasizes the active role played by the private sector, and its imperfections, in the accomplishment of monetary policy targets, where the private sector is far from that described by general equilibrium theory since it is mostly characterized by *imperfections*, like rigidities and economic agents endowed with monopolistic powers. Moreover, the traditional border on the Private and the Public Sector is vague as far as the *social planner* seems to be an ingenuous tool to represent a world where agents aggregate themselves in interest groups to promote their wants at all levels.

2.  On a methodological ground, several new analytical tools are now available to study economic interrelations between distinct agents. Game theory has provided a key to make the behavior of economic agents endogenous. By extending the traditional single agent optimization problem to a multi-agent context, policy games are able, in fact, to rationalize the behavior of public and private sectors according to some assumptions about the information distribution among economic agents and the way according to which they form conjectures about strategies of their *rivals*. In this sense, relationships or propositions among economic variables derived from this approach can be defined endogenous since they (explicitly) derive from the strategic interactions among economic agents.

By considering the above claims, our aim is to assume—along the lines of the political economy literature—policymakers in a broad sense which also includes *private policymakers*, who are assumed to set the values of crucial economic instruments as, for example, the wage rate, thus considering the economic process as the result of the interplay of different institutions. We will then focus on the interrelation among these and model monetary policy as the outcome of a game between monetary authorities and other institutional agents which represent different groups of interests. Of course, our aim is not to build a new theory of policymaking but simply to explore some relevant issues of monetary policy from a different point of view. In doing so we hope to be able to switch on a bit of new light on the explanation of some still debated issues.

In exploring the interaction among policymakers we consider their "interests" as parametrically given, and therefore, we will not investigate the political process from which these interests derive. The limitation is vast, but we are aware of the problem. The parametric assumption and the existence of several rival political bodies, however, allow us to consider a situation different from the orthodox social welfare approach, e.g. electoral competition between right and left wing parties, labor unions' political partisanship, and "clashes" between the central bank and the government.

We plan to extend and generalize the results of policy game literature on monetary policy seeking to put many disperse contributions into a common framework. We seek to build a simple general model where some aspects of recent economic debates on monetary policy management can be investigated from an endogenous point of view, in the sense that they can be read as outcomes of strategic interrelations among policymakers derived according to some initial assumptions.

We investigate the different effects of monetary policy management on economic performance by considering:

1. Governments' political ideologies.
2. Labor market institutions (union centralization, corporatism, union partisanship).

In our model some stylized facts can be derived from the policymakers' behavior. Then we can highlight the theoretical assumptions (on policymakers' preference and economic-structure features) which are compatible with the empirical results and with their policy implications. In such a sense, our study is deeply influenced by Tarantelli's pharmacist's approach to economic policy: each sick person (economy) is different, and therefore, each person needs different medical care (economic policy), a particular drug can be useful for one person but can even be dangerous for another.

The rest of the chapter is organized as follows. The next section describes the effects of political and union partisanship. Section 3 describes the industrialized industrial relation system in industrialized economies. Section 4 outlines a simple policy game that takes an account of the institution interplay on the monetary policy management. Section 3 closely examines and discusses the institutional setting structure. Section 4 solves the model. Section 5 analyses partisanship. Section 6 analyses corporatism. Section 7 analyses various hump-shaped relationships among variables related to the industrial relations. Section 8 studies the monetary policy management by highlighting an endogenous Phillips curve that depends on the parameters describing the exogenous labor market and political institutions. Section 9 provides concluding remarks.

## 2 Government and Political Partisanship

Between 1947 and 1992, the United States faced nine recessions (one every 5 years). In these 46 years the Republicans were in office for 10 more years than the Democrats, but there were two recessions in the 18 Democratic years, or one every 8 years, and seven in the 28 Republican years, or one every 4 years, on average (Kreech, 1995: 72-73).

One can argue that the Republicans focus on inflation when they take office because it is the most serious macro problem the country faced at that time, and for the same reason the Democrats concentrate on employment. But—as pointed out by Muller (1989: 292)—since the Republicans take over from the Democrats, and the Democrats from the Republicans, this observation hardly contradicts the hypothesis (the Republicans endogenously create extra-inflation whereas the Democrats extra-unemployment). A significant example is represented by the Reagan administration. Both unemployment (7.1%) and inflation (12.5%) were serious problem when Ronald Reagan took office. Inflation received the highest priority. After two years the inflation rate was cut by more than five percent, while unemployment had risen to the highest level in the postwar period (9.5%). The unemployment level was reduced only five years after the beginning of the Republicans' administration.

Good evidence exists that similar differences are present in other countries. Saint-Paul (1996), for example, underlines the strong link between policy objectives and government ideologies. He analyses 40 changes in European employment-protection legislation since 1960, classifying each one according to whether it was a step towards or away from more job protection and according to whether it affected all workers or just a specific group. Ideology, not surprisingly, plays a role: across-the-board reforms tend to happen under right-wing governments just as targeted increases in protection are associated with left-wing governments.[1]

The theoretical framework joining policy objectives with government ideologies is the partisan theory. Douglas Hibbs (1977) first formulated this theory in a very influential article published in 1977 and in a successful book published ten years later. Hibbs (1977) contrasted his partisan model to the political business cycle theory of Nordhaus (1975). Partisanship models in fact emphasize the nature of the choice between alternatives presented in majority-rule elections instead of a principal-agent problem between voters and elected public officials as in the electoral business cycle models. The partisan theory of macroeconomic policy is based on the idea that political parties weigh nominal and real economic performance differently. Left-wing governments are assumed to be more inclined than right-wing ones to pursue expansionary policies designed to yield lower unemployment and higher growth, but running the risk of extra inflation.[2]

The assumption of partisanship can be justified by the consequences of unemployment for income distribution. In periods of high (low) unemployment, low (high) growth and low (high) inflation the relative income of the upper-middle class increases (decreases). However, having different preferences is a necessary but not a sufficient condition for observing that political parties act differently when in office. In fact, in two-party elections, candidates may converge towards the center in order to win the election: even a partisan politician cannot implement his/her desired policies if he loses. A possible justification can be found in the uncertainty of electoral results. Parties trade off the potential gain in the probability of victory if they converge towards the center against the potential loss in their preference dimension if they move away from their preferred position. By contrast, Douglas Hibbs points out that the distribution of the voter preferences is not unimodal. Therefore, median voter theorem does not apply. We will not explore the question of policy convergence in a two-party system with partisan policymakers and will stick to the original formulation.[3]

Relationships among political parties, unions, and labor markets are also clearly strong. In most European countries, members of different unions can be found in the same

---

[1] Similar statistical relationships between policies and ideologies are found by Krischen (1974) and Hibbs (1977). Other studies are collected in Kreech (1995) for the United States and Alesina et al. (1997) for OECD countries. Furthermore, empirical evidence shows that political ideologies are also related to the labor market structure (Alvarez et al., 1991; Hibbs, 1992; Franzese, 1999; and Di Bartolomeo, 2001) and to the central bank (Chappel et al., 1993; and Oatley, 1999)—see below.

[2] See Hibbs (1992) for a review of the voluminous literature.

[3] For a discussion of these and other related issues, see Wittman (1983), Calavert (1985), and Alesina and Rosenthal (1995: Chapter 2).

establishment and, sometimes, labor unions compete among each other to raise their membership. In Belgium, France, Italy, and other countries rival unions are tied to different political parties. Furthermore, in the same countries, labor unions' leaders often become candidates in the elections and/or take important offices in the government or in other political institutions. For example, the former Dutch premier (Win Kock) was before leader of an important national labor union, as well as the former Italian Ministry of Finance Ottaviano Del Turco. In Italy, Sergio D'Antoni has recently attempted to create a new political party after leaving the CISL leadership.[4]

On a theoretical point of view, sociologists and political scholars traditionally consider labor unions' actions as inspired by three different ideologies from which three forms of unionism can be derived:

1. The business unionism.
2. The reformist unionism.
3. The Marxist unionism.

The fathers of the business unionism are Samuel Gompers and John Commons. The former is also the father of the *American Labor Federation*. In their view the union is the "technical" instrument by which workers and other "inferior" classes can exercise a constant pressure on the central power to achieve a larger participation in the social decisions, higher incomes, and more freedom and security for their members.

The union of Sidney and Beatrice Webb is a stable association of workers that has as its scope the achievement of better conditions for the workers. Thus the union's role is to contrast and correct the initial unfair distribution of the bargaining powers between the individual workers, on one side, and monopolistic firms, on the other (Adam Smith perceived the argument of the unfair distribution, already, in the 18th century). Several different schools form the reformist unionism: from the Fabian one to the German revisionist school. Notwithstanding diversities, a feature that reformist schools share is the idea of a gradual transformation of the actual society to a socialist system by a democratic process. This last feature is the main distinction between the reformist unionism and the Marxist one.

Karl Marx and Friedrich Engels were interested in union action mainly for its historical mission. The role of the Marxist unionism is mainly that of a political instrument in the contrast among social classes. The ultimate scope of unions has to be the workers' government of society. Nowadays it is probably difficult to define a labor union as Marxist. Even once extremist left-oriented unions as the Italian CGIL and the French CGT are since a long time closer to a Webbs's reformist position. The Marxist view is, however, important to understand our past (e.g. the French May and the Italian "Autunno Caldo") and a possible future when, e.g., the less developed countries are considered. Furthermore, notwithstanding the new international asset (after the crash of the communist system), the issue of the political conflict has not disappeared at all. European governments should not fail to note that politics of imposition was likely to run into massive social unrest that could wreck the reform efforts and the promised electoral fortune. Examples of "doomed" politics of imposition are those tried by Mr. Silvio Berlusconi and his center-right coalition in Italy in 1994, and later by

---

[4] The CISL (*Confederazione Italiana Sindacati dei Lavoratori*) is one of the three Italian largest national labor unions

President Jaques Chirac and Prime Minister Alain Juppé in France. Similar public failures were observed in Denmark for the reform of pension legislation and in Greece for the measures about flexibility in the labor market unilaterally instituted by the government.

Notwithstanding the remarkable differences, in all the definitions of unionism the importance of the political dimension of union's action is straightforward. Furthermore, each ideology shares with the others its aim, which is the modification of the income distribution, of the wealth, and of the social power distribution. These targets are pursed by following different strategies: reducing the competition among workers (business unionists), reforming the society and safeguarding the jobs (reformists), or modifying the social relations of the production (Marxists).

The ideology of the union plays a crucial role to understand the unions' influence on the economy. Furthermore, political issues are closely related to the other ones expressed by the structural and cooperative dimensions of the industrial relation centralization. Two examples follow.

First, business unionism tend to negotiate wages at the level of the single firm since this way can be the most suitable way to achieve "as much as possible" for each given individual worker. By contrast, Marxist unionism tends to be more centralized since its main aim is the conflict with the political system. Probably, the Marxist optimal level of wage bargaining is the industry level. In fact, here, (political) strike actions can be easily organized and supported. Finally, the reformist unionism should prefer to bargain wages at a centralized level trying to find an agreement not only with firms but also with the government to put the social reforms on the other scale of the balance. This argumentation is related to—and it can affect—the traditional interpretation of the Calmfors and Driffill's (1988) relationship.

Second, the ideology of unions also plays a crucial role in social cooperation issues. An agreement between the government (firms) and Marxist unions is unlikely to be observed whereas it is expected when a reformist union is considered. In the terms of Tarantelli (1986a) in the first case the political "residual" is not negotiable whereas it is in the second one. Furthermore, for a reformist union an agreement with a left-wing government is more likely to be achieved since both the reformist union and the left-wing government pursues similar reforms—in principle. An agreement between the government's representatives and the business unionists will be possible only for specific issues, and therefore, business unions probably prefer to base their relationship with the government more on informal channels (e.g. the lobbyist way) than on the formal ones (e.g. social pacts).

Relations and links between politics and labor unions can be very strong in some countries. Notwithstanding the evidence of the man in the street and empirical economists (see, among others, Alvarez *et. al.*, 1991; and Oatley, 1999), seminal contributions—based on aggregate or empirical models—were forgotten after the micro-foundation revolution and the emergence of a labor union theory based on methodological individualism.

Recent models developed by Detken and Gärtner (1994), Franzese (1999), and Di Bartolomeo (2001) have tried to fill this theoretical gap in economic theory by opening a new angle in the institutional analysis of labor markets. The unions' partisanship theory is linked to the idea that unions act as institutional agents, and therefore, they can support or not the government's action. According to this view left-wing governments have a political influence on labor unions. The underlying assumption is that the unions' members, or their leaders, can support a left wing government. This assumption is also sustained by a large amount of empirical literature, which finds that unionized workers or unskilled and low-income workers (who are good candidates to be union members) support left-wing parties.[5]

Outside a context of perfect information between union members and union leaders, the assumption that union leaders support left wing government is, however, a sufficient condition to consider the partisanship of unions. Furthermore, this context opens a new ground unexplored for agency problems. In fact, it is possible to assume that unions' leader are bureaucrats, which aim to enter in the political arena or long for achieving some personal advantages from politicians. Therefore, in a context of asymmetric information (where workers do not know how much the outcome of bargaining depends on the action of their delegates) a representation problem emerges: the preference function of unions represents not the workers' interest, but the private interest of unions' leaders. The problem becomes larger as the size of the representative union is enlarged since the interrelations between the unions' delegates and the firms' representatives during the negotiations become more difficult to be observed by the workers.

Unions can commit themselves to support (or adverse) a desired (undesired) government. On the other hand, an inverse causality, going from the government to unions, is also possible. Interests of left-wing governments could be more aligned with unions, and therefore, left-wing governments could be more responsive to the demands of unions than right-wing governments are. This causality is mainly due to the described possible political nature of the labor union and the close connection between its organization and that of the political parties. In fact, all largest European labor unions are associated with political parties and often share offices, personnel, and leaders with them.[6]

The relations between firms, lobbies and the government are also important. The links between politicians (in particular those of right-wing parties) and the (large) firms are also straightforward. The Italian Prime Minister Silvio Berlusconi represents a relevant example. Furthermore, recent scandals about corruption and hidden financial aid emerged in some European countries (e.g. France, Germany, and Italy) emphasize how large firms can support political parties. Finally, another important channel of relationship between governments and firms is determined by the role that multinationals can have in the political system. This issue is particularly, but not exclusively, relevant for less-developed countries.

## 3   Industrial Relations

The political relationships discussed above influence monetary policy since they affect the context where it takes place. In particular political relationships may affect the preferences of government and unions and, therefore, reactions of those policymakers to monetary policies. However, the power of governments and unions to react to the monetary authorities also depends on their constraints determined by the institutional context where the wages are set, i.e. the industrial relation system. Empirical studies show that different partisan alternatives lead, under different setting of the domestic economy, to a different performance. In particular, economic policies achieve a better performance in terms of growth, inflation, and unemployment in countries where there are strong and centralized unions and left-wing governments; whereas right-wing governments achieve a better result when labor movements

---

[5] See Hibbs (1992) and references in Muller (1998).
[6] See Ebbingaus and Visser (2000) for the European unions' orientation.

are weak. Economic performances are poor in countries where there is not the above consistency between winning parties and labor market structures (Alvarez *et al.*, 1991).

The most famous example of the effects of industrial relationship on the economic performance is, however, probably given by the Calmfors and Driffills (1988) relationship: a reverse humped-shaped relationship between the degree of centralization and indicators of macroeconomic performance. According to this relationship, the indicators of macroeconomic performance turn out to be higher at both the high and the low level of centralization of wage-negotiations. Moving towards intermediate levels—that is, towards negotiation taken at the industry level—macroeconomic indicators worsen. The empirical relationship and its theoretical foundations have been questioned from a long time.[7] Soskice (1990) probably gives the strong foundations to the relationship by arguing that it derives from two separate factors: coordination and unions' strength. These factors have a negative and a positive effect on the performance, respectively. These factors are generally, but not always, correlated with centralization.[8]

Cooperation is a crucial issue in industrial relations. The reasons of cooperation among unions at different levels and between unions and the other social partners are different. We will generally use the term social cooperation (and social pact) to refer to the cooperation among the social partners and coordination to refer to the cooperation within union, or firms, or policymakers. Coordination among unions is the answer to an externality. The type of externality that unions face is mainly related to a price or quantity competition, i.e. if unions are rivals in nominal wages determination or if they are rivals in employment determination. The prevalent externality is strongly related to the level at which the negotiation between employers and employees takes place. In fact, workers tend to associate, seeking to increase their bargaining power, and therefore, to balance the "unfair" competition against the employers. By contrast, "unions" tend to federate themselves to eliminate the negative externality that the wage claims produce over the prices, and therefore, over the real wages.

The relations between the level at which wage-negotiations take place and the externality associated with a non-coordinated setting of nominal wages are summarized as follows.

1.  Workers organize themselves into plant unions for increasing their bargaining power—by a larger and compact representation—against the employers. Therefore, the aim of plant unions is to overtake the negative externality associated with the one-to-one bargaining that leaves the single workers always in the worst position but that allowed the worker to follow a free-rider behavior (i.e. to offer its work at a lower wage). A necessary condition to observe plant unions is, therefore, a real anti-discrimination law between unionized and non-unionized workers.

---

[7] Recent contributions place the Calmfors and Driffill's relationship in an analytical context that is coherent with the microeconomic theory of labor unions and with its policy game extensions (e.g. Cukierman and Lippi, 1999). Results of this strand are not robust, since they hold only if unions are sufficiently inflation averse. Moreover, by introducing monopolistic competition in the good market, Coricelli *et al.* (2006) find a linear instead of a humped-shaped relationship. The relation has been also challenged by empirical studies that show its instability (see e.g. Fabiani *et al.*, 1997; OECD, 1997; or Appelbaum and Schettkat, 1996).

[8] This view of Calmfors and Driffill's relationship is in line with that proposed, among others, by Layard *et al.* (1991) and Bleaney (1996), who also provides some empirical evidence. On the one hand, economic literature has emphasized the role of the degree of the centralization of the wage-negotiation level; on the other hand, the same literature has emphasized that importance of centralization was also over estimated. Considering only the degree of the centralization of the wage-negotiation level can imply misleading results and conclusions (see, among others, Soskice, 1990; Bleneay, 1996; Oatley, 1999; Di Bartolomeo, 2001).

2. Plant unions associate themselves into firm unions for increasing their bargaining power against the employers by coordinating their strike action. Unions belonging to the same industry associate themselves for a reason similar to that of the workers. However, industry unions can have a national relevance since, in this case, strikes affect the whole economy. Therefore, industry unions can bargain over more aspects related to their sector (e.g. public investment and legislation concerning safety, working hours, and so on within the sector). Furthermore, another common reason that often explains the emergence of the unionism at the sector level is the large impact of industry level on the government associated with the possible political nature of unions (see below).

3. Industry unions organize themselves into federations to coordinate their actions with respect to the price externality associated with a decentralized wage negotiation and to become a social body able to affect the economic policy determination. Just as sector unions, the federations of unions can bargain more aspects than the mere wage, but their action is not limited to issues related to a specific economic sector. In fact unions can influence economic policy and general legislation by threats or agreements. Furthermore, since unions represent just a part of the citizens, their considerations about price externalities associated with wage bargaining are different from those of the society. This difference leaves a margin for a further "political exchange:" wage moderation exchanged with a chair in the determination of economic policies and legislation (see Tarantelli, 1986a).

In this paper we are mainly interested in the last form of cooperation, cooperation among social partners, since in our macroeconomic context and political economic perspective it the most relevant of the three. Examples of policy involving social partners and government are many. Recently, e.g., the Social Democrat/Green German government was able to revive the idea of an employment pact leading to a new national "Alliance for Jobs" that includes the formation of a tripartite body. Similar pacts and labor market policy reform agreements have also been reached at national and regional levels in countries such as Belgium, Ireland, Italy, and Portugal.

The Wassenaar agreement of 1982 in the Netherlands, with the government ostensibly present behind the scene threatening wage controls and other norms (Boeri *et al.*, 2001: 76), is a perfect example of government threats tending to facilitate social pacts. The pact has been signed in a period of particularly economic crisis of the Dutch system (see Ebbinghaus and Visser, 1997). Dutch government with the support of employers and unions has cut public spending as a share of GDP from 60% to 50%. Part of the money saved has been used to reduce employers' social-security contributions to only 7.9% from almost 20% in 1989 in order to help job-creation. With the same goal, the bottom rate of income tax was halved to 7% in 1994 while top marginal income-tax rates remained at 60%. In the labor market, the Dutch have tried to combine the flexibility of North America with the security of Germany. They have made part-time work easier by permitting part-timers to be paid less than full-timers for the same job. This has helped Dutch companies to adjust their work force to the demand for labor and has helped unemployed people to get back into work. At the same time, centralized wage bargaining has helped to build a consensus in favor of wage restraint. Dutch wages in manufacturing have been moderate compared to Germany and France, where bargaining occurs sector by sector.

On the other hand, the negative impact of a lack of consultation with social partner organizations was arguably demonstrated when a number of national-level policy reforms ran into trouble. In Denmark, for example, there was significant disagreement over the reform of pension legislation, which had been drawn up prior to consultation. Similarly, in Greece unilateral decisions about labor market flexibility measures instituted by the government caused significant unrest in the industrial relations sphere.[9]

Policies, involving government and social partners, are often referred as "corporatist policies" and the systems where they are made "corporatist systems". Corporatism however is also used as synonymous of cooperation among unions. More in general, corporatism is an ambiguous concept, which has been defined in a variety of ways. Therefore, its meaning in this writing needs to be clarified.

A frequently quoted definition by political scientists is that of Katzenstein (1985). This author defines corporatism as a form of social partnership between the government and centralized interest groups, which voluntary and informally coordinate conflicting objectives. This definition is consistent with Olson's (1982) theories on encompassing organization. Olson (1982) argues that encompassing organizations have some incentives to make the society in which they operate more prosperous, and an incentive to redistribute income to their members with as little excess burden as possible, and to cease such redistribution unless the amount redistributed is substantial to the social cost of the redistribution.

Katzenstein's (1985) definition is closer to that used by several authors in economic investigations. Burda (1997) defines corporatism as measures, which improve upon non-cooperative interactions between union and government. Among others, Bruno and Sachs (1985) define corporatism as an institutional arrangement that involve negotiation, bargaining, collaboration and accord between major economic groupings in the society and especially between unions and governments. Many other economist identify consensus as an element of corporatism,[10] but often also different definition are proposed. For example, among others, Newell and Symons (1987) and Glyn and Rowthorn (1988) suggest that a distinctive feature of corporatism is real wage restraint to keep high the employment level. Alogoskoulfis and Manning (1988) and Layard et al. (1991) also discuss this wage restraint argument. Cubitt (1995) gives a multi-dimensional definition of corporatism that attempts to generalize those presented above in a game theoretical context.[11]

Henceforth, in order to eliminate any ambiguity, we will refer to corporatism by considering it as form of cooperation where at least the public sector and unions are involved.[12] The nature of the agreement can be different. Government can play the role of a

---

[9] See Rhodes (2001) for further evidence.

[10] See Di Bartolomeo (2001) and his references.

[11] According to this author corporatism is formed by several elements. Assuming that unions care about inflation and that the employment target of the unions is lower that that of the government, Cubitt (1995: 248-249) measures corporatism by using four dimensions. These dimensions can be defined as follows. i) CORP1 rises when the weight attached by the unions to inflation rises. ii) CORP2 rises when the representative union's employment target rises. iii) CORP3 rises when the difference between the employment target of the labor unions and that of the government falls. iv) CORP4 rises when the policymaker and the unions set the demand and wage policies in a cooperative manner.

[12] The definition is not straightforward. For instance, when labor unions moderate their wage claims because they consider inflation a public good, we say that unions coordinate their wage policy to prevent increases in the price level. By contrast, when unions moderate their action because of an explicit agreement with the

*super partes* authority to avoid the free riding problem or unions can sign a "contract" with the government with whom they exchange the wage moderation with "something" related to the workers' satisfaction, e.g. a "good" pension reform.[13]

## 4 The Basic Model

After having discussed informally the partisanship and the main features of industrial relation systems, we built a simple model that formally describes the most important effects of these concepts on monetary policy management. We assume that four agents (central bank, government, unions, and firms) operate in a closed economy. The central bank sets nominal money supply. Firms maximize profit. The central bank influences the aggregate demand by monetary policy. Nominal wages are set by the interaction between monopoly unions and the government.[14] Firms determine employment by the labor demand constraint.[15]

Preference functions of central bank, government and unions are the following:

$$V = \frac{1}{2} E_{-1} \left[ -\beta \left( \pi - \pi_B \right)^2 - \left( y - y_B \right)^2 \right] \tag{1}$$

$$G = \frac{1}{2} E_{-1} \left[ -\gamma \left( \pi - \pi_G \right)^2 - \left( y - y_G \right)^2 \right] \tag{2}$$

$$U = E_{-1} \left[ \alpha \left( w - p \right) - \frac{1}{2} \left( y - y_U \right)^2 \right] \tag{3}$$

where $E_{-1}$ is the expectation operator (i.e. the pre-shocks expectation); $\pi$ is the inflation rate, defined as $(p - p_{-1})$; $y$ is the real output (employment) level; $\pi_B$ and $\pi_G$ are the inflation rates desired by the central bank and by the government; $(w - p)$ represents the real wage (equal to the nominal wage less the price level); $y_B$, $y_U$ and $y_G$ are the central bank's, unions' and government's desired real output levels.

In the literature $\beta$ is often called the central bank's degree of conservativeness, which can be considered a central bank's independence index (Cukierman and Lippi, 1999). Parameter

---

government, we say that unions cooperate in setting the wage to prevent increases in the price level and we refer to this situation as a corporatist one.

[13] Both the free riding and the political exchange issues are described in Tarantelli (1986a, and 1986b).

[14] The government participates to nominal wage determination in many ways. There are specific tools that the government can use to affect the outcome of collective bargaining, e.g. compulsory mediation of labor market disputes, public employment or taxation. In addition, it may control the bargaining power of labor unions by making easy or hard unions' formation. See Blanchard and Giavazzi (2003) and Palokangas (2003). On the importance of including the government in wage negotiation, see also Bruno and Sachs (1985), Calmfors and Driffill (1988), and Pekkarinen *et al.* (1992).

[15] The introduction of *right to manage* assumption complicates the algebra of the model but do not substantially alter its results. By contrast, the relevant assumption is the possibility that the government influence nominal wages because this assumption implies the non-neutrality of monetary policy. See Acocella and Di Bartolomeo (2004) for a full discussion.

$\alpha$ is an index of the distortion of labor market as it measures the importance of the wage premium for the unions, which mainly depends on the reservation wage (therefore, e.g., from the unemployment benefits).

The economy is synthesized in equations [4] and [5].[16]

$$p = w + \frac{y}{\eta} + \varepsilon \qquad\qquad [4]$$

$$y = m - p + v \qquad\qquad [5]$$

Equation [4] represents the aggregate supply with real wage elasticity equal to $\eta$; $\varepsilon \sim iid\ (0, \sigma_\varepsilon)$ is a production shock. Equation [5] represents the aggregate demand where the real money supply elasticity is equal to one; $v \sim iid\ (0, \sigma_v)$ is a demand white noise term (i.e. the velocity shock).

Notice that since there is an inverse relationship between the real wage and output equation [3] implies that the desired expected output target for the union is:

$$E_{-1}(y) = y_U - \frac{\alpha}{\eta} \qquad\qquad [6]$$

Equation [6] is obtained by simply maximizing equation [3] subject to the labor demand constraint [4]. We will refer to equation [6] as the (expected) output desired by the unions.[17]

## 5  Institutional Settings

We assume that government and unions bargain the nominal wage.[18] The bargaining process is usually complex. Nevertheless, its results can be easily circumvented by assuming that the two players maximize a common utility function, which is a linear convex combination of the logarithms of their respective utility functions.[19] We have, however, chosen this specification to generalize the results of Detken and Gärtner (1994), Gylfason and Lindbeck (1994), Cubitt (1995), and Acocella and Ciccarone (1997), which can be easily derived as particular case of a bargaining procedure used by us (see, e.g., Sections 6 and 7, and below).

We assume the weight associated with the unions in the bargaining equals its economic power, determined by the labor market forces, discounted by some factors that take account of political and social relationships between unions and the government.

The union power in wage-bargaining varies across countries and time. It depends on historical, social and cultural factors that are reflected in the economic conditions under

---

[16] The economic structure is taken from Cubitt (1995).

[17] See Acocella and Di Bartolomeo (2004) and (2006).

[18] A next task of our research is to formalize the wage bargaining between the government and unions by introducing taxation.

[19] Notice, however, that the described *bargaining technology* does not strictly represent a Nash bargaining solution. See Acocella *et al.* (2003b) for a discussion.

which unions operate. We capture it by an exogenous parameter $\sigma$. According to Naylor and Raaum (1993) and Corneo (1997) unions' bargaining power can be seen as an increasing function of the membership. Therefore, a possible economic interpretation of $\sigma$ is to consider it as an element of wages-bargaining centralization, and refer to it as "degree of unionization." We follow this interpretation.

As said, the degree of unionization is discounted by the political influence of political system on unions' behavior ($\Phi$), and the degree of corporatism ($\Sigma$). Hence, formally the government's bargaining power, $\delta$, can be expressed as.

$$\delta = 1 - (1 - \Sigma)(1 - \Phi)\sigma \qquad [7]$$

The reader should note that we use different discount factors (unless their effects on the model are the same) because they capture different aspects of the bargain process and, therefore, imply different consequences.[20] More in detail, $\Sigma$ and $\Phi$ can be interpreted as follows.

Parameter $\Sigma$ represents the *degree of corporatism*. It is an index of cooperation in line with Cubitt's CORP1-3 definitions (see Cubitt, 1995: 249). Remark that, according to Tarantelli (1986b) and Soskice (1990), we are implicitly assuming that corporatism has a monotonic effect on government's performance. In spite of that, in Section 9 we will show how hump-shaped curves in Calmfors and Driffill's style can also be derived.

Parameter $\Phi$ represents the political influence of the government on unions, which is, according to Detken and Gärtner (1994), linked to the *ideological animus* of the unions. The implicit assumption is that the unions' members, or their leaders, are left-wing party supporters. When a right-wing party wins the election, we set the political influence parameter equal to zero. Hence we restrict our attention on positive partisanship. Detken and Gärtner (1994) also investigate the possibility of negative $\Phi$, when a right-wing party wins the election.

## 6   Game Solution

The monetary authority plays at the same time as the wage are negotiated. Preference function of the central bank [1] is maximized with respect to the nominal money supply subject to the reduced form of the model [4] and [5]. Corresponding central bank's optimal wage-contingent policy rule is:

$$m = -\frac{\beta - \eta}{\beta + \eta^2}\eta w + \frac{1 + \eta}{\beta + \eta^2}(\eta y_B + \beta p_B) \qquad [8]$$

---

[20] In order to avoid confusion, it should be noted that, in this paper, the discount factors are not inter-temporal discounts, but static discounts, i.e. *x-discount* indicates the reduction (increase) in unions' (government's) bargaining power according to *x-reason*.

The bargaining between unions and the government is expressed by a maximization of a linear convex combination of the logarithms of the preference functions of the government and unions subject to the reduced form of the model [4] and [5]:[21]

$$\max_{w} E_{-1}\left\{\delta \ln\left[-\frac{\gamma}{2}(\pi-\pi_G)^2 -\frac{1}{2}(y-y_G)^2\right]+(1-\delta)\ln\left[\alpha(w-p)-\frac{1}{2}(y-y_U)^2\right]\right\} \quad [9]$$

From the above expression, the nominal wage contingent to $m$ can be obtained as:

$$w = \frac{\eta-\delta\gamma}{1+\delta\gamma}\frac{m}{\eta} - \frac{1+\eta}{1+\delta\gamma}\left[\delta(y_G-\gamma p_G)+(1-\delta)(y_U-\alpha\eta^{-1})\right] \quad [10]$$

By solving the two-equation system [9] and [10], we obtain the controls equilibrium values:

$$w^N = (\eta-\delta\gamma)\frac{y_B+\beta\eta^{-1}p_B}{\beta+\delta\eta\gamma} - (\beta+\eta^2)\frac{\delta(y_G-\gamma p_G)+(1-\delta)(y_U-\alpha\eta^{-1})}{\eta(\beta+\delta\eta\gamma)} \quad [11]$$

$$m^N = (\delta\gamma-\eta)\frac{y_B+\beta\eta^{-1}p_B}{\beta+\delta\eta\gamma} - (\beta+\eta^2)\frac{\delta(y_G-\gamma p_G)+(1-\delta)(y_U-\alpha\eta^{-1})}{\eta(\beta+\delta\eta\gamma)} \quad [12]$$

Finally, we derive the equilibrium values for output and inflation by substituting equations [11] and [12] in the reduced form.

$$y^N = \frac{\delta\eta\gamma y_B+\beta\left[\delta y_G+(1-\delta)(y_U-\alpha\eta^{-1})\right]}{\beta+\delta\eta\gamma} + \frac{\beta\delta\gamma(\pi_B-\pi_G)}{\beta+\delta\eta\gamma} + \frac{\eta(v-\varepsilon)}{1+\eta} \quad [13]$$

$$\pi^N = \frac{\beta\pi_B+\delta\eta\gamma\pi_G}{\beta+\delta\eta\gamma} + \frac{y_B-\left[\delta y_G+(1-\delta)(y_U-\alpha\eta^{-1})\right]}{\beta+\delta\eta\gamma} + \frac{v+\eta\varepsilon}{1+\eta} \quad [14]$$

The Nash equilibrium employment [13] is equal to the sum of three terms. The first term is the weighted average between the two macro-players' output targets, where the weights are the players' inflation-aversions (notice that the government's aversion is always discounted by its bargaining power). The second term is the central bank and government's desired

---

[21] The two players determine nominal wage that is a common control variable. Possible losses in the bargain (e.g., caused by the duration of workers' strikes) are implicitly discounted in the bargaining power index.

inflation difference multiplied by a factor, which is a measure of the players' inflation aversions. The third term is a linear combination of the demand and supply shocks.

Similarly, equilibrium inflation is also equal to the sum of three terms: the weighted average between the desired inflation levels, the difference between the optimal output levels multiplied by an inflation-aversion factor and a linear combination of the shocks. The more the players are inflation-averse, the less relevant in inflation determination the second term of equation [14] is.[22]

The meaning of the results is clear. When government is introduced in a unions-central bank game, unions are no longer able to impose their optimal output level as it occurs in the Barro-Gordon standard games.[23] Therefore, the equilibrium output depends on all the players bargaining powers and desired targets. Monetary policy is no longer neutral since increases in the inflation aversion reduce the inflation bias but also affect the employment as well as change in the monetary authority or government targets. We will closely analyze the economic sense of our results in the following sections.

# 7  Partisanship and Economic Performance

This section introduces the Alesina-Hibbs' partisanship hypothesis, which implies that government's political orientation may be different according to the nature of the political party in office. Political parties can have a right- or left-wing attitude in the sense we are going to specify.

We introduce the following assumptions:

(a) Right- and left-wing parties have different opportunity costs of low inflation in terms of employment. We assume that a left-wing government is more averse to the utility losses caused by unemployment. We suppose that a right-wing government is more averse to the utility losses caused by an inflation rise. See Hibbs (1977).

(b) The central bank is more averse to the utility losses caused by inflation than the government (right- or left-wing).

(c) The bliss points of the central bank and of the government (right- or left-wing) are full employment and zero inflation; unions care about real wage and desire full employment.[24]

(d) Corporatism (or political exchange) is not considered. This implies $\Sigma = 0$. We will remove this assumption in the next Section.

(e) Shocks are not considered and the output elasticity of the real wage is set equal to one. These assumptions are only introduced for the sake of exposition. The reader should only note that the assumption $\eta = 1$ guarantees that we are always considering a stable solution, without this assumption the equilibrium could be unstable (see Di Bartolomeo and Pauwels, 2006).

---

[22] Notice that without unions ($\delta = 1$) the game collapses in a traditional coordination problem between the central bank and government (see Andersen and Schneider, 1985). By contrast, when the unions are really monopolists ($\delta = 0$), the game is the same presented by Acocella and Ciccarone (1997). As said, our framework nests different models.

[23] See Acocella and Di Bartolomeo (2004) and Acocella et al. (2003a) for a full discussion.

[24] We introduce these assumptions only as exposition devices.

Given the above assumptions, the preference functions of the central bank and right-(left-) wing government only diverge for their marginal substitution rate between inflation and unemployment. From assumptions (a) and (b) we obtain that the central bank is more inflation-averse than the right-wing government, and that the right-wing government is more inflation-averse than the left-wing government. Therefore, the inequalities $\beta > \gamma^R > \gamma^L$ hold (superscripts identify right and left governments).

Equations [13] and [14] becomes:

$$y^{NN} = \overline{y} - \left( \frac{\beta(1-\delta)}{\beta + \delta\gamma^i} \right) \frac{\alpha}{2}, \; i \in \{R,L\} \qquad [15]$$

$$\pi^{NN} = \left( \frac{1-\delta}{\beta + \delta\gamma^i} \right) \frac{\alpha}{2}, \; i \in \{R,L\} \qquad [16]$$

where $\overline{y}$ is the full employment output. Equations [15] and [16] now describe output and inflation under two political alternatives.

First, notice that, when a non-partisan monopolist union is assumed (i.e. the government has not any bargaining power), we obtain the standard result of policy neutrality that is already largely discussed and considered in Gylfason and Lindbeck (1994) and Acocella and Ciccarone (1997). Furthermore, when a non-partisan monopoly union is assumed the Rogoff's standard proposition holds (i.e. the higher the central bank's conservativeness is, the lower the inflation rate is). However, when, in line with Detken and Gärtner (1994), rational-partisan monopolist unions are assumed (i.e. $\sigma = 1$, but $\Phi \neq 0$), monetary policy is no longer neutral since $\delta \neq 0$.

Second, if unions are not monopolists, neutrality vanishes. In general terms (i.e. without specifying the government nature), if the government's bargaining power *ceteris paribus* increases, employment arises and inflation decreases. The positive effect on employment occurs because the government's optimal level is higher than that of unions, since the government does not take account of the real wages. Therefore, the lower the unions bargaining power is, the higher employment is. The positive effect on inflation occurs because the higher the employment level that government-unions follows, the lower the inflation bias is. This is because the inflation bias is the cost that unions impose on the central bank's willingness to reach full employment by an inflationary policy. Then, the more the economy nears full employment, the lower the central bank's willingness to inflate the real wage becomes. The same holds when government's inflation-aversion rises. A rise in the unions' preference for the real wage has the negative effect on inflation and employment. Furthermore, the Rogoff's proposition holds in the following terms: the higher the central bank's conservativeness is, the lower (higher) inflation (output) is.

The above results are summarized in Table 1, which can be easily derived by differentiation of equations [15] and [16].

Table 1 also reports the effects of parameter changes in terms of performance in the following sense. In comparative static analysis, when the effects of preference parameters are clear and opposite in inflation and output determination, we can generally speak of performance (or social performance) meaning any social loss function that decreases in unemployment and inflation (see Cubitt, 1995: 249-50). According to the above view, e.g., we can state that, *ceteris paribus*, the higher the government's inflation-aversion is, the higher the performance is. By contrast, the effects of increases of the degree of conservativeness cannot be analyzed in terms of the social performance above described without specifying it since higher levels of central bank's inflation-aversion imply lower inflation but lower employment

Table 1 – Summary of the parameters effects

| | inflation | unemployment | performance |
|---|---|---|---|
| degree of conservativeness ($\beta$) | − | + | ? |
| degree of unionization ($\sigma$) | + | + | − |
| Labor market rigidities ($\alpha$) | + | + | − |
| Corporatism ($\Sigma$) | − | − | + |
| Partisanship ($\Omega$) for a left-wing government only | − | − | + |
| government's bargaining power ($\delta$) | − | − | + |
| government's inflation-aversion degree ($\gamma$) | − | − | + |

When government's nature is introduced, by comparing both [15] and [16] for $i \in \{R, L\}$ (i.e. $y^L - y^R > 0$ and $\pi^L - \pi^R < 0$) it is easy to check that the best (worst) performance of a left- (right-) wing governments is driven, in both cases, by the following condition (crossing condition, henceforth):[25]

$$\sigma > \frac{\left(\gamma^R - \gamma^L\right) - \Phi\left(\beta + \gamma^R\right)}{\left(1 - \Phi\right)\left(\gamma^R - \gamma^L\right)} \qquad [17]$$

Since the condition is the same for the best (worst) performance in terms of both employment and inflation, we can again talk of social performance.

The crossing condition synthesizes two different forces.

i) The left-wing government tends to achieve a better performance since its bargaining power is always higher than that of a right-wing government because of the unions' partisanship. This effect depends on the existence of a positive bargaining power difference between left- and right-wing governments (i.e. $\delta^L - \delta^R > 0$). We refer to this effect as left-wing effect (LWE, henceforth).

ii) The right-wing government tends to achieve a better performance since its inflation-aversion is higher than that of the left-wing government. Thus this effect depends on the existence of a positive inflation-aversions difference between right- and left-wing governments (i.e. $\gamma^R - \gamma^L > 0$). We refer to this effect as right-wing effect (RWE, henceforth).

---

[25] We derive the condition of the best (worst) performance for a left- (right-) wing government just for an expositional reason. It is clear that is exactly equivalent to derive the best (worst) performance condition for a right- (left-) wing government by inverting the above inequality.

The RWE and LWE are not symmetric. The LWE is decreasing in the bargaining power of the union since the governments' bargaining powers difference is a constant fraction of the unions' bargaining power. By contrast, the RWE is unaffected by changes in the degree of centralization. Hence the crossing condition will be more likely to be satisfied when the unions' bargaining power is high.

We can draw a generic performance curve by considering different degree of unionization for both left- and right-wing governments. Both curves are decreasing in the degree of unionization, but they are associated with different shapes. The right-wing government's performance curve tends to be steeper than that of the left-wing government. Moreover, the higher is the inflation-aversion difference, the higher is the right-wing initial performance. The higher is the unions' partisanship, the higher is the left-wing final performance.

In graphical terms, the above sentence is represented in Figure 1(a) where the $LL$ and $RR$ curves represent the performance curves of left-wing and right-wing governments, respectively. Curves are convex because as the degree of unionization decreases, the central bank's preference (zero inflation and full employment) becomes more important than the joint preference of unions and government. However, curves can be also linear or concave depending on the unknown function of welfare, but for any welfare function equation [17] holds with equality in point B. On the left of point B, the right-wing performance is higher than that of the left-wing government; and on the right of B, the contrary occurs.

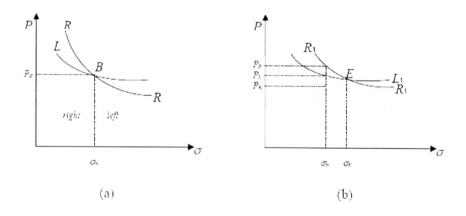

Figure 1 – Government performance curves $(P, \sigma)$

In other words, left-wing governments achieve a better economic performance than those of right-wing governments in countries where large workers' associations are present. Right-wing governments obtain better results than those of left-wing governments in countries with weak unions. Notice that performance curves are not defined in $\delta = 1$ (see footnote 24).

# 8    Corporatism

Let us insert corporatism into our model by removing assumption (d). We show the effect of corporatism on crossing condition in Figure 1(b) and 2.

In Figure 1(b), an increase in the degree of corporatism shifts the performance curves of both parties upward, respectively, leading the crossing condition far from the y-axis.

The performance curve of the left-wing government shifts from $LL$ to $L_1L_1$ while the right-wing one moves from $RR$ to $R_1R_1$. Hence, point E represents the new crossing point where the degree of unionization is higher than that at the initial point B.

The crossing condition then becomes:

$$\sigma > \frac{\left(\gamma^R - \gamma^L\right) - \Phi\left(\beta + \gamma^R\right)}{\left(1 - \Phi\right)\left(1 - \Sigma\right)\left(\gamma^R - \gamma^L\right)} \qquad [18]$$

Now equation [18] is, for a left-wing government, more restrictive than euqation [17]. Therefore, in a corporatist system, a left-wing government needs a higher degree of unionization to achieve a better economic performance than in a non-corporatist one. This occurs because a rise in the degree of corporatism has the same effect of as a reduction in the degree of unionization.[26] Therefore, it is positive for both left and right governments, but the government with a preference function closer to that of the central bank (which is the right government by assumption) tends to gain more.

Figure 2 shows the relationship between corporatism and government's performance. An increase in the degree of corporatism allows, *ceteris paribus*, the government (right or left) to achieve a better performance. However, a right-wing government gains more than a left-wing government. The right-wing government's performance curve (DA) has a stepper slope than that of left-wing government (CB) for the reasons discussed above.

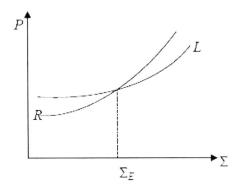

Figure 2 – Government performance curves $(P, \Sigma)$

Notice again that the right-wing government's performance curve could cross the performance curve of the left-wing party outside of the domain of $\Sigma$. If the curves cross for a value of $\Sigma$ greater than one, a right-wing government could never achieve a better economic performance than a left-wing government, but our propositions still hold.

---

[26] Because it affects the differential between right-left wing governments' power markets, i.e. $(\delta^R - \delta^L)$, and not the differential between right-left wing governments' anti-inflationary preferences, i.e. $(\gamma^R - \gamma^L)$.

The results of this section show that corporatism is crucial in the interpretation of economic performance. However, it is not correct to reckon that the government can fine-tune performance by varying the degree of corporatism for the following reasons.

1.  No precise account of the determination of the corporatism has been given here. There is no suggestion that the degree of corporatism is a policy variable under the control of the government.
2.  In addition, if we suppose that the government can influence the degree of corporatism by law, this policy will be strongly opposed by a non-government party, or by the same government when it allows the opposition-party to achieve a possible future better performance.
3.  Like most policy games, our investigation is based on a static model. It contains no account of disequilibrium dynamics that might be important in the short-run analysis.

Our aim only is, however, to underline the complexity of the institutional analysis and the relevance of considering their interplay. The lack of the account for the institutional interaction may, in fact, leads to misunderstand the economic determinants of the performance as we will show in the next Section.

## 9   Hump-Shaped Relationships

Our results can be interpreted in various ways. In the previous section, we implicitly interpret them as a prediction of difference in performance of a given country under different governments and/or labor market structures. Results can be also seen as a prediction of difference in countries in which the degree of corporatism, unionization, partisanship and the *color* of the government changes exogenously. In this context of multi-country comparison, a left-wing government is just a government supported by a partisan union, whereas a right-wing government is one with a high degree of inflation-aversion. In Figure 3, we draw two hump-shaped relationships derived from our model.

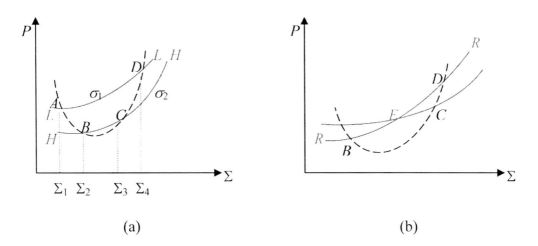

(a)                                                      (b)

Figure 3 – Reverse hump-shaped relationships

Figure 3(a) underlines the difference in the unions' bargaining power by analyzing the influence of institutional setting on corporatism. *LL* is the performance curve associated with a low degree of unionization ($\sigma_1$) and *HH* is the performance curve associated with a high degree of unionization ($\sigma_2$).[27] Therefore, points A, B, C, and D represent an example of different combinations between the degrees of corporatism and of unionization on economic performance.

A high corporatist system (point D) can achieve a better performance than low less unionized corporatist systems can (point B and C). In addition, a weakly unionized and corporatist system (point A) may obtain better economic performance than more corporatist and unionized systems (point B and C).

In Figure 3(a), different degrees of unionization allow a hump-shaped relationship between corporatism and economic performance. Observe, however, that Calmfors and Driffill (1988) consider centralization instead of corporatism. The centralization of wage bargaining does not necessarily imply cooperation. Nevertheless, the adoption of a high employment target and/or the consideration of inflationary consequences of their action by the representatives of organized labor are sometimes seen as implications of centralization (see Cubitt, 1995). Therefore, using the definition of corporatism adopted in this paper,[28] we can consider point A as a system with weak uncoordinated unions (fully decentralized). Point B represents a system with strong uncoordinated unions (medium centralized); and point c represents a system of strong coordinated unions (centralized).

Figure 3(a) is close to the view of Calmfors and Driffill's curve proposed by Soskice (1990) and supported, among others, by Layard *et al.* (1991) and Bleaney (1996). Soskice (1990) argues that the Calmfors and Driffill's hump-shaped relationship may derive from two separate factors: coordination and unions' strength, with negative and positive effect on performance, respectively. These factors are generally, but not always, correlated with centralization.

Figure 3(b) represents an alternative interpretation of Calmfors and Driffill's relationship based on the relationship between political parties and unions. High corporatist systems (as, e.g., those represented in points D and C) achieve better economic results than low corporatist ones (as, e.g., in point B). However, low corporatist systems (as, e.g., in point A) can also achieve better economic results than more corporatist ones (as, e.g., in point B).

This result may hold if two conditions are met: i) in the low corporatist system the government is a left-wing government and in the high corporatist system the government is a right-wing government; ii) in the high corporatist system, the positive effect of corporatism does not compensate for the positive that left-wing government has on unions in the low corporatist system.[29] However, a higher degree of corporatism always allows the government to achieve a better economic performance. The analysis of Figure 3(b) is not in contrast to the interpretation of Figure 3(a), but is an extension of that traditional interpretation. Consideration of also Figure 3(b) makes compatible the theoretical interpretation with the OECD's (1997) study that point out the instability of the Calmfors and Driffill's relationship.

---

[27] The reader should note that here we are considering two performance curves without introducing assumptions about the government's political side.

[28] Recall that here corporatism can be see as a measure of how much unions take into account full employment and low inflation (Cubitt's CORP 1-3 definitions).

[29] It is obvious that if the unionization degree is high, this situation is possible. This occurs because the political influence is expressed in terms of the bargaining power of the unions.

Several empirical studies underline the hump-shaped relationship instability, i.e. the shape of the relationship between unemployment (and other macroeconomic performance indicators) and the degree of centralization has not always been confirmed in the empirical studies. This instability of the Calmfors and Driffill's hump-shaped relationship (and, more in general, of relationships between the industrial relations and the economic performance) is well known since a long time (see, among others, Tarantelli 1986b; Bean, 1994; Appelbaum and Schettkat, 1996; and OECD, 1997).

Fabiani *et al.* (1997) underline the role of the nature of shocks. They argue that this instability of the relationship may derive from the interaction between the bargaining structure and the nature of the shocks experienced by an economy. A centralized structure may be better suited to offset aggregate and undifferentiated shocks, while a more decentralized one may more promptly respond to structural and micro-based shocks. In this case, the empirical estimates may lead to robust results only if appropriate variables controlling for the nature of the shocks are introduced. Bean (1994) and Blanchard and Wolfers (2000) also argue that the role that shocks play in determinate the economic performance is important, but both also argue that the differences in the domestic institution are the key to understand the differences in the performance.

By combining the analyses of the above sections, we can obtain an unstable hump-shaped relationship without considering asymmetric shocks.[30] The instability is driven by the instability of the political parameters, which are subject to higher degrees of volatility than the labor market parameters.

Other linear (as that proposed among other by Tarantelli, 1986b) or hump-shaped relationships can be easily derived. According to Tarantelli (1986b) and Calmfors (1993) several facets of a bargaining system may not easily be synthesized by a single index meant to measure the degree of centralization. Our model, in its own simplicity, shows how the effects of the bargaining system on aggregate wage formation and macroeconomic performance are more complex than originally acknowledged. The factors that influence economic performance are many and interrelated. Different political environments, labor market structures, degree of cooperation, and social preference contribute to achieve a better or worse economic performance.

## 10 Monetary Policy management: The Phillips Curve

A Phillips relationship can be directly derived from equations [15] and [16]:[31]

$$u = -\frac{\delta\gamma b(1-\delta)}{(1-\delta)+\upsilon_2}\pi + \frac{\alpha(1-\delta)}{b} + \upsilon_1 \qquad [19]$$

---

[30] It is also possible to consider the impact of the shocks structure on the hump-shaped relationship since shocks are included in the model. In this paper we prefer to focus on the deterministic differences in the institutional set-up for reason of conciseness leaving to future developments the analysis of the shock structure effects.

[31] In particular, equation [19] is derived by solving equations [15] and [16] for $\beta$, equalizing, and solving for the unemployment.

Equation [19] represents unemployment rates consistent with any rate of inflation. In other words equation [19] is the constraint that the central bank faces in minimizing its preferences when it manages monetary policy. Equation [19] can be also interpreted a sort of NAIRU, if the inflation/output adjustment is described by best response dynamics (see, e.g., Sargent 2000; or Di Bartolomeo and Pauwels, 2006).

Equation [19] implies an endogenous Phillips curve that depends on social and political parameters. Our Phillips curve is endogenous in the following sense. Inflation is determined by the central bank's preferences according to its inflation aversion (by equation [16]) and the output consistent with inflation rate is then obtained by equation [19]. In such a way, both inflation and output are endogenously determined by taking account of the public/private agent interplay, hence, our Phillips curve is unaffected by the Lucas kind critique.

As said Phillips curve shape depends on social, economic, and political parameters. Different curves are represented in the following figure. In line with our previous discussion, panel (a) shows that corporatist countries are consistent with better performance of monetary policy since their Phillips curve are closer to the origin. Panel (b) shows how better (worsen) performance of tight monetary policy under right- (left-) wing government.

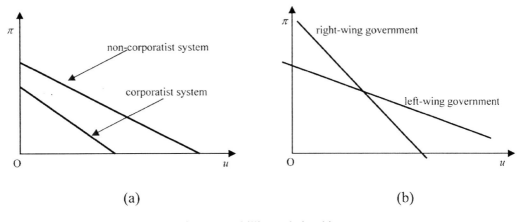

(a)                                                         (b)

Figure 4 – Phillips' relationships

The shape of the Phillips curve has an important implication on the relative cost of policy management. In high inflation times, costs of disinflation (in terms of unemployment variation) are clearly higher in non-corporatist countries. By contrast, in high unemployment time, costs of expansionary policy are lower in such countries.

In a similar way, in periods of high inflation (unemployment), the costs of disinflation (expansionary policy) are lower (higher) under right-wing governments rather than left-wing ones. This observation supports an inverse causality for the political business cycle; by assuming partisan political parties, political business cycle can be explained not on the basis of parties' preferences but on the basis of their effects on the monetary policy efficiency. Since tight monetary policy implies a lower cost under right-wing government, in period of high inflation is rational for the electors to vote for the right-wing government, while in period of recession it is rational to vote for left-wing government.

# 11 Conclusions

We have exhibited how monetary policy can be associated with different performances according to the nature of the government in office. In large unionized economies, monetary authorities can lead to better economic performance under a left-wing government rather than a right-wing one, and vice versa in weakly unionized countries. The result is in line with recent empirical studies.

Two different forces drive different performances of different political parties in office: the LWE and RWE. The former supports a left-wing government's performance through unions' partisan action. The latter supports a right-wing government's performance under the assumption that its aversion to inflation is larger than that of the left-wing government. Both these effects are strictly dependent on the degree of unionization, the corporatist level of the economy, and the central bank's degree of conservativeness. We have identified and studied the condition that permits the left-wing government to achieve a better (or worse) performance than that of the right-wing government.

By analyzing the effects of the degree of corporatism and partisan preferences, we have achieved an innovative conclusion. The right-wing government's economic performance improves when the degree of corporatism increases. The more workers perceive low inflation as a public good, the higher are the chances for a right-wing government to obtain better performance than that of a left-wing government. This occurs because an increase in the degree of corporatism reduces the LWE, but it does not affect the RWE. The increase of the degree of corporatism supports the right government under the condition that the preferences of the right government are the closest to those of the central bank.

Finally, after having described the traditional Calmfors and Driffill's hump-shaped relationship in our context, we have found an alternative interpretation of the empiric hump-shaped relationship by using the Alesina-Hibbs' assumption of partisanship. In our model, a low corporatist system can achieve a better economic performance than a more corporatist one, when two conditions apply. First, either in low corporatist systems the government is a left-wing one or in high corporatist system the government is a right-wing one. Second, in the high corporatist systems the positive effect of corporatism does not compensate the positive effect for the left-wing government of political influence (that the left party has on unions) in the low corporatist system.

Our finding opens an interesting new angle in the analysis of the Calmfors and Driffill's hump-shaped relationship and the analysis of labor market performance. However, it should be also noted that our interpretation is based on players' different preferences. Hence, it is an alternative to the traditional interpretation proposed in the literature, but – as we have shown – it is not incompatible with this. More in general, we have shown how it is possible to derive an empirical hump-shaped performance curve à la Calmfors and Driffill in various ways.

Our aim has been to build a simple model, consistent with several empirical findings, to underline the complexity of the relationship between the economic performance and the institution interplay effects on it. We can conclude by asserting that the factors that influence the economic performance through industrial relations are many and interrelated. The interactions among political variables, labor market structures, degrees of cooperation, and social preferences soundly contribute to explain the economic performance. Therefore, any analysis, which takes them into account only partially, might lead to misunderstand the economic result determinants by ignoring part of the complex interrelations among the above concepts.

# References

Acocella N. and Ciccarone G. (1997), "Trade Unions, Nonneutrality and Stagflation", *Public Choice* **91**: 161-198.

Acocella, N. and Di Bartolomeo G. (2004), "Non-Neutrality of Monetary Policy in Policy Games," *European Journal of Political Economy* **20**: 695-707.

Acocella, N. and Di Bartolomeo G. (2006), "Tinbergen and Theil Meet Nash: Controllability in Policy Games," *Economics Letters*, **90**: 213-18.

Acocella N., Di Bartolomeo G., Hibbs D.A. (2003a), "Labor Market Regimes and Monetary Policy", Public Economics Department, University of Rome *La Sapienza*, *Working Paper* No. 58. *Journal of Macroeconomics* (forthcoming).

Acocella N., Di Bartolomeo G., Pauwels W. (2003b), "Does the Public Good Nature of Economy Stabilization Support Corporatist Policy?", Public Economics Department, University of Rome *La Sapienza*, mimeo.

Alesina A., Cohen G.D. and Roubini N. (1997), *Political Cycles and Macroeconomy*, MIT Press, Cambridge.

Alesina A. and Rosenthal H. (1993), *Partisan Politics, Divided Government and the Economy*, Cambridge University Press, Cambridge.

Alogoskoulfis G.S. and Manning A. (1988), "Wage Setting and Unemployment Persistence in Europe, Japan and the USA", *European Economic Review*, **32**: 698-706.

Alvarez M.R., Garrett G. and Lange P. (1991), "Government Partisanship, Labour Organization and Macroeconomic Performance", *American Political Science Review* **85**: 539-556.

Andersen T.N. and Schneider F. (1985), "Coordination of Fiscal and Monetary Policy under Different Institutional Arrangements", *European Journal of Political Economy* **2**: 169-191.

Appelbaum E. and Schettkat R. (1996), "The Importance of Wage-Bargaining Institutions for Employment Performance" in *International Handbook of Labour Market Policy and Evaluation* edited by Schmid G., J. O'Reilly and K. Schömann, Edward Edgar, Cheltenham: 791-810.

Bean C.R. (1994), "European Unemployment: A Retrospective", *European Economic Review* **38**: 523-534.

Blanchard O. and Wolfers J. (2000), "The Role of Shocks and Institutions in the Rise of European Unemployment: The Aggregate Evidence", *The Economic Journal* **110**: C1-C33.

Blanchard, O. and Giavazzi F. (2003), "The Macroeconomic Effects of Regulation and Deregulation in Goods and Labor Markets", *Quarterly Journal of Economics*, 118-3: 879-909.

Bleaney M. (1996), "Central Bank Independence, Wage-Bargaining Structure, and Macroeconomic Performance in OECD Countries", *Oxford Economic Papers* **48**: 20-38.

Boeri T., Brugiavini A., and Calmfors L. (2001), eds., *The Role of Unions in the Twenty-First Century*, Oxford University Press, Oxford

Bruno M. and Sachs J.D. (1985), *The Economic of World-wide Stagflation*, Basil Blackwell, Oxford.

Burda M.C. (1997), "Whither Corporatism? Corporatism, Labor Union and the Safety Net", *European Economic Review* **41**: 653-646.

Calavert R. (1985), "Robustness of the Multidimensional Voting Model: Candidates' Motivations, Uncertainty, and Convergence", *American Journal of Political Science* **29**: 69-95.

Calmfors L. (1993), "Centralisation of Wage Bargaining and Macroeconomic Performance. A Survey", *OECD Economic Studies* **21**: 161-191.

Calmfors L. and Driffill J. (1988), "Bargaining Structure, Corporatism and Macroeconomic Performance", *Economic Policy* **6**: 14-61.

Calmfors L., Booth A., Burda M., Checchi D., Naylor R. and Visser J. (2001), "The Future of Collective Bargaining in Europe", in The Role of Unions in the Twenty-First Century edited by Boeri T., Brugiavini A. and Calmfors L., Oxford University Press, Oxford.

Chappel H.W. Jr., Havrilesky T.M. and MacGregor R.R. (1993), "Partisan Monetary Policies: Presidential Influence through the Power of Appointment", *Quarterly Journal of Economics* **108**: 185-219.

Corneo G. (1997), "The Theory of the Open Shop Trade Union Reconsidered", *Labour Economics* **4**: 71-84.

Cubitt R.P. (1995), "Corporatism, Monetary Policy and Macroeconomic Performance: a Simple Game Theoretic Analysis", *Scandinavian Journal of Economics* **97**: 245-259.

Cukierman A. and Lippi F. (1999), "Central Bank Independence, Centralization of Wage Bargaining, Inflation and Unemployment", *European Economic Review* **43**: 1395-1434.

Coricelli, F., Cukierman A., and Dalmazzo A. (2006), "Monetary institutions, monopolistic competition, unionized labor markets and economic performance", *Scandinavian Journal of Economics*, **108**: 39-63.

Detken C. and Gärtner M. (1994), "Governments, Trade Unions and the Macroeconomy: an expository analysis of the Political Business Cycle", *Public Choice* **73**: 37-53.

Di Bartolomeo G. (2001), "Corporatism, partisanship and economic performance", Faculty of Applied Economics UFSIA-RUCA, University of Antwerp, *Working Paper* No. **4.**

Di Bartolomeo G. and Pauwels W. (2006), "Is the Conservative Central Banker's Proposition Unbounded?," *Public Choice*, **126**: 275-296.

Ebbinghaus B. and Visser J. (1997), *A Dutch Miracle*, Amsterdam University Press, Amsterdam.

Ebbinghaus B. and Visser J. (2000), *Trade Unions in Western Europe since 1945*, Macmillan, London.

Fabiani S., Locarno A., Oneto G.P. and Sestito P. (1997), "NAIRU: Income Policy and Inflation", Economic Department, OECD Paris, *Working Paper* No. **187**.

Gylfason T. and Lindbeck A. (1994), "The Interaction of Monetary Policy and Wages", *Public Choice* **79**: 33-46.

Glyn A. and Rowthorn R.E. (1988), "West European Unemployment: Corporatism and Structural Change", *American Economic Review* **78**: 194-199.

Hibbs D.A. (1977), "Political Parties and Macroeconomic Policy", *American Political Science Review* **71**: 1467-1487.

Hibbs, D.A. (1992), "Partisan Theory after Fifteen Years", *European Journal of Political Economy* **8**: 361-373.

Katzenstein P.J. (1985), *Small States in World Markets, Industrial Policy in Europe*, Cornell University Press, Ithaca.

Kreech W.R. (1995), *Economic Politics*, Cambridge University Press, Cambridge.

Layard R., Nickell S. and Jackman R. (1991), *Unemployment*, Oxford, Oxford University Press.

Mueller, D.C. (1989), *Public Choice II*, Cambridge University Press, Cambridge.

Naylor R. and Raaum O. (1993), "The Open Shop Union, Wages and Management Opposition", *Oxford Economic Papers* **45**: 589-604.

Newell A. and Symons J.S.V. (1987), "Corporatism, Laissez-Faire and the Rise in Unemployment", *European Economic Review* **31**: 567-601.

Nordhaus W.D. (1975), "The Political Business Cycle", *Review of Economic Studies* **42**: 169-190.

Oateley T. (1999), "Central Bank Independence and Inflation: Corporatism, Partisanship, and Alternative Indices of Central Bank Independence", *Public Choice* **98**: 399-313.

OECD (1997), "Economic Performance and Structure of Collective Bargaining", *Employment Outlook*, OECD, Paris: 63-92.

Olson, M. (1982), *The Rise and Decline of Nations: Economic Growth, Stagflation, and Economic Rigidities*, Yale University Press, New Haven.

Palokangas T. (2003), "The Political Economy of Collective Bargaining," *Labour Economics*, **10**: 253-264.

Pekkarinen J., Pojhola M., and Rowthorn R.E. (1992), *Social Corporatism: A Superior Economic System*, Clarendon Press, Oxford.

Soskice D. (1990), "Wage Determination: The Changing Rule of Institutions in Advanced Economized Economies", *Oxford Review of Economic Policy* **6**: 36–61.

Rhodes M. (2001), "The Political Economy of Social Pacts: 'Competitive Corporatism' and European Welfare Reform" in *The New Politics of the Welfare State* edited by Pierson P., Oxford University Press, Oxford: 165-194.

Tarantelli E. (1986a), Economia Politica del Lavoro, Utet, Turin.

Tarantelli E. (1986b), "The Regulation of Inflation and Unemployment" in *Industrial Relations* 25: 1-15. Reprinted in *Economic Models of Trade Union* edited by Garonna P., Mori P. and Tedeschi P., 1996, Chapman&Hall, London: 305–318.

Traxler F. and Kittel B. (2000), "The Bargaining System and Performance: A Comparison of 18 OECD countries", *Comparative Political Studies*, **33**: 1154-1190.

Wittman D. (1983), "Candidate Motivation: a Synthesis of Alternatives", *American Political Science Review* **77**: 142-157.

Visser J. (1998), "Two Cheers for Corporatism, One for Market: Industrial Relations, Wage Moderation and Job Growth in the Netherlands", *British Journal of Industrial Relations* **36**: 269-292.

In: International Finance and Monetary Policy
Editor: Gleb P. Severov, pp. 29-59

*Chapter 2*

# GLOBAL DIVERGENCE[†]

## *David Mayer-Foulkes*
Centro de Investigación y Docencia Económicas[‡]
Mexico

## Abstract

I show that the evolution of cross-country incomes during the period 1960-1997 is characterized by global divergence. To do this, the sample of non-mainly-petroleum-exporting countries having market economies during this period is divided into five clusters of countries by a regression clustering algorithm according to the levels and rates of change of income and life expectancy. The five clusters correspond to advanced countries, especially fast growing countries, and three tiers of less developed countries with qualitatively different development paths. The following properties hold for these clusters. 1) Growth rates across groups of countries are globally divergent; some successive groups converge while most diverge. 2) Income inequality *between* these groups of countries has *increased* while income inequality *within* the groups has remained almost *unchanged*. 3) The five groups of countries exhibit β and σ income *divergence between groups* and *convergence within groups*. Besides, the implied steady state growth rates across groups of countries are globally divergent, the five-club convergence model is much more significant than the one-club model, and the *distributions* of country-specific convergence regression *coefficients* are significantly different across groups of countries. The convergence found within groups is consistent with the relative convergence (to steady state trajectories) found in the literature. However, relative convergence only means that there are a series of perhaps distinct, local equilibrium processes going on. Indeed, these may themselves be due to economic forces that *prevent* global convergence. The empirical facts are consistent only with theories of economic growth *explaining divergence and proposing multiple steady states* or other explanations for prolonged transitions Such models usually reflect advantages of the rich and disadvantages of the poor. A descriptive study of the five groups of countries suggests, as a stylized fact, that there are three large-scale steady states or convergence clubs, *semi-stagnation* (low income and life expectancy), *semi-development* (middle income and high life expectancy) and *development* (high income and life expectancy), according to whether countries have

---

[†] This paper was awarded Silver Medal for Research on Development in Growth, Inequality and Poverty category at Global Development Network Conference, Cairo, 2003.

[‡] División de Economía, Carretera México-Toluca 3655, Lomas de Santa Fé, 01210, México D.F., México. Telephone: (52) 5727-9800, Fax: (52) 5727-9878, e-mail:. david.mayer@cide.edu.

overcome barriers to human development and to technological innovation. Three of the five groups lie in each of these steady states and the other two transit between them.

# Introduction

The discussion of convergence has occupied a prominent place in the study of economic growth across countries for over a decade. The finding of a significant, negative "convergence coefficient" has been one of the most robust in cross-country growth regressions (Barro, 1991, 1997; Barro and Sala-i-Martin, 1991, 1992a, see Levine and Renelt, 1992, for a comparative sensitivity analysis covering many studies). Evans (1995) confirms convergence in a large group of medium- to high-income countries, at least to parallel growth paths. However, empirical studies have also found evidence for divergence in the data. Cross-country per capita income differences widened dramatically during the twentieth century (Pritchett, 1997). Quah's (1993, 1996, 1997) finding of an emerging twin-peaked cross-country income distribution can be interpreted as a continuation of this divergence. Mayer-Foulkes (2003) finds evidence for convergence-clubs in life expectancy dynamics over the period 1962-1997, with three groups of countries; those remaining in a lower peak, those changing to the higher peak, and those in the higher peak throughout. Other anomalies of "convergence" are the following. First, the presence of especially fast-growing countries, either at higher levels of income, like Singapore, Hong Kong and Korea, or at lower levels of income, like Botswana. Second, continent-wide growth slow-downs since the 80's, in the case of Latin America, which slowed from an average of 2.5% to –0.5%, and Sub-Saharan Africa, which slowed from 1.5% to –0.8%. These phenomena add to the already complex panorama of convergence and divergence. I show in this paper that these diverse empirical facts can be reconciled by examining convergence clusters of countries. I define a convergence clustering as a subdivision of countries into groups or clusters showing convergence within groups; a partial empirical counterpart of the concept of convergence clubs.[1] Using a specially defined clustering algorithm, I find a subdivision of countries which is simultaneously an income and a life expectancy convergence clustering. Between these groups, a series of tests show that there is global divergence, while within the groups there is convergence. As I show below, the presence of these convergence clusters serves as a qualitative test for the theories explaining economic growth, showing that these can only account for the empirical facts if they involve *multiple steady states and explain divergence.*

Up to the middle of the twentieth century, economic growth was viewed fundamentally as a process of capital accumulation, or industrialization (Harrod, 1939; Domar, 1946). This point of view has shifted, giving technological change a more prominent role. First, the recognition of decreasing returns to capital implied that technological change plays a fundamental role in the long run (Solow, 1956; Swan, 1956). Capital accumulation was now conceptualized as playing a transitional role encompassing at least part of the process of development, and its decreasing returns supported and came to be the focus of the convergence hypothesis. Capital flows between developed and underdeveloped countries,

---

[1] I take the position that showing the existence of convergence clubs includes determining the economic phenomena originating them, in correspondence with the theory. Also, the clusters represent significantly different trajectories, but not necessary different steady states, for example in the case of NIC's versus developed countries.

however, were inconsistent with the theory. This led to including human capital as an essential component of growth, both as an input complementary with physical capital and as knowledge. Knowledge could lead to endogenous growth, originated as an externality of capital accumulation, or through the purposeful application of human capital (Arrow, 1962; Uzawa, 1965; Frankel, 1962; Romer 1986; Lucas, 1988; Romer, 1990). Using an augmented Solow model, Mankiw, Romer and Weyl (1992) argued that just including the role of human capital as an input could account for an important proportion of cross-country income variation. However, evidence for the importance of productivity differences across countries has accumulated (Knight, Loayza and Villanueva, 1993; Islam, 1995; Caselli, Esquivel and Lefort, 1996; Klenow and Rodriguez Clare, 1997; Hall and Jones, 1999; Easterly and Levine, 2000). Martin and Mitra (2001) show that total factor productivity in both agriculture and manufacturing grew more rapidly in developed than in less developed countries during the period 1967-1992. Parente and Prescott (2000) show by simulation that barriers to increasing total factor productivity may result in amplified differences in income. Dollar and Wolff (1994) argue that technological convergence rather than factor accumulation was behind the catch up of the OECD countries to the U.S. Feyrer (2000) finds that although the distribution of output per capita is single-peaked, and the distribution of human capital is almost flat, the distribution of the productivity residual is increasingly twin-peaked, calling for a technological explanation of cross-country income disparities and dynamics. From the theoretical point of view, the Schumpeterian (1934) conceptualization of growth through purposeful innovation and creative destruction has been modeled by Aghion and Howitt, (1992, 1998), who distinguish clearly between knowledge and human capital inputs and describe the basic dynamics of technological change, conceptualized now as a driving force complementary to capital accumulation. Howitt's (2000) multi-country model shows that convergence and growth could be driven by the diffusion and spillover of ideas. Thus the changing theoretical perspective means that convergence is now viewed as a process that might result not only from decreasing returns to capital accumulation, but also from technological catch-up and other processes. The strong convergence that was found to hold for some specific cases, such as the U.S. states, European regions or the Japanese prefectures (Barro and Sala-i-Martin, 1995), may result from technological, institutional and other types of convergence as well as from capital accumulation.

Besides these central theoretical and empirical developments, the practical difficulties of development and economic growth, and the evidence for income divergence across countries, as well as inequality within countries, has motivated a series of models explaining these phenomena in terms of multiple steady states in income dynamics that might lead to convergence clubs, an idea originated by Baumol (1986). These are based on multiple equilibria in physical capital accumulation (such as Becker, Murphy and Tamura, 1990; Galor and Weil, 1996; Becker and Barro, 1989; Murphy, Shleifer and Vishny, 1989) and in human capital accumulation (such as Azariadis and Drazen, 1990; Benabou, 1996; Durlauf, 1993, 1996; Galor and Zeira, 1993; Galor and Tsiddon, 1997; Tsiddon, 1992). Other phenomena that may lead to persistent income differences or multiple equilibria in development have also been discussed. These include threshold externalities (Azariadis and Drazen, 1990), and the effects of nutrition and health on persistent educational inequality (Galor and Mayer-Foulkes, 2002). More recently, taking the viewpoint of endogenous technological change, Howitt and Mayer-Foulkes (2005) note that R&D is limited to just a few countries, and extend the Schumpeterian approach to include both innovation and technology implementation. They show that convergence clubs of countries carrying out innovation, or trapped in implementation or stagnation, can exist in which productivity levels can be quite different and may be influenced by a series of country-specific productivity and policy parameters. They thus give a technological explanation for the large-scale divergence of incomes that occurred through the 20th century, as well as for the convergence of middle- and high-income countries in the second half of that century. These multiple steady state dynamics also suggest explanations for the growth anomalies mentioned above. Discussing another low technology trap Acemoglu, Aghion and Zilibotti (2002) show that political economy traps can exist in which large industrial conglomerates preclude reforms promoting the selection of entrepreneurial ability that would advance strong, innovation-based growth.

Kremer, Onatski and Stock (2001) propose a modification to steady state theory in which there is a low but permanent probability of moving from a low, otherwise steady state to a high steady state, in a prolonged transition. In theories of multiple steady states, transitions between states can arise from the disappearance of an attractor. Multiple steady states are often also meant to be suggestive of barriers giving rise to long transitions. Thus, for the purpose of this paper I regard Kremer, Onatski and Stock's (2001) model of prolonged transition as one explanation (finding appropriate policies) of how such transitions may arise.

The wide panorama presented by the theory of economic growth means that different countries or groups of countries are likely to be undergoing quite different processes whose dynamical features correspond to different economic phenomena. These may include processes of physical and human capital accumulation, or technological and institutional change, perhaps affected by geography (e.g. Bloom and Sachs, 1998; Sachs and Warner, 1997; Krugman, 1991a, 1991b, 1994) or policy choice (Kremer, Onatski and Stock, 2001), that may be confronting different problems at different stages or levels of development. In spite of this wide theoretical panorama, empirical cross-country studies are usually designed to confront only a *single* theory, describing a single economic phenomenon, with the empirical facts. Here instead I test a wide class of theories by asking whether the empirical facts, including the robust convergence coefficient, correspond to a single or to multiple convergence clubs. The conclusion favors multiple convergence clubs, something that has strong implications for both theory and policy.

Before proceeding with the discussion it is necessary to distinguish between *conditional* and *relative* convergence, which are different concepts in the context of multiple steady states. Galor (1996) defines conditional convergence to mean that countries with the same characteristics converge to the same growth path. According to this definition, if countries with identical parameters find themselves in different steady states, as in multiple steady state models, then conditional convergence does not hold. However, this distinction is not made by studies deducing conditional convergence from a negative convergence coefficient, (e.g. Barro 1991, 1997, Barro and Sala-i-Martin, 1991, 1992a). Instead, what is assumed is what I shall call relative convergence, that each country tends to its own steady state path (which may be of a certain type thus belonging to a club) and that growth slows when income increases towards the steady state levels. Two countries with identical parameters tending to different steady states would exhibit relative convergence (with a negative convergence coefficient) but not conditional convergence. A panel study with country-specific effects (e.g. Islam, 1995) includes information on the steady state type in these effects, as well as country-specific parameters. An essential implication of multiple steady states is that, under certain conditions, relatively small differences in endowments, or the application of specific policies, can result in important differences in economic performance. Countries on one side of the divide will diverge from countries on the other side.

According to the definition above, cross-country studies usually test for *relative* convergence. It is usually assumed that each country's economic trajectory tends towards some steady state trajectory. Then it is assumed, without discussion, that there is a single type of steady state or convergence club. Instead, I assume that there may be several convergence clubs. Consider a set of theories in which each country is following some dynamical system toward some type of steady state or, alternatively, a theory in which each country lies in different basins of attraction of one grand system. In such a situation the typical convergence study will find relative convergence. This *only* means that there *are* a series of *perhaps distinct* equilibrium processes going on. Indeed, it may be precisely these local equilibria that *prevent* global convergence. I subdivide a wide sample of countries into five groups that meet the criteria for convergence clusters, that is, there is convergence within groups. These also exhibit global divergence.

For these five groups of countries, *between* group income inequality has increased while *within* group income inequality has remained almost unchanged. Also, there is mean and variance divergence of income *between* groups and convergence *within* groups. In the case of life expectancy, for which global convergence can be expected, since it is closely bounded above, the result is that there is convergence within groups and convergence between groups except for Group 5 (the poorest), whose life expectancy improved much less than convergence would imply throughout the period, and stagnated in the 1990's.[2] Inequality of life expectancy between and within groups decreased until the 1980's, but then increased again in the 1990's. Thus, the divergence of income across groups of countries is confirmed in one test after another. Except for the fast-growing countries, it is found that richer groups of countries have higher average and steady-state growth rates. Besides, in several different tests, the hypothesis of a single convergence club is *rejected* when contrasted with the hypothesis of five convergence clusters, for both income and life expectancy. Each of the five clusters is found to differ significantly from the others in at least one respect: steady state levels, steady state growth and convergence coefficients, or the distribution of country-specific effects. The results can be interpreted as a qualitative test for a wide class of theories, by asking how many convergence clubs these support, and whether they explain divergence.

The empirical evidence thus supports theories involving multiple convergence clubs, rather than a single club. As reviewed above, the multiple steady state theories that have been advocated theoretically often result from advantages of the rich over the poor, as individuals, as classes of people or as countries, originating in production, education, technology, institutions or market failures.[3] To be consistent with the facts, theories must explain global divergence as well as the presence of multiple steady states or prolonged transitions.

A descriptive study of the five groups of countries suggests, consistently with Ranis, Stewart and Ramírez (2000), that there are three large-scale steady states, according to whether countries have overcome barriers to human development, as indicated by life expectancy, and to technological innovation (as indicated by high levels of income). *Developed* countries in Group 1 have overcome both barriers. *Semi-developed* countries in

---

[2] Wars and Aids in Africa are amongst the causes.

[3] These advantages often result from or are induced by nonconvavities in the models. There are a few cases in which multiple steady states may be argued to arise from phenomena not directly related to these types of advantages. These include multiple equilibria due to expectations and to political and economic institutions.

Group 3 have overcome only the human development barrier. *Semi-stagnant* countries in Group 5 have overcome none. Group 2 was in transit from semi-development to development, and Group 4 from semi-stagnation to semi-development.

The remainder of the paper is organized as follows. First, we summarize an antecedent study in life expectancy convergence clubs to explain why the clustering is defined in *five* groups. Next, the clustering algorithm is described. Then descriptive statistics are given for the five groups of countries. These are followed by a battery of tests on divergence and convergence. The first three tests do not depend on convergence regression models. The next tests apply convergence regressions by groups of countries, finding further evidence for divergence between and convergence within groups. These tests are further supported by tests on the distribution of country-specific convergence regression coefficients across groups of countries. The final section sets out the conclusions.

## Life Expectancy Convergence Clubs

This study builds upon a previous study finding convergence clusters in the patterns of life expectancy dynamics (Mayer-Foulkes, 2003). There it is shown that the cross-country distribution of life expectancy for 163 countries is very distinctly twin-peaked in 1962 and 1997. Approximately half the countries belonged to the lower peak in 1962, and approximately half of these migrated to the higher peak during the 35-year period. This unusually clear empirical subdivision gives rise to three groups of countries, 40 Low-Low, 42 Low-High, and 81 High-High countries. The trajectories followed by the life expectancy levels are quite distinct, and convergence in life expectancy levels is found within the groups. This broad characterization of countries according to life expectancy trajectories is informative only for the countries lying in the lower peak in 1962. Any further subdivision of the 81 High-High countries according to development paths must necessarily involve income data. In this paper we find that such a subdivision is possible. By combining income and life expectancy information the resulting subdivision reflects both income growth and human development. The hope is that, even though categorizations into groups are often somewhat arbitrary, this subdivision can be further studied to shed some light on the actual, distinct growth process going on at different levels of income and life expectancy. The 81 High-High life expectancy cluster contains many less-developed Latin American countries, the newly industrialized countries (NIC's), and the whole developed world. Generating a subdivision of this cluster that distinguishes between these three categories thus demands a total of at least five groups of countries, namely the developed countries, the fast-growing countries and three tiers of less-developed countries corresponding to the Low-Low, Low-High and High-High life expectancy convergence clusters described before.

To this purpose, I exclude both ex-socialist block countries and mainly-petroleum-exporting countries. The reason is that these countries followed very different processes. Most theories for economic growth over the period 1960-1997 are not geared to explain growth in these countries. Socialist countries followed a non-market process that is addressed only vaguely by the theory of development for countries with market economies, and the economic interrelationship they held with market economies was very weak. Thus they naturally form a separate club that may or may not converge. The income of mainly oil exporting countries evolves according to petroleum prices, and these countries have highly distorted relationships between their per capita income and human development variables, which must be addressed in more specific terms and would introduce noise in the data if included.

It must be mentioned here that there is a very close, mutually causal micro and macro relationship between income and health that has been studied intensely (Preston, 1975; Pritchett and Summers, 1996; Anand and Ravallion, 1993; Fogel, 1994; Barro, 1991; Arora, 2001; Mayer-Foulkes, 2001a; Schultz, 1992, 1997, 1999; Thomas, Schoeni and Strauss, 1997; Strauss and Thomas, 1998; Savedoff and Schultz, 2000; Steckel, 1995, amongst many others. For a further review of this interrelationship see Mayer-Foulkes, 2001b). Life expectancy is an excellent indicator of development with a wider coverage across countries than income per capita. Thus use of income and life expectancy data as joint indicators of growth and development is quite appropriate.

As mentioned above, the five groups of countries do not necessarily correspond to different steady states. Two of them are more likely to represent accelerated transitions between steady states, respectively overcoming barriers to human development and to technological innovation. Because the trajectories are quite distinct, I nevertheless treat the five groups as convergence clusters that do indeed exhibit convergence within groups. Treating the clusters in transition distinctly brings out divergence and convergence more clearly.

## The Clustering Algorithm

The choice of groups is carried out by a clustering algorithm using both income and life expectancy data. For this to work it was necessary to take both level and rate of change data into account.[4] The clustering algorithm maximizes the $R^2$ of four regressions describing the level and growth rate trajectories of income and life expectancy data by groups of countries in terms of time trends. These descriptive regressions take the form

$$X_{it} = \alpha_j^0 D_{ji} + \alpha_j^1 D_{ji}t + \alpha_j^2 D_{ji}t^2 + u_{it} \qquad \text{(RC)}$$

Here $D_{ji} = 1$ if country $i$ belongs to group $j$, so that $\alpha_j^0, \alpha_j^1, \alpha_j^2$ are coefficients of a quadratic expression describing the path of $X_{it}$ for each group $j$. The dependent variables $X_{it}$ are log income per capita, log life expectancy and their rates of change.[5] t ranges quinquenially over 1960-1995 for income, 1962-1997 for life expectancy, and one period less for the rates of change. The algorithm maximizes the average of the four R-squares of these estimates over joint partitions of the sample of countries into five groups. This is equivalent to maximizing their joint R-square once the four dependent variables are normalized to the same variance. See Appendix 1 for a further description of the clustering algorithm and its properties. The sample consists of all counties for which the full quinquenial data is complete for income for 1960-1995 or life expectancy for 1962-1997. The regressions for income and

---

[4] In Mayer-Foulkes (2003) level data for life expectancy was sufficient.
[5] The life expectancy and income (Penn World Table 5.6, real GDP at constant 1985 purchasing power parity dollars) data were obtained from the World Bank data base at http://www.worldbank.org/research/growth/GDNdata.htm collected by Easterly and Sewadeh.

life expectancy were run for countries for which the full respective data is available. Thus the group definitions are shaped by all the available complete data in income and life expectancy and by all of the available complete data on their joint evolution. Once the socialist block and the mainly-petroleum-exporting countries were excluded, the algorithm produced a very reasonable subdivision that accords quite well with a commonsense appraisal of the facts. The result was a partition of the sample of 126 countries into five groups that will be shown to define a convergence clustering for both income and life expectancy simultaneously. Although any subdivision into groups may be argued to be somewhat arbitrary, the five groups of countries correspond quite closely to a common-sense classification of countries. In any case, the subdivision is neutral to the relationship between levels and rates of growth across the distribution of income and life expectancy.

## The Groups of Countries: A Descriptive View

Table I. The five clusters of countries by continents.

| Group | West Europe and North America | East Asia Pacific | Latin America and Caribbean | Middle East, North Africa and Turkey | South Asia | Sub-Saharan Africa | Total |
|---|---|---|---|---|---|---|---|
| 1 | 19 | 3 | 7 | 1 | 0 | 0 | 30 |
| 2 | 3 | 7 | 2 | 0 | 0 | 2 | 14 |
| 3 | 0 | 3 | 15 | 5 | 1 | 3 | 27 |
| 4 | 0 | 2 | 4 | 3 | 5 | 13 | 27 |
| 5 | 0 | 0 | 1 | 0 | 1 | 26 | 28 |
| Total | 22 | 15 | 29 | 9 | 7 | 44 | 126 |

Table I shows the composition of the groups by continents.[6] Group 1 consists mainly of developed countries, with the exception of Argentina and Uruguay, characterized by high

---

[6] The membership of the groups including groups of excluded countries, is the following:

**Group 1**: Argentina; Australia; Austria; Bahamas; Barbados; Belgium; Bermuda; Canada; Denmark; Finland; France; Fed. Rep. of Germany (former); Italy; Japan; Luxembourg; Netherlands; Netherlands Antilles; New Zealand; Norway; Puerto Rico; Spain; Sweden; Switzerland; United Kingdom; United States; Uruguay.

**Group 2**: Botswana; Cyprus; Guadeloupe; Hong Kong; Rep. of Korea; Macao; Malaysia; Malta; Martinique; Portugal; Seychelles; Singapore; Taiwan; Thailand.

**Group 3**: Belize; Brazil; Chile; Colombia; Costa Rica; Dominican Republic; Ecuador; El Salvador; Fiji; Guyana; Jamaica; Jordan; Lebanon; Mauritius; Mexico; New Caledonia; Panama; Paraguay; Peru; Philippines; Reunion; South Africa; Sri Lanka; Suriname; Syrian Arab Republic; Tunisia; Turkey.

**Group 4**: Bangladesh; Benin; Bolivia; Cameroon; Cape Verde; Comoros; Egypt; Equatorial Guinea; Gambia; Ghana; Guatemala; Honduras; India; Indonesia; Lesotho; Maldives; Mauritania; Morocco; Namibia; Nepal; Nicaragua; Pakistan; Papua New Guinea; Senegal; Sudan; Swaziland; Yemen.

**Group 5**: Afghanistan; Burkina Faso; Burundi; Central African Republic; Chad; Dem. Rep. of Congo; Cote d'Ivoire; Djibouti; Eritrea; Ethiopia; Guinea; Guinea-Bissau; Haiti; Kenya; Liberia; Madagascar; Malawi; Mali; Mozambique; Niger; Rwanda; Sierra Leone; Somalia; Tanzania; Togo; Uganda; Zambia; Zimbabwe.

**Group 6** (Ex-Soviet block): Armenia; Azerbaijan; Belarus; Bulgaria; Czech Republic; Estonia; Georgia; Hungary; Lithuania; Poland; Romania; Slovenia; Tajikistan; Turkmenistan; Ukraine; Yugoslavia (Serbia/Montenegro).

**Group 7** (Other socialist or ex-socialist): Albania; Angola; Cambodia; China; Dem. Rep. of Korea; Laos; Latvia; Mongolia; Myanmar; Vietnam.

**Group 8** (Mainly petroleum exporting): Algeria; Bahrain; Brunei; Rep. of Congo; Gabon; Iran; Iraq; Kuwait; Libya; Nigeria; Oman; Qatar; Saudi Arabia; Trinidad and Tobago; United Arab Emirates; Venezuela.

levels of income and life expectancy throughout the period, and relatively high income growth and low life expectancy growth. Group 2 consists of exceptionally fast growers at various income levels. Group 3 has many Latin American, Middle Eastern and North African middle income countries. Group 4 has South Asian, Latin American and Sub-Saharan countries with low incomes but high, transitional life expectancy growth. India accounts for about 58% of the population of this group. Group 5 consists mainly of Sub-Saharan countries whose average income declined and whose life expectancy remained very low.

Table II shows the average income and life expectancy levels and growth rates through the respective periods, together with the number of countries for which income or life expectancy data is available in each group.

Some of the characteristics of the countries excluded from the clustering algorithm are the following. Group 6 consists of ex-Soviet block countries, which arguably could form a convergence cluster, since these countries had close economic and political ties which mostly continue due to their geographical and historical proximity. However, the corresponding convergence coefficient was neither negative nor significant. Group 7 are the remaining socialist or ex-socialist countries, with about 80% of the population in China. Group 8 are the mainly-petroleum-exporting countries. Groups 1 to 5 contain about 63% of the world population while Groups 6 to 8 contain about 37%. The population of Groups 1 to 8 accounts for 99.9% of the world population.

Table II. Average Income and Life Expectancy for the five groups of countries: initial and final levels and growth rates. Number of countries in each group with complete respective data also indicated.

| | Income | | | Life Expectancy | | |
|---|---|---|---|---|---|---|
| | **Balanced Obs.** | **Levels** | | **Growth Rate** | **Balanced Obs.** | **Levels** | | **Growth Rate** |
| **Group** | | **1960** | **1995** | **1960-1995** | | **1962** | **1997** | **1962-1997** |
| 1 | 27 | 5631 | 13064 | 2.48% | 28 | 70 | 77 | 0.27% |
| 2 | 10 | 1409 | 8891 | 5.04% | 13 | 62 | 73 | 0.49% |
| 3 | 24 | 1739 | 3483 | 1.91% | 25 | 57 | 71 | 0.62% |
| 4 | 24 | 926 | 1500 | 1.36% | 27 | 43 | 60 | 0.94% |
| 5 | 23 | 693 | 610 | -0.32% | 28 | 39 | 47 | 0.49% |

Apart from Group 2, which consist of fast-growing countries, the average growth rate of Group 1 to 5 is increasing in the income levels, confirming that income has diverged between groups of countries.[7] In the case of life expectancy, for which the returns to wealth decrease very strongly (Group 1 had 21.4 times the average income per capita of Group 5 in 1995, but average life expectancy was only 64% higher in 1997), increases in average life expectancy were absolutely higher for groups with lower life expectancies, except for Group 5, which improved very slowly.

---

[7] The significance of this finding is confirmed below.

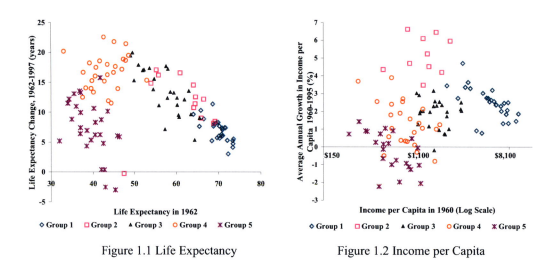

Figure 1.1 Life Expectancy           Figure 1.2 Income per Capita

Figure 1. Empirical Phase Diagrams: Change against Initial Levels

Figures 1.1 and 1.2 show the empirical phase diagrams plotting changes against levels in log-income for 1960-1995 and log life expectancy for 1962-1997 by groups. The life expectancy phase diagram (Figure 1.1) is clearly arch-shaped. Countries and groups begin on the left with low levels and low (even negative) changes, with a high dispersion of rates of change. Fortunate countries then move to the region of somewhat higher levels and high rates of change at the top left of the arch. Finally they transit diagonally downwards converging towards high levels and moderate but sustained improvement. The transition from low to high life expectancy levels involves, according to this cross-sectional view, an initial transitional period of rapid change. In the case of income, if we exclude Group 2, countries shift, in general terms, form the low dispersed income, low growth region, to the high income, high growth region. Group 2 is distinct in that it has faster growth. Excluding the socialist block and mainly oil exporting countries, as well as plotting the convergence clustering obtained in conjunctions with life expectancy data, clarifies this diagram, presented elsewhere as a mysterious stochastic plot (see for example, Barro, 1997, page 10).

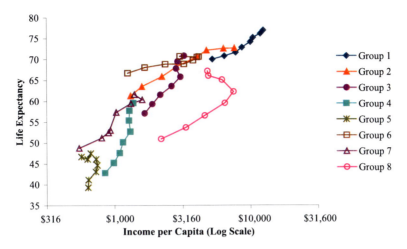

(The trajectories run through the following years, with life expectancy trending upwards: Life
Expectancy, 1962, 1967, ...,1997; income per capita, 1960, 1965, ...,1995, in 1985 PPP US dlrs.)

Figure 2. Average Life Expectancy versus Income per Capita by Groups of Countries

It is notable that the transition to higher life expectancies occurs, as a rule, ahead of the
transition to higher incomes, as can be corroborated by the relatively lagged positioning of the
groups in the income phase diagram as compared to the life expectancy phase diagram. This
pattern corroborates Ranis, Stewart and Ramírez' (2000) results, who finds that the transition
to a 'virtuous cycle' in human development is both usually more stable and a propitious
antecedent to the transition to a 'virtuous cycle' in income growth. It is also consistent with
studies affirming the causality from health improvements to economic growth during this and
other historical contexts (Fogel, 1994; Arora, 2001; Mayer-Foulkes, 2001a, 2001b).

Thus the evidence is suggestive of the three large-scale convergence clubs mentioned
above. The lowest steady state (*semi-stagnation*) is almost stagnant in income but observes
some life expectancy growth. The middle steady state (*semi-development*) has much higher
life expectancies and a middle level of income. The highest steady state (*development*) has
high levels of income and life expectancy. Group 2 transits from semi-development to
development. This may explain its fast rates of growth. Group 4 transits from semi-stagnation
to semi-development. These three steady states are compatible with the technological
convergence club model proposed by Howitt and Mayer-Foulkes (2005). The higher steady
state corresponds to he ability to perform or to imitate R&D. The middle steady state
correspond to the ability only to implement technologies, with R&D imitation requiring levels
of science that remain inaccessible due to low educational levels. The lower steady state
corresponds to stagnation, interpreted to mean that only very low cost technologies can be
implemented. These nevertheless lead to rises in life expectancy. Under such and
interpretation, long term forces may lead to the disappearance of the lower steady states in a
prolonged transition. What may not be explained sufficiently in the Howitt and Mayer-
Foulkes (2005) model is the degree and continuity of global divergence that is observed
across Groups 1 to 4.

Figure 2 plots average life expectancy[8] for 1962, 1967, ...,1997 against average log income per capita for 1960, 1965, ..., 1995, including all eight groups of countries. It is interesting to note that, together, the five groups of countries in the convergence clustering almost conform a functional relationship between life expectancy and income. However, each group of countries achieves a higher life expectancy at the end of the period than the next richer group obtained at some earlier time when it had and equal or higher level of income, confirming Preston's (1975) study. The following descriptive estimation for life expectancy in terms of income is a reestimation of this relation confirms this relationship (run with fixed effects and White's heteroskedasticity correction; t-statistics in parenthesis; R-squared: 0.966).

$$\log(LE_{it}) = 0.252 \log(y_{it}) + 0.073\ t - 0.015 \log(y_{it})^2 - 0.04 \log(y_{it})\ t - 0.002\ t^2 + c_i + u_{it}$$
$$\quad\quad (5.39) \quad\quad\quad (13.16) \quad (-5.02) \quad\quad\quad (-4.38) \quad\quad\quad (-4.73)$$

According to the regression, log life expectancy was decreasing in log per capita income and increased with time, in an effect which was stronger for lower income countries and decreasing through time.

It is notable that the ex-Soviet block countries (Group 6) and other socialist or ex-socialist countries (Group 7, mainly China) enjoyed better life expectancy at comparable income levels than their market counterparts until the 1970's and 1980's respectively. The reverse holds for the mainly-petroleum-exporting countries, which had much higher income for given life expectancy levels. This, by the way, supports their exclusion from the sample.

Figures 3.1 and 3.2 show three standard deviation corridors for the log life expectancy and log income of each group of countries at five year intervals. It is quite clear that each group of countries is following its own significantly different pattern of economic growth. The health improvement pattern followed by the less-developed Groups 3, 4, and 5 reproduces the convergence clustering found for life expectancy in the antecedent study mentioned above (Mayer-Foulkes, 2003), with Group 4 changing from the level of Group 5 toward that of Group 3.

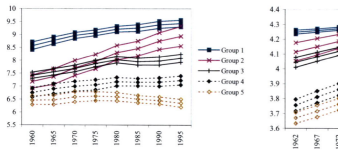

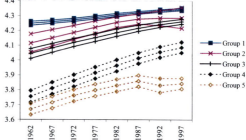

Figure 3.1 Income per Capita                    Figure 3.2 Life Expectancy

Figure 3. Income per Capita and Life Expectancy Three Standard Deviation Corridors by Groups of Countries (Constructed on the Logarithmics of the Variables)

---

[8] (Actually, the exponent of average log life expectancy for each Group.)

It is noteworthy that income also follows this pattern, with Group 4 tending to catch up on Group 3, and Group 5 staying behind, actually experiencing negative average growth after 1980. On the other hand, Group 2, the fast-growing countries, starts from levels comparable to Group 3 and almost catches up with Group 1, the developed world.

These different growth experiences are grounded in conditions originating long before 1960. Acemoglu, Johnson and Robinson (2000) give evidence that the current distribution of income has substantive long-term determinants, being correlated with mortality data from the colonial era. Howitt and Mayer-Foulkes (2005) point out that their econometric results are consistent with long-term technologically-caused convergence clubs giving rise to persistence in the cross-country distribution of income. The correlation that exists between group membership and geographical location by continents (see Table II) also underlines the long-term antecedents of group membership, independently of whether the main transmission channels are historical, institutional, technological or geographical, or whether the transmission mechanisms have changed over time. These proposed mechanisms explaining the persistence of the income distribution across countries could in any case work in succession, because they each deliver the appropriate initial conditions for the succeeding mechanism in a new historical period dominated by different economic forces.

## Convergence and Divergence Across Groups of Countries

It is not difficult to obtain a first tests of the convergence and divergence properties across the five groups of countries that is independent of regression models. This consists of testing for a trend across ordered groups, by applying Cuzick's (1985) non parametric test. The results are shown in Table III. When the test is applied to the full subdivision into five groups, a highly significant divergence trend is found (represented by a negative sign because higher income groups have a lower index number). This trend is independent of the inclusion of Group 2, as is shown by excluding this Group from the sample. In the case of life expectancy, the overall pattern is one of convergence, independently of the inclusion of Group 2. Next, we examine neighboring groups in succession. Groups 1 and 2 converge in income and life expectancy. Groups 2 and 3 diverge in income and exhibit a somewhat significant life expectancy convergence. Groups 3 and 4 converge in life expectancy and exhibit a somewhat significant income divergence. Groups 4 and 5 diverge in income and life expectancy. This pattern of convergence and divergence is inconsistent with a view that would have each country belong to its own club. First, because it would remain to explain the evidence for global divergence, and second, because there are significant common phenomena across groups that cannot be due simply to random differences between countries. The convergence and divergence pattern supports the stylized fact of three large-scale convergence clubs mentioned above.

Table III. Test for the divergence and convergence of income and life expectancy growth rates across groups of countries and by pairs of successive groups.

| Groups | Income per Capita z | p | Life Expectancy z | p |
|---|---|---|---|---|
| 1, 2, 3, 4, 5 | -6.89 | 0 | 5.45 | 0 |
| 1, 3, 4, 5 | -6.45 | 0 | 5.23 | 0 |
| 1,2 | 4.45 | 0 | 4.01 | 0 |
| 2,3 | -4.54 | 0 | 1.68 | 0.09 |
| 3,4 | -1.75 | 0.08 | 5.01 | 0 |
| 4,5 | -3.85 | 0 | -5.37 | 0 |

# Within and between Group Inequality in Income and Life Expectancy

I now decompose income and life expectancy inequality by groups of countries, following method 1 of Cowell and Jenkins (1995). The results are very similar for $\alpha = -1/2$, 0 and 1, indexes of the family of the generalized entropy class of inequality measures. $\alpha = 0$ is reported in Figures 4.1 and 4.2. Income inequality between groups of countries increased, while inequality within groups decreased. According to this methodology, the evolution of income inequality is mainly explained by what is happening *between* the groups, that is, by differences in the growth pattern followed by the different groups of countries, providing evidence for a pattern of global divergence of income across groups of countries. Quah's (1993, 1996, 1997) findings of an increasingly twin-peaked distribution also express the increase in income inequality observed between 1970 and 1985.

In the case of life expectancy, inequality between groups of countries first decreased but this trend ended in the late 1980's mainly because of life expectancy problems in Group 5. Figures 4.3 and 4.4 show the evolution of the proportion of variance that is between groups.

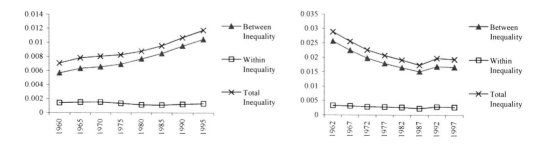

Figure 4.1 Income per Capita        Figure 4.2 Life Expectancy

Proportion of Inequality that is Between Groups

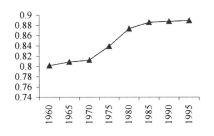

Figure 4.3 Income per Capita

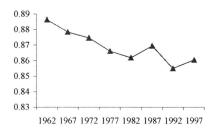

Figure 4.4 Life Expectancy

Figure 4. Within and Between Group Inequality Decomposition (Generalized Entropy Inequality Measure, alpha = 0) (Constructed on the Logarithms of the Variables)

# Within and between Group Variance of Income and Life Expectancy

Next, I examine $\sigma$-convergence by decomposing variance between and within groups of countries. The results, shown in Figures 5.1 to 5.4, are very similar to those obtained for the inequality decompositions. Variance of income between groups of countries increased, while variance within groups decreased. In the case of life expectancy, variance between groups of countries first decreased but this trend ended in the late 1980's mainly because of life expectancy problems in Group 5.

## Convergence and Divergence in Regression Models

The above three sections give econometric evidence for income divergence between groups and convergence within groups, as well as specific regions of divergence and convergence, independently of a regression model. Here we turn to convergence regression models.

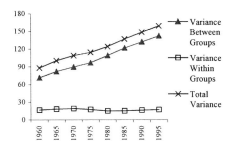

Figure 5.1 Income per Capita

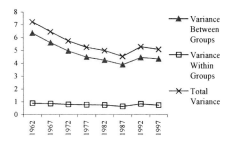

Figure 5.2 Life Expectancy

Proportion of Variance that is Between Groups

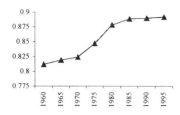

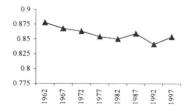

Figure 5.3 Income per Capita          Figure 5.4 Life Expectancy

Figure 5. Within and Between Group Variance Decomposition (Constructed on the Logarithms of the Variables)

Each of the theories of economic growth mentioned in the introduction models economic processes tending to states of equilibria represented by a single or multiple steady states. Thus, to analyze convergence I assume that each country's economic trajectory tends to some steady state trajectory. By analyzing the properties of these steady states, it is usually possible, for economic indicator functions such as income and life expectancy (as shown in Appendix 2), to arrive at a convergence equation of the form

$$\frac{1}{T}\left(y_{it+T} - y_{it}\right) = c_i + \gamma_i t + B_i y_{it} + \eta_{it} \tag{C}$$

Here $y_{it}$ represents log income per capita, $B_i$ represents the rate of convergence to the steady state trajectory, $\gamma_i$ is a multiple of the characteristic growth rate of the steady state, and $c_i$ are country-specific fixed effects. Equation (C) implies that as the income trajectory $y_{it}$ approaches the steady state trajectory $y_{it}^*$ from below, growth tends to slow down. If it is assumed that life expectancy is a function of the underlying economic variables, then it also obeys an analogous convergence equation.

## Constant Coefficients by Groups of Countries: Convergence Clusters

Cross-country empirical studies of convergence usually assume that there is a single convergence club. Here we test the hypothesis that there is divergence between the five groups of countries, convergence within them, and also that the five groups have significantly distinct convergence properties.

I begin by assuming that all steady states have the same rate of growth, and that the convergence rates are the same. Then a simple regression can be applied to distinguish if the different groups have different steady states: group specific dummies and also a dummy for each time period are introduced in equation (C). This regression is compared to the single club model in which the group specific dummies are excluded. The results are in Table IV. The single club model obtains absolute divergence (as opposed to absolute convergence). The five club model obtains a negative convergence coefficient and highly significant group-specific constant terms representing different steady states, expressed in comparison to Group 1. The magnitudes are strictly ordered (according to the group index), except that Group 2's constant is higher than Group 1's. Wald tests show that all of the coefficients are different with p-value less than 0.001, supporting the hypothesis that the five groups have significantly different steady states. An F-test finds the five club model to be more significant than the single club model at better than one in a million, although the significance may be biased upward by the clustering by levels.

In the case of life expectancy there is absolute convergence, and life expectancy improves fastest in Groups 3 and 2. Group 4's rate of improvement is statistically indistinguishable from Group 1, while Group 5's life expectancy deteriorated significantly, and is responsible for the negative sign in the only significant time dummy. The five club model is also much more significant than the one-club model.

However, steady states growth rates and convergence coefficients need not be the same. To estimate them properly, it is necessary to include country fixed effects. Hence convergence properties independent of country-specific steady state levels will be tested. I assume that each of the five groups of countries has common coefficients (instead of the usual assumption that *all* countries have the same coefficients).[9] Although Group 2 may be transiting to the same steady state as Group 1, so that they would belong to the same convergence club, testing this hypothesis is beyond the scope of this paper, because it probably involves several kinds of non-linearities. The same holds for the relationship between Groups 4 and 3. Thus I analyze each group separately, even if these two pairs may each belong to the same broad convergence club. For this reason, the concept of *convergence clustering* is restricted to mean only that its group-specific convergence coefficient is negative. Thus I estimate:

$$\frac{1}{T}(y_{it+T} - y_{it}) = c_i + \sum_j \gamma_j D_{ji} t + \sum_j B_j D_{ji} y_{it} + \eta_{it}$$

$$(1)$$

Here $D_{ji}$ is 1 if country $i$ is in group $j$ and 0 otherwise, and a similar equation for log life expectancy. The first column in Table V shows the income results. Each of the groups has a significant negative convergence coefficient for income per capita. They also have significant, positive steady-state growth coefficients, except for Group 4, which is near 0 with a similar standard deviation, and Group 5, for which the coefficient is negative. The growth coefficients rise with the income level of the groups, except for Group 2, which grows faster. To test for this tendency I estimate the following regression:

$$\frac{1}{T}(y_{it+T} - y_{it}) = c_i + \sum_j B_j D_{ji} y_{it} + \delta_0 t + \delta_2 D_{2i} t + \delta_G \sum_j j D_{ji} t + \eta_{it}$$

$$(2)$$

Here $\delta_0$ represents a parallel growth term, $\delta_2$ represents additional growth in Group 2, and $\delta_G$ represents additional group-specific growth, parameterized by the group index $j$. Since this index is decreasing in income, a significant, negative $\delta_G$ implies divergence of growth rates across groups of countries. The results, column 2 of Table V show that there is

---

[9] Below we drop this assumption and investigate the coefficient distributions, showing that they differ significantly between groups.

indeed highly significant divergence between groups of countries, and that Group 2 grows even faster. Because modeling by the group index is somewhat arbitrary, I also tested the model given by the coefficients of regression (1) as follows:

$$\frac{1}{T}(y_{it+T} - y_{it}) = c_i + \sum_j B_j D_{ji} y_{it} + \delta_0 t + \delta_{DIV} \sum_j \gamma_j D_{ji} t + \eta_{it}$$
(3)

Here $\sum_j \gamma_j D_{ji}$ is the divergence pattern estimated in regression (1). The significance of $\delta_{DIV}$ (whose value must be 1) is the joint significance of this divergence pattern, which is higher than the significance of $\delta_G$, as can be seen in column 3 of Table V. $\delta_0$ obtains a value of 0, and is completely insignificant, as is to be expected.

Column 4 of Table V has the results for life expectancy. The steady state growth coefficients are not very significant, as is to be expected, since life expectancy must tend to a bounded steady state. The convergence coefficients, however, are significant for all of the groups except Group 2.

Tables VI.1 and VI.2 show the results of Wald tests for the pair-wise equality the coefficient vectors ($B_j$, $\gamma_j$) between groups of countries for the income and life expectancy regressions in columns 1 and 4 of Table V. The pairs of coefficient vectors are mostly significantly different. Tables VII.1 and VII.2 show the results of a Kruskal-Wallis equality of populations rank test (adjusted for ties) for the fixed effects of these regressions by groups of countries. The fixed effects distributions are always significantly different. These two sets of test show that the group of countries follow significantly different income and life expectancy dynamics. However, that the presence of a strong, significant divergence pattern means that steady states cannot be readily compared across groups of countries, since the steady state growth rates involved in their definition are different.

Finally, an F-test comparing the single-club model for income and life expectancy with the five-club model found that the five-club structure was significant at better than one in a million in both cases. The significance may nevertheless be biased upwards by the clustering by levels.

The convergence observed within groups, which recovers the robust relative convergence finding, is evidence that there are equilibrium processes keeping group members to their group trajectories.[10] This supports the hypothesis of a convergence club structure, or multiple steady states, since the evidence for divergence implies that there are economic forces maintaining income differences in spite of the forces that lead to convergence. Evidence for these forces has been found in the case of OECD countries, for instance, corresponding approximately to convergence within Group 1 in this study.

---

[10] The convergence coefficient found by cross-country studies assuming a single convergence club arises as a weighted average of group-specific convergence coefficients, with divergence factored in.

## Distribution of Convergence Properties by Groups of Countries

I now drop the assumption that each group of countries has common convergence coefficients, maintained in the previous section, and look at the distributions of the coefficients $c_i$, $B_i$, $\gamma_i$ to test if these are the same across groups of countries. One of the reasons it is necessary to drop this assumption is that each group of countries may itself be subdividable into clubs. Differences in the distributions of the coefficients of the convergence equations between groups reflect differences in their economic dynamics. I test for these differences by applying the Kruskal-Wallis equality of populations rank test (adjusted for ties) of the hypothesis that the several subsamples are from the same population.

The first pair of columns in Table VIII shows that the steady state growth rates, convergence coefficients, and fixed effects of income per capita and life expectancy for the five groups of countries are very unlikely to belong to the same distribution. To eliminate the possibility that these results are driven by Group 2 (which is shown to differ significantly from the other groups in Table VIII) the second pair of columns shows that Group 1 can be distinguished from the joint group formed by Groups 3, 4 and 5 (i.e. developed from underdeveloped countries), mainly by the convergence coefficients and life expectancy fixed effects. When Group 5 is eliminated, the same results hold except that for income convergence the significance is reduced (recall that the sample is down to 75). The final pair of columns shows that Groups 3, 4 and 5 differ significantly amongst each other, mainly in their growth rates.

Table IX shows the results for pair-wise Kruskal-Wallis tests between the groups of countries, applied to the coefficient distributions for the convergence equations for income and life expectancy. All pairs can be distinguished on some count. Pairs of groups 1 and 3, 3 and 4 and 4 and 5 can only be distinguished in terms of life expectancy. Every other pair-wise distinction has some significant difference in the behavior of the income growth.

To test for divergence, I apply Cuzick's (1985) nonparametric test for a trend across ordered groups in the steady-state growth rates $g_i = -\gamma_i / B_i$ for income and life expectancy.[11] The results are in Table X. The significant negative relationships imply that the income and life expectancy steady state growth rates of higher income groups are higher (because the group index is decreasing in income), independently of whether Group 2 is included or not.[12] Also the coefficient for life expectancy fixed effects was found to be higher for higher income countries.

---

[11] This is an extension of the Wilcoxon rank-sum test and incorporates a correction for ties (Altman, 1991).

[12] Divergence of the growth rate coefficients $\gamma_i$ was also found for income per capita, independently of the inclusion of Group 2.

Table IV. Single and Five-Club Convergence Regressions (White Heteroskedasticity Correction)

|  | Income per Capita | | Life Expectancy | |
|---|---|---|---|---|
|  | Single Club | Five-Club | Single Club | Five-Club |
| **Constant** | **-0.0264** | **0.1185** | **0.0362** | **0.0623** |
|  | **(0.001)** | **(0)** | **(0)** | **(0)** |
| **Dummy for Group 2** |  | **0.0159** |  | **0.0011** |
|  |  | **(0)** |  | **(0.017)** |
| **Dummy for Group 3** |  | **-0.0177** |  | **0.0015** |
|  |  | **(0)** |  | **(0.006)** |
| **Dummy for Group 4** |  | **-0.0299** |  | 0.0015 |
|  |  | **(0)** |  | (0.264) |
| **Dummy for Group 5** |  | **-0.0525** |  | **-0.0048** |
|  |  | **(0)** |  | **(0.014)** |
| **Initial log income per capita or life expectancy** | **0.0072** | **-0.0098** | **-0.0073** | **-0.0138** |
|  | **(0)** | **(0)** | **(0)** | **(0)** |
| **Dummy for 1965 or 1967** | 0.0034 | 0.0056 | 0.0002 | 0.0004 |
|  | (0.362) | (0.109) | (0.66) | (0.308) |
| **Dummy for 1970 or 1972** | -0.0066 | -0.0015 | 0 | 0.0005 |
|  | (0.127) | (0.72) | (0.915) | (0.28) |
| **Dummy for 1975 or 1977** | -0.0046 | 0.0024 | -0.0001 | 0.0006 |
|  | (0.292) | (0.556) | (0.804) | (0.298) |
| **Dummy for 1980 or 1982** | **-0.0324** | **-0.0234** | -0.0005 | 0.0004 |
|  | **(0)** | **(0)** | (0.356) | (0.522) |
| **Dummy for 1985 or 1987** | **-0.0174** | **-0.0091** | **-0.0039** | **-0.0028** |
|  | **(0)** | **(0.017)** | **(0.001)** | **(0.008)** |
| **Dummy for 1990 or 1992** | **-0.0202** | **-0.0107** | **-0.0028** | -0.0016 |
|  | **(0)** | **(0.007)** | **(0.002)** | (0.161) |
| **R-Squared** | 0.152 | 0.316 | 0.152 | 0.259 |
| **Adjusted R-Squared** | 0.144 | 0.307 | 0.145 | 0.249 |
| **Durbin-Watson** | 1.707 | 1.944 | 1.797 | 1.999 |
| **F-Statistic** | 20.2 | 33.1 | 21.7 | 26.8 |
| **Prob (F-Statistic)** | 0 | 0 | 0 | 0 |

(p-value in parenthesis, 5% significance in bold, 10% in italics)

Table V. Five-Club Convergence Regressions (Fixed Effects, White Heterosk. Correction)

| | Income | Income | Income | Life Expectancy |
|---|---|---|---|---|
| **Steady State Growth Decomposition Coefficients** | | | | |
| **Group 1** | **0.0055** **(0.001)** | | | **0.001** **(0)** |
| **Group 2** | **0.0206** **(0)** | | | -0.0011 (0.492) |
| **Group 3** | **0.0042** **(0.006)** | | | *0.0005* *(0.095)* |
| **Group 4** | -0.0001 (0.963)* | | | 0.0006 (0.379) |
| **Group 5** | **-0.0046** **(0)** | | | 0.0003 (0.741) |
| **Parallel Growth** | | **0.0111** **(0)** | 0 (1) | |
| **Group 2 Additional Growth** | | **0.0154** **(0.005)** | | |
| **Group Index Additional Growth** | | **-0.003** **(0)†** | | |
| **Divergence Pattern Growth** | | | **1** **(0)‡** | |
| **Convergence Coefficients** | | | | |
| **Group 1** | **-0.0793** **(0)** | **-0.0956** **(0)** | **-0.0793** **(0)** | **-0.0724** **(0)** |
| **Group 2** | **-0.0793** **(0)** | **-0.0793** **(0)** | **-0.0793** **(0)** | -0.0068 (0.886) |
| **Group 3** | **-0.0798** **(0)** | **-0.0679** **(0)** | **-0.0798** **(0)** | **-0.0344** **(0)** |
| **Group 4** | **-0.0557** **(0)** | **-0.0517** **(0)** | **-0.0557** **(0)** | **-0.0255** **(0.045)** |
| **Group 5** | **-0.0661** **(0)** | **-0.0666** **(0)** | **-0.0661** **(0)** | **-0.0706** **(0.003)** |
| **R-Squared** | 0.472 | 0.468 | 0.472 | 0.415 |
| **Adjusted R-Squared** | 0.371 | 0.369 | 0.374 | 0.307 |
| **Durbin-Watson** | 2.075 | 2.091 | 2.075 | 2.103 |
| **F-Statistic** | 66.424 | 84.541 | 100.083 | 56.850 |
| **Prob (F-Statistic)** | 0.000 | 0.000 | 0.000 | 0.000 |

(p-value in parenthesis, 5% significance in bold, 10% in italics)
* The std. devs. for these coefficients for Groups 1 to 5 are: 0.0017, 0.0054, 0.0015, 0.0012, 0.0012.
† t-statistic: -5.628.   ‡ t-statistic: 6.605.

### Single-Club Convergence Regression
### (Fixed Effects, White Heteroskedasticity Correction)

| | Income | Life Expectancy |
|---|---|---|
| **Steady State Growth Coefficient** | **-0.0008** **(0.227)** | 0.0003 (0.37) |
| **Convergence Coefficient** | **-0.0329** **(0)** | **-0.0378** **(0.001)** |
| **R-Squared** | 0.400 | 0.353 |
| **Adjusted R-Squared** | 0.295 | 0.242 |
| **Durbin-Watson** | 2.199 | 2.145 |
| **F-Statistic** | 451.842 | 396.770 |
| **Prob (F-Statistic)** | 0.000 | 0.000 |

(p-value in parenthesis, 5% significance in bold)

Table VI. Wald Test for Equality of Steady State Growth and Convergence Coefficients Between Groups of Countries for Five-Club Model

### Table VI.1. Income per Capita

|         | Group 1 | Group 2 | Group 3 | Group 4 |
|---------|---------|---------|---------|---------|
| Group 2 | **31.5** **(0)** | | | |
| Group 3 | 0.8 (0.447) | **25.2** **(0)** | | |
| Group 4 | **4.3** **(0.014)** | **16.9** **(0)** | *2.4* *(0.091)* | |
| Group 5 | **14.2** **(0)** | **20.4** **(0)** | **11.2** **(0)** | **4.5** **(0.012)** |

(F-test with p-value in parenthesis, 5% significance in bold, 10% in italics)

### Table VI.2. Life Expectancy

|         | Group 1 | Group 2 | Group 3 | Group 4 |
|---------|---------|---------|---------|---------|
| Group 2 | 0.9 (0.402) | | | |
| Group 3 | **8.5** **(0)** | **4** **(0.019)** | | |
| Group 4 | **15.8** **(0)** | **4.1** **(0.016)** | **3.6** **(0.028)** | |
| Group 5 | 1.6 (0.194) | 2 (0.136) | **7.9** **(0)** | **10.6** **(0)** |

(F-test with p-value in parenthesis, 5% significance in bold)

Table VII. Kruskal-Wallis Equality of Populations Rank Test (Corrected for Ties) for Fixed Effects by Groups of Countries for Five-Club Model

### Table VII. Kruskal-Wallis Equality of Populations Rank Test (Corrected for Ties) for Fixed Effects by Groups of Countries for Five-Club Model

### Table VII.1. Income per Capita

|         | Group 1 | Group 2 | Group 3 | Group 4 |
|---------|---------|---------|---------|---------|
| Group 2 | **0.0001** | | | |
| Group 3 | **0.0001** | *0.077* | | |
| Group 4 | **0.0001** | **0.0001** | **0.0001** | |
| Group 5 | **0.0001** | **0.0001** | **0.0001** | **0.0001** |

(p-value, 5% significance in bold)

### Table VII.2. Life Expectancy

|         | Group 1 | Group 2 | Group 3 | Group 4 |
|---------|---------|---------|---------|---------|
| Group 2 | **0.0001** | | | |
| Group 3 | **0.0001** | **0.0001** | | |
| Group 4 | **0.0001** | **0.0001** | **0.0001** | |
| Group 5 | **0.0001** | **0.0001** | **0.0001** | **0.0001** |

(p-value, 5% significance in bold)

Table VIII. Results of Kruskal-Wallis equality of populations rank test (corrected for ties) for the distributions of coefficients of the convergence estimates for income per capita and life expectancy by countries: a) divided into the five groups of countries; b) Group 1 compared with all countries in Groups 3, 4 and 5; c) Group 1 compared with all countries in Groups 3 and 4; d) Groups 3, 4 and 5 compared.

| Groups Tested | a) 1,2,3,4,5 | | b) 1, {3,4,5} | | c) 1, {3,4} | | d) 3,4,5 | |
|---------------|--------------|------|---------------|------|-------------|------|----------|------|
| **Coefficients** | **Income per Capita** | **Life Expect.** | **Income per Capita** | **Life Expect.** | **Income per Capita** | **Life Expect.** | **Income per Capita** | **Life Expect.** |
| $\gamma_i$ | **0.0001** | **0.0423** | 0.5441 | 0.1717 | 0.4332 | 0.7881 | **0.0126** | **0.0415** |
| $B_i$ | **0.0112** | **0.017** | **0.0297** | **0.0007** | *0.0851* | **0.0012** | 0.5922 | 0.8577 |
| $C_i$ | **0.0402** | **0.0048** | 0.4248 | **0.0001** | 0.5008 | **0.0003** | 0.5984 | 0.899 |

(p-value; bold used for better than 5% significance, italics for 10%.)

Table IX. Test of Equality of the Distributions of Country-Specific Regression Coefficients by Groups of Countries. (Pair-Wise Kruskal-Wallis Equality of Populations Rank Test, Corrected for Ties)

## Income per Capita          Life Expectancy

### Convergence Coefficients

| Group | 1 | 2 | 3 | 4 | Group | 1 | 2 | 3 | 4 |
|-------|---|---|---|---|-------|---|---|---|---|
| 2 | **0.005** | | | | 2 | **0.0053** | | | |
| 3 | 0.2575 | **0.0022** | | | 3 | **0.0031** | 0.9142 | | |
| 4 | **0.07** | **0.0257** | 0.3223 | | 4 | **0.0088** | 0.4105 | 0.4922 | |
| 5 | 0.1824 | **0.0077** | 0.5513 | 0.6396 | 5 | **0.0325** | 0.6141 | 0.9715 | 0.8137 |

(P-values, 5% signif in bold)          (P-values, 5% signif in bold)

### Steady State Growth Coefficients

| Group | 1 | 2 | 3 | 4 | Group | 1 | 2 | 3 | 4 |
|-------|---|---|---|---|-------|---|---|---|---|
| 2 | **0.0001** | | | | 2 | **0.0115** | | | |
| 3 | 0.8209 | **0.0001** | | | 3 | 0.1217 | 0.6334 | | |
| 4 | 0.1173 | **0.0001** | 0.1609 | | 4 | 0.3115 | *0.0912* | *0.0511* | |
| 5 | **0.0094** | **0.0001** | **0.0036** | 0.1058 | 5 | *0.08* | 0.8227 | 0.2932 | **0.0286** |

(P-values, 5% signif in bold)          (P-values, 5% signif in bold, 10% in italics)

### Fixed Effects

| Group | 1 | 2 | 3 | 4 | Group | 1 | 2 | 3 | 4 |
|-------|---|---|---|---|-------|---|---|---|---|
| 2 | **0.034** | | | | 2 | **0.0049** | | | |
| 3 | 0.7199 | **0.0052** | | | 3 | **0.0017** | 0.9142 | | |
| 4 | 0.428 | **0.0156** | 0.6207 | | 4 | **0.0024** | 0.4441 | 0.6405 | |
| 5 | 0.8381 | **0.0013** | 0.5371 | 0.3382 | 5 | **0.0061** | 0.7157 | 0.8307 | 0.7491 |

(P-values, 5% signif in bold)          (P-values, 5% signif in bold)

Table X. Test for the divergence of steady state income growth rates and for a trend in life expectancy fixed effects across groups of countries.

| Groups | Income per Capita Steady State Growth Rates | | Life Expectancy Fixed Effects | |
|--------|------|------|------|------|
| | z | p | z | p |
| 1, 2, 3, 4, 5 | -1.92 | 0.05 | -5.22 | 0 |
| 1, 3, 4, 5 | -1.95 | 0.05 | -5.49 | 0 |

The tests applied to the distributions of the convergence regression coefficients support the finding of global income divergence across groups of countries. They also show that each group follows its own distinct income and life expectancy dynamics, though the possibility of non-linearities is not being taken into account.

# Summary

A whole sequence of tests has been applied to examine convergence and divergence within and between the five groups of countries. First, the pattern of convergence and divergence found for growth rates across groups of countries shows that there is global divergence, and supports the existence of the large scale, three club structure mentioned above. Second, inequality and variance decompositions show that inequality between groups has increased, while inequality within groups has decreased. This gives direct evidence of divergence between groups of countries, independently of any theoretical modeling. Third, if it is assumed that countries share steady-state growth rates and convergence coefficients, then the five club model is much more significant than the single club model and implies each group has different steady states. Fourth, it is assumed that instead countries move along trajectories tending to country-specific steady states, but that otherwise countries in each of the five groups follow the same dynamics. Then it is found that income growth rates are significantly divergent and that there is a significant negative convergence coefficient within each group of countries, both for income and life expectancy. Thus, the groups of countries form a diverging set of convergence clusters. The five group model is very significantly better than the single club model, and the dynamics followed by each group of countries are significantly distinct. Fifth, the convergence regressions are estimated separately for each country. Tests on the coefficients of these regressions then show that average and steady state income growth rates are significantly divergent, independently of Group 2, while life expectancy fixed effects were significantly higher for the higher income groups. Also, the convergence regression coefficients were significantly different across groups of countries, showing that they follow distinct income and life expectancy dynamics.

The income and life expectancy trajectories (Figure 3, Table III) suggest the presence of three large-scale convergence clubs. The poorest, semi-stagnant countries face barriers to human development. When these are overcome, income and especially life expectancy rise quickly. At this level, the trajectories suggest a further set of barriers to high income that may involve the process of technological change, distinguishing semi-developed from developed countries, which have overcome them.

# Conclusions

The subdivision of non-mainly-petroleum-exporting market economies into five groups of countries presented herein provides the opportunity to test the conditional convergence hypothesis. In fact, what is found is global divergence. The convergence hypothesis is rejected even in its weakest form, which is convergence to parallel paths. Instead, what is observed is that convergence occurs within groups of countries, consistently with the robust finding of relative convergence across countries, while the groups themselves diverge.

Our findings confirm Pritchett's (1997) findings of divergence in the cross-country distribution of income. Pritchett's method is to find a minimum level of income for the less developed countries in 1870, and to therefore infer a maximum rate of growth for these countries during the period 1870-1990. The data I use covers the last portion of this period and exhibits this divergence directly, in manner consistent with the relative convergence that has also been observed, once countries are subdivided appropriately into groups. The results also show that divergence and inequality rose to even higher levels after 1980, consistently with Quah's (1993, 1996, 1997) findings. Thus, the divergence observed by Pritchett continues to this day.

The recognition of multiple convergence clubs allows the definition of *states of development*, which in the language of dynamics correspond to lying in the basin of attraction of a specific configuration of economic of growth. A fuller knowledge of the underlying economics can lead to policies aimed at dissolving specific physical and human capital, technological, institutional and other low income traps, perhaps involving geography, and therefore at *changing states of development*, rather than just policies seeking macroeconomic stability and poverty alleviation. The descriptive statistics suggest, as stylized facts, the existence of three large-scale convergence clubs, *semi-stagnation* (low income and life expectancy), *semi-development* (middle income and high life expectancy) and *development* (high income and life expectancy). These are broadly consistent with the Howitt and Mayer-Foulkes (2005) model. However the monotonic relation that exists between levels of income and rates of growth between the remaining Groups 1, 3, 4 and 5 is not sufficiently explained.

It cannot be helped but to observe that the explanations for economic growth that were current during the period failed to be consistent with the facts. Perhaps countries compete for growth or growth-producing resources, and richer countries have an advantage in this competition.

The existence of multiple convergence clusters is only consistent with multiple convergence clubs or prolonged transitions, rather than a single convergence club, or a club for each country, and has important implications for policy. Multiple steady states tend to arise from disadvantages faced by the poor or from advantages enjoyed by the rich, either individually, as classes of people, or as countries, originating in production, education, technology, institutions, geography or market failures. These give rise to non-convexities in the process of growth and lead to barriers that markets cannot remove on their own. This need not be considered a question of orthodoxy. What is needed, first of all, is to understand the main kinds of barriers that exist. This will make it possible to propose the policies, and perhaps to find the resources that may be required to achieve the miracle rises in human well-being that are so badly needed.

# Appendix 1. The Regression Clustering Algorithm

The algorithm for finding the partition of the sample of countries into N groups with the minimum joint R-squared for the four equations (RC) mentioned above works as follows. Given an initial partition into N groups, the algorithm passes through each country and switches it to that group of countries for which the highest R-squared improvement is obtained. This procedure is applied successively until no country can be changed to another group in such a way that the joint R-squared increases. The maximum to the problem is not unique, as can be ascertained by considering a problem with sufficient symmetry. However, the solutions obtained (see Figures 1.1 and 1.2) do look unique, because there is no obvious way in which the clusters could be arranged differently other than by shifting their boundaries, which the algorithm can do. In any case it is sufficient for the purposes of this article to produce any partition yielding the results. The initial partitions were obtained by splitting optimal partitions for lower N. The algorithm is implemented in a Delphi program (the Windows version of Pascal) written for the purpose by the author.

# Appendix 2. The Convergence Equation

Assume that the economic growth experienced by the countries in the sample over the period under consideration obeys some dynamic model in which each country is tending to some steady state. Each country $i$ is described at time $t$ by a vector $x_{it}$ of fundamental variables, such as human and physical capital, and two observed variables, log income $y_{it}$ and log life expectancy $LE_{it}$, which the model describes as functions of the underlying economic variables $x_{it}$, such as $y_{it} = g(x_{it}, \theta_i)$ and $LE_{it} = h(x_{it}, \theta_i)$ where $\theta_i$ are country-specific parameters.[13] Suppose further, for example by using a log-linearization, that near the steady state

$$\hat{x}_{it+T} - \hat{x}_i^* = M_i(\hat{x}_{it} - \hat{x}_i^*),$$

$$y_{it} = a_i' x_{it} + \varepsilon_{it}^y$$

$$LE_{it} = b_i' x_{it} + \varepsilon_{it}^{LE},$$

where $M_i$ is a country-specific matrix (for example a Jacobian matrix in the case of a differential model), and $a_i$, $b_i$ are fixed, country-specific vectors. Each steady state has a characteristic growth rate $g_i$. The fundamental variables and their steady states levels are expressed in terms of transformed variable $\hat{x}_{it}, \hat{x}_{it}$ defined in terms of $g_i$ by the following relation: $x_{it} = \hat{x}_{it} + g_i et$ where $e = (1,...,1)'$, in such a way that the steady states $\hat{x}_i^*$ are constant. These equations can be derived for most growth models, so long as life expectancy is considered to depend on the underlying economic variables and country-specific parameters.

Suppose for simplicity that cycles have been excluded from the theory (as is usually the case), and that the steady states are stable, so that $M_i$ has real negative eigenvalues. Let $\beta_i$ be the eigenvalue with the smallest absolute value. Near the steady state, $\hat{x}_{it} - \hat{x}_i^*$ is close to being an eigenvector of $\beta_i$ and so the log-linearized model becomes:

$$\frac{1}{T}(\hat{x}_{it+T} - \hat{x}_i^*) = \frac{1}{T}e^{\beta_i T}(\hat{x}_{it} - \hat{x}_i^*) + \mu_{it}$$

---

[13] For example, life expectancy can be considered a function of one or several of income, capital, technology, inequality, etc., see Mayer-Foulkes (2003).

where $\mu_{it}$ is an error term. Hence

$$
\begin{aligned}
\frac{1}{T}(y_{it+T} - y_{it}) &= \frac{1}{T}a_i'(x_{it+T} - x_{it}) + \Delta\varepsilon_{it}^y \\
&= a_i'(\frac{1}{T}(\hat{x}_{it+T} - \hat{x}_{it}) + g_i e) + \Delta\varepsilon_{it}^y \\
&= B_i a_i'(\hat{x}_{it} - \hat{x}_i^*) + g_i a_i' e + v_{it} \\
&= B_i a_i'(x_{it} - g_i te - \hat{x}_i^*) + g_i a_i' e + v_{it} \\
&= B_i a_i'(-g_i te - \hat{x}_i^*) + B_i y_{it} + g_i a_i' e + \eta_{it} \\
&= c_i + \gamma_i t + B_i y_{it} + \eta_{it}
\end{aligned}
\qquad \text{C)}
$$

where $\quad \Delta\varepsilon_{it}^y = \frac{1}{T}(\varepsilon_{it+T}^y - \varepsilon_{it}^y)$, $\qquad v_{it} = a_i'\mu_{it} + \Delta\varepsilon_{it}^y$, $\qquad B_i = -\frac{1}{T}(1 - e^{\beta_i T}) < 0$,

$\eta_{it} = v_{it} - B_i\varepsilon_{it}^y$, $c_i = g_i a_i' e - B_i a_i' \hat{x}_{it}^*$ and $\gamma_i = -B_i g_i a_i' e$. If the fundamental variables

$x_{it}$ have the same steady state growth rate as income, as is usually assumed, then $a_i'e = 1$. I

shall refer to $c_i$, $\gamma_i$, and $B_i$ as the fixed effect, steady state growth rate and convergence coefficients respectively. Although the error term derived here has an order one autoregressive structure, turn out to be insignificant. This is the equation that we estimate for income. An analogous derivation holds for life expectancy.

# References

Acemoglu, D., Aghion, P. and Zilibotti, F. (2002). "Distance to Frontier, Selection, and Economic Growth", mimeo.

Acemoglu, D., Simon Johnson, and James A. Robinson (2001). "The Colonial Origins of Comparative Development: An Empirical Investigation." *American Economic Review* **91** (December): 1369-1401.

Aghion, P. and P. Howitt (1992). "A Model of Growth through Creative Destruction." *Econometrica, (March),* **60** (2), pp. 323-51.

Anand, S. and Ravallion, M. (1993) "Human Development in Poor Countries: On the Role of Private Incomes and Public Services", *Journal of Economic Perspectives* **7**.

Arora, S. (2001) "Health, Human Productivity and Long-Term Growth", *Journal of Economic History*, (forthcoming).

Arrow, Kenneth J. (1962). "The Economic Implications of Learning by Doing." *Review of Economic Studies*, **29** (June), pp. 155-73.

Azariadis and Drazen (1990). "Threshold Externalities in Economic Development." *Quarterly Journal of Economics*, May, 5 (105), 501-526.

Barro, R. (1991) "Economic Growth in a Cross Section of Countries. " *Quarterly Journal of Economics* **196** (2/May): 407–443.

Barro, R. (1997). *Determinants of Economic Growth: A cross-country emprirical study.* Lionel Robbins Lectures. Cambridge and London: MIT Press.

Barro, R. J. and Sala-i-Martin, X. (1991). "Convergence Across States and Regions." *Brookings Papers on Economic Activity* **(1),** pp. 107-58.

Barro, R. J. and Sala-i-Martin, X. (1992a). "Convergence." *Journal of Political Economy* April, **100**(2), pp. 223-51.

Barro, R. J. and Sala-i-Martin, X. (1995), *Economic Growth*, McGraw-Hill, Inc.

Baumol, William. (1986), "Productivity Growth, Convergence, and Welfare." *American Economics Review*, December, **76**, 1072-1085.

Becker, Gary and Robert J. Barro (1989). "Fertility choice in a model of economic growth." *Econometrica*, **76**, 481-501.

Benabou, Roland (1996). "Equity and Efficiency in human capital investment: the local connection." *Review of Economic Studies*.

Bloom, David E. and Jeffrey D. Sachs (1998). "Geography, Demography, and Economic Growth in Africa", *Brookings Papers on Economic Activity*, Vol. 1998, No. 2. pp. 207-273.

Caselli, F., Esquivel, G. and Lefort, F (1996). "Reopening the Convergence Debate: A New Look at Cross-Country Growth Empirics", *Journal of Economic Growth*, September, **1**(3), 363-389.

Cowell, F. and Jenkins, S. (1995). "How Much Inequality Can We Explain? A Methodology and an Application to the United States", *Economic-Journal*, vol.105, pp. 421-430.

Dollar, David, and Edward N. Wolff (1997). "Convergence of Industry Labor Productivity among Advanced Economies, 1963-1982." In Edward N. Wolff, ed. *The Economics of Productivity*, 2: 39-48. Cheltenham, U.K.: Elgar Reference Collection

Domar, E. (1946), "Capital Expansion, Rate of Growth, and Employment." *Econometrica*, **14**(2): 137-47.

Durlauf, S. (1993). "Nonergodic economic growth." *Review of Economic Studies*, **60**, 349-367.

Durlauf, S. (1996). "A theory of persistent income inequality." *Journal of Economic Growth*, **1**, 75-94.

Easterly, W. (2001) *The Elusive Quest of Growth: Economists" Adventures And Misadventures in the Tropics*, MIT Press: Cambridge MA.

Evans, Paul. (1996). "Using Cross-Country Variances to Evaluate Growth Theories." Journal of Economic Dynamics and Control 20 (June-July): 1027-49.

Feyrer, James (2001). "Convergence by Parts", November, mimeo.

Fogel, R. (1994) "Economic Growth, Population Theory, and Physiology: The Bearing of Long-Term Processes on the Making of Economic Policy", *American Economic Review*, Vol.84(3):369-95.

Frankel, M. (1962). "The Production Function in Allocation and Growth: A Synthesis." *American Economic Review*, **52**, pp. 995-1022.

Galor, O. and Mayer-Foulkes, D. (2002), "Food for Thought: Basic Needs and Persistent Educational Inequality", mimeo.

Galor, Oded (1996). "Convergence? Inferences from Theoretical Models." *Economic Journal* **106**, July, pp. 1056-69.

Galor, Oded and David Weil (1996). "The Gender Gap, Fertility, and Growth." *American Economic Review*, June.

Galor, Oded, and D. Tsiddon(1997). "The distribution of human capital and economic growth." *Journal of Economic Growth*, March, pp. 93-124.

Galor, O. and Zeira, J. (1993). "Income Distribution and Macroeconomics." *Review of Economic Studies*, pp. 35-53.

Hall, R.E., and Jones, C.I. (1999). "Why Do Some Countries Produce so Much More Output per Worker than Others?" *Quarterly Journal of Economics*, **114**(1): 83-116.

Harrod, R. (1939). "An Essay in Dynamic Theory." *Economic Journal*, **49**(193): 14-33.

Howitt, P. (2000) "Endogenous growth and cross country income differences", *American Economics Review* **90**(4):829-46.

Howitt, P. and Mayer-Foulkes, D. (2005). "R&D, Implementation and Stagnation: A Schumpeterian Theory of Convergence Clubs", Journal of Money, Credit and Banking, Vol. 37, No. 1, Feb.

Howitt, P., and Aghion, P. (1998) "Capital Accumulation and Innovation as Complementary Factors in Long-Run Growth." *Journal of Economic Growth*, **3**(2):111-30.

Islam, N. (1995). "Growth Empirics: A Panel Data Approach", *Quarterly Journal of Economics*, pp. 1127-1170.

Klenow, P.J., and Rodríguez-Clare, A. (1997) "The Neoclassical Revival in Growth Economics: Has it Gone too Far?" in B. Bernanke and J. Rotemberg (eds) *NBER Macroeconomics Annual 1997*, MIT Press: Cambridge, MA.

Knight, Malcolm; Loayza, Norman; Villanueva, Delano (1993). "Testing the Neoclassical Theory of Economic Growth: A Panel Data Approach", *IMF Sta. Papers*, September, **40**(3), 512-41.

Kremer, M, Onatski, A. and Stock, J., (2001). "Searching for Prosperity." *National Bureau of Economic Research*, Working Paper 8250, (April).

Krugman, Paul (1991a). "Increasing Returns and Economic Geography", *The Journal of Political Economy*, Vol. 99, No. 3. (Jun., 1991), pp. 483-499.

Krugman, Paul (1991b). "History and Industry Location: The Case of the Manufacturing Belt (in Path Dependence in Economics: The Invisible Hand in the Grip of the Past)", *The American Economic Review*, Vol. 81, No. 2, Papers and Proceedings of the Hundred and Third Annual Meeting of the American Economic Association. (May, 1991), pp. 80-83.

Krugman, Paul (1994). "Complex Landscapes in Economic Geography (in Complexity in Economic Theory)", *The American Economic Review*, Vol. 84, No. 2, Papers and Proceedings of the Hundred and Sixth Annual Meeting of the American Economic Association. May, pp. 412-416.

Levine, R. & Renelt, D. (1992). "A Sensitivity Analysis of Cross-Country Growth Regressions." *American Economic Review* **82** (4/Sept.): 942–963.

Lucas, Robert E., Jr. (1988). "On the Mechanics of Development Planning." *Journal of Monetary Economics*, **22**, 1 (July), pp. 3-42.

Mankiw, N. Gregory, David Romer and David N. Weil (1992). "A Contribution to the Empirics of Economic Growth." *Quarterly Journal of Economics*, **107**, 2 (May), pp. 407-37.

Martin, Will and Mitra, Devashish (2001). "Productivity Growth and Convergence in Agriculture and Manufacturing" *Economic Development and Cultural Change*, **49**(2): 403-422.

Mayer-Foulkes, D. (2001a). "The Long-Term Impact of Health on Economic Growth in Mexico, 1950-1995", *Journal of International Development*, **13**(1), pp. 123-126.

Mayer-Foulkes, D. (2001b). "The Long-Term Impact of Health on Economic Growth in Latin America", *World Development*, **29**(6) pp. 1025-1033.

Mayer-Foulkes, D. (2003). "Convergence Clubs in Cross-Country Life Expectancy Dynamics", in Perspectives on Growth and Poverty, Rolph van der Hoeven and Antony Shorrocks (editors), United Nations University Press, pp. 144-171.

Murphy, Kevin M., Andrei Shleifer, and Robert W. Vishny (1989). "Industrialization and the Big Push." *Journal of Political Economy* **97** (October): 1003-26.

Parente, Stephen L., and Edward C. Prescott. 2000. *Barriers to Riches*. Cambridge, Massachusetts : The MIT Press.

Preston, S. (1975). "The Changing Relation between Mortality and Level of Economic Development", *Population Studies*, **29**(2):231-48.

Pritchett, L. and Summers, L. (1996) "Wealthier is Healthier", *Journal of Human Resources* **31**(4): 842-68.

Pritchett, Lant (1997). "Divergence, Big Time." *Journal of Economic Perspectives*, 11(3), Summer 1997, pp. 3-17.

Quah, Danny T. (1993). "Empirical cross-section dynamics in Economic Growth." *European Economic Review* **37**(2/3), 426-434.

Quah, Danny T. (1996). "Convergence empirics across countries with (some) capital mobility." *Journal of Economic Growth* **1** (1), 95-124.

Quah, Danny T. (1997). "Empirics for Growth and Distribution: Stratification, Polarization and Convergence Clubs." *Journal of Economic Growth 2*, pp. 27-59.

Ranis, Stewart and Ramírez (2000). "Economic Growth and Human Development", *World-Development*, vol 28 (2), pages 197-219.

Romer, Paul M. (1986). "Increasing Returns and Long-Run Growth." *Journal of Political Economy*, **94**, 5 (October), pp. 1002-37.

Romer, Paul M. (1990). "Endogenous Technological Change." *Journal of Political Economy*, **98**, 5 (October), part II, pp. S71-S102.

Sachs, Jeffrey D. and Andrew M. Warner (1997). "Fundamental Sources of Long-Run Growth (in What Have we Learned from Recent Empirical Growth Research?)", *The American Economic Review*, Vol. 87, No. 2, Papers and Proceedings of the Hundred and Fourth Annual Meeting of the American Economic Association. May, pp. 184-188.

Savedoff, W.D., and Schultz, T.P. (eds) (2000) *Wealth from Health: Linking Social Investments to Earnings in Latin America*, Inter-American Development Bank: Washington.

Schultz, T.P. (1992) "The Role of Education and Human Capital in Economic Development: An Empirical Assessment", *Yale Economic Growth Center Discussion Papers* No.**670**.

Schultz, T.P. (1997) "Assessing the Productive Benefits of Nutrition and Health: An Integrated Human Capital Approach", *Journal of Econometrics* **77**(1):141-58.

Schultz, T.P. (1999) "Health and Schooling Investments in Africa", *Journal of Economic Perspectives* **13**(3):67-88.

Schumpeter, Joseph A. (1934), *The Theory of Economic Development.* Cambridge MA, Harvard University Press.

Solow, R. M. (1956). "A Contribution to the Theory of Economic Growth." *Quarterly Journal of Economics*, **70**(1): 65-94.

Steckel, R. (1995) "Stature and the Standard of Living", *Journal of Economic Literature* **33**(4):1903-40.

Strauss, J., and Thomas, D. (1998) "Health, Nutrition, and Economic Development". *Journal of Economic Literature* **36**(2):766-817.

Swan, T. W. (1956). "Economic Growth and Capital Accumulation." *Economic Record*, **32**: 334-361.

Thomas, D.; Schoeni, R.F., and Strauss, J. (1997) "Parental Investments in Schooling: Gender and Household Resource Allocation in Urban Brazil", *RAND Labor and Population Program Working Paper*.

Tsiddon, D. (1992). "A moral hazard trap to growth." *International Economic Growth*, **33**, 299-322.

Uzawa, Hirofumi (1965). "Optimal Technical Change in an Aggregative Model of Economic Growth." *International Economic Review*, 6 (January), pp. 18-31.

In: International Finance and Monetary Policy
Editor: Gleb P. Severov pp. 61-85

ISBN 1-60021-103-8

*Chapter 3*

# LEARNING TO LIVE WITH THE FLOAT: TURKEY'S EXPERIENCE 2001-2003

*Faruk Selçuk*[1][*] *and Oya Pinar Ardic*[2][†]
[1]Department of Economics, Bilkent University,
Bilkent 06800, Ankara, Turkey
[2]Bogazici University, Department of Economics,
Bebek 34342, Istanbul, Turkey

## Abstract

The conduct of policy under floating exchange rates is becoming an increasingly important concern for developing countries. The challenge facing the central banks is to contain the volatility of the exchange rate while achieving low inflation and stimulating output growth. As a complement, the governments must implement sound policies to bring the fiscal and legal environments close to those of the advanced economies so as to enhance long-term economic growth. One recent example of an emerging economy that confronts this challenge is Turkey with a history of high inflation and a collapse of a fixed exchange rate based stabilization program that resulted in a market-forced devaluation. After a review of the literature, this chapter analyzes the developments in the foreign exchange market in Turkey in light of the Central Bank's policies during the floating exchange rate system between February 2001 - November 2003. The results indicate that the Central Bank had been successful in containing volatility and reducing the average inflation rate. However, the accumulated risks in the economy, such as the extreme appreciation of the currency and high real interest rates make the system vulnerable to adverse shocks.

**Keywords:** exchange rate systems, emerging markets, financial volatility

**JEL No:** C32, E31, E58, E65, F31

---

[*]E-mail address: faruk@bilkent.edu.tr, http://www.bilkent.edu.tr/~faruk, Tel: +90 (532) 294 8796, Fax: +1 (208) 694 3196.

[†]E-mail address: pinar.ardic@boun.edu.tr, http://www.econ.boun.edu.tr/ardic. Corresponding Author. Tel: +90 (212) 359 7650, Fax: +90 (212) 287 24 53.

# 1  Introduction

The choice of an exchange rate regime under free capital mobility has become an important concern for the emerging market economies. The Asian crisis in 1997-1998 and the
turmoil in Brazil, Russia, Turkey and Argentina afterwards have played a crucial part in
raising this question. Furthermore, the increasing degree of globalization has sped up the
international integration of capital markets, augmenting the difficulty of policy conduct for
the developing economies.

The crises in the international capital markets that had affected the emerging economies
since the last decade of the twentieth century had adverse impacts especially on the countries that have some form of pegged exchange rate regimes. Since then, the policy discussions on the choice of exchange rate regimes have been in favor of corner solutions, namely
hard pegs and free floats. The intermediate regimes, or soft pegs, have lost their attractiveness to a certain extent. Tavlas (2003) argues that the increase in the international flows
of capital is the factor that made the management of exchange rate difficult. In addition,
the unpredictable reversal of capital flows and contagion as the other two sources besides
the expansion of capital flows that had led to the departure from the intermediate foreign
exchange rate regimes.

Even if a country declares that the exchange rate regime is a "free float", it should be
expected that the country will not remain indifferent to wide fluctuations in the exchange
rates, a behavior which Calvo and Reinhart (2002) call the "fear of floating." Fischer (2001)
argues that the "fear of floating" is understandable. He points out that although the soft pegs
are unsustainable for countries that experience high capital mobility, there still exists a range
of flexible exchange rate arrangements. The excluded arrangements from his "acceptable
regimes" are certain forms of fixed, adjustable peg, and narrow band exchange rate systems. In these excluded regimes, the government is committed to defending a particular
value of the exchange rate, or a narrow range of exchange rates without any required institutional commitment, although the country is open to international capital flows. Thus,
free and managed floats, as well as currency unions, currency boards, and dollarization (or
Euroization) are acceptable in this "bipolar view" as long as the country backs the system
with necessary institutional changes. On the other hand, as the recent Argentine experience
shows, the absence of mechanisms other than the nominal exchange rate to create flexibility
in the system to absorb negative shocks can lead to a severe crisis under a currency board.

The majority of the emerging market economies still suffer the "fear of floating" although the consensus is that soft pegs are not sustainable for a long period of time, and
hard pegs have harmful effects on economic performance when there is lack of sufficient
flexibility. The question, then, is the following: Is it possible for an emerging economy
to conduct a monetary policy to contain the volatility in the exchange rate and to achieve
success in lowering (and/or controlling) inflation and in enhancing output growth under a
floating exchange rate regime?

In order to provide a partial answer to this question from an emerging country experience, this chapter analyzes the developments in the foreign exchange market in light of
the Central Bank's policies during the floating exchange rate system in Turkey between
February 2001 and November 2003. The main finding is that the Central Bank had been
successful in containing volatility and reducing the average inflation rate while there was

a surge in output growth. However, the accumulated risks in the economy, such as the extreme appreciation of the currency and high real interest rates makes the country vulnerable to adverse shocks.

The rest of this chapter is organized as follows. The next section reviews the exchange rate regimes and policies, and discusses the implications for the emerging market economies. The third section provides an account of the recent experiences of the Turkish economy. The empirical analysis is presented in Section 4. Section 5 concludes.

## 2   Exchange Rate Regimes and Policy in Emerging Market Economies

The volatility of the exchange rate is a crucial issue for an emerging economy due to liability dollarization and the sensitivity of domestic prices to fluctuations in the exchange rate. It has important implications on domestic prices and the inflation rate, interest rates, and investment. Thus, containing the volatility of the exchange rate is a crucial aspect of enhancing stability, and the choice of the exchange rate system is a critical issue in this respect.[1]

Exchange rate regimes range from free floats to hard pegs, of which free floats put no restrictions on monetary policy but has the problem of volatility while hard pegs reduce the damages of volatility at the expense of the abandonment of monetary policy as a tool. Soft pegs lie between these two extreme cases, and have served as a tool for stabilization in developing economies. Thus, there is a trade-off between exchange rate volatility and the ability to use monetary policy. For expositional purposes, a summary of the types of exchange rate systems are summarized below.[2,3]

- *Free Float* Under a free float regime, the value of the exchange rate is determined by the demand and supply in the market, and the monetary authority does not intervene for the purpose of affecting the value of the exchange rate. Thus, the exchange rate does not restrict macroeconomic policies. Australia, Canada, Chile, Colombia, Japan, the United Kingdom, and the United States are examples of countries using free float.

- *Managed Float* Other than the intervention of the monetary authority to contain volatility or to correct the long run misalignment of the exchange rate, there is no specific exchange rate target, and macroeconomic policies are not restricted that much by efforts to set the value of the exchange rate. Algeria had a managed float as of the end of 2001.

---

[1]See Minella *et al.* (2003) for a recent account of monetary policy under exchange rate volatility in Brazil. Calderon and Schmidt-Hebbel (2003) provide an analysis of macroeconomic policies in Latin America. Both studies stress the importance of the credibility of the Central Banks in inflation targeting, exchange rate volatility, and the ability to conduct counter-cyclical policies.

[2]For more details, see Tavlas (2003) who provides a review of exchange rate regimes. His summary emphasizes the choice of an exchange rate regime for an emerging economy. He suggests inflation targeting along with managed float for emerging market economies.

[3]The country examples for each type of exchange rate system are taken from Bubula and Otker-Robe (2002) who use the recent IMF de facto classification of exchange rates (in effect since 1998) to compile historical data (pre-1998) for the classification of exchange rate systems. Before 1998, IMF classifications were based on official announcements by each country (de jure classification). The classification is as of the end of 2001.

- *Soft Pegs* Under a soft peg, there is a particular exchange rate target, and the monetary authority conducts policy to achieve it. Types of soft pegs include adjustable pegs where the target rate might seldom be altered if the target differs from the equilibrium exchange rate and capital controls are used to support the system, and crawling pegs where there is a set path for the exchange rate and the target rate is adjusted frequently. Bolivia, Costa Rica and Israel were among the countries that had some form of a soft peg by the end of 2001.

- *Fixed Exchange Rates* Under a fixed exchange rate system, the monetary authority fixes the value of the domestic currency against a foreign currency or a basket of foreign currencies. Malaysia adopted a fixed exchange rate regime in 1998.

- *Currency Boards* Under this system, which restricts the conduct of monetary policy, the local currency is convertible to the anchor currency on demand at a preset (by law) fixed exchange rate, and this is guaranteed by backing the domestic monetary base with the foreign currency. In Argentina, a currency board system was in effect between 1991-2002.

- *Dollarization (or Euroization)* The country adopts US dollars (or euros) as the official currency. The examples of countries that have adopted US dollars as their official currency include Panama, Ecuador, and El Salvador.

- *Monetary Union* This is an agreement by a group of countries to adopt a common currency and to have a common central bank to conduct monetary policy for the whole group. Monetary policy can no longer be used for the needs of individual members of the group. The Euro area is an example of a monetary union.

The choice of an exchange rate regime has long been a concern for economists. See, for example, Mundell (1961), McKinnon (1963), and Kenen (1969). Obstfeld and Rogoff (1995) argue that a fixed exchange rate has costs in terms of developing and maintaining credibility, and that the exchange rate should not be the target of the monetary policy, but rather can be used as an indicator. The alternative to fixed exchange rates as a tool for reducing inflation and exchange rate volatility is to establish sound monetary institutions. Reinhart (2000) and Calvo and Reinhart (2002) state that although there seems to be an observed shift in the world toward floating exchange rate regimes, the "fear of floating" is pervasive, and in practice, except for a few developed nations, the countries do conduct policies to affect their exchange rates.

Most emerging market economies are characterized by economic problems including high inflation, and current account deficits. The majority of the domestic debt in these countries is denominated in terms of a foreign currency (usually the US dollar), elevating the importance of having a stable exchange rate. In addition, there is evidence that the pass-through from exchange rates to prices is higher in emerging economies (Calvo and Reinhart, 2001). Thus, some form of a peg appears to be the most attractive exchange rate regime. Furthermore, by restricting the use of monetary policy, pegged regimes have been used as a tool in developing countries to enhance the credibility of the monetary authority in stabilizing the economy.

Until recently, soft pegs were desirable, and were widely adopted by the developing economies, in many cases as a part of a stabilization program. The crises of the last decade and a half, however, resulted in a departure away from pegged exchange rates, which is basically attributable to the increased integration of the international capital markets. The concept of the "impossible (or unholy) trinity" provides an explanation for this phenomenon. This concept states that it is impossible for a country to have fixed exchange rates, capital mobility, and monetary policy as a tool for domestic goals at the same time. Soft pegs can be thought of as a means for having fixed exchange rates and domestic monetary policy for a country with capital mobility (Fischer, 2001). However, in a world with increased openness of capital accounts, responding to domestic and external shocks that shift the equilibrium exchange rate has become increasingly difficult, and such countries have been objects of speculative attacks. The Asian crisis of the 1997-1998 is the major example of this phenomenon when Malaysia imposed capital controls in order to control the exchange rate. But, although capital controls under such situations can provide some short term relief, they are ineffective in the long term.

The preference for the pegged systems by the developing economies stems from the idea that pegged systems implicitly call for fiscal discipline under capital mobility, since bad policies by the government would lead to the worsening of the external balance, eventually forcing the abandoning of the peg. In practice, however, this fiscal discipline is not observed since the eventual outcome, devaluation, may come long afterwards leaving the authorities very little incentive to take the necessary fiscal measures. As put forth by Tornell and Velasco (2000), flexible exchange rate regimes, on the other hand, provide an incentive for the authorities to enhance fiscal discipline since the costs of bad policies are immediate. Examples of crises due to insufficient fiscal discipline under pegged systems include the Mexican crisis of 1994, the Asian crisis of 1997, the Brazilian crisis of 1999 and the Turkish crisis of 2001. Argentina can also be included in this list since one of the major reasons for the collapse of the currency board regime was the lack of fiscal discipline in local governments.

The case against the currency boards was demonstrated by the dramatic collapse of the Argentine economy in 2001. While labor market rigidity and lack of fiscal discipline were the two main factors contributing to this collapse, perhaps the most important reason was the wrong choice for the anchor currency that lead to the loss of international competitiveness. The lesson of the collapse of the Argentine currency board is that the use of a proper peg, fiscal sustainability, and credibility are crucial for success while over the long term maintaining the peg comes at high costs. Also, fiscal sustainability not only means reducing primary spending or raising taxes, but also conducting policies to correct the mismatch between debt composition and output composition in terms of tradables versus non-tradables.[4]

Eichengreen (2001) provides an account of the 2001 crises in Argentina and Turkey. Although Argentina and Turkey had differences in terms of the underlying inflation history, and the timing and the type of the exchange rate regime used in their stabilization programs (currency board in Argentina, crawling peg in Turkey), the two countries shared

---

[4]See Calvo *et al.* (2003) for more on the collapse of the Currency Board in Argentina. In addition to the points outlined in this paragraph, Calvo *et al.* (2003) emphasize the role of liability dollarization besides the smaller share of tradables in output relative to the share of non-tradables in the effects of a sudden stop of capital flows.

many aspects such as experiencing an extended period of depressed growth followed by a short-lived boom after the initiation of the stabilization program, increased exports and imports, need for capital inflows to finance the increased imports, and efforts to privatize the state enterprises, to strengthen the banking system and to balance public sector accounts. However, in both Argentina and Turkey, incomplete fiscal consolidation and lack of political support for reduced public spending still continued to be problems. In addition, the increase in domestic demand proved to be temporary, and once the problem of competitiveness that arose from the exchange rate anchor was added, financing the current account became difficult, and a one-time adjustment of the exchange rate was necessary to improve competitiveness. But, this would diminish the stability of the banking system in both countries as the banks had large foreign currency liabilities. Furthermore, it would hurt the credibility of the policy-makers. Thus, short-term foreign liabilities and rollover risk increased as maturities shortened. Both economies became vulnerable to deteriorating external conditions, and eventually were not able to avoid the crises.

According to Eichengreen (2001) there are eight lessons of the crises in Argentina and Turkey. First, exchange-rate based stabilizations are risky as exit from a peg is difficult. Second, the existence of large short-term debt creates fears of crisis. Third, debt swaps only delay the problems, they do not provide a solution. Fourth, fiscal stability requires reduced public spending, which in turn implies reduced aggregate demand and growth. The decline in growth decreases the tax base, and thus the tax revenues, worsening the fiscal position. Therefore, engineering fiscal consolidation while maintaining output growth is difficult. Fifth, under circumstances in which market-based solutions are not viable, it is not easy to overcome the problem of moral hazard in international lending, and thus the international financial institutions found themselves bailing out both countries in fears of a more widespread crisis. Sixth, in both countries, the governments adopted fiscal and financial reforms to catalyze private lending in the aftermath of the crises, and the international financial institutions provided necessary funds in the meantime, until the markets react. However, market reaction was delayed as investors waited for evidence of commitment to stabilization policies. Seventh, as the Argentine case shows, there are limitations to private contingent lines since the collateral bonds were limited in supply as a result of the debt swap prior to the crisis. Thus, the governments may have a tendency to think it unlikely to ever be drawing those lines. Eighth, and last, it is difficult to get the private sector involved in the bail out as the market is unwilling to hold new claims after a crisis. Thus, Eichengreen (2001) claims that there is still much to be done in terms of formulating policies to prevent and to resolve the crises.

The common features of the crises that the emerging markets have experienced since the 1990s are the collapse of some form of pegged exchange rate regime and an accompanying sudden stop of capital inflows. These crises resulted in a sharp currency depreciation, a decline in the stock market, and contraction in output in the short run. Cespedes et al. (2000) model a small open economy that has liability dollarization,[5] sticky wages, and where the net worth of domestic entrepreneurs play a crucial role in capital flows to the economy, and find that flexible exchange rates help the adjustment process in the immediate aftermath of a financial crisis which results in a large depreciation and sudden stop. A high

---

[5]See Cespedes et al. (2000), Cavallo et al. (2002), Allen et al. (2002), Calvo et al. (2003) and the references therein for details on the magnifying effects of liability dollarization on the emerging market financial crises.

degree of liability dollarization acts as a magnifier of external shocks through balance sheet effects, which diminishes the risk premium of the country and lead to the reversal of capital inflows. Allen *et al.* (2002) also consider the balance sheet effects of the emerging market crises, and discuss how liability dollarization can eventually trigger the crisis. They stress the importance of the maturity and the denomination of domestic debt, and claim that the solution to the problems of currency and maturity mismatches are limited.

Cavallo *et al.* (2002) also model this phenomenon, and claim that the sudden stop of capital inflows and output contraction are related to the degree of liability dollarization in the economy. They find that the cause of the overshooting of the exchange rate is the existence of large foreign currency denominated debt stock and the need for hedging open foreign currency positions after the collapse of the peg. Exchange rate overshooting, together with large foreign currency debt create balance sheet effects and result in a decline in the stock market, leading to a contraction in output. Then, Cavallo *et al.* (2002) evaluate the cost of the crisis in a country with a high degree of liability dollarization. Exchange rate overshooting and the decline in the stock market force the investors to leave the economy. However, this induces further depreciation of the exchange rate and the fall in the stock market, creating a cycle which results in large, adverse wealth effects for the economy. Their findings indicate, contrary to the findings of Cespedes *et al.* (2000), that if the authorities maintain the peg for at least a temporary period in the immediate aftermath of the crisis, they can reduce overshooting and its negative wealth effects, but at the expense of additional output contractions in the short run. The mechanism that ensures this is the presence of margin constraints imposed on the domestic economy.

In order to analyze alternative exchange rate regimes and monetary policy options for an emerging market economy that experiences shocks to world interest rates and terms of trade, and is subject to risk premia in external financing, Devereux and Lane (2003) calibrate a model and find that financial distortions do not have a major impact on alternative policy options. They conclude that liability dollarization does not necessarily make fixed exchange rates desirable for macroeconomic stabilization, but the degree of pass-through in import prices has important consequences for price stabilization.

Mussa *et al.* (2000) consider the effects of increased capital mobility and integration of developing economies into world markets on the exchange rate regimes of the advanced economies as well as of the developing and transition economies. For developing economies that are closely integrated to the world economy, they conclude that maintaining pegged exchange rates have become difficult, and more flexible exchange rate regimes have become more desirable. In order for an emerging market country to opt for a form of hard peg, it needs to have established institutional structures and sufficient policy discipline to support the peg.

Putting special emphasis on the Turkish experience, Alper and Yılmaz (2003) argue that the best choice for the exchange rate regime for a developing economy with capital mobility is a floating system, supporting the conclusions of Mussa *et al.* (2000). A floating system would provide immediate costs to the governments that do not undertake serious fiscal measures. In addition, Alper and Yılmaz (2003) claim that as the foreign exchange risk will be transferred to the investors from the Central Bank under a free float, this would reduce the volume of short term capital flows and reduce the risk of speculative attacks (see also the arguments put forth by Eichengreen and Hausmann (1999) below for reducing the moral hazard problem). Further, if there is significant dollarization in the economy, the depreciation of the domestic currency implies a redistribution with undesirable political consequences, forcing the government to achieve fiscal discipline.

The high degree of currency substitution is another problem inherent in emerging market economies which has important consequences for the conduct of monetary policy and the implementation of stabilization programs, as currency substitution makes the use of monetary policy more difficult in fighting inflation since the demand for domestic money becomes unstable. Selçuk (2003) provides empirical evidence that the degree of currency substitution in emerging economies in the European Union periphery is indeed high. Domaç and Bahmani-Oskooee (2002) study the effects of currency substitution on inflation dynamics in Turkey. They find that the higher the degree of currency substitution is, the lower the monetary base will be, and thus, the fiscal authority needs to raise the administered prices in order to compensate for the decline in inflation tax. In the meantime, the domestic currency depreciates with the increases in the degree of currency substitution. Thus, the monetary authority would experience credibility problems more under a flexible exchange regime than it would under fixed exchange rates. In conclusion, Domaç and Bahmani-Oskooee (2002) indicate the emergence of inflation targeting as a suitable policy as it could limit the degree of currency substitution through leading to a higher exchange rate volatility than price volatility.

Eichengreen and Hausmann (1999) consider three problems that most emerging market economies suffer - moral hazard, original sin, and commitment problems - and examine the implications of exchange rate regimes in providing solutions to them. The bailing out of a troubled emerging market economy by the international financial institutions gives the investors incentives to take on excessive risks since they do not face the full risk of their investments. This creates moral hazard problem in international lending. Eichengreen and Hausmann (1999) argue that the solution is to require the private sector to share part of the burden of the bail-out. Pegged exchange rates in this case are undesirable as they reinforce the moral hazard problem, while flexible exchange rated are preferred as they limit short-term capital inflows.

The incompleteness in financial markets in emerging market countries may result in the inability of the country to borrow in terms of domestic currency in international markets and/or to borrow long-term domestically in terms of domestic currency. This "original sin" problem leads to currency mismatch where borrowing is in terms of foreign currency while revenues are in terms of domestic currency, and to maturity mismatch where liabilities are short-term and revenues are generated by long-term contracts. Eichengreen and Hausmann (1999) claim that dollarization (or euroization) is the best choice if original sin is the problem because flexible exchange rates cause bankruptcies by increasing the degree of currency mismatch and hard pegs cause defaults on short-term debt by increasing the degree of maturity mismatch.

The third problem Eichengreen and Hausmann (1999) consider for emerging markets is the commitment problem, which arises due to weak institutions that address commitment issues. Financial transactions are not self-enforcing by nature of being intertemporal, and in order to ensure commitment and enforce financial contracts, the economy needs to strengthen its financial infrastructure. Eichengreen and Hausmann (1999) argue that, in this case, both flexible and fixed exchange rates would increase financial fragility. Thus, taking these three problems into consideration, they suggest two options for emerging market economies. The first option is to dollarize while the second is to build well-structured domestic markets in which long-term domestic currency denominated instruments are traded. The second option, they state, takes longer and is harder, and therefore, most emerging market economies may rather choose to dollarize.[6]

Whether emerging market economies should float and whether they should adopt inflation targeting is considered by Eichengreen (2002). Under inflation targeting, the primary goal of monetary policy is price stabilization, and this goal and the policy tools are openly communicated to the public. Once the commitment to stable prices is institutionalized, credibility of the monetary authority would improve, leaving it room for pursuing policy to achieve the target. Eichengreen (2002) concludes that inflation targeting is not infeasible but complicated for emerging markets due to openness, liability dollarization, and lack of credibility. Openness adds to the challenge as it makes the economy vulnerable to external shocks, and the presence of liability dollarization would lead the monetary authority to refrain from movements in the exchange rate. However, when the economy is less open, the degree of liability dollarization is not very high, and credibility is easier to construct, inflation targeting would be attractive.

Domaç and Mendoza (2002) investigate whether the policy makers in emerging market economies should take into account the movements in exchange rates under inflation targeting. Although the primary goal under inflation targeting is the stability of prices, emerging economies would also be willing to contain the shocks to exchange rates in order to enhance stability. On the other hand, too much intervention in foreign exchange may alter inflation target as the primary goal. They suggest that policies aimed at containing the volatility of the exchange rate, but not affecting its level, can be useful under inflation targeting as they would reduce the adverse effects of exchange rate shocks on inflation and financial stability.

## 3   Turkish Economy: An Overview

This section provides an overview of the economic developments in Turkey, leading to the collapse of the most recent fixed exchange rate based stabilization program. The year 1980 had been the beginning of the period of liberalization and integration of the Turkish economy to the world economy. The structural change and reform plan of 1980 called for abandoning the barriers to trade, adopting export-led growth strategy, reducing the controls on foreign exchange, transition to the flexible exchange regime, lifting the controls on interest rates, easing bureaucracy, subsidizing foreign capital, and adopting price mechanism were among the main economic reforms introduced in this period. In the immediate aftermath of the implementation of this program, the economy experienced high output growth, low inflation and a healthy balance of payments situation.

The period since the late 1980s is characterized by increasing inflation and several stabilization programs. Nominal anchoring and monetary tightening were used in these programs without any serious effort to reduce the public sector borrowing requirement. In 1989, the capital account was liberalized and high nominal interest rate and low depreci-

---

[6]The conclusion of Eichengreen and Hausmann (1999) (supporting a form of hard peg) agrees with Calvo and Reinhart (2001) who suggest that some form of a peg is attractive for emerging economies.

ation rate were used to attract short term foreign capital to roll-over the public debt. By the end of 1993, the fiscal and external deficits were viewed by the market participants as no longer sustainable. These developments led to the crisis of April 1994. The stabilization program adopted after the crisis was not pursued vigorously and eventually abandoned (Ertuğrul and Selçuk, 2002).

The next stabilization attempt was in 1999 when the Russian crisis of 1998, the general elections and the earthquakes of 1999 deteriorated the fiscal balance. In December of 1999, a stand-by agreement was signed with the IMF with the crawling peg regime being the major disinflation tool.[7] The initial phase of this program was successful in reducing the interest rates and slowing down inflation which in turn led to increased consumption of consumer durables. However, the overvaluation of the exchange rate and lower real interest rates led to increased imports of consumption goods as well as intermediate goods. Increased world oil prices and the depreciation of the euro against the US dollar were the developments in the international markets that had adverse effects on the trade balance.

On the fiscal side, the program failed to achieve its targets which led the IMF and the World Bank to postpone the release of funds in the second half of 2000. In the meantime, inefficiencies and increased risk in the banking sector resulted in increased interest rates and reduced confidence in the financial markets. The slow pace of the government in undertaking the necessary steps to solve the financial problems of the state-owned banks and to implement other reforms, the lack of consensus and action in terms of privatization, the record levels of the current account deficit due to appreciation and negative domestic real interest rates, the deterioration of relations between Turkey and the European Union, and political instability are among the factors that contributed in this reduced confidence. In addition, the history of unsuccessful stabilization programs made it more difficult for the authorities to build up credibility, and the inability to deal with the fundamental problems of the economy resulted in an erosion of credibility.

There was a short-lived crisis in November 2000 which started with the inability of a commercial bank with a risky position to borrow from the money market. In two days, the overnight interest rates increased while the international investors started to get out. In order not to give up the parity, the Central Bank had to use its reserves to meet the increased demand for foreign currency. Later, to restore confidence in the program, the Central Bank had announced that such an action would not be repeated. However this only increased the interest rates. In December 2000, the IMF supplied extra funds, which provided temporary relief. There was short-term capital inflow to the economy for a while, and the reserves of the Central Bank returned to their pre-crisis level. Nevertheless, there were still concerns about the developments in the economy. In the end, the adverse political developments of February 2001 triggered another crisis and led the Central Bank to finally abandon the parity.

This last crisis, on February 19, 2001, was triggered by domestic political issues and led to an 18% drop in the stock market and the loss of approximately one-third of the total official reserves of the Central Bank in one day (USD 7.5 billion). When the Central Bank refused to provide Turkish Lira (TRL) liquidity to the two state banks that were not able to meet their obligations or other banks the following day, the banks were forced to

---

[7]The percentage change of the Turkish lira against a basket of euro and the US dollar was fixed.

give up USD 6 billion foreign exchange buying contracts with the Central Bank. The daily average overnight interest rates shot up to (simple annual) 2000 percent on February 20, and 4000 percent on February 21.[8] The government could not resist and dropped its exchange rate controls early February 22 and the TRL/USD exchange rate went up 40% in one week. Monthly inflation was 10% and 14% in March and April of 2001 respectively. The government prepared a new letter of intent to the IMF, emphasizing a major overhaul in the banking system and a promise of further acceleration of structural reforms outlined in the earlier letters of intent. On May 15, 2001, the IMF approved this revision of Turkey's three-year Stand-By arrangement by USD 8 billion with an understanding that the country moved into a floating exchange rate regime, and would stick to this policy.

Following the crisis, the challenge for the Central Bank was to re-establish confidence and contain volatility in financial markets while pursuing an implicit inflation targeting policy in a free floating exchange rate system. It was a challenge in the sense that the country had a long history of high inflation, and had never experienced a free float. Nominal exchange rates almost always increased in line with high inflation. The recent collapse of the fixed exchange rate based stabilization program further eroded the credibility of the Central Bank and led economic agents to think that any policy announcement by the authorities is not credible.[9]

## 4  Policy Under Floating Exchange Rate Regime in Turkey

In the aftermath of February 2001, the Central Bank of Turkey repeatedly stressed that it would stick to the floating exchange rate regime, and the volatility of the nominal exchange rate will be a concern rather than its level or direction. Meanwhile, an implicit inflation targeting policy would be pursued by controlling the monetary aggregates and setting an indicative interest rate (CBT, 2002, 2003).

In order to control the volatility of the exchange rate, the Central Bank conducted several buying and selling auctions. During the early stages of the float, between March 29, 2001 and November 30, 2001, all interventions were in the form of selling auctions, and the Central Bank sold a sum of USD 6,553 million. All other episodes of preannounced interventions had been in the form of buying auctions, the first one running from April 4 through June 6, 2002, and the second which started on May 5, 2003 and ended on October 22, 2003. The total amount bought back in these auctions were USD 6,447.3 million. The Bank also directly intervened in the market four times between May 12 and July 18, 2003 buying USD 2,083 million.[10] Thus, since the immediate aftermath of the float, the Central

---

[8]These are *weighted average* interest rates. The highest realized overnight interest rates during these two days were 2300 and 6200 percent (simple annual).

[9]Gençay and Selçuk (2006) provide an anecdotal story of the February 2001 crisis in Turkey. For a detailed account of the recent developments in the Turkish economy from different perspectives, see Ertuğrul and Selçuk (2002), Metin-Özcan et al. (2001), Öniş and Rubin (2003) and references therein. A series of articles in Kibritçioğlu et al. (2002) provides a detailed analysis of inflation dynamics and disinflation efforts in Turkey. For earlier studies, see Metin (1995) and Lim and Papi (1997). More recent studies are Celasun et al. (2003) and Domaç and Bahmani-Oskooee (2002).

[10]There were three direct interventions in 2002 (one buying and two selling). However, the amounts involved in these interventions as well as the amounts involved in two direct buying interventions in September 10-25, 2003 are not known.

Table 1: Granger causality probabilities. Sample period: March 13, 2001 - October 30, 2003 (667 business days). The rows show equations. The reported probabilities are probabilities that the column variable does not Granger cause the row variable.

|                | Return | Volatility | Interest Rate | Buying Auction | Selling Auction |
|----------------|--------|------------|---------------|----------------|-----------------|
| Return         | 0.00   | 0.13       | 0.56          | 0.19           | 0.00            |
| Volatility     | 0.00   | 0.00       | 0.00          | 0.46           | 0.00            |
| Interest Rate  | 0.09   | 0.00       | 0.89          | 0.10           | 0.46            |
| Buying Auction | 0.89   | 0.95       | 0.25          | 0.00           | 1.00            |
| Selling Auction| 0.04   | 0.06       | 0.18          | 0.96           | 0.00            |

Bank had sold USD 6,553 million, and bought at least USD 8,530 million. One crucial aspect of the Central Bank policies since May 2003 is that, the level and the direction of the exchange rate seem to have become the target of the policies rather than its volatility, implying a possible deviation from the free float. There were arguments that recent buying auctions, along with two direct buying interventions in September 2003 were a response to the nominal (and real) appreciation of the Turkish lira during the float period.

In this part, we extend the analysis conducted by Selçuk (2005), employing a larger sample size. In addition, we look at the developments in the foreign exchange market during two separate periods. In our analysis, a five variable VAR system is estimated using daily data in order to investigate the interaction among the exchange rate, its volatility, and the Central Bank policies. The variables in the system are the TRL/USD exchange rate return (log difference, percent), the absolute value of the exchange rate return as a measure of volatility (percent), the change in the Central Bank overnight interest rates (simple annual, percent), the daily total amount bought by the Central Bank in USD buying auctions and the amount sold by the Central Bank in USD selling auctions (million USD). To assess a possible change in the direction of the policy in recent months, the VAR system is estimated for the whole sample, between March 2001 and October 2003, and also for the two sub-samples, pre-May 2003 and post-May 2003, a possible break point reflecting an implicit change in exchange rate policy of the Central Bank.

The VAR model for the whole sample is estimated by using a constant term and 7 lags as indicated by Sims' Likelihood Ratio (LR) test (Sims, 1980) for the period between March 13, 2001 - October 30, 2003 (667 business days).[11] Adjusted R-squares lie between 0.04 (change in the interest rate equation) and 0.79 (buying auctions equation). The results of the Granger causality tests indicate that exchange rate return and selling auctions cause volatility of the exchange rate at 1% level of significance. Exchange rate return and selling auctions, and changes in the interest rate and volatility of the exchange rate exhibit feedback at 5% and 1% levels of significance respectively. See Table 1 for the results of Granger causality tests.

Figure 1 plots the response of exchange rate return to shocks to different variables in the system, along with 95 percent bootstrap confidence intervals. Normally, one would

---

[11]We excluded the first 8 business days of the floating regime period to avoid any "start-off" effects. As shown by Selçuk (2004a), after a large shock in a financial market, the cumulative number of aftershocks increases at an exponential rate and converges after a certain period of time. These aftershocks, which are not part of the normal system, may cause some bias in our estimations if they are not excluded.

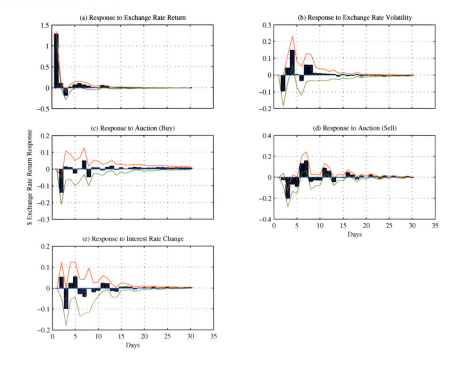

Figure 1: TRL/USD daily exchange rate return (log difference) response to shocks to different variables in the system. (a) Response to a shock (1.36 percent increase) in TRL/USD daily exchange rate return. (b) Response to a shock (1.06 percent increase) in TRL/USD daily volatility (absolute return). (c) Response to a shock (21 Million USD increase) in Central Bank USD buying auction. (d) Response to a shock (30 Million USD increase) in Central Bank selling auction. (e) Response to a shock (0.60 percent increase) in change in overnight interest rates. 95 percent bootstrap confidence intervals are plotted as straight lines. Sample period: March 13, 2001 - October 30, 2003 (667 business days).

expect the response of exchange rate return to shocks to Central Bank buying auctions to be positive since there is an increase in overall demand for the foreign currency. The results, however, indicate that this response is negative and statistically significant for one period. On the other hand, the response of the exchange rate return to a shock in selling auction is negative, as expected, for the first four periods. However, the response is reversed afterward and the overall response is very close to zero. The response of the exchange rate return to a shock to the change in interest rate is not statistically significant. Thus, it is possible to conclude that the Central Bank policies in the form of buying and selling auctions and changes in interest rate did not influence the direction (log return) of the exchange rates. In passing, we also note that a shock to the volatility of the exchange rate does not have any effect on the exchange rate return.

The response of exchange rate volatility to different shocks in the system is plotted in Figure 2. Panel (a) shows that an unexpected increase in exchange rate return increases volatility, and this impact prevails for several periods. Notice that the symmetric nature of the impulse response function implies that a fall in the foreign exchange rate return reduces volatility. However, the symmetric response of volatility to the shocks to the exchange rate

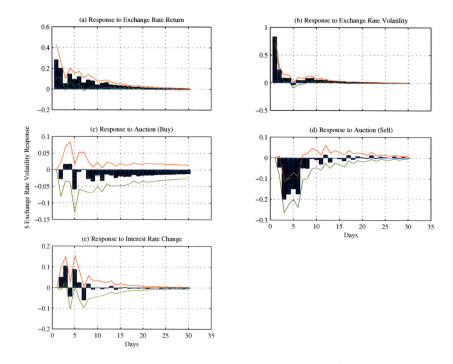

Figure 2: TRL/USD daily exchange rate volatility response to shocks to different variables in the system. (a) Response to a shock (1.36 percent increase) in TRL/USD daily exchange rate return. (b) Response to a shock (1.06 percent increase) in TRL/USD daily volatility (absolute return). (c) Response to a shock (21 Million USD increase) in Central Bank USD buying auction. (d) Response to a shock (30 million USD increase) in Central Bank selling auction. (e) Response to a shock (0.60 percent increase) in change in overnight interest rates. 95 percent bootstrap confidence intervals are plotted as straight lines. Sample period: March 13, 2001 - October 30, 2003 (667 business days).

return is not warranted. In an asymmetric stochastic volatility framework, Selçuk (2004b) shows that there is strong positive correlation between the shocks to the foreign exchange rate return at time $t$ and the shocks to volatility (defined as the standard deviation of the exchange rate return) at time $t + 1$ during the floating exchange rate system in Turkey. However, Selçuk (2004b) implies that the response of volatility is actually asymmetric: the same magnitude of shocks to the exchange rate return cause different effects on the volatility, depending on the sign of shocks.

Response of volatility to selling auction is negative and statistically significant, implying the Central Bank is able to reduce volatility through selling auctions while buying auctions do not seem to influence volatility. In addition, unexpected increases in the interest rate raise volatility, which makes it possible to say that unexpected interest rate cuts reduce the volatility of the exchange rate. These findings are in line with the Central Bank's argument that its policies are not aimed at the level or the direction of the exchange rate but rather the goal is to contain volatility.[12]

---

[12]The full estimation results in this section are not reported. They are available from the authors.

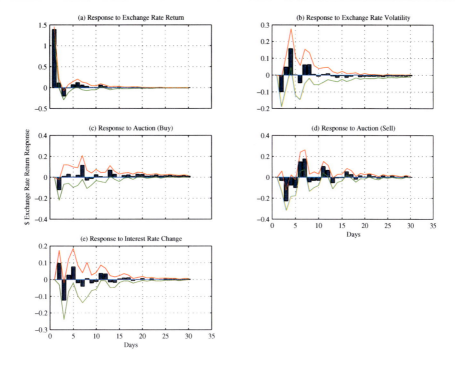

Figure 3: TRL/USD daily exchange rate return (log difference) response to shocks to different variables in the system. (a) Response to a shock (1.48 percent increase) in TRL/USD daily exchange rate return. (b) Response to a shock (1.15 percent increase) in TRL/USD daily volatility (absolute return). (c) Response to a shock in Central Bank USD buying (6 Million USD increase) auction. (d) Response to a shock (33 Million USD increase) in Central Bank selling auction. (e) Response to a shock (0.60 percent increase) in change in overnight interest rates. 95 percent bootstrap confidence intervals are plotted as straight lines. Sample period: March 13, 2001 - April 30, 2003 (538 business days).

The period before May 2003 is also investigated by means of the same five variable VAR system. The system is estimated using 11 lags as indicated by the likelihood ratio tests. Adjusted R-squares for this system lie in the range of 0.03, for the change in the interest rate equation, and 0.45, for selling auctions equation. Granger causality tests indicate that, as in the previous case, exchange rate return and selling auctions cause volatility of the exchange rate at 1% level of significance. Changes in the interest rate and volatility exhibit feedback at 1% level of significance. However, the feedback between selling auctions and exchange rate return is no longer observed: selling auctions cause exchange rate return at 1% significance level. Table 2 reports the results of Granger causality tests. This causality should be interpreted with impluse responses below before reaching a conclusion on the Central Bank policies.

Figure 3 depicts the impulse responses of the exchange rate return to various shocks in the system. These are analogous to the responses of the exchange rate return when the last part of the sample is also included. Similar arguments can be put forth for the responses of volatility to different shocks in the system by observing Figure 4. Thus, one may conclude that the Central Bank's policies from the start of the float until May 2003 targeted volatility

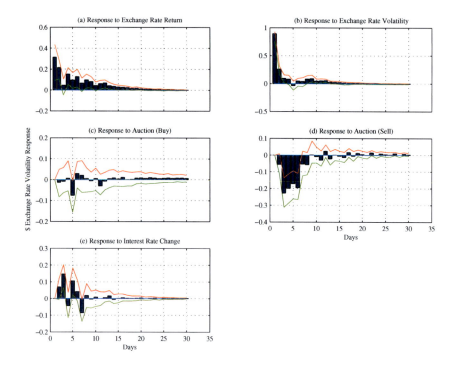

Figure 4: TRL/USD daily exchange rate volatility response to shocks to different variables in the system. (a) Response to a shock (1.48 percent increase) in TRL/USD daily exchange rate return. (b) Response to a shock (1.15 percent increase) in TRL/USD daily volatility (absolute return). (c) Response to a shock (6 Million USD increase) in Central Bank USD buying auction. (d) Response to a shock (33 Million USD increase) in Central Bank selling auction. (e) Response to a shock (0.60 percent increase) in change in overnight interest rates. 95 percent bootstrap confidence intervals are plotted as straight lines. Sample period: March 13, 2001 - April 30, 2003 (538 business days).

rather than the direction or the level of the exchange rate.

The VAR model is estimated using four lags as indicated by the likelihood ratio test for the post-May 2003 period as well.[13] Adjusted R-squares range from 0.04 (change in the interest rate equation) to 0.48 (buying auctions equation). Granger causality tests indicate that exchange rate volatility and buying auctions cause exchange rate return at 5% and 1% significance levels respectively. The results of Granger causality tests are reported in Table 3.

In the period after May 2003, we observe that the response of the exchange rate return to a shock to buying auctions is negative (see Figure 5). Thus, this again confirms that the buying auctions of the Central Bank did not influence the exchange rate positively. This contradicts the claim that the Central Bank was actually intervening in the market to affect the direction of the exchange rate upwards. Even if the bank had such an intention, it was not successful. Panel (d) of Figure 5 depicts the effects of an unexpected increase in the interest

---

[13]This model includes four variables: exchange rate return, exchange rate volatility, buying auctions, and changes in overnight interest rates. The bank conducted only buying actions during the period.

Table 2: Granger causality probabilities. Sample period: March 13, 2001 - April 30, 2003 (538 business days). The reported probabilities are probabilities that the column variable does not Granger cause the row variable.

| | Return | Volatility | Interest Rate | Buying Auction | Selling Auction |
|---|---|---|---|---|---|
| Return | 0.00 | 0.26 | 0.34 | 0.13 | 0.00 |
| Volatility | 0.01 | 0.00 | 0.00 | 0.53 | 0.00 |
| Interest Rate | 0.16 | 0.00 | 0.62 | 0.98 | 0.46 |
| Buying Auction | 0.44 | 0.82 | 0.67 | 0.00 | 1.00 |
| Selling Auction | 0.08 | 0.12 | 0.18 | 0.92 | 0.00 |

Table 3: Granger causality probabilities. Sample period: May 1, 2003 - October 30, 2003 (129 business days). The reported probabilities are probabilities that the column variable does not Granger cause the row variable.

| | Return | Volatility | Interest Rate | Buying Auction |
|---|---|---|---|---|
| Return | 0.17 | 0.02 | 0.60 | 0.00 |
| Volatility | 0.06 | 0.10 | 0.06 | 0.38 |
| Interest Rate | 0.17 | 0.53 | 0.84 | 0.01 |
| Buying Auction | 0.35 | 0.60 | 0.19 | 0.00 |

rate on the exchange rate. The initial impact is negative and statistically significant. Most of the positive responses in the following period are not statistically significant. The response of the exchange rate return to interest rate changes during this period is stronger and more immediate than what it was before May 2003. Previously, we found that the response was either not statistically significant (for the entire sample) or significant after one period (pre-May 2003). Here, the first period response is negative and statistically significant. That is, the exchange rate return responds positively (depreciation) to an unexpected interest rate cut. Finally, Figure 6 shows that impulse responses of the volatility to shocks to different variables after May, 2003 are not statistically significant, except a positive response to a positive shock to the exchange rate return. This indicates that the return-volatility relation is still strong in the foreign exchange market in Turkey.

The results of the VAR analysis indicate that the Central Bank policies were aimed at controlling the volatility of the exchange rate since the beginning of the float, but not to influence the level or the direction of the exchange rate. Contrary to the claims that the Central Bank had been responding to the direction of the exchange rate since May 2003, the results indicate that the policies affected volatility rather than the exchange rate itself. Even if the Central Bank implicitly aimed at the level of the exchange rates in recent months, there is no statistical evidence to determine such a policy change from the sample information.

The results in this part are in line with previous findings. Selçuk (2005) estimated the same model with a shorter sample from the free float period and found similar results. Domaç and Mendoza (2002) estimated an Exponential GARCH model using daily data on foreign exchange intervention in Turkey and Mexico. Using a smaller sample (February 2001 - May 2002), they showed that both the amount and frequency of foreign exchange intervention decreased the volatility of the exchange rates in Turkey. Domaç and Mendoza

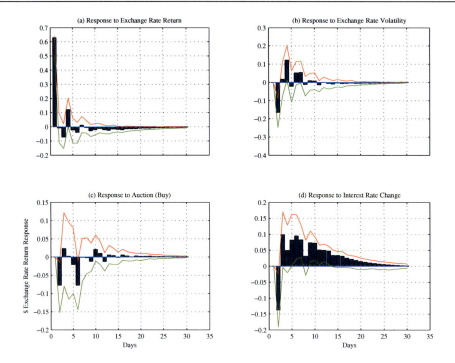

Figure 5: TRL/USD daily exchange rate return (log difference) response to shocks to different variables in the system. (a) Response to a shock (0.70 percent) in TRL/USD daily exchange rate return. (b) Response to a shock (0.43 percent increase) in TRL/USD daily volatility (absolute return). (c) Response to a shock (27 Million USD increase) in Central Bank USD buying auction. (d) Response to a shock (0.58 percent increase) in change in overnight interest rates. 95 percent bootstrap confidence intervals are plotted as straight lines. Sample period: May 1, 2003 - October 30, 2003 (There was no selling auction during this period). (129 business days).

(2002) reported that their results also imply that sale operations are effective in influencing the exchange rate and its volatility, while purchase operations are found to be statistically insignificant in affecting the exchange rate and its volatility. Finally, Selçuk (2004b) shows, in an asymmetric stochastic volatility framework, that there is strong positive correlation between the shocks to the foreign exchange rate return at time $t$ and the shocks to volatility (defined as the standard deviation of the exchange rate return) at time $t + 1$ during the floating exchange rate system in Turkey. We also found that shocks to the return and shocks to the volatility are indeed positively related. This finding itself implies that even if the Central Bank aimed at reducing volatility, the bank was in favor of nominal appreciations as compared to nominal depreciations since these two have opposite effects on the volatility.

# 5  Accumulated Risks

Although the Central Bank has been successful in containing the volatility of the exchange rates, the economy is not free from significant risks. Among these, the record level of real appreciation of the domestic currency and the total public debt with high real interest rates

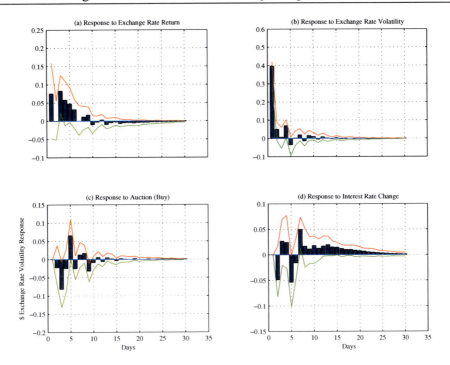

Figure 6: TRL/USD daily exchange rate volatility response to shocks to different variables in the system. (a) Response to a shock (0.70 percent increase) in TRL/USD daily exchange rate return. (b) Response to a shock (0.43 percent increase) in TRL/USD daily volatility (absolute return). (c) Response to a shock (27 Million USD increase) in Central Bank USD buying auction. (d) Response to a shock (0.58 percent increase) in change in overnight interest rates. 95 percent bootstrap confidence intervals are plotted as straight lines. Sample period: May 1, 2003 - October 30, 2003 (There was no selling auction during this period). (129 business days).

are the most important ones.

According to two real effective exchange rate indices published by the Central Bank, the overall real appreciation of the Turkish lira during the float (March 2001 - October 2003) is in between 26 and 34 percent. This appreciation is not as a result of the initial large depreciation (overshooting) in February 2001. The current level of both indices indicate that the real appreciation is in between 28 and 42 percent as compared to 1995 which was a "normal" year in terms of the real exchange rate level. However, the economy did not register a large current account deficit: it is expected to be around 3 percent of GDP in 2003. The record level of the real appreciation may be explained in part by the productivity increase in tradeable goods sector (the so-called "Balassa-Samuelson effect"). Labor productivity in private manufacturing industry increased 20 percent between 2001 and 2003 (second quarter). In addition, there was a fall in hourly nominal wages (in USD terms) during the same period. As a result, the unit wage index fell 30 percent as compared to 2000. This development partially explains why the competitiveness of the country did not suffer much from the record level of real appreciation. However, both the productivity growth and the fall in unit wages (in USD terms) seem to have slowed down during the second half of 2003. As a result, there might be a higher than expected current account deficit in 2004, unless the government takes further actions to increase the productivity and to contain the current account deficit.

Another reason behind the appreciation seems to be an external factor. Ardic and Selçuk (2006) report that the change in the spread between emerging market bonds and US treasury bills is a significant variable in explaining the TRL/USD dynamics. Particularly, they find that a decrease in the spread causes a decrease in TRL/USD while an increase is followed by a nominal depreciation of the Turkish lira. Currently, this spread is at its historical lows and the cycle is expected to reverse following an increase in interest rates in developed markets and a "flight-to-quality". Therefore, another risk for the Turkish economy is a reversal of foreign capital flows. This development, along with an increasing current account deficit, signals that there might be an upward pressure on the nominal exchange rates in year 2004.

One positive consequence of the appreciation manifested itself on inflation rates: During the float, monthly inflation rates went down from an average of 4 percent to and average of less than 1 percent. For a country with a long history of high inflation, this development is considered as a big success. Selçuk (2005) reports that the exchange rate pass through in Turkey is around 35 to 50 percent. Consequently, a slow down in nominal exchange rate depreciation would result in a smaller inflation. Similarly, nominal appreciation would have some deflationary effect on prices. Although it is a free floating exchange rate regime, the positive correlation between the exchange rate and price level may cause a bias in the Central Bank's approach to the developments in the exchange rate market. In other words, the Bank would favor exchange rate appreciations in its policy design since it also follows an implicit inflation targeting policy. If the risks with the current account deficit and its finance are realized, there would be an upward pressure on prices, and consequently an increase in inflation. This potential risk is possibly one reason why both indicative interest rates determined by the Central Bank and the market determined interest rates remain high in the economy. If the real interest rates are stalled at their current level (around 15 percent), the economy faces a much higher risk in another front: public debt rollover and an unsustainable fiscal position.

Table 5 gives the recent history of the public debt in Turkey.[14] It shows that the total public debt, as a percentage of the Gross National Product (GNP), doubled during the last 5 years. Particularly, the increase in total domestic debt is alarming: it was 21.9 percent of GNP in 1998 while it is 57.7 percent in 2003. What is more, foreign exchange (FX) denominated or FX linked component of the domestic debt is also increasing: it was just 7 percent of the total domestic debt in 1998 while it is now 23 percent. The public foreign debt stock, on the other hand, increased from USD 52 billion in 1998 to USD 89.8 billion in 2003, reaching 46 percent of GNP. Foreign public debt and FX denominated/linked component of the domestic debt together (USD 118 billion) is 60 percent of GNP which implies that a nominal depreciation of the domestic currency would increase the foreign debt burden of the country on impact. This concern might be another contributing factor in viewing real appreciations as a positive development from the policy makers' point of view.

Even if we assume that the country would face no difficulties in rolling over the existing

---

[14]These figures reflect the "gross" public debt of the central government in Turkey. For a detailed debt sustainability analysis, net public debt figures should be calculated. That is, the net foreign assets of the Central Bank and the other public sector should be included in the foreign debt calculation. Similarly, the rest of the public sector and the public deposits should be included in domestic debt figures.

Table 4: Public Debt in Turkey. Source: The Central Bank and the Treasury.

| Public Debt (Billion USD) | 1998 | 1999 | 2000 | 2001 | 2002 | 2003* |
|---|---|---|---|---|---|---|
| Domestic | 37.1 | 42.4 | 54.2 | 84.9 | 91.7 | 120.8 |
| Foreign | 52.0 | 52.7 | 61.2 | 70.1 | 85.4 | 89.8 |
| Total | 89.1 | 95.1 | 115.4 | 155 | 177.1 | 210.6 |
| | | | | | | |
| % of GNP | | | | | | |
| Domestic | 21.9 | 29.3 | 29.0 | 69.2 | 54.8 | 57.7 |
| Foreign | 25.3 | 28.3 | 30.4 | 48.7 | 47.1 | 46.1 |
| Total | 47.2 | 57.6 | 59.4 | 117.9 | 101.9 | 103.8 |

*As of September 2003.

foreign debt, the domestic debt situation is very fragile. In its simplest form, sustainable fiscal policy condition requires that the total debt as a percentage of the total income should not be increasing forever. That is, the following equation should not be positive under the fiscal policy of a country

$$\Delta\beta = (r - g)\beta - x \tag{1}$$

where $\beta$ is the debt-income ratio, $r$ is the real interest rate, $g$ is the real growth rate of the economy, and $x$ is the primary surplus (non-interest budget surplus). If the current path of the fiscal policy implies that the change in debt-income ratio ($\Delta\beta$) will be positive, the policy is said to be unsustainable, i.e., the fiscal policy at some point must change.

If we assume a 5 percent real growth and a 15 percent real interest rate, the current domestic debt/income ratio (58 percent) implies that the required primary surplus to keep the domestic debt/income ratio constant is 5.8 percent of GDP. So far, the Turkish government is keen to give this much primary surplus. However, an adverse shock to the system may increase the real interest rate while decreasing the growth rate and worsen the fiscal position. For example, if the real interest rate-real growth differential ($r - g$) increases from its assumed level of 10 percent to 15 percent (2-3 percentage point increase in real interest rate and 2-3 percent decrease in the growth rate), the required primary surplus would increase to 9 percent. Given the fact that the government is currently operating at the limit (in terms of tax revenues and public expenditures), it would be extremely unlikely to obtain a 9 percent primary surplus. In this case, some other policy options to put the fiscal policy into a sustainable path may come into effect in the economy. Otherwise, Anne Kruger, First Deputy Managing Director of IMF, warns that even an IMF assistance could not be helpful:

> Suppose, for instance, that the debt is truly unsustainable and that, for whatever reason, a government fails to introduce economic reforms of the kind needed to rebalance the economy. It is difficult to see how, in such circumstances, a program of Fund financial assistance could help. If the structure of the existing debt does not change, the total amount that a country can repay will not change. It is bound to be less than that needed to service the debt. Additional lending from the Fund will simply displace private debt and, in practice, increase the size of the 'haircut' that private creditors will, eventually, have to accept (Krueger, 2003).

In sum, the high real appreciation during the float along with a recently slowed down productivity in manufacturing industry may result in a large current account deficit in Turkey. This development, coupled with external financing difficulties, may lead to an upward correction in nominal exchange rates. This risk increases the risk premium of the country, and prevents the Central Bank from cutting interest rates further down because of the higher inflation risk. High real interest rates, on the other hand, make the fiscal position of the government very fragile.

## 6  Conclusion

The choice of an exchange rate regime under high capital mobility has become an important concern for the emerging market economies, especially after the Asian crisis, and the subsequent ones in Brazil, Russia, Turkey and Argentina. Furthermore, the increasing degree of globalization in the world has sped up the international integration of capital markets, augmenting the difficulty of policy conduct for the developing economies.

Recent policy discussions on the choice of exchange rate regimes have been in support of corner solutions, namely hard pegs and floats. In the aftermath of the February 2001 crisis, Turkey has let the Turkish lira float, and the policies of the Central Bank since then have been aimed at controlling the volatility of the exchange rate rather than targeting its level or direction while trying to lower the inflation rate.

This chapter has analyzed the developments in the foreign exchange market in light of the Central Bank's policies during the floating exchange rate system in Turkey between 2001-2004. The main finding is that the Central Bank had been successful in containing volatility and reducing the average inflation rate. The estimation results show that the Central Bank did not target the level nor the direction of the exchange rate, and was successful in containing volatility. Despite the arguments that the Central Bank policies after May 2003 were aimed at preventing the appreciation of the Turkish lira, the results of the empirical analysis indicate no evidence to support this claim.

It is important to note, however, that the accumulated risks in the economy, such as the extreme appreciation of the currency and high real interest rates along with large debt burden suggest that the economy is fragile. More drastic economic policies to restructure the economy would lessen the negative impact of unexpected adverse shocks.

## References

Allen, M., Rosenberg, C., Keller, C., Setser, B., and Roubini, N. (2002). A balance sheet approach to financial crisis. *IMF Working Paper,* WP/02/210.

Alper, C. E. and Yılmaz, K. (2003). Domestic needs for foreign finance and exchange rate choice in developing countries with special reference to the Turkish experience. *Turkish Studies,* **4**, 67–91.

Ardic, O. and Selçuk, F. (2006). The dynamics of a newly floating exchange rate: the Turkish case. *Applied Economics,* **38**, 931–941.

Bubula, A. and Otker-Robe, I. (2002). The evolution of exchange rates since 1990: Evidence from de facto policies. *IMF Working Paper,* WP/02/155.

Calderon, C. and Schmidt-Hebbel, K. (2003). Macroeconomic policies and performance in Latin America. *Journal of International Money and Finance*, **22**, 895–923.

Calvo, G. A. and Reinhart, C. M. (2001). Fixing for your life. *Brookings Trade Forum 2000. Policy Challenges for the Next Millennium,* edited by S. Collins and D. Rodrik. Washington DC: Brookings Institution.

Calvo, G. A. and Reinhart, C. M. (2002). Fear of floating. *The Quarterly Journal of Economics*, **117**, 379–408.

Calvo, G. A., Izquierdo, A., and Talvi, E. (2003). Sudden stops, the real exchange rate, and fiscal sustainability: Argentina's lessons. *NBER Working Paper,* WP9828.

Cavallo, M., Kisselev, K., Perri, F., and Roubini, N. (2002). Exchange rate overshooting and the costs of floating. *Mimeo,* New York University.

CBT (2002). Monetary policy and exchange rate policy in 2002 and prospective developments. *The Central Bank of the Republic of Turkey. Basic Policy Readings.* http://www.tcmb.gov.tr.

CBT (2003). General framework of the monetary and exchange rate policy in 2003. *The Central Bank of the Republic of Turkey. Basic Policy Readings.* http://www.tcmb.gov.tr.

Celasun, O., Gelos, R. G., and Prati, A. (2003). Would "cold turkey" work in Turkey? *IMF Working Paper,* WP/03/49.

Cespedes, L. F., Chang, R., and Velasco, A. (2000). Balance sheets and exchange rate policy. *NBER Working Paper,* WP7840.

Devereux, M. B. and Lane, P. R. (2003). Exchange rates and monetary policy in emerging market economies. *Mimeo,* http://http://www.arts.ubc.ca/econ/devereux/hkimr.pdf.

Domaç, İ. and Bahmani-Oskooee, M. (2002). On the link between dollarization and inflation: evidence from Turkey. *The Central Bank of the Republic of Turkey, Discussion Paper.*

Domaç, İ. and Mendoza, A. (2002). Is there room for forex interventions under inflation targeting framework? Evidence from Mexico and Turkey. *The Central Bank of the Republic of Turkey, Discussion Paper.*

Eichengreen, B. (2001). Crisis prevention and management: Any new lessons from Argentina and Turkey? *Background paper written for the World Banks Global Development Finance 2002,* University of California, Berkeley.

Eichengreen, B. (2002). Can emerging markets float? Should they inflation target? *Mimeo,* University of California, Berkeley.

Eichengreen, B. and Hausmann, R. (1999). Exchange rates and financial fragility. *NBER Working Paper,* WP7418.

Ertuğrul, A. and Selçuk, F. (2002). Turkish economy: 1980-2001. *Inflation and Disinflation in Turkey,* edited by A. Kibritçioğlu, L. Rittenberg and F. Selçuk. Aldershot: Ashgate Publishing Company.

Fischer, S. (2001). Exchange rate regimes: Is the bipolar view correct? *Journal of Economic Perspectives*, **15**, 3–24.

Gençay, R. and Selçuk, F. (2006). Overnight borrowing, interest rates and extreme value theory. *European Economic Review*, **50**, 547–563.

Kenen, P. B. (1969). The theory of optimum currency areas: An eclectic view. *Monetary Problems of the International Economy,* edited by R. A. Mundell and A. K. Swoboda. Chicago: University of Chicago Press.

Kibritçioğlu, A., Rittenberg, L., and Selçuk, F. (2002). *Inflation and Disinflation in Turkey.* Edited by A. Kibritçioğlu, L. Rittenberg and F. Selçuk, Ashgate Publishing Company, Aldershot.

Krueger, A. O. (2003). The difference is in the debt: Crisis resolution in Latin America. *Luncheon Address,* Latin America Conference on Sector Reform, Stanford Center for International Development, Stanford, CA. November 14, 2003.

Lim, C. H. and Papi, L. (1997). An econometric analysis of determinants of inflation in Turkey. *IMF Working Paper,* WP/97/170.

McKinnon, R. I. (1963). Optimum currency areas. *American Economic Review*, **53**, 717–725.

Metin, K. (1995). An integrated analysis of Turkish inflation. *Oxford Bulletin of Economics and Statistics*, **57**, 513–531.

Metin-Özcan, K., Voyvoda, E., and Yeldan, A. E. (2001). Dynamics of macroeconomic adjustment in a globalized developing economy: growth, accumulation and distribution, Turkey 1969-1999. *Revue Canadienne d'Etudes du Developpement*, **22**, 219–253.

Minella, A., Freitas, P. S., Goldfajn, I., and Muinhos, M. K. (2003). Inflation targeting in Brazil: constructing credibility under exchange rate volatility. *Journal of International Money and Finance*, **22**, 1015–1040.

Mundell, R. A. (1961). A theory of optimum currency areas. *American Economic Review*, **51**, 657–665.

Mussa, M., Masson, P., Swoboda, A., Jadresic, E., Mauro, P., and Berg, A. (2000). Exchange rate regimes in and increasingly integrated world economy. *IMF Occasional Paper,* No:193.

Obstfeld, M. and Rogoff, K. (1995). The mirage of fixed exchange rates. *Journal of Economic Perspectives*, **9**, 73–96.

Öniş, Z. and Rubin, B. (2003). *Turkish Economy in Crisis.* Edited by Ziya Öniş and B. Rubin, Frank Cass & Co., London.

Reinhart, C. M. (2000). The mirage of floating exchange rates. *American Economic Review Papers and Proceedings*, **90**, 65–70.

Selçuk, F. (2003). Currency substitution: new evidence from emerging economies. *Economics Letters*, **78**, 219–224.

Selçuk, F. (2004a). Financial earthquakes, aftershocks and scaling in emerging stock markets. *Physica A*, **333**, 306–316.

Selçuk, F. (2004b). Free float and stochastic volatility: the experience of a small open economy. *Physica A*, **342**, 693–700.

Selçuk, F. (2005). The policy challenge at floating exchange rates: Turkey's recent experience. *Open Economies Review*, **16**, 295–312.

Sims, C. A. (1980). Macroeconomics and reality. *Econometrica*, **48**, 1–48.

Tavlas, G. (2003). The economics of exchange rate regimes: A review essay. *The World Economy*, **26**, 1215–1246.

Tornell, A. and Velasco, A. (2000). Fixed versus floating exchange rates: Which provide more fiscal discipline? *Journal of Monetary Economics*, **45**, 399–436.

In: International Finance and Monetary Policy
Editor: Gleb P. Severov, pp. 87-115

ISBN: 1-60021-103-8
© 2006 Nova Science Publishers, Inc.

*Chapter 4*

# MANAGING EXTERNAL VOLATILITY: CENTRAL BANK OPTIONS IN LOW-INCOME COUNTRIES

## *Stephen O'Connell*[*], *Christopher Adam, Edward Buffie and Catherine Pattillo*

Swarthmore College; University of Oxford; University of Indiana; and International Monetary Fund African Department

## Abstract

Low-income countries have participated in the worldwide move towards greater *de jure* flexibility of exchange rates since the late 1980s. In practice, however, the move to exchange rate flexibility has been fairly cautious, both by comparison with public pronouncements and by the standards of the more decisive legacy of the period, the abandonment of tight exchange controls and disequilibrium exchange rates. Our own interpretation of the African experience since the early 1990s places a heavier emphasis on the desire to reconcile low inflation with a competitive and stable real exchange rate. In Buffie *et al* (2004) we focused on the large increases in aid received by a number of African countries starting in the late 1990s. Using a calibrated general equilibrium model, we showed that a persistent surge in aid can produce distinctly unpleasant macroeconomic outcomes under floating exchange rates, given structural conditions typical of low-income economies. We showed that a strategy of substantial and non-sterilized foreign exchange intervention is warranted in this situation. Section 1 of the paper introduces the core model. In Section 2 we specify policy behavior, including the response of government spending to aid and the intervention and sterilization behavior of the central bank. In Section 3 we linearize the model and calibrate it to Uganda, Tanzania and Mozambique in the later 1990s. Section 4 contains a set of simulation results for an aid-only version of the model, and in Section 5 we expand the analysis to include commodity price shocks. Section 6 concludes.

[*] E-mail address: steve_oconnell@swarthmore.edu. Corresponding author: Stephen A. O'Connell, Department of Economics, Swarthmore College, Swarthmore, PA 19081

# Introduction

Low-income countries have participated in the worldwide move towards greater *de jure* flexibility of exchange rates since the late 1980s. Table 1 documents this for Sub-Saharan Africa (SSA), where outside of monetary unions there has been a strong trend towards the adoption of intermediate or more flexible regimes. In many cases the move to greater exchange rate flexibility accompanied a concerted effort to establish monetary aggregates as inflation anchors, via the application of tight limits on budgetary financing and a strengthening of the institutional independence of the central bank. As a result of these developments, the majority of non-CFA central banks in SSA now publicly embrace a market-determined exchange rate. Monetary policy is formally conducted within a variant of reserve-money programming, with an eye on an eventual transition to formal inflation targeting.

In practice, however, many African central banks appear to retain strong views about appropriate exchange rates. The move to exchange rate flexibility has therefore been fairly cautious, both by comparison with public pronouncements and by the standards of the more decisive legacy of the period, the abandonment of tight exchange controls and disequilibrium exchange rates.[1] In the terminology of Calvo and Reinhart (2000a), "fear of floating" is widespread in SSA. Table 1 uses the Reinhart and Rogoff (2004) *de facto* classification to show that heavy foreign exchange intervention remains the practice even among African countries reporting the strongest commitments to flexible exchange rates.

Why such reluctance to float? In emerging-market economies, explanations for fear of floating tend to emphasize balance-sheet effects that discourage real depreciation and/or high degrees of exchange-rate pass-through that create a tight link between exchange rate changes and inflation. But the first of these considerations is not obviously relevant for low-income countries, where neither the private nor the public sector would appear to be highly leveraged in foreign currency. The exposure of African banking systems to currency mismatch remains very limited, for example, in part the result of tight regulatory limits on open positions. Nor do private firms tend to be highly exposed, given their limited access to direct foreign borrowing and the reluctance of banks to lend in foreign exchange against domestic currency revenues (Čihák and Podpiera 2005). The African private sector as a whole, of course, is a large net holder of foreign exchange assets (Collier, Hoeffler and Pattillo 2001). The public sector is a net borrower in foreign currency, suggesting that conventional concerns over the fiscal burden of real depreciation may be relevant; but as emphasized in an earlier literature on exchange-rate unification, many African public sectors receive more foreign exchange in the form of aid and/or mineral revenues than they spend on imports and debt service (Kiguel and O'Connell 1995, Agénor and Ucer 1999). Real depreciation therefore confers, if anything, a fiscal bonus, a tendency reinforced by the tradable bias of the domestic tax base, at least among non-CFA countries (Adam, Bevan and Chambas 2001), and – since the mid-1990s – by successive official debt-reduction exercises.

---

[1] Exceptions to the abandonment of exchange controls are limited to a few countries, like Zimbabwe, suffering acute macroeconomic instability.

Table 1. Non-CFA Countries: IMF De Jure Classification Compared to Reinhart-Rogoff Classification (in percent of total *de jure* observations available)

| *De jure* Classification | Reinhart-Rogoff Classification | | | | | | Average # of countries by *de jure* Classification |
|---|---|---|---|---|---|---|---|
| | Pegged | Limited Flexibility | Managed Float | Free Float | Free Falling | Dual w/ limited data* | |
| 1980-84 | | | | | | | |
| Hard Pegs | . | . | . | . | . | . | 0 |
| Other Pegs | 27.3 | 14.4 | 15.5 | 0.9 | 3.4 | 5.3 | 23.4 |
| Intermediate | 0.0 | 0.0 | 43.3 | 11.7 | 35.0 | 0.0 | 3.2 |
| Floating | 0.0 | 0.0 | 75.0 | 0.0 | 0.0 | 0.0 | 0.6 |
| 1985-89 | | | | | | | |
| Hard Pegs | . | . | . | . | . | . | 0 |
| Other Pegs | 23.3 | 6.0 | 19.2 | 5.1 | 3.1 | 3.9 | 19.8 |
| Intermediate | 11.7 | 0.0 | 61.7 | 5.0 | 21.7 | 0.0 | 3.2 |
| Floating | 6.2 | 0.0 | 12.9 | 30.7 | 9.0 | 14.2 | 5.0 |
| 1990-94 | | | | | | | |
| Hard Pegs | 0.0 | 0.0 | 0.0 | 0.0 | 0.0 | 0.0 | 0.8 |
| Other Pegs | 19.3 | 9.6 | 17.5 | 3.3 | 11.0 | 6.4 | 16.2 |
| Intermediate | 4.0 | 40.0 | 8.0 | 0.0 | 14.0 | 0.0 | 2.2 |
| Floating | 0.0 | 6.4 | 16.1 | 8.5 | 24.7 | 11.9 | 9.8 |
| 1995-01 | | | | | | | |
| Hard Pegs | . | . | . | . | . | . | 0 |
| Other Pegs | 34.4 | 11.5 | 9.4 | 0.0 | 1.3 | 2.9 | 8.9 |
| Intermediate | 7.3 | 16.0 | 31.8 | 0.0 | 8.5 | 0.0 | 5.0 |
| Floating | 2.5 | 17.0 | 22.2 | 11.6 | 10.5 | 0.9 | 16.1 |

**Source**: Authors' calculations, Reinhart and Rogoff (2004), IMF data.

**Notes**: 1. Entries should be interpreted as follows (first block, for example): In 27.3% of the country-year observations where the IMF *de jure* scheme classified a regime as *Other Peg*, Reinhart and Rogoff (2004) classified the regime as *Pegged*. 2. *"Dual w/ limited data" refers to dual market arrangements for which there are no data on the parallel market rate. 2. Rows do not sum to zero across the six Reinhart-Rogoff categories because there are some countries and years for which the *de jure* classification exists but for which Reinhart and Rogoff did not provide a classification.

Our own interpretation of the African experience since the early 1990s places a heavier emphasis on the desire to reconcile low inflation with a competitive and stable real exchange rate. In Buffie *et al* (2004) we focused on the large increases in aid received by a number of African countries starting in the late 1990s. Using a calibrated general equilibrium model, we showed that a persistent surge in aid can produce distinctly unpleasant macroeconomic outcomes under floating exchange rates, given structural conditions typical of low-income economies. In particular, if currency substitution is active and a portion of aid receipts is expected to substitute for domestic financing of the fiscal deficit, the reduction in expected future seigniorage creates strong pressures for portfolio substitution in favor of the domestic currency. The real exchange rate overshoots strongly, and if the prices of nontraded goods are not perfectly flexible, a sharp demand-switching recession takes place. We showed that a strategy of substantial and non-sterilized foreign exchange intervention is warranted in this situation.

This analysis captures key features of the experience of Tanzania and Uganda in the late 1990s. In both countries, aid surges drew the central bank into substantial foreign exchange intervention, on fears of an excessive real appreciation. Intervention was initially sterilized via sales of domestic securities, in a pattern reminiscent of responses to private capital inflows among emerging-market economies in the early 1990s. But domestic debt and real interest rates rose so sharply that sterilization was abandoned within a few months.[2] Intervention continued, and as inflows persisted the *de facto* exchange rate regime increasingly resembled a crawling peg rather than a flexible exchange rate.

The experiences of Uganda and Tanzania suggest that at least in the face of persistent fluctuations in aid, "learning to float" may be a painful process for low-income countries. But how general is the appeal of a heavily managed exchange rate in the face of other sources of macroeconomic volatility relevant for low-income countries? The literature on exchange rate arrangements and monetary policy in emerging-market economies is vast but of limited relevance, given the distinctive structural features of low-income countries, where official capital flows still dominate private capital flows, exports remain dominated by a few primary commodities, and a substantial share of the labor force remains in agriculture. We therefore pose a broad and largely unsettled question in this paper: How should the conventional monetary policy instruments increasingly available to central banks in low-income countries be deployed to manage the particular patterns of external volatility characteristic of these countries, while maintaining a commitment to a long-run inflation target?

We focus on shocks to aid and commodity prices. In the Buffie *et al* (2004) analysis, private capital mobility plays a crucial role in tipping the scales in favor of intervention. This result recalls an earlier literature that favored fixed exchange rates in the face of portfolio shocks (Garber and Svensson 1995). But in reality, aid shocks compete with other shocks for policymakers' attention, and aid flows may themselves include responses to other shocks. Policymakers seek intervention and sterilization rules that are robust to the entire structure of exogenous shocks. To study this broader problem we develop a discrete-time model in which aid shocks arrive as a stochastic process that may or may not be correlated with a separate process for export prices.[3] We tie down the long-run inflation rate by studying only the stationary component of external shocks, so that the economy returns to its original inflation rate even in the face of a large and persistent shock to aid or the terms of trade. Short-run policy responses will nonetheless have a major impact on how the economy absorbs a given shock.

While the model may ultimately lend itself to solving for "approximately optimal" policy rules given an explicit loss function, our objectives at this initial stage are more modest. We seek intervention and sterilization rules that are straightforward and operationally clear, that avoid excessive instability in the central bank's balance sheet, and that generate acceptable levels of short-run volatility in real exchange rates, real interest rates, inflation, and output given the pattern of exogenous shocks and the impact of shocks on government spending. To

---

[2] In the Buffie *et al* (2004) analysis, sterilization is feasible because capital mobility is imperfect. But there is no useful role for it in the face of an aid surge that lowers expected future seigniorage. Sales of government securities merely generate very high real interest rates, with adverse feedback effects on inflation.

[3] It will be straightforward to incorporate agricultural supply shocks in a subsequent version.

locate such rules we restrict attention to a simple class of linear reaction functions that express alternative degrees of commitment to exchange rate and monetary targets. We embed these in the nonlinear optimizing model and linearize the resulting model around a reference steady state. We then use stochastic simulations to generate volatilities in the variables of interest as functions of the government spending responses and the parameters of these reaction functions.

The analysis generates a set of important insights, of which we briefly mention two, leaving further discussion to the body of the paper. First, currency substitution gives rise to endogenous private capital flows that can play an important role in the macroeconomic response to external shocks even in a stationary stochastic framework. Aid shocks are ultimately temporary in our analysis, and therefore have no impact on the steady-state inflation rate. But unless aid has very low persistence or is fully spent as it is received, the portfolio-substitution effects of inflation variability significantly weaken the case for floating exchange rates, certainly by comparison with a Mundell-Fleming benchmark that would favor flexible rates in the face of real shocks. Second, observed patterns of covariation between aid and the terms of trade vary substantially across countries and have an important bearing on the effectiveness of alternative monetary policy rules; where aid provides partial insurance against terms of trade shocks, the case for a float is in some respects significantly stronger.

Section 1 of the paper introduces the core model. In Section 2 we specify policy behavior, including the response of government spending to aid and the intervention and sterilization behavior of the central bank. In Section 3 we linearize the model and calibrate it to Uganda, Tanzania and Mozambique in the later 1990s. Section 4 contains a set of simulation results for an aid-only version of the model, and in Section 5 we expand the analysis to include commodity price shocks. Section 6 concludes.

# 1   The Model

Following Buffie *et al* (2004), we adopt a currency-substitution framework in which bonds are non-traded and currencies are imperfect substitutes in the provision of liquidity services. We incorporate terms of trade shocks by adopting a three-good structure in which the domestic economy produces nontraded goods and export goods and consumes nontraded goods and non-competitive imports. The representative household maximizes an expected utility function of the form

$$E_t \sum_{s=t}^{\infty} \beta^{s-t} \left( \frac{C_s^{1-\tau^{-1}}}{1-\tau^{-1}} + \frac{hL_s^{1-\tau^{-1}}}{1-\tau^{-1}} \right),$$

where $\tau$ is the intertemporal elasticity of substitution, $\beta \equiv (1+\rho)^{-1}$ is the discount factor, and the consumption and liquidity aggregates $C$ and $L$ are CES functions of the underlying goods and currencies:

$$
C_t \equiv \left( k_N C_{Nt}^{\frac{\alpha-1}{\alpha}} + k_I c_{It}^{\frac{\alpha-1}{\alpha}} \right)^{\frac{\alpha}{\alpha-1}}
\qquad
L_t \equiv \left\{ k_M \left( \frac{M_t}{P_t} \right)^{\frac{\sigma-1}{\sigma}} + k_F \left( \frac{E_t f_t}{P_t} \right)^{\frac{\sigma-1}{\sigma}} \right\}^{\frac{\sigma}{\sigma-1}}.
$$

Here $C_{Nt}$ and $c_{It}$ are consumption of nontraded and imported goods, $M_t$ and $f_t$ are end-of-period holdings of domestic and foreign currency, $E_t$ is the nominal exchange rate, and $P$ is a consumption-based price index.[4]

Along with domestic and foreign currency, households have access to government bonds whose yield is indexed to $P$. Financial wealth acquired in period $t$ is given by $W_t = M_t + P_t b_t^P + E_t f_t$. Using $Y$ to denote the non-interest income of the household sector and $T$ to denote taxes net of transfers received from the government, the household sector's overall budget constraint in nominal terms is

$$
W_t = M_{t-1} + R_{t-1} P_t b_{t-1}^P + E_t f_{t-1} + Y_t - T_t - P_t C_t,
$$

where $P_t C_t = (P_{Nt} C_{Nt} + P_{It} c_{It})$ and where $R_{t-1} = 1 + r_{t-1}$ is the real interest factor applicable to bonds carried over from period $t$–1. Assuming PPP for traded goods and normalizing the foreign price of importables to 1, we can divide by $E_t$ to express this in terms of imports. Using lower-case letters to denote stocks or flows measured in terms of imported goods, this yields

$$
w_t = m_t + p_t b_t^P + f_t = X_t^{-1} m_{t-1} + R_{It} p_{t-1} b_{t-1}^P + f_{t-1} + y_t - t_t - p_t C_t,
$$

where $\Pi_t = 1 + \pi_t = P_t / P_{t-1}$ and $X_t = 1 + x_t = E_t / E_{t-1}$ are the current-period inflation and depreciation factors and $R_{It} = 1 + r_{It} = R_{t-1} \Pi_t / X_t$ is the real interest factor in terms of importables (note that as of period $t$–1, the real yield $R_{It}$ is uncertain even though $R_{t-1}$ is known). The price of the consumption aggregate in terms of imported goods, $p_t$, is a function of the real exchange rate for imports, $e_t \equiv P_{Nt} / E_t$:

$$
p_t \equiv \frac{P_t}{E_t} = \left( k_N^\alpha e_t^{1-\alpha} + k_I^\alpha \right)^{\frac{1}{1-\alpha}}.
$$

(1)

---

[4] $P$ is the minimum nominal expenditure required to achieve a value of 1 for the consumption index $C$. In the CES case $P$ takes the form $P_t = \left( k_N^\alpha P_{Nt}^{1-\alpha} + k_I^\alpha P_{It}^{1-\alpha} \right)^{\frac{1}{1-\alpha}}$.

Rearranging terms and using $R_{It} = I_t / X_t$ (for $I_t = 1 + i_t = R_{t-1}\Pi_t$) to simplify further, we can write the household sector's budget constraint as

$$\Delta w_t = r_{It} w_{t-1} - \frac{i_t}{1+x_t} m_{t-1} - \frac{i_t - x_t}{1+x_t} f_{t-1} + y_t - t_t - p_t C_t.$$

(2)

Equation (2) says that spending (measured in importables) can be transferred from period $t$ to period $t+1$ at the rate $R_{I,t+1}$, and that the opportunity costs of holding domestic and foreign currency rather than bonds are $i_{t+1}/(1+x_{t+1})$ and $(i_{t+1} - x_{t+1})/(1+x_{t+1})$, respectively.

The first-order conditions for maximizing utility subject to the sequence of budget constraints (2) include, along with appropriate transversality conditions, the consumption Euler equation

$$C_t^{-\tau^{-1}} = \beta E_t \left[ \frac{R_{I,t+1} P_t}{P_{t+1}} C_{t+1}^{-\tau^{-1}} \right] = \beta R_t E_t C_{t+1}^{-\tau^{-1}},$$

(3)

the CES commodity demands

$$c_{I,t} = (1 - \gamma_t) p_t C_t \quad \text{and} \quad \frac{e_t C_{N,t}}{c_{I,t}} = \frac{\gamma_t}{1 - \gamma_t},$$

(4)

where $\gamma_t \equiv \dfrac{k_N^\alpha P_{Nt}^{1-\alpha}}{k_N^\alpha P_{Nt}^{1-\alpha} + k_I^\alpha P_{Tt}^{1-\alpha}} = \dfrac{k_N^\alpha e^{1-\alpha}}{k_N^\alpha e^{1-\alpha} + k_I^\alpha}$ is the share of spending allocated to nontraded goods, and the currency demand conditions

$$L_t^{-\tau^{-1}} h k_M \left( \frac{m_t}{p_t L_t} \right)^{-\frac{1}{\sigma}} = \beta E_t \left[ \frac{i_{t+1}}{1+\pi_{t+1}} C_{t+1}^{-\tau^{-1}} \right]$$

(5)

and

$$L_t^{-\tau^{-1}} h k_F \left( \frac{f_t}{p_t L_t} \right)^{-\frac{1}{\sigma}} = \beta E_t \left[ \frac{i_{t+1} - x_{t+1}}{1+\pi_{t+1}} C_{t+1}^{-\tau^{-1}} \right].$$

(6)

Under certainty, the latter two conditions can be expressed in the form of a money demand equation and a relative currency demand equation:

$$\frac{m_t}{p_t L_t} = (h k_M)^\sigma \left(\frac{i_{t+1}}{1+i_{t+1}}\right)^{-\sigma} \left(\frac{C_t}{L_t}\right)^{\frac{\sigma}{\tau}}, \qquad \frac{m_t}{f_t} = \frac{k_M^\sigma}{k_F^\sigma} \left(\frac{i_{t+1} - x_{t+1}}{i_{t+1}}\right)^\sigma.$$

When $i_{t+1}$ and $x_{t+1}$ are stochastic, however, this simplification is unavailable and we must proceed with (5) and (6).[5]

## Aggregate Supply

Full-employment GDP, measured in importables, is given by

$$y_t = e_t \cdot \varphi_{Nt} \overline{Q}_N + p_{Xt} \cdot \varphi_{Xt} \overline{q}_X,$$

where $\overline{Q}_N$ and $\overline{q}_X$ are the expected values of nontraded and exportable goods at full employment, $\varphi_N$ and $\varphi_X$ are stochastic productivity shocks with expected values of unity, and $p_X$ is the world price of the exportable in terms of the importable (the barter terms of trade).[6] While our PPP assumption rules out sticky prices for exports, the assumption of flexible domestic prices is less appealing for nontraded goods. To accommodate the possibility of price stickiness, we follow Calvo (1983) in assuming that an individual firm's opportunity to change its price arrives as a Poisson process with parameter $\lambda$. Rotemberg (1987) shows that if firms with the opportunity to change prices in period $t$ choose a price that minimizes a quadratic loss function defined over current and subsequent deviations of the log of the firm's price from a sequence of target log prices $\log P_{N,t+k}^*$, the price level chosen by adjusting firms in period $t$ satisfies

$$\log P_{Nt}^A = [1 - (1 - \lambda)\beta] \log P_{Nt}^* + (1 - \lambda)\beta E_t \log P_{N,t+1}^A.$$

Since a proportion $\lambda$ of (the large number of) firms ends up changing prices in period $t$, the aggregate price level for nontraded goods satisfies

$$\log P_{Nt} = \lambda \log P_{Nt}^A + (1 - \lambda) \log P_{N,t-1}.$$

In the meantime, the actual output of nontraded goods is demand determined. We model the optimal price as a function of the aggregate price level and the gap between the output of nontraded goods and their supply at full employment. Thus

---

[5] In the certainty case, the household's portfolio problem separates into two distinct two stages (as its consumption problem does in (3) and (4)), with the household first choosing overall liquidity services and then allocating these between $m$ and $f$ according to the opportunity costs of the two currencies.

[6] Allowing supplies to respond to sectoral relative prices would reduce the volatility of the real exchange rate in all of our experiments, but would not change anything of substance in our analysis.

$$\log P_{Nt}^* = \log P_{Nt} + \zeta \cdot \left[ \frac{C_{Nt}(e,C_t) + G_{Nt} - \varphi_{Nt}\overline{Q}_N}{\varphi_{Nt}\overline{Q}_N} \right], \qquad \zeta > 0.$$

where the function $C_{Nt}(e_t, C_t)$ is defined by (4). These three equations yield the sector-specific Phillips Curve

$$\log P_{Nt} - \log P_{N,t-1} = \beta E_t [\log P_{N,t+1} - \log P_{Nt}] + \psi \cdot \left[ \frac{C_{Nt}(e_t,C_t) + G_{Nt} - \varphi_{Nt}\overline{Q}_N}{\varphi_{Nt}\overline{Q}_N} \right], \quad (7)$$

where $\psi \equiv \dfrac{\zeta\lambda}{1-\lambda}[1-(1-\lambda)\beta] > 0$. High values of $\psi$ imply greater price flexibility, and as $\psi \to \infty$ equation (12) approaches the flexible-price market-clearing condition in the nontraded goods market, $\varphi_{Nt}Q_N(e_{Xt}) = C_{Nt}(e_t,C_t) + G_{Nt}$. To ensure that the Natural Rate Hypothesis holds, we impose $\beta = 1$ in equation (7).

## Government

The central bank's balance sheet, in nominal terms, reads $\Delta M_t = E_t\Delta z_t + P_t\Delta b_t^C$, where $z$ and $b^C$ are international reserves and government securities held by the central bank. If the central bank transfers its operating surplus to the non-bank budget, the non-bank public sector's budget constraint takes the form

$$P_t(\Delta b_t^P + \Delta b_t^C) = P_{Nt}G_{Nt} + E_t g_{It} + P_t r_{t-1} b_{t-1}^P - T_t - E_t a_t,$$

where we are assuming no interest on reserves and no foreign debt accumulation, and where $a$ is foreign aid net of interest payments on any existing foreign debt of the public sector. The consolidated public sector budget constraint is therefore

$$M_t + P_t b_t^P - E_t z_t = M_{t-1} + P_t R_{t-1} b_{t-1}^P - E_t z_{t-1} + P_{Nt}G_{Nt} + E_t g_{It} - T_t - E_t a_t$$

or, in terms of importables,

$$\Delta m_t + p_t\Delta b_t^P - \Delta z_t = def_t - a_t - \frac{x_t}{1+x_t}m_{t-1}, \tag{8}$$

where the fiscal deficit is defined as $def_t \equiv g_t - t_t + p_t r_{t-1} b_{t-1}^P$. Equation (8) can be combined with the household sector's flow budget constraint (2) to yield the current account identity $\Delta f_t + \Delta z_t = y_t - g_t - p_t C_t + a_t$. Imposing the condition $Q_N = C_N + G_N$, we can re-express this as

$$\Delta f_t + \Delta z_t = p_{Xt}\varphi_{Xt}q_{Xt} - [c_{lt}(e_t, C_t) + g_{lt}] + a_t. \tag{9}$$

## External Shocks

To close the model, we need a stochastic specification for the external shocks and a set of fiscal and monetary policy reaction functions. We characterize the former by assuming that the vector $v_t = [\log a_t - \log \overline{a}, \log p_{Xt} - \log \overline{p}_X]'$ follows a stationary vector AR($p$) process, for given unconditional means $\overline{a}$ and $\overline{p}_X$. Thus

$$v_t = \sum_{i=1}^{p} N_i v_{t-i} + \varepsilon_{ut}, \qquad E_t \varepsilon_{ut} \varepsilon_{ut}' = \begin{bmatrix} \sigma_a^2 & \sigma_{a\tau} \\ \sigma_{a\tau} & \sigma_\tau^2 \end{bmatrix}, \tag{10}$$

where $N_i$ is a 2x2 matrix of coefficients, $\varepsilon_{ut}$ is serially uncorrelated, and the roots of the lag polynomial are all stable.

## A Reference Steady State

Denoting steady-state values by an over-bar and setting $C_t = C_{t+1} = \overline{C}$, a non-stochastic, steady-state version of the consumption Euler equation yields $\overline{r} = \rho$. The values of $\overline{e}$ and $\overline{C}$ are determined as functions of government spending, aid, and the terms of trade by the conditions

$$C_N(\overline{e}, \overline{C}) = \overline{\varphi}_N Q_N(\overline{p}_X \cdot \overline{e}) + \overline{G}_N$$
$$c_T(\overline{e}, \overline{C}) = \overline{\varphi}_T q_T(\overline{p}_X \cdot \overline{e}) + \overline{a} - \overline{g}_T.$$

The first of these equations is the Phillips curve in the nontraded goods market (equation (7)), while the second is a combination of (7) and the current account equation (9).

Given $\overline{e}$ and $\overline{C}$, steady-state inflation is determined by conventional tax revenue, which ties down the fiscal deficit and therefore the inflation tax requirement. Imposing the steady-state condition $\overline{x} = \overline{\pi}$, the inflation tax requirement is

$$\left(\frac{\overline{\pi}}{1 + \overline{\pi}}\right)\overline{m} = \overline{e}\overline{G}_N + \overline{g}_T - \overline{i} + \rho\overline{p}\overline{b}^P - \overline{a}. \tag{11}$$

To preserve the stationary structure of the analysis, we will require that any sterilization operations undertaken by the central bank be unwound over time. For given steady-state values of government spending and taxation, this ties down the right-hand side of (11). The steady-state demand for money, in turn, is determined by

$$\overline{m} = k_M^\tau \left(\frac{k_M}{\xi}\right)^{\frac{\tau-\sigma}{\sigma-1}} \left(1 - \frac{1}{(1+\rho)(1+\overline{\pi})}\right)^{-\tau} \overline{p}\overline{C},$$

where

$$\xi \equiv \frac{\overline{i}\,\overline{m}}{\overline{i}\,\overline{m} + \rho\overline{f}} = \frac{k_M^\sigma(\overline{\pi}+\rho)^{1-\sigma}}{k_M^\sigma(\overline{\pi}+\rho)^{1-\sigma} + k_F^\sigma\rho^{1-\sigma}}$$

is the long-run share of domestic currency in the opportunity cost of liquidity services. The two above equations jointly determine $\overline{\pi}$ and $\overline{m}$ as functions of the fiscal variables, aid, and the inelastic long-run supply of government bonds. Given $\overline{m}$ and $\overline{\pi}$, foreign currency balances are determined by a steady-state version of the non-stochastic relative currency demand equation.

## 2  Fiscal and Monetary Rules

The fiscal and monetary authorities each have access to four potential instruments, of which at most three can be chosen independently. The Treasury controls government purchases of imported and nontraded goods ($g_I$, $G_N$), revenue ($T$), and net domestic borrowing $\Delta B^C + \Delta B^P$. The central bank controls the exchange rate and the three asset stocks $M$, $B^C$ and $z$. We will require that policy choices be compatible with a long-run inflation target.

As emphasized by Buffie, *et al* (2004), low-income countries typically devote a significant portion of aid inflows to deficit reduction. To capture this we allow an aid-receiving government to expand its primary deficit by a fraction $0 < \phi \leq 1$ of every additional dollar of aid. The remainder serves as financing support, reducing the government's domestic financing requirement. A set of fiscal policy reaction functions with this property is

$$t_t = \overline{t} - (1 - b_N - b_I)\phi(a_t - \overline{a})$$
$$eG_{N,t} = \overline{e}\,\overline{G}_N + b_N\phi(a_t - \overline{a})$$
$$g_{I,t} = \overline{g}_I + b_I\phi(a_t - \overline{a})$$

(12)

with slope coefficients satisfying

$$0 \leq \phi \leq 1, \quad b_N \geq 0, \quad b_I \geq 0, \quad 0 \leq b_N + b_I \leq 0.$$

Equation (12) states that on the margin, an increase in aid is spent partly on tax reductions, partly on spending increases, and partly on financing the pre-existing fiscal deficit. Steady-state inflation is determined by the intercepts in (12), via the steady-state seigniorage equation (11).

The immediate monetary impact of this fiscal behavior is straightforward. We will assume that the government deposits aid receipts in the central bank and immediately draws down the domestic-currency "counterpart" to the extent specified in (12). Domestic credit to the government therefore falls by the amount of budget support, $(1-\phi)(a_t - \overline{a})$. What happens to international reserves and the monetary base depends on whether the central bank retains the aid inflow or not. If it does, international reserves increase by $(1 - b_t \phi)(a_t - \overline{a})$ and the monetary base rises by $(1 - b_t)\phi(a_t - \overline{a})$. If it chooses, instead, to sell the foreign exchange on the private market (as under money-targeting system with a flexible exchange rate), then reserves are unchanged and the monetary base falls by the amount of budget support.

In general, of course, the central bank may choose to retain some intermediate portion of aid proceeds or to sterilize some portion of changes in the monetary base via bond sales; and in any case, new tradeoffs will emerge over time, based on the private sector's response to the inflow. To characterize the behavior of the monetary authority, we treat the aid management problem as a subset of the more general problem of choosing the appropriate degree of commitment to monetary and exchange rate targets. Our approach is to specify intuitively appealing rules for intervention and sterilization and study their behavior for alternative parameter values.[7]

The instruments at the disposal of the monetary authority are foreign exchange intervention and open market operations in government bonds. To preserve the stationary structure of the analysis we assume that the government maintains long-run targets for government bonds $\overline{b}^P$ and international reserves $\overline{z}$. Intervention behavior embodies at least a partial commitment on the part of the monetary authority to a predetermined rate of crawl. Thus

$$\frac{z_t - z_{t-1}}{\overline{z}} = z_1 \cdot \frac{\overline{\pi} - x_t}{\overline{X}} + \left[ \frac{z_2}{z_1 + z_2} \right] \cdot \frac{\overline{z} - z_{t-1}}{\overline{z}},$$

$$z_1 \geq 0, \quad z_2 > 0. \tag{13}$$

where the target rate of crawl is tied down by the steady-state inflation rate. As $z_1 \to \infty$ the regime approaches a predetermined crawl $(x_t = \overline{\pi})$. Lower values of $z_1$ represent looser

---

[7] In the background, we think of the monetary authority as seeking to minimize some weighted sum of the variances of inflation, output, the real exchange rate, and perhaps the real interest rate. Using the linearized version of the model, we could in principle specify a quadratic loss function and solve for optimal instrument rules, as in the recent literatures on monetary policy rules and inflation targeting (e.g., Taylor (1999), Svensson (2000)). Note that in contrast to these literatures, which suppress portfolio behavior and assume that the central bank can set the nominal interest rate directly, we retain a detailed description of portfolio behavior and focus on quantity (i.e., balance sheet) rather than price instruments.

commitments to the reference path for the nominal exchange rate, and for $z_1 = 0$ the central bank operates a purely floating exchange rate $(z_t = \bar{z})$.

Any net foreign exchange intervention that is pursued using (13) changes the monetary base. To allow the monetary authority to sterilize a portion of this impact on a temporary basis, we specify a bond-sterilization function of the form

$$p_t(b_t^P - b_{t-1}^P) = b_1(z_t - z_{t-1}) + b_2 p_t(\bar{b}^P - b_{t-1}^P). \tag{14}$$

where $0 < b_2 \le 1$. For $b_1 > 0$, open-market operations are used to offset at least a portion of the impact of foreign exchange intervention on the monetary base. These operations are then unwound over time, at a rate determined by $b_2$. We also consider a generalization of (14) that allows the monetary authority to target the domestic credit component of overall growth in the monetary base. In a steady-state equilibrium, the fiscal deficit net of aid is financed by the inflation tax, which is provided to the government in the form of domestic credit growth. The following specification allows the monetary authority to offset a portion of the difference between the government's current borrowing requirement and the steady-state growth in domestic credit:

$$p_t(b_t^P - b_{t-1}^P) = b_0\left[ def_t - a_t - \frac{\pi}{1+x_t} m_{t-1} \right] + b_1(z_t - z_{t-1}) + b_2 p_t(\bar{b}^P - b_{t-1}^P). \tag{15}$$

where $0 \le b_0 < 1$. Note that setting $b_0 = b_1$ amounts to offsetting a constant fraction $b_0 = b_1$ of excess growth in the monetary base, whether such excess arises from foreign exchange purchases or from central bank credit to the government.

## 3    Linearization and Calibration

The stochastic model is nonlinear and cannot be solved analytically. We therefore follow Campbell (1994) and others in linearizing the model around its non-stochastic steady state and studying the properties of the resulting stochastic linear model. The linearization is performed within Dynare (Julliard 1996), along with the calculation of impulse responses and theoretical variances of the endogenous variables, using a first-order Taylor approximation. In assessing macroeconomic responses we focus particularly on the inflation rate, the real exchange rate, the real interest rate, and in the case of sticky prices, the output of nontraded goods.

To tie down steady-state asset stocks, inflation, public spending, and aid we use rough averages of values observed for Uganda, Tanzania and Mozambique in the late 1990s. As ratios to GDP,

$$\bar{m} = 0.08, \quad \bar{f} = 0.12, \quad \bar{b}^P = 0.09, \quad \bar{z} = 0.04, \quad \bar{\pi} = 0.10, \quad \bar{g} = 0.25, \quad \bar{a} = 0.10.$$

We use 1/2 for the steady-state shares of nontraded goods in private consumption $(\bar{\gamma})$ and nontraded output in GDP. For the semi-elasticity of nontraded goods inflation with respect to the output gap, we use $\psi = 5.0$, which implies a very modest degree of price stickiness.

We adopt the following preference parameters, consistent with the limited microeconomic evidence summarized by Buffie *et al* (2004):

$$\alpha = 0.50, \quad \rho = 0.10, \quad \tau = 0.50, \quad \sigma = 2.0.$$

For the elasticities of intertemporal $(\tau)$ and currency $(\sigma)$ substitution, these values fall in the middle of the ranges used by Buffie *et al*.

To parameterize the stochastic process for aid and commodity prices, the natural approach is to estimate a version of equation (10) as a VAR and retain the implied information about the stationary components of the vector $v$. Our preliminary work suggests that after transformation to stationarity, a first-order VAR provides an adequate representation of the annual data for low-income African countries.[8] Individual VARs uniformly generate a very small value for the contemporaneous covariance $\sigma_{ac}$ and we impose $\sigma_{ac} = 0$ in what follows (the *a* and *c* subscripts denote aid and commodity prices respectively). Commodity prices also tend to show uniformly low persistence; mean-group estimation places the autogregressive coefficient at roughly 0.11, and we adopt this value for all simulations. Where countries differ more substantially is with respect to the *persistence* of aid flows and the degree to which they provide (*ex post*) *insurance* for commodity price shocks. Thus while the stationary component of aid generally shows positive serial correlation, we can distinguish country groups with relatively low and relatively high persistence. Stretching a bit on the high end, we report results below for $n_{aa} = 0.26$ and $n_{aa} = 0.72$. With respect to insurance, we use $n_{at} = -0.50$ and $n_{aa} = 0.50$, again stretching a bit with respect to the latter value in order to study the implications of "unusually" poor insurance.

A final calibration step involves setting the parameters of fiscal and monetary behavior. We begin by distinguishing the case in which all aid is spent from the empirically more relevant case in which aid is "partially deficit-reducing" or *PDR*. We therefore allow $\phi$ to take the values 1 and 0.75; in the latter case, a quarter of aid is devoted to reducing the Treasury's domestic financing requirement. In Buffie *et al* (2004), it was the *PDR* component of aid that generated the most difficult short-run macroeconomic tradeoffs, as the prospect of lower inflation generated short-run private capital inflows that in some cases rivaled the official flows in magnitude.

---

[8] We estimated single-country VARs using annual data for aid (net ODA excluding technical assistance grants, as a share of GDP), real export commodity prices (deflated by a general index of developing country import prices), and rainfall, for 16 Sub-Saharan African countries for the period 1970-2000 (rainfall shocks were intended to proxy for agricultural supply shocks, which we have omitted from the current paper). We first transformed the variables to stationarity using the Hodrick-Prescott filter, and then estimated separate country-by-country third-order VARs (with rainfall recursively prior to commodity prices and aid, and commodity prices prior to aid), and tested these down to first-order representations which were accepted for all countries. We used a mean-group approach to identify a small set of archetypes within the country-level results.

Given the fiscal reaction functions (12), government spending patterns differ from those of the private sector in two respects. First, the government does not wish to smooth its spending on goods and services relative to its receipts, while the private sector does. Second, the government's marginal spending may be biased towards imported or nontraded goods, while the private sector adopts a half-and-half split (at steady state relative prices). For most of the paper we suppress these distinctions by setting $b_N = b_I = 0$. Government spending out of aid therefore takes the form solely of transfers to the private sector, which are spent according to the preferences of private households. At the end of the paper, however, we briefly consider the case in which a portion of government spending is on goods and services and is import-biased ($b_N = 0, b_I = 0.75$) or nontraded-biased ($b_N = 0.75, b_I = 0$) on the margin.

Intervention and sterilization behavior are governed by $z_1, z_2, b_0, b_1$ and $b_2$. We set $b_2 = 0.25$ throughout, so that any bond operations are unwound at the rate of 25 percent per year. We get a pure float by setting $z_1 = 0$, and in this case $z_2$ and $b_1$ are irrelevant because the level of international reserves never changes (aid is immediately sold for domestic currency, whether or not the counterpart funds are spent on goods and services). To capture a crawl we set $z_1 = z_2 = 20$. A policy of no sterilization of foreign exchange intervention is given by $b_1 = 0$, and to investigate modest and aggressive sterilization of intervention we use $b_1 = 0.5$ and $b_1 = 0.75$. To capture partial money-base targeting, we use $b_0 = b_1 = 0.5$. Table 2 shows the alternative parameters settings used in the experiments reported below.

# 4    Managing Aid Shocks

To convey the basic structure of the analysis, we begin with a stripped-down version of the model in which commodity price shocks have been eliminated ($Var(p_{Xt}) = 0$) and all government spending takes the form of transfers to the private sector ($b_N = b_I = 0$ in equations (12)). In this simplified version, macroeconomic volatility is driven solely by shocks to foreign aid. We treat these shocks as highly persistent ($n_{aa} = 0.72$). Note that by limiting government spending out of aid to income transfers, we are aligning any ultimate impetus to spending with the preferences of the private sector, including the private sector's desire to smooth consumption relative to the temporary component of transfers.

Table 2. Alternative parameter values.

| Category | Parameter settings |
|---|---|
| Flexibility of $N$-goods prices | *Flex* $(\psi = 1000)$ or *Sticky* $(\psi = 5)$. |
| *Fiscal policy:* | |
| PDR component of aid | *PDR* $(\phi = 0.75)$ or *No PDR* $(\phi = 0)$. |
| $N$ or $I$ bias in public spending (relative to private) at the margin | *Neutral* $(b_N = b_I = 0)$, <br> *N-bias* $(b_N = 0.75, b_I = 0)$, <br> or *I-bias* $(b_N = 0, b_I = 0.75)$. |
| *Monetary policy:* | |
| Foreign exchange intervention | *Clean* $(z_1 = 0)$ or *Dirty* $(z_1 = z_2 = 20)$ float. |
| Sterilization of intervention | *None* $(b_1 = 0)$ or *Partial* $(b_1 = 0.5, b_2 = 0.25)$. |
| Domestic credit targeting | *None* $(b_0 = 0)$ or *Partial Monetary Base Targeting* $(b_0 = b_1 = 0.5, b_2 = 0.25)$ |
| *Structure of shocks:* | |
| Persistence of aid | *Low* $(n_{aa} = 0.26)$ or *High* $(n_{aa} = 0.72)$. |
| Insurance role of aid** | *Counter-* $(n_{at} = -0.5)$ or *Pro-* $(n_{at} = 0.5)$ cyclical. |

**The contemporaneous covariance of aid and commodity prices is set to zero as discussed in the text. The term "insurance" refers to the impact of lagged commodity prices on aid.

## 4.1   Drawbacks of a Clean Float under Persistent PDR Aid

Tables 3a and 3b report impulse responses to a one-time aid shock equivalent to 2% of GDP, not an unrealistic value for countries receiving HIPC and PRSP-related relief starting in the late 1990s. Aid is stationary but persistent: the initial increase of 20 percent is followed by a gradual return to the initial steady state. Table 3a shows the pattern of responses when aid is fully spent, while Table 3b assumes a *PDR* component of 25%. In each case we compare responses under full price flexibility with responses under a modest degree of price stickiness in the nontraded goods sector. We consider two alternative exchange rate arrangements. Under a *clean* float, the central bank immediately recycles all aid receipts through the foreign exchange market and international reserves never change. Under a *dirty* float, the central bank intervenes continuously and (given our chosen parameters) relatively aggressively, allowing only minor deviations of the depreciation rate from its steady-state value. In these initial runs, the central bank foregoes any bond operations, so that money growth reflects the joint influence of fluctuations in domestic credit and intervention in the foreign exchange market.

Note first that there are circumstances under which the exchange rate arrangement has little impact on how the economy absorbs an aid shock:

- The exchange rate regime is neutral in the long run, a basic property of the model.

- Aid that is fully spent (Table 3a) is absorbed with minor and transitory real effects including a modest real appreciation. Inflation tends to fall persistently regardless of exchange rate regime, but the real appreciation requires an modest initial inflationary spike under a dirty float. These observations hold regardless of the degree of price stickiness, although real exchange rate movements are somewhat smaller and real interest rate movements somewhat larger under sticky prices than when markets clear instantaneously. Under sticky prices, the aid inflow creates a small transitory boom in the nontraded goods market.

Potentially serious macroeconomic impacts begin to emerge, however, when a portion of aid is devoted to reducing the seigniorage requirement (Table 3b, *PDR* aid). Expected inflation now falls very substantially under a floating exchange rate, driving up the demand for domestic currency and inducing a desired private capital inflow that creates acute short-run pressure in the foreign exchange market. Under a clean float, nontraded prices must fall very dramatically to reconcile the large nominal appreciation that is required by maintain portfolio equilibrium with the much smaller real appreciation needed to absorb the aid. If the prices of nontraded goods are even moderately sticky, the real exchange rate overshoots by a large margin, producing a sharp demand-switching recession in the nontraded goods sector.

Table 3b shows that when aid has a substantial *PDR* component, a dirty float that aggressively targets the steady-state depreciation rate dramatically out-performs a clean float. In part this is because intervention allows the desired portfolio adjustment to take place through foreign exchange intervention rather than through nominal appreciation. With nominal appreciation now roughly in line with the required real appreciation, the aid inflow is no longer highly disinflationary, and what would have been a sharp recession in the nontraded goods sector under sticky prices is in fact converted into a small boom. But the desired portfolio adjustment is also considerably smaller under the dirty float, because targeting the crawl at its steady-state level limits the fall in expected inflation and therefore the desired shift into domestic currency. The result of these considerations is that the heavily managed float allows macroeconomic adjustment to take place with considerably less volatility in inflation and the real exchange rate, and with a moderate to substantial reduction in real interest rate volatility. Table 4a makes these points precise by showing the theoretical standard deviations implied by the linearized model. When aid has a *PDR* component, the dirty float clearly dominates, producing lower volatility in all variables except the current account and international reserves (the volatiles of the real interest rate and private consumption are very close across regimes in the sticky price case). The conclusion is straightforward: *If PDR aid shocks are the dominant source of short-run macroeconomic volatility, there is very little to recommend a clean float.*

Table 3a. Impulse responses to an aid shock when all aid is spent.

| Period<br>Variable | 0 | 1 | 2 | 3 | 4 | 5 | 15 |
|---|---|---|---|---|---|---|---|
| *Flex* prices, *Clean* float, *No PDR* | | | | | | | |
| $\pi$ | 0.27 | -0.35 | -0.93 | -1.03 | -0.94 | -0.78 | -0.04 |
| $e$ | 4.07 | 3.78 | 3.18 | 2.54 | 1.96 | 1.49 | 0.06 |
| $r$ | -0.37 | -0.72 | -0.77 | -0.69 | -0.57 | -0.45 | -0.02 |
| $C$ | 2.23 | 2.06 | 1.73 | 1.38 | 1.07 | 0.81 | 0.03 |
| $ca$ | 0.62 | 0.16 | -0.04 | -0.11 | -0.12 | -0.11 | -0.01 |
| $y_N$ | 0.01 | 0.00 | 0.00 | 0.00 | 0.00 | 0.00 | 0.00 |
| $z$ | 0.00 | 0.00 | 0.00 | 0.00 | 0.00 | 0.00 | 0.00 |
| $x$ | -1.97 | -0.20 | -0.60 | -0.68 | -0.62 | -0.52 | -0.03 |
| $mg$ | 0.07 | -0.42 | -0.92 | -1.00 | -0.90 | -0.74 | -0.04 |
| *Flex* prices, *Dirty* float, *No PDR* | | | | | | | |
| $\pi$ | 2.03 | -0.02 | -0.26 | -0.35 | -0.37 | -0.36 | -0.18 |
| $e$ | 3.79 | 3.58 | 3.05 | 2.47 | 1.94 | 1.49 | 0.08 |
| $r$ | -0.29 | -0.63 | -0.70 | -0.64 | -0.54 | -0.43 | -0.02 |
| $C$ | 2.08 | 1.95 | 1.66 | 1.34 | 1.05 | 0.81 | 0.04 |
| $ca$ | 0.71 | 0.23 | 0.01 | -0.09 | -0.12 | -0.11 | -0.01 |
| $y_N$ | 0.01 | 0.00 | 0.00 | 0.00 | 0.00 | 0.00 | 0.00 |
| $z$ | 1.08 | -1.29 | -1.12 | 0.06 | 1.47 | 2.78 | 6.04 |
| $x$ | -0.06 | 0.10 | 0.03 | -0.03 | -0.08 | -0.11 | -0.16 |
| $mg$ | 0.82 | -1.51 | -0.43 | 0.04 | 0.20 | 0.21 | -0.16 |
| *Sticky* prices, *Clean* float, *No PDR* | | | | | | | |
| $\pi$ | -1.03 | -0.57 | -0.91 | -0.94 | -0.84 | -0.71 | -0.04 |
| $e$ | 3.07 | 3.20 | 2.96 | 2.54 | 2.07 | 1.64 | 0.08 |
| $r$ | -0.88 | -0.99 | -0.86 | -0.70 | -0.55 | -0.42 | -0.02 |
| $C$ | 2.57 | 2.17 | 1.72 | 1.32 | 1.01 | 0.76 | 0.03 |
| $ca$ | 0.55 | 0.16 | -0.01 | -0.08 | -0.11 | -0.10 | -0.01 |
| $y_N$ | 0.69 | 0.33 | 0.08 | -0.04 | -0.09 | -0.10 | -0.01 |
| $z$ | 0.00 | 0.00 | 0.00 | 0.00 | 0.00 | 0.00 | 0.00 |
| $x$ | -2.72 | -0.64 | -0.78 | -0.70 | -0.59 | -0.47 | -0.03 |
| $mg$ | -0.06 | -1.19 | -1.31 | -1.12 | -0.90 | -0.70 | -0.04 |
| *Sticky* prices, *Dirty* float, *No PDR* | | | | | | | |
| $\pi$ | 1.18 | 0.30 | -0.12 | -0.31 | -0.38 | -0.39 | -0.23 |
| $e$ | 2.12 | 2.69 | 2.61 | 2.27 | 1.87 | 1.49 | 0.10 |
| $r$ | -0.93 | -0.88 | -0.78 | -0.66 | -0.53 | -0.42 | -0.02 |
| $C$ | 2.49 | 2.07 | 1.68 | 1.32 | 1.02 | 0.78 | 0.04 |
| $ca$ | 0.66 | 0.25 | 0.04 | -0.06 | -0.10 | -0.10 | -0.02 |
| $y_N$ | 1.04 | 0.47 | 0.20 | 0.07 | 0.00 | -0.02 | -0.01 |
| $z$ | -0.29 | 0.22 | 1.44 | 2.90 | 4.31 | 5.50 | 7.81 |
| $x$ | 0.02 | -0.02 | -0.07 | -0.12 | -0.16 | -0.18 | -0.21 |
| $mg$ | -0.03 | -0.70 | -0.19 | 0.05 | 0.12 | 0.11 | -0.21 |

The aid shock is 2% of GDP, with persistence parameter $n_{aa} = 0.72$. To interpret other parameter settings see Table 2. Key: $\pi$ = inflation rate; $e$ = real exchange rate; $r$ = real interest rate; $ca$ = current account as share of GDP; $y_N$ = nontraded output; $z$ = international reserves; $x$ = depreciation rate; $mg$ = nominal money growth rate. IRs are reported in annualized percentage point deviations from SS for all growth rates and the real interest rate; in percentage deviations from SS for $e$, $C$, $y_N$, and $z$; and in percentage-points-of-GDP deviations for $ca$.

Table 3b. Impulse responses to an aid shock with a 25% PDR component

| Period Variable | 0 | 1 | 2 | 3 | 4 | 5 | 15 |
|---|---|---|---|---|---|---|---|
| *Flex* prices, *Clean* float, *PDR* aid | | | | | | | |
| $\pi$ | -20.91 | -5.29 | -3.88 | -2.84 | -2.06 | -1.50 | -0.06 |
| $e$ | 5.78 | 4.23 | 3.09 | 2.25 | 1.64 | 1.19 | 0.05 |
| $r$ | -1.77 | -1.35 | -1.00 | -0.74 | -0.54 | -0.39 | -0.02 |
| $C$ | 3.10 | 2.29 | 1.68 | 1.22 | 0.89 | 0.64 | 0.03 |
| $ca$ | 0.07 | 0.02 | -0.01 | -0.01 | -0.01 | -0.01 | 0.00 |
| $y_N$ | -0.04 | -0.01 | 0.00 | 0.00 | 0.00 | 0.00 | 0.00 |
| $z$ | 0.00 | 0.00 | 0.00 | 0.00 | 0.00 | 0.00 | 0.00 |
| $x$ | -24.09 | -4.43 | -3.26 | -2.37 | -1.72 | -1.25 | -0.05 |
| $mg$ | -8.71 | -8.68 | -6.36 | -4.61 | -3.34 | -2.42 | -0.09 |
| *Flex* prices, *Dirty* float, *PDR* aid | | | | | | | |
| $\pi$ | 0.71 | -1.10 | -1.34 | -1.45 | -1.48 | -1.48 | -1.11 |
| $e$ | 3.23 | 2.97 | 2.51 | 2.03 | 1.61 | 1.25 | 0.15 |
| $r$ | -0.35 | -0.55 | -0.57 | -0.51 | -0.43 | -0.34 | -0.02 |
| $C$ | 1.77 | 1.62 | 1.37 | 1.11 | 0.88 | 0.68 | 0.08 |
| $ca$ | 0.90 | 0.44 | 0.19 | 0.06 | -0.01 | -0.04 | -0.04 |
| $y_N$ | 0.01 | 0.00 | 0.00 | 0.00 | 0.00 | 0.00 | 0.00 |
| $z$ | 19.49 | 27.04 | 33.38 | 38.28 | 41.81 | 44.18 | 40.95 |
| $x$ | -1.07 | -0.95 | -1.09 | -1.19 | -1.25 | -1.28 | -1.10 |
| $mg$ | 3.95 | -1.59 | -1.10 | -0.96 | -0.97 | -1.04 | -1.22 |
| *Sticky* prices, *Clean* float, *PDR* aid | | | | | | | |
| $\pi$ | -16.35 | -4.75 | -3.79 | -2.84 | -2.09 | -1.53 | -0.06 |
| $e$ | 9.67 | 6.26 | 4.55 | 3.36 | 2.48 | 1.82 | 0.07 |
| $r$ | 0.24 | -0.95 | -0.86 | -0.66 | -0.49 | -0.36 | -0.02 |
| $C$ | 1.83 | 1.94 | 1.51 | 1.12 | 0.82 | 0.60 | 0.02 |
| $ca$ | 0.34 | 0.01 | -0.05 | -0.06 | -0.05 | -0.05 | 0.00 |
| $y_N$ | -2.65 | -1.13 | -0.75 | -0.55 | -0.41 | -0.30 | -0.01 |
| $z$ | 0.00 | 0.00 | 0.00 | 0.00 | 0.00 | 0.00 | 0.00 |
| $x$ | -21.67 | -2.87 | -2.85 | -2.18 | -1.60 | -1.17 | -0.05 |
| $mg$ | -8.25 | -5.74 | -5.68 | -4.32 | -3.16 | -2.29 | -0.09 |
| *Sticky* prices, *Dirty* float, *PDR* aid | | | | | | | |
| $\pi$ | -0.04 | -0.82 | -1.22 | -1.41 | -1.49 | -1.50 | -1.15 |
| $e$ | 1.76 | 2.20 | 2.12 | 1.86 | 1.55 | 1.26 | 0.19 |
| $r$ | -0.91 | -0.76 | -0.64 | -0.53 | -0.42 | -0.33 | -0.02 |
| $C$ | 2.14 | 1.73 | 1.38 | 1.09 | 0.85 | 0.66 | 0.08 |
| $ca$ | 0.85 | 0.45 | 0.22 | 0.08 | 0.01 | -0.03 | -0.04 |
| $y_N$ | 0.91 | 0.41 | 0.18 | 0.06 | 0.01 | -0.02 | -0.02 |
| $z$ | 18.29 | 28.36 | 35.60 | 40.76 | 44.30 | 46.58 | 42.54 |
| $x$ | -1.01 | -1.06 | -1.18 | -1.26 | -1.32 | -1.34 | -1.14 |
| $mg$ | 3.20 | -0.87 | -0.89 | -0.95 | -1.03 | -1.12 | -1.27 |

The aid shock is 2% of GDP, with persistence parameter $n_{aa} = 0.72$. To interpret other parameter settings see Table 2. Key: $\pi$ = inflation rate; $e$ = real exchange rate; $r$ = real interest rate; $ca$ = current account as share of GDP; $y_N$ = nontraded output; $z$ = international reserves; $x$ = depreciation rate; $mg$ = nominal money growth rate. IRs are reported in annualized percentage point deviations from SS for all growth rates and the real interest rate; in percentage deviations from SS for $e$, $C$, $y_N$, and $z$; and in percentage-points-of-GDP deviations for $ca$.

Table 4a. Standard deviations under alternative exchange rate regimes.

| Varia-ble | Aid fully spent | | | | PDR aid | | | |
|---|---|---|---|---|---|---|---|---|
| | Flex prices | | Sticky prices | | Flex prices | | Sticky prices | |
| | Clean | Dirty* | Clean | Dirty* | Clean | Dirty* | Clean | Dirty* |
| | (1) | (2) | (3) | (4) | (5) | (6) | (7) | (8) |
| $\pi$ | 2.13 | 2.38 | 2.26 | 1.89 | 22.30 | 6.81 | 17.93 | 6.91 |
| $e$ | 7.50 | 7.17 | 6.75 | 5.71 | 8.46 | 6.04 | 13.34 | 4.81 |
| $r$ | 1.59 | 1.46 | 1.92 | 1.83 | 2.67 | 1.21 | 1.63 | 1.59 |
| $C$ | 4.09 | 3.91 | 4.27 | 4.18 | 4.56 | 3.29 | 3.48 | 3.53 |
| $ca$ | 0.69 | 0.79 | 0.61 | 0.74 | 0.08 | 1.04 | 0.36 | 1.01 |
| $y_N$ | 0.01 | 0.01 | 0.80 | 1.16 | 0.04 | 0.01 | 3.09 | 1.02 |
| $z$ | 0.00 | 31.27 | 0.00 | 41.33 | 0.00 | 234.68 | 0.00 | 244.33 |
| $X$ | 2.41 | 0.87 | 3.13 | 1.14 | 24.95 | 6.52 | 22.27 | 6.78 |
| $mg$ | 2.05 | 1.98 | 2.52 | 1.31 | 15.37 | 7.94 | 13.15 | 7.71 |
| $b$ | 0.00 | 0.00 | 0.00 | 0.00 | 0.00 | 0.00 | 0.00 | 0.00 |

*Intervention is not sterilized (see left panel of Table 3b for partial sterilization). For units of the standard deviations see note to Table 3a. For parameter values corresponding to cases in italics (e.g., *Clean* vs. *Dirty*) see Table 2. The standard deviation of the aid shock is .02 and aid persistence is *High* at $n_{aa} = 0.72$. Government spending is *Neutral*. The standard deviation of the commodity price shock is set to .00001, so commodity prices have no impact on these results.

Table 4b. Volatility impact of bond operations: partial sterilization of foreign exchange intervention and money base targeting.(increase in standard deviation due to bond operations)

| Varia-ble | Partial sterilization of foreign exchange intervention* (Dirty float) | | | | | | Money base targeting** (PDR case) | | | |
|---|---|---|---|---|---|---|---|---|---|---|
| | Moderate* | | | | Aggressive* | | Clean float | | Dirty float | |
| | Aid fully spent | | PDR aid | | PDR Aid | | | | | |
| | Flex prices | Sticky prices | Flex prices | Sticky prices | Flex prices | Sticky prices | Flex prices | Sticky prices | Flex prices | Sticky prices |
| | (9) | (10) | (11) | (12) | (13) | (14) | (15) | (16) | (17) | (18) |
| $\pi$ | -0.01 | -0.11 | -1.07 | -1.10 | -0.01 | -0.44 | 2.25 | 3.18 | 1.23 | 1.32 |
| $e$ | -0.02 | 0.01 | 0.03 | 0.64 | 0.27 | 1.22 | 1.55 | 0.35 | 0.07 | 0.15 |
| $r$ | 0.01 | 0.00 | -0.02 | -0.27 | 1.84 | 7.34 | 0.45 | 0.64 | 0.03 | -0.14 |
| $C$ | -0.01 | -0.02 | 0.01 | -0.12 | 0.15 | 0.49 | 0.85 | 0.99 | 0.04 | 0.01 |
| $ca$ | 0.00 | 0.01 | 0.18 | 0.19 | 0.32 | 0.49 | 0.49 | 0.13 | 0.01 | 0.00 |
| $y_N$ | 0.00 | 0.01 | -0.01 | -0.50 | 0.02 | 1.27 | -0.01 | -0.57 | 0.00 | -0.14 |
| $z$ | -3.10 | -4.34 | -30.78 | -37.15 | -42.45 | -46.75 | 0.00 | 0.00 | 49.87 | 49.83 |
| $x$ | -0.06 | -0.12 | -0.65 | -0.84 | 0.04 | 1.16 | 2.10 | 2.41 | 1.38 | 1.37 |
| $mg$ | -0.44 | -0.18 | 0.39 | 0.40 | -1.89 | -0.49 | 1.84 | 2.27 | 1.03 | 1.18 |
| $b$ | 1.90 | 1.97 | 13.32 | 13.46 | 25.86 | 32.94 | 26.73 | 23.98 | 13.11 | 13.42 |

For units of the standard deviations see note to Table 3a. For parameter values corresponding to cases in italics (e.g., *Clean* vs. *Dirty*) see Table 2. The standard deviation of the aid shock is .02 and aid persistence is *High* at $n_{aa} = 0.72$. The standard deviation of the commodity price shock is set to .00001, so commodity prices have no impact on these results.

*The table shows differences between the standard deviation under partial sterilization of foreign exchange intervention and the standard deviation under no sterilization (the latter appears in the appropriate dirty float column of Table 3a). For moderate partial sterilization we set $b_0=0$, $b_1=0.5$, and $b_2=0.25$. For aggressive partial sterilization, $b_1=0.75$.

**The table shows differences between the standard deviation under partial money base targeting and the standard deviation under no targeting (the latter appears in the appropriate PDR aid column of Table 3a). For money base targeting we set $b_0=b_1=0.5$ and $b_2=0.25$.

A striking feature of Table 4a is the distinctly higher volatility of base money growth under a clean float. Since the Central Bank is not intervening in foreign exchange markets under a float, this volatility arises from fluctuations in domestic credit to the government. The source of these fluctuations is the *PDR* component of aid: assuming no change in private holdings .of government securities, net domestic credit must fall by an amount equal to the *PDR* component of the aid inflow. This generates a sharp monetary contraction (in the first year, dated 0 in the impulse responses, money growth falls nearly to zero from its baseline value of 10 percent). Under a dirty float, foreign exchange intervention is substantial, but its net impact is to offset the contractionary impulse of deficit-reduction and therefore to reduce, rather than increase, the volatility of the monetary base.

These findings on the superiority of a managed float are consistent with those of Buffie *et al* (2004), in which permanent aid shocks produced dynamics similar to those of the persistent shocks studied here. While it remains to be seen how general this conclusion is (see below), the analysis suggests that two time-honored rationales for managed exchange rates may need to be revived if we are to understand the prevalence of fear of floating (Calvo and Reinhart 2000a, 2000b) within the structural and financial context of low-income countries. The first focuses on the superiority of intervention when portfolio shocks are dominant, a robust feature of the Mundell-Fleming model (Obstfeld and Rogoff 1996). In our case the precipitating shock is a real shock, but in the PDR case the deficit-financing component alters expected inflation and, in the presence of active currency substitution, leads to potentially large adjustment in private portfolios. As indicated in columns 6 and 8 of Table 4a, a policy that stabilizes the crawl around its steady-state level allows these otherwise disruptive portfolio adjustments to take place smoothly.

A second rationale for heavily managed exchange rates was introduced by Fischer (1976) and Lipschitz (1978), who argued that the Mundell-Fleming model provided a poor approximation to macroeconomic conditions in low-income countries. These authors showed that if output was supply-determined (as in our flexible price case), capital mobility was relatively low (bonds are nontraded in our analysis, although there is active currency substitution), and welfare was measured by the volatility of private spending, the standard assignment of flexible exchange rates to real shocks was reversed. Private spending would be less volatile under managed exchange rates, because consumption smoothing could take place via a procyclical trade surplus supported by movements in international reserves. This effect is evident in columns 1-2 and 5-6 of Table 4a, where a dirty float modestly reduces the volatility of private spending when prices are flexible. The buffering role of intervention is evident in the greater volatility of reserves and the current account under a dirty float.

## 4.2  Bond Operations: Sterilized Intervention and Money-Base Targeting

Central banks operating managed exchange rates routinely reach for sterilization as a first response to balance of payments shocks (Schadler *et al*, 1993), and the central banks of both Tanzania and Uganda did precisely this in response to the aid surges of the late 1990s. We saw above, however, that when aid has a nontrivial *PDR* component, a policy of non-sterilized intervention already delivers a smoother path for base money than one that foregoes foreign exchange intervention altogether (Table 4a). It is not clear, therefore, that there is any rationale for bond sterilization in the case of *PDR* aid. Table 4b underscores this point by reporting the increase in standard deviations due to bond sterilization operations relative to the corresponding standard deviations reported in Table 3a. The left panel shows the impact, within a dirty float regime, of sterilizing half or more of any foreign exchange intervention. The effect of sterilization on volatility is small as long as the share of intervention sterilized remains modest (though it is larger in the sticky price case than under flexible prices). Aggressive sterilization, in contrast, is problematic. An attempt to sterilize three-fourths of any intervention creates severe volatility in the real interest rate and bond holdings (as occurred in both Tanzania and Uganda, leading to the abandonment of bond operations; see Buffie, *et al* 2004).

Aggressive sterilization delivers very little gain in terms of the volatility of inflation, which actually increases relative to the no-sterilization case if the sterilization share is pushed above 0.75 (not shown). The fiscal burden of interest payments is what causes the volatility of inflation to increase under an aggressive sterilization policy. In the case of an aid inflow, this burden becomes acute both because bond sales are substantial and because the real interest rate, which is not tethered to the world interest rate as it would be in an emerging-market economy, rises sharply. The size of bond sales, in turn, reflects the operation of an offset coefficient that is close to 0.90 despite the lack of perfect capital mobility. The source of this offset is straightforward: initial bond sales reduce domestic currency holdings, producing a sharp contraction in liquidity services; but when this occurs, the private sector restores a portion of liquidity services through a private capital inflow, i.e., by exchanging foreign currency for domestic currency at the central bank.[9] Renewed reserve accumulation then requires further bond sales.

In the second half of Table 4b we consider the use of bond operations to directly target the growth rate of the monetary base. Here the central bank simply shifts a portion of any change in the government's overall domestic financing requirement (the fiscal deficit net of aid, plus reserve accumulation) into the domestic bond market. This is a perilous exercise, however, given the impact of bond operations on the fiscal deficit. Table 4b shows that in the case of a floating exchange rate (where domestic credit is the sole source of base money growth), the use of bond operations to maintain a tight adherence to a money growth anchor creates severe volatility in the key macroeconomic variables. Even money growth itself fails to be stabilized, even though bond operations are being used to limit the full monetization of each year's fiscal deficit after grants.

## 5   Shocks and Intervention Policy

In this section we broaden the analysis to incorporate commodity price shocks. This analysis is preliminary and we emphasize a few important points rather than attempting a comprehensive treatment. To limit the dimensionality of the discussion we restrict attention to the sticky-price, *PDR* case, which presents the most difficult macroeconomic tradeoffs in the

---

[9] As long as the rate of crawl of the exchange rate is positive in steady state, domestic currency has a higher opportunity cost than does foreign currency and therefore delivers higher liquidity services on the margin. A private capital outflow therefore constitutes a way of restoring lost liquidity services. The offset coefficient associated with a 1-time sale of government securities, for example, is 0.884. In other words, nearly 90 percent of the monetary contraction is offset in the first year through currency transactions with the central bank. The offset coefficient falls to 0.580 if the elasticity of currency substitution is 0.75 rather than 2.0.

aid-only situation; and for the present we focus on intervention policy, leaving sterilization aside. Our interest is in how alternative structures of external shocks alter the relative efficacy of clean and dirty floats in managing volatility. As emphasized above, the empirical evidence suggests a grouping of countries along two dimensions: first, the *persistence* of aid (given by its autoregressive parameter $n_{aa}$), and second, the degree to which aid flows provide *insurance* against commodity price shocks (given by the lag parameter $n_{at}$).

We begin with a benchmark case in which aid and commodity prices are mutually independent and aid shows *low* persistence (we uniformly treat commodity prices as non-persistent, with an autoregressive parameter of only 0.11). We deliberately calibrate the aid and commodity price innovations so as to generate an equivalent initial windfall in terms of foreign exchange. Since exports are 5 times the size of aid, this requires setting the standard deviation of commodity export prices to 1/5 that of aid (4 percent as against 20 percent, in each case generating an initial shock equal to 2% of GDP).

Tables 5a and 5b show the impulse responses to aid and commodity export price shocks in the benchmark specification. Differences reflect the divergent fiscal impacts of the two shocks: *PDR* aid reduces the domestic financing requirement, while export price shocks have no direct fiscal impact. Under a floating exchange rate, inflation falls by much more in the face of an aid shock than in the case of a commodity price boom, and the nominal and real exchange rates appreciate by more. As a result of the latter, the "switching" recession familiar from the persistent *PDR* aid case (Table 3b) appears here, although the fall in nontraded output is smaller. The real interest rate falls by more under commodity price shocks than *PDR* aid, regardless of exchange rate arrangement: this is because the *PDR* component reduces the shock to private disposable income, so that the impetus to smooth consumption is weaker in the aid case than with an otherwise-equivalent export price shock.

Table 5. IRs to aid and commodity export price shocks under sticky prices and PDR aid (Entries give percentage deviations from steady-state values)

| Period<br>*Variable* | 0 | 1 | 2 | 3 | 4 | 5 | 15 |
|---|---|---|---|---|---|---|---|
| **Table 5a.** *Clean* float (Note $z$ has zero IR) | | | | | | | |
| Impulse responses to an aid shock (Note $p_X$ has zero IR) | | | | | | | |
| $\pi$ | -7.59 | -2.23 | -1.49 | -0.91 | -0.55 | -0.32 | 0.00 |
| $e$ | 4.86 | 3.16 | 2.05 | 1.28 | 0.78 | 0.47 | 0.00 |
| $r$ | -0.85 | -0.83 | -0.48 | -0.27 | -0.16 | -0.09 | 0.00 |
| $C$ | 1.28 | 0.89 | 0.52 | 0.30 | 0.17 | 0.10 | 0.00 |
| $ca$ | 1.00 | -0.16 | -0.28 | -0.21 | -0.14 | -0.09 | 0.00 |
| $y_N$ | -1.06 | -0.64 | -0.46 | -0.31 | -0.19 | -0.12 | 0.00 |
| $x$ | -10.26 | -1.29 | -0.88 | -0.49 | -0.28 | -0.16 | 0.00 |
| $mg$ | -7.51 | -3.01 | -1.54 | -0.72 | -0.36 | -0.19 | 0.00 |
| $a$ | 20.00 | 5.20 | 1.35 | 0.35 | 0.09 | 0.02 | 0.00 |
| Impulse responses to a commodity export price shock (Note $a$ has zero IR) | | | | | | | |
| $\pi$ | -1.38 | -2.04 | -1.21 | -0.69 | -0.41 | -0.24 | 0.00 |
| $e$ | 1.84 | 2.12 | 1.52 | 0.95 | 0.58 | 0.35 | 0.00 |
| $r$ | -2.87 | -1.05 | -0.41 | -0.20 | -0.11 | -0.07 | 0.00 |
| $C$ | 2.18 | 0.88 | 0.40 | 0.22 | 0.13 | 0.08 | 0.00 |
| $ca$ | 1.07 | -0.34 | -0.29 | -0.18 | -0.11 | -0.06 | 0.00 |
| $y_N$ | 0.91 | -0.21 | -0.33 | -0.23 | -0.15 | -0.09 | 0.00 |

| | | | | | | | |
|---|---|---|---|---|---|---|---|
| $x$ | -2.39 | -2.20 | -0.88 | -0.38 | -0.20 | -0.11 | 0.00 |
| $mg$ | -0.10 | -3.83 | -1.34 | -0.50 | -0.24 | -0.13 | 0.00 |
| $p_X$ | 4.00 | 0.44 | 0.05 | 0.01 | 0.00 | 0.00 | 0.00 |

**Table 5b.** *Dirty* float

Impulse responses to an aid shock (Note $p_X$ has zero IR; $a$ follows pattern above)

| | | | | | | | |
|---|---|---|---|---|---|---|---|
| $\pi$ | 0.02 | -0.63 | -0.81 | -0.80 | -0.75 | -0.70 | -0.47 |
| $e$ | 1.08 | 1.15 | 0.91 | 0.64 | 0.44 | 0.30 | 0.06 |
| $r$ | -1.38 | -0.88 | -0.48 | -0.25 | -0.14 | -0.08 | 0.00 |
| $C$ | 1.53 | 0.90 | 0.50 | 0.28 | 0.17 | 0.11 | 0.02 |
| $ca$ | 1.20 | 0.00 | -0.17 | -0.15 | -0.11 | -0.07 | -0.01 |
| $y_N$ | 0.72 | 0.21 | 0.01 | -0.05 | -0.05 | -0.04 | -0.01 |
| $z$ | 10.43 | 17.29 | 20.85 | 22.34 | 22.77 | 22.67 | 17.40 |
| $x$ | -0.57 | -0.66 | -0.67 | -0.66 | -0.64 | -0.62 | -0.46 |
| $mg$ | -1.12 | 0.34 | 0.36 | -0.05 | -0.33 | -0.48 | -0.53 |

Impulse responses to a commodity export price shock ($p_X$ follows pattern above)

| | | | | | | | |
|---|---|---|---|---|---|---|---|
| $\pi$ | 1.05 | -0.17 | -0.40 | -0.40 | -0.35 | -0.30 | -0.17 |
| $e$ | 1.03 | 1.19 | 0.91 | 0.62 | 0.40 | 0.25 | 0.02 |
| $r$ | -2.11 | -1.10 | -0.52 | -0.25 | -0.13 | -0.07 | 0.00 |
| $C$ | 1.96 | 1.00 | 0.50 | 0.26 | 0.15 | 0.09 | 0.01 |
| $ca$ | 1.24 | -0.32 | -0.28 | -0.17 | -0.10 | -0.06 | -0.01 |
| $y_N$ | 1.06 | 0.27 | 0.00 | -0.06 | -0.05 | -0.04 | 0.00 |
| $z$ | -8.33 | -0.07 | 4.49 | 6.53 | 7.41 | 7.75 | 6.32 |
| $x$ | 0.46 | -0.23 | -0.25 | -0.24 | -0.23 | -0.22 | -0.17 |
| $mg$ | -4.48 | 2.44 | 1.39 | 0.56 | 0.16 | -0.03 | -0.19 |

See Table 3a for definitions and units of the variables. Details of the experiment appear in the text.

Table 6. Volatility implications of floating when aid shocks or commodity price shocks are dominant. (theoretical standard deviations from linearized model)

| Varia-ble | *PDR* Aid shocks only | | | | | | Export price shocks only | | |
|---|---|---|---|---|---|---|---|---|---|
| | *High* persistence | | | *Low* persistence | | | | | |
| | *Clean* float (1) | *Dirty* float (2) | Differ-ence = (2) – (1) (3) | *Clean* float (4) | *Dirty* float (5) | Differ-ence = (5) – (4) (6) | *Clean* float (7) | *Dirty* float (8) | Differ-rence = (8)–(7) (9) |
| $\pi$ | 17.93 | 6.91 | -11.02 | 8.13 | 3.04 | -5.09 | 2.88 | 1.60 | -1.28 |
| $e$ | 13.34 | 4.81 | -8.54 | 6.35 | 2.04 | -4.31 | 3.40 | 2.02 | -1.38 |
| $r$ | 1.63 | 1.59 | -0.04 | 1.32 | 1.73 | 0.41 | 3.09 | 2.45 | -0.64 |
| $C$ | 3.48 | 3.53 | 0.06 | 1.68 | 1.88 | 0.19 | 2.40 | 2.28 | -0.13 |
| $ca$ | 0.36 | 1.01 | 0.65 | 1.08 | 1.23 | 0.15 | 1.18 | 1.33 | 0.15 |
| $y_N$ | 3.09 | 1.02 | -2.07 | 1.37 | 0.76 | -0.61 | 1.04 | 1.09 | 0.06 |
| $z$ | 0.00 | 244.33 | 244.33 | 0.00 | 106.11 | 106.11 | 0.00 | 37.55 | 37.55 |
| $x$ | 22.27 | 6.78 | -15.49 | 10.40 | 2.96 | -7.43 | 3.40 | 1.15 | -2.25 |
| $mg$ | 13.15 | 7.71 | -5.44 | 8.27 | 3.11 | -5.16 | 4.10 | 5.40 | 1.31 |

See Table 3a for definitions and units of the variables. Nontraded prices are *sticky*. Government spending is *neutral*. The aid shock has standard deviation 0.02 (20 percent); the commodity price shock, 0.04 (4 percent), so a 1-standard deviation innovation in each has the same impact effect on foreign exchange earnings.

Table 7a. Volatility implications of floating under alternative shock structures (theoretical standard deviations from linearized model)

| Variable | *Low* Persistence, *Counter*-cyclical aid | | | Alternative shock structures | | |
| | *Clean* float | *Dirty* float | Difference =(2)–(1) | Difference between standard deviation under dirty and clean float | | |
| | | | | *High, Counter-* | *Low, Pro-* | *High, Pro-* |
| | (1) | (2) | (3) | (4) | (5) | (6) |
| $\pi$ | 10.07 | 3.70 | -6.37 | -14.75 | -7.78 | -16.36 |
| $e$ | 7.03 | 2.14 | -4.89 | -10.52 | -6.65 | -12.58 |
| $r$ | 4.56 | 3.41 | -1.14 | -1.68 | 0.04 | -0.22 |
| $C$ | 2.38 | 2.25 | -0.13 | -0.16 | 0.10 | -0.07 |
| $ca$ | 2.57 | 2.73 | 0.16 | 0.17 | 0.34 | 0.99 |
| $y_N$ | 2.66 | 1.12 | -1.54 | -3.71 | -0.12 | -2.18 |
| $z$ | 0.00 | 126.78 | 126.78 | 327.57 | 175.30 | 378.94 |
| $x$ | 12.79 | 3.61 | -9.18 | -20.38 | -11.59 | -22.91 |
| $mg$ | 9.11 | 13.31 | 4.19 | 0.42 | -8.33 | -9.33 |

See notes to Table 6.

Table 7b. Volatility implications of alternative shock structures (increases in theoretical standard deviations from linearized model)

| Variable | *Dirty* float (Increase in standard deviation relative to column (2) of Table 6a) | | | *Clean* float (Increase in standard deviation relative to column (1) of Table 6a) | | |
| | Alternative shock structure: | | | Alternative shock structure: | | |
| | *High, Counter-* | *Low, Pro-* | *High, Pro-* | *High, Counter-* | *Low, Pro-* | *High, Pro-* |
| $\pi$ | 5.55 | 1.55 | 7.15 | 13.93 | 2.97 | 17.14 |
| $e$ | 4.00 | 2.67 | 6.47 | 9.63 | 4.44 | 14.16 |
| $r$ | 0.32 | -0.17 | -0.63 | 0.85 | -1.36 | -1.56 |
| $C$ | 2.15 | 2.11 | 4.20 | 2.17 | 1.88 | 4.14 |
| $ca$ | 0.09 | -0.90 | -1.26 | 0.08 | -1.09 | -2.09 |
| $y_N$ | 0.20 | 0.57 | 0.81 | 2.37 | -0.86 | 1.45 |
| $z$ | 200.78 | 48.51 | 252.16 | 0.00 | 0.00 | 0.00 |
| $x$ | 5.51 | 1.28 | 6.90 | 16.70 | 3.68 | 20.63 |
| $mg$ | 4.46 | -7.52 | -1.32 | 8.24 | 5.01 | 12.21 |

See notes to Table 6.

Table 8. Volatility implications of alternative government spending patterns

| Variable | Clean float Government spending is: | | | Dirty float Government spending is: | | |
|---|---|---|---|---|---|---|
| | Import-biased | Neutral* | Nontraded-biased | Import-biased | Neutral* | Nontraded-biased |
| | (standard deviations) | | | (increases in standard deviations relative to a clean float) | | |
| $\pi$ | 17.01 | 17.93 | 16.19 | -10.83 | -11.02 | -9.46 |
| $e$ | 9.92 | 13.34 | 16.37 | -8.26 | -8.54 | -8.00 |
| $r$ | 0.98 | 1.63 | 1.13 | -0.42 | -0.04 | 0.06 |
| $C$ | 1.11 | 3.48 | 2.44 | 0.08 | 0.06 | 0.11 |
| $ca$ | 0.10 | 0.36 | 0.46 | 0.54 | 0.65 | 0.59 |
| $y_N$ | 3.48 | 3.09 | 2.15 | -3.11 | -2.07 | -0.20 |
| $z$ | 0.00 | 0.00 | 0.00 | 221.84 | 244.33 | 229.78 |
| $x$ | 20.59 | 22.27 | 21.30 | -14.42 | -15.49 | -14.91 |
| $mg$ | 12.07 | 13.15 | 12.22 | -4.86 | -5.44 | -3.99 |

See Table 3a for definitions and units of the variables. Nontraded prices are *sticky*. Government spending is *neutral*. The aid shock has standard deviation 0.02 (20 percent). *The *neutral* cases correspond to columns (7) and (8) of Table 4a.

Our main interest is in the impact of alternative regimes on volatility. Going step by step, Table 6 first reports the volatilities of key variables in aid-only and export-price-only versions of the model. We find the following:

- While the disadvantages of a clean float are more dramatic when aid is highly persistent, they remain present even under very low aid persistence.
- When export price shocks are dominant, the appeal of a heavily managed float is less dramatic than when *PDR* aid shocks are dominant (even when aid shows low persistence). But a dirty float nonetheless delivers lower volatilities for inflation, the real exchange rate, and the real interest rate than does a clean float.
- Dirty floating produces a Fisher/Lipschitz "buffer stock" effect – apparent in an increase in the volatility of reserves and a reduction in the volatility of real interest rates and private consumption – when export price shocks are dominant. The same effect is not present when the dominant shocks are low-persistence shocks to *PDR* aid. The contrast is consistent with the greater need for smoothing in the commodity price case.

Tables 7a and 7b take up the general case in which both shocks are present. We begin in columns 1-3 of Table 7a by comparing clean and dirty floats in the benchmark specification with both shocks operative. In this specification, aid persistence is low and aid is countercyclical, providing a kind of *ex post* insurance with respect to commodity price shocks. Columns 4-6 compares clean and dirty floats under alternative shock structures. Our earlier conclusion with respect to PDR aid proves robust:

- The severe short-run volatility associated with absorbing *PDR* aid shocks in a clean float continues to be present when transitory commodity price shocks are incorporated, as does the clear superiority of a heavily managed float. This holds regardless of the cyclical association of aid with lagged commodity prices.

In Table 7b we look at the impact of alternative shock structures on the volatilities generated by clean and dirty floats. The following conclusions emerge:

- Aid that provides partial *ex post* insurance for commodity price shocks significantly reduces the volatility in inflation, real exchange rates, and private consumption that is associated with a clean float, regardless of the degree of persistence of aid (column 7b(11) versus 7a(1), and 7b(12) versus 7b(10)).
- Counter-cyclical aid also produces lower volatilities of key variables under dirty float, and the improvement now extends to nontraded output. But counter-cyclical aid has a considerably smaller ameliorative effect on the volatilities of inflation and the real exchange rate in a dirty float regime than in a clean float. If these are the dominant preoccupations of monetary policy, then the insurance component of aid enhances the relative attractiveness of a clean float.

Further work will be required to assess the robustness of these implications.

We close by briefly returning to the aid-only model to see whether the case for intervention is significantly altered by differences public and private spending patterns out of aid. Table 8 reports volatilities in response to persistent *PDR* aid shocks, under neutral, import-biased, and nontraded-biased government spending. Column 1 of Table 8 corresponds exactly to column 7 of Table 4a: it considers a clean float with sticky prices and *PDR* aid. Columns 2 and 3 consider import-biased and nontraded-biased government spending, respectively. Not surprisingly, the volatility of the real exchange rate is smaller the larger is the share of imports in aid-financed spending. More importantly, however, the conclusions reached earlier about the desirability of a heavily managed float in the face of persistent PDR aid are robust to differences in public sector spending patterns. In the right-side panel of Table 8, a dirty float out-performs a clean float regardless of the disposition of government spending between transfers, traded goods, and nontraded goods.

# 6  Conclusions

How should central banks in low-income countries deploy the increasingly conventional monetary policy instruments at their disposal? We have leveraged recent institutional developments by assuming that policymakers can credibly commit to a variety of alternative rules consistent with a given inflation target. Our aim has been to locate rules that deliver acceptable levels of volatility in key macroeconomic variables, given the structure of these economies and the shocks that buffet them. While this is a familiar problem, shocks to aid and commodity export prices are largely 'beneath the radar' of the contemporary monetary policy literature, given its preoccupation with industrial and emerging-market economies. Nor does uncovered interest parity provide a useful benchmark for the economies we have in mind, although currency substitution is increasingly nimble. Understanding the operating characteristics of alternative rules therefore requires a model that is tailored to a novel set of structural circumstances.

The model we have developed makes a start. In meeting this challenge we intentionally depart from an increasingly dominant trend in the monetary policy literature (e.g., Svensson (2000)), by retaining the "LM" curve (i.e., a detailed description of portfolio behavior). This allows us to specify policy rules at the level of the central bank's balance sheet, where intervention and sterilization operations actually take place and reserve money programs are carried out and modified on the fly.

Our clearest result relates to the relative attractiveness of clean and dirty floats. We have shown that when current account shocks – whether aid shocks or commodity price shocks that accrue substantially to the public sector – give rise to sustained movements in seigniorage, private portfolio adjustments greatly complicate macroeconomic management and produce distinctly unpleasant outcomes under floating exchange rates. From this perspective, "fear of floating" is readily interpretable, given the structure of financial markets in countries like Tanzania and Uganda, as fear of avoidable volatility in inflation, real exchange rates, real interest rates and real GDP.

This work can be taken in a variety of directions, of which we close by mentioning three. First, supply shocks to agriculture are a formidable source of volatility in low-income economies. We can incorporate them in the current model by identifying the traded/nontraded structure of agriculture and developing empirical proxies for supply shocks. To the degree that agriculture is nontraded (as suggested by the sensitivity of consumer prices to agricultural conditions in low-income countries), the tradeoffs associated with droughts and other agricultural shocks will be distinct from those associated with international commodity prices. Second, the analysis suggests a high return to further empirical work on the time-series structure of current account shocks in low-income countries, as well as on the relationship between the simulated volatilities generated by the model and observed volatilities in inflation, real exchange rates, and other variables. Finally, the linearized model lends itself to a more formal approach to deriving optimal rules, using a quadratic loss function defined over expected deviations of inflation and other key variables from steady-state values. Progress in any of these areas would sharpen our understanding of the volatility tradeoffs facing low-income countries and the appropriate stances of monetary and exchange rate policy.

# References

Adam, C., D. Bevan and G. Chambas (2001), "Exchange rate regimes and revenue performance in Sub-Saharan Africa" *Journal of Development Economics* **64**: 173-213.

Agénor, P-R. and E.Ucer (1999) "Exchange Market Reform, Inflation and Fiscal Deficits" *Journal of Policy Reform* 3: 81-96.

Buffie, E., C. Adam, S. O'Connell, and C. Pattillo (2004), "Exchange Rate Policy and the Management of Official and Private Capital Inflows in Africa," *IMF Staff Papers* **51**(Special Issue): 126-160.

Calvo, G. A. (1983), "Staggered prices in a utility-maximizing framework," *Journal of Monetary Economics* **12**: 383-398.

Calvo, G. A. and C. Reinhart (2000a), "Fear of floating," *Quarterly Journal of Economics* **117**(2): 379-408.

Calvo, G. A. and C. Reinhart (2000b), "Fixing for your life," NBER Working Paper No. 8006 (Cambridge, MA: National Bureau of Economic Research).

Campbell, J. Y. (1994), "Inspecting the mechanism: an analytical approach to the stochastic growth model," *Journal of Monetary Economics* **33**: 463-506.

Čihák, M. and R. Podpiera (2005), "Bank Behaviour in Developing Countries: Evidence from East Africa", *IMF Working Paper* **05**/129.

Collier, P., A.Hoeffler, and C.Pattillo (2001) "Flight Capital as a Portfolio Choice" *World Bank Economic Review* **15**: 55-80.

Fischer, S. (1976), "Stability and exchange rate system in a monetarist model of the balance of payments," in R. Z. Aliber, ed, *The Political Economy of Monetary Reform* (Montclair, NJ: Allenhel, Osmund and Company).

Garber, P. and L. E. O. Svensson (1995), "The operation and collapse of fixed exchange rate regimes," in G. M. Grossman and K. Rogoff, eds, *Handbook of International Economics, Volume 3*. Amsterdam: North Holland.

Julliard, M. (1996) "Dynare: a program for the resolution and simulation of dynamic models with forward variables through the use of a relaxation algorithm," *CEPREMAP Working Paper* **9602**.

Kiguel, M. and S.O'Connell (1995) "Parallel Exchange Rates in Developing Countries" *World Bank Research Observer* **10**(1): 21-52.

Lipschitz, L. (1978), "Exchange Rate Policies for Developing Countries: Some Simple Arguments for Intervention," *IMF Staff Papers* **25**(4): 650-675.

Marimon, R. and A. Scott, eds (1999), *Computational Methods for the Study of Dynamic Economies* (Oxford: Oxford University Press).

Obstfeld, M. (1999), "Foreign resource inflows, saving, and growth," In K. Schmidt-Hebbel and L. Servén, eds, *The Economics of Saving and Growth* (Cambridge: Cambridge University Press).

Obstfeld, M. and K. Rogoff (1996), *Foundations of International Macroeconomics* (Cambridge, MA: MIT Press).

Reinhart, C. and K.Rogoff (2004) "The Modern History of Exchange Rate Arrangements: A Reinterpretation" *Quarterly Journal of Economics* **119**(1): 1-48.

Roberts, J. M. (1995), "New Keynesian economics and the Phillips curve," *Journal of Money, Credit, and Banking* **27**(4), November, Part I: 975-84.

Rotemberg, J. J. (1987), "New Keynesian microfoundations," In S. Fischer (ed), *NBER Macroeconomics Annual, 1987* (Cambridge, MA: MIT Press, 1987), pp. 69-104.

Rotemberg, J. J. and M. Woodford (1997), "An optimization-based econometric framework for the evaluation of monetary policy," In B. S. Bernanke and J. J. Rotemberg, eds, *NBER Macroeconomics Annual 1997*. Cambridge, MA: MIT Press: 297-345.

Schadler, S. M. Carcovic, A. Bennett, and R. Kahn (1993), *Recent Experiences with Surges in Capital Inflows*. IMF Occasional Paper No. 108 (Washington, DC: International Monetary Fund).

Svensson, L. E. O. (2000), "Open-economy inflation targeting," *Journal of International Economics* **50**: 155-183.

Taylor, J.B, ed. (1999), *Monetary Policy Rules*. Chicago: University of Chicago Press.

In: International Finance and Monetary Policy
Editor: Gleb P. Severov, pp. 117-133

ISBN: 1-60021-103-8
© 2006 Nova Science Publishers, Inc.

*Chapter 5*

# THE CHOICE OF EXCHANGE RATE REGIMES IN TRANSITION ECONOMIES: EVOLUTION AND DETERMINATION

*Jizhong Zhou*[*]

Shanghai University of Finance and Economics, ZEI, and University of Bonn

*Jürgen von Hagen*[**]

ZEI, University of Bonn, Indiana University, and CEPR

## Abstract

We provide an empirical analysis for the evolution and determination of the choice of exchange rate regimes in 25 transition economies. We apply the IMF's new regime classification scheme backwards to classify exchange rate regimes in these countries during the 1990s. We estimate transition matrices to study the evolution of exchange rate regimes. We also run tests for various implications of the "hollowing-out" hypothesis, but do not find supporting evidences. We develop a multinomial logit model to analyze the choice of exchange rate regimes and estimate both static and dynamic version of the model. We find that past regime choices have strong influences on current choices. Both versions of the model provide some support for the relevance of the traditional OCA guidelines for the choice of exchange rate regimes. The variables related to macroeconomic stabilization and the risks of currency crises are also found playing some role in the determination of exchange rate regimes. There are evidences, however, that these influences may not be monotonic, since in some cases intermediate regimes are preferred to both fixed and flexible regimes.

---

[*] E-mail address: jzzhou@mail.shufe.edu.cn, Tel: +86+21+65904611. Fax: +86+21+65103925. School of Finance, Shanghai University of Finance and Economics, 777 Guoding Road, Shanghai 200433, China
[**] E-mail address: vonhagen@uni-bonn.de. Tel: +49+228+739199. Fax: +49+228+731809. ZEI, University of Bonn, Walter-Flex-Strasse 3, 53113 Bonn, Germany

# 1  Introduction

Exchange rate regimes have always fascinated both economists and policy makers. In the transition economies in Central and Eastern Europe (CEE) and in the Former Soviet Union (FSU), the choice of an appropriate exchange rate regime has been given particular attention. Such a decision is not just a choice of a framework for the conduct of monetary policy, but usually regarded as an important part of the overall reform strategy, since it is widely believed that an appropriate exchange rate regime can help establish monetary credibility and macroeconomic stability. As the economic transition turned out to be bumpy, and the monetary authorities of the newly independent countries had to build their credibility from scratch, the choice of an appropriate exchange rate regime becomes a critical and acute issue for the transition economies.

But how should a country choose its exchange rate regime? Over the past 40 years, economists have developed various answers to this question. Early literature on the theory of optimal currency areas (OCA) stressed fundamentals related to the ability to cope with demand shocks and the usefulness of monetary policy for aggregate demand management (Mundell, 1961; McKinnon, 1963; Kenen, 1969). Then the focus of research shifted to the role exchange rate regimes can play in economic stabilization. This literature examined the type and source of the dominant shocks to which an economy is exposed as possible determinants of the choice of exchange rate regimes (Boyer, 1978; Henderson, 1979; McKinnon, 1981). The literature of the 1980s developed the idea that exchange rate pegs could help import credibility of low inflation policies from a foreign central bank (Melitz, 1988; Fratianni and von Hagen, 1992). Most recent literature drew lessons from the currency crises of the 1990s and concluded that countries exposed to large capital flows are left with two corner solutions: a very hard currency peg (such as a currency board or dollarization) or flexible exchange rates, a view that has been dubbed the "hollowing-out" hypothesis (Eichengreen, 1994; Fischer, 2001).

How relevant are these guidelines for the actual selection of an exchange rate regime? The empirical studies emerged after the collapse of the Bretton Woods System have addressed this question in various ways. The early literature found that the fundamentals identified by the OCA approach provided some guidance for observed regime choices (Heller, 1978; Dreyer 1978). Later studies introduced considerations of optimal macroeconomic stabilization, adding proxies for various types of shocks (Melvin, 1985; Savvides, 1990). These authors find that the presence of domestic nominal shocks raises the likelihood of a currency peg, while real shocks reduce it. More recent empirical literature considers the influence of political and institutional variables on regime choices and suggests that political instability tends to increase the likelihood of flexible exchange rate regimes (Edwards, 1996; Berger et al., 2000).

This chapter is aimed to provide an empirical analysis of the evolution and determination of the choice of exchange rate regimes for a group of 25 transition economies in the 1990s. Despite of the similarity in their economic background and policy tasks, there is quite a variety of exchange rate regimes among these countries. The main question of this chapter is, therefore, how this variety can be explained. Moreover, as these countries are increasingly integrated into the world financial market, the "hollowing-out" hypothesis predicts a move away from intermediate exchange rate regimes. Whether it is relevant for the evolution of exchange rate regimes in transition economies will also be addressed in this chapter.

The rest of the chapter is organized as follows. In section 2, we describe our classification of exchange rate regimes and provide a formal test for various implications of the "hollowing-out" hypothesis. Section 3 develops a multinomial logit model of exchange rate regime choices and present estimates of this model. Section 4 concludes.

## 2 Exchange Rate Regimes in Transition Economies: Classification and Evolution

### 2.1 Classification of Exchange Rate Regimes

Any meaningful discussion of the choice of exchange rate regimes requires as the first step an appropriate classification of these regimes. The traditional textbook dichotomy of fixed-vs.-flexible exchange rates cannot account for the diversity of actual regime choices observed in reality. There are various intermediate exchange rate regimes lying somewhere between the two corner regimes of either completely fixed or freely floating rates. As a result, we will not use the rough binary regime classification, as has been frequently used in empirical studies; instead, we will use a three-regime classification consisting of fixed, intermediate, and flexible exchange rate regimes as three regime options.

Table 1 Exchange Rate Regimes: The IMF's Classification System

|   | Exchange Rate Regime | Descriptions |
|---|---|---|
| 1 | Dollarization, euroization | No separate legal tender |
| 2 | Currency Board | Currency fully backed by foreign exchange reserves |
| 3 | Conventional Fixed Pegs | Peg to another currency or currency basket within a band of at most +/- 1% |
| 4 | Horizontal Bands | Pegs with bands larger than +/-1% |
| 5 | Crawling Pegs | Pegs with central parity periodically adjusted in fixed amounts at a pre-announced rate or in response to changes in selected quantitative indicators |
| 6 | Crawling Bands | Crawling pegs combined with bands larger than +/- 1% |
| 7 | Managed Float with No Pre-announced Path for the Exchange Rate | Active intervention without precommitment to a pre-announced target or path for the exchange rate |
| 8 | Independent Float | Market-determined exchange rate with monetary policy independent of exchange rate policy |

**Source**: IMF (1999).

Our main source of information on the choice of exchange rate regimes is the International Monetary Fund (IMF). Each member country report its exchange rate regime to the IMF, and the latter classifies these regimes according to a scheme and publishes this information. The classification scheme used by the IMF before 1998 was essentially a fixed-or-flexible dichotomy and could not classify appropriately many intermediate exchange rate regimes. As an attempt to address this problem, the IMF has adopted a new eight-regime classification scheme since 1998, which ranges from monetary union to independently floating regimes. Table 1 provides an overview of this classification scheme. Based on information from the IMF, the European Bank for Reconstruction and Development (EBRD), and national central banks of the transition economies, we apply this classification scheme to the pre-1998 period and construct an eight-regime classification for 25 transition economies during the 1990s (see Appendix for details).

For the analysis presented below, we condense this eight-regime classification into a three-regime one. The reason is two-folds. On the one hand, because our sample is small, many regimes from the detailed scheme have few or no observations. On the other hand, a three-regime classification still captures the main advantage of the eight-regime scheme in the sense that intermediate regimes are explicitly allowed, which contrasts sharply to the binary structure of only fixed or flexible exchange rate regimes. All these suggest that summarizing a detailed eight-regime classification into a broad three-regime one might be a reasonable simplification. Using the regime codes listed in Table 1, the basic classification for in our analysis includes regimes with code 1, 2, and 3 as fixed regimes; those with code 4, 5, 6, and 7 in the intermediate group; and independent floating regimes as flexible ones. We also try an alternative classification, which reclassifies managed floating regimes (with code 7) as flexible ones.

## 2.2  Evolution of Exchange Rate Regimes: Is There "Hollowing-out" of the Middle?

The "hollowing-out" hypothesis was first discussed by Eichengreen (1994). This hypothesis argues that, in a world of increasingly integrated financial markets and high degree of international capital mobility, intermediate exchange rate regimes are intrinsically less viable than both hard pegs and flexible regimes. As a result, only the two corner regimes are sustainable in the long run; the middle ground for intermediate regimes is hollowing out. The empirical evidence presented by Masson (2001), however, does not render support to this hypothesis. It will be interesting to see whether there is "hollowing-out" of intermediate regimes in transition economies as these countries are increasingly involved in international capital transactions. Therefore, we follow the methodology used by Masson (2001) to test the relevance of the "hollowing-out" hypothesis for our sample. [1]

### Transition Matrix
Assuming that countries can choose their exchange rate regime every year, we can look at the evolution of these choices as a Markov process. Denote the probability that a country chooses regime $j$ in period $t$ given that it chose regime $i$ in period $t-1$ by $p_{ij}$. The transition matrix $P = \{p_{ij}\}$ indicates the probabilities of moving from one exchange rate regime to another over time. The order of the transition matrix $P$ is $N \times N$ with $N$ equal to the number of available regimes. As we are interested in the evolution between two polar regimes and the intermediate regime, we set $N$ to 3. We estimate this matrix for transition economies using both the basic and the alternative classifications.

---

[1] This section draws heavily from Zhou (2002), chapter 2.

The estimated transition matrices are reported in Table 2. The two matrices share some common features. Firstly, because the diagonal elements of a transition matrix measure the chance that a country stays in the previous exchange rate regime, it provides a simple indicator of regime persistence. It is clear from Table 2 that all the three regimes tend to be persistent, with more than 70% of cases having the same exchange rate regime as in the previous year. In particular, the intermediate regimes tend to be quite persistent, indicating that the "hollowing-out" hypothesis might not be relevant in these countries. Secondly, both matrices show that fixed regimes are less persistent than either intermediate or flexible regimes. Thirdly, under both classifications the probability of going from a fixed directly to a flexible regime is much larger than the probability of going to an intermediate regime, while under the alternative classification the probability of going from a flexible directly to a fixed regime is higher than that of going to an intermediate regime. These results seem to suggest that intermediate regimes tend to be less favored than the two corner regimes, which is consistent with the "hollowing-out" hypothesis, especially when the alternative classification is applied.

Table 2 Transition Matrix

| ERR in t-1 | Basic Classification: ERR in t | | | Alternative Classification: ERR in t | | |
|---|---|---|---|---|---|---|
| | FIX | INTER | FLEX | FIX | INTER | FLEX |
| FIX | 0.698 | 0.111 | 0.191 | 0.698 | 0.064 | 0.238 |
| INTER | 0.032 | 0.921 | 0.048 | 0.000 | 0.769 | 0.231 |
| FLEX | 0.067 | 0.167 | 0.767 | 0.062 | 0.041 | 0.897 |

Note: ERR: exchange rate regimes; FIX: fixed regimes; INTER: intermediate regimes; FLEX: flexible regimes.

## Tests for the "Hollowing-Out" Hypothesis

A casual look at the transition matrices does not provide decisive evidence for or against the relevance of the "hollowing-out" hypothesis in transition economies. In order to run a formal test for the hypothesis, we need first derive some testable implications from the hypothesis. Let fixed, intermediate, and flexible exchange rate regimes be denoted by 1, 2, and 3, respectively. One implication of the "hollowing-out" hypothesis is that fixed regimes form an absorbing state. A corresponding transition matrix should have $p_{12} = p_{13} = 0$, indicating that countries will stay with fixed regimes once such regimes are ever adopted. Another implication, symmetrically, is that flexible regimes form an absorbing state, with a relevant transition matrix having $p_{31} = p_{32} = 0$. The third implication is that fixed and flexible regimes together form a closed set, with a corresponding transition matrix having $p_{12} = p_{32} = 0$, which means that there is no exit from these to intermediate regimes.

For an estimate of the transition matrix, $P = \{p_{ij}\}$, Bhat (1972) shows that the associated log-likelihood can be written as:

$$L(P) = \ln B(n_{ij}) + \sum_i \sum_j n_{ij} \ln p_{ij}$$
,

where $n_{ij}$ is the sample frequency of transition from regime $i$ in period $t-1$ to regime $j$ in period $t$, and $B$ is a function of $n_{ij}$. The maximum likelihood estimate of the transition matrix corresponds to the sample frequencies of transitions between regimes. Based on this log-likelihood function, we can compute likelihood ratios (LR) to test various implications of the "hollowing-out" hypothesis. Denoting the transition matrix conforming the "hollowing-out" hypothesis by $P^* = \{p_{ij}^*\}$, the LR statistic is given as:[2]

$$-2\left[L(P) - L(P^*)\right] = 2\sum_i \sum_j n_{ij} \ln(p_{ij}^* / p_{ij})$$

The LR statistic has a chi-square distribution with degrees of freedom equal to the number of restrictions. Since each hypothetical transition matrix $P^*$ involves two zero restrictions, the LR statistic has two degrees of freedom. A significant LR statistic will lead to the rejection of the related hypothesis.

We run the LR tests for various implications of the "hollowing-out" hypothesis based on the estimated transition matrices reported in Table 2. The test results are shown in the upper panel of Table 3. The empirical evidence does not support the hypothesis. All test statistics are highly significant, indicating that the "hollowing-out" hypothesis should be rejected. These evidences suggest that all regimes are free to switch back and forth among themselves. In particular, there is no evidence, at least in the short period under consideration, that the intermediate regimes will disappear from the menu of exchange rate regimes. They seem to remain a viable option for many countries in transition. In short, the "hollowing-out" hypothesis is less relevant for the transition economies.

Table 3 Hollowing-out: Some Tests

|  | Basic Classification | Alternative Classification |
|---|---|---|
| *Likelihood-ratio tests* |  |  |
| Fixed regimes as an absorbing state | 31.587*** | 31.587*** |
| Flexible regimes as an absorbing state | 24.445*** | 18.932*** |
| Fixed and flexible regimes forming a closed set | 31.424*** | 15.573*** |
|  |  |  |
| *Steady-state distribution, in %* |  |  |
| Fixed regimes | 11.9 | 14.3 |
| Intermediate regimes | 65.1 | 16.3 |
| Flexible regimes | 23.0 | 69.4 |

**Note**: *** denotes significance at 1% level.

## Steady-State Distributions

Another approach to examine the "hollowing-out" issue is to look at the steady-state distribution of exchange rate regimes, $\pi$, a $1 \times 3$ row vector containing the steady-state distribution of probabilities for fixed, intermediate, and flexible regimes. Such a distribution

---

[2] Since the $B$ term is common to both likelihood functions, it is cancelled out. The summation is taken only over the non-zero elements of the transition matrices. See Bhat (1972).

has the defining property that $\pi P = \pi$, and it is also called the invariant distribution. The $\pi$ vector should be properly normalized to ensure that its elements are all non-negative and sum up to unity. It is clear from the defining property that $\pi$ is the row eigenvector of $P$ associated with the eigenvalue of unity. It can be shown that the existence of $\pi$ depends on the existence of a limit for $P^n$ when $n$ goes to infinity, which in turn depends on the existence of a limit for $\Lambda^n$, where $\Lambda$ is a diagonal matrix containing eigenvalues of $P$ on the main diagonal. The last condition requires that, except for the eigenvalue(s) equal to unity, the other eigenvalues should be smaller than unity in modules. If this is true, then the (normalized) row eigenvector associated with the unity eigenvalue represents a steady-state distribution.[3] We use this methodology to estimate the steady-state distributions for the basic and alternative classifications and report the results in the lower panel of Table 3.

Under the basic classification, $\pi = (11.9\%, 65.1\%, 23.0\%)$, so the intermediate regimes will not only exist in the steady state, but also dominates the two corner regimes, exactly the opposite of the "hollowing-out" hypothesis. Using the alternative transition matrix, the steady-state distribution becomes $\pi = (14.3\%, 16.3\%, 69.4\%)$. Now the flexible regimes dominate the distribution, but intermediate regimes still account for a reasonable mass of probability, which is even higher than that of fixed regimes. As a result, intermediate regimes will not be the first to disappear from the menu of viable regimes.

# 3 Determination of Exchange Rate Regimes in Transition Economies

## 3.1 The Model

We consider a multinomial logit model for the choice of exchange rate regimes in transition economies. The main advantage of a multinomial model lies in its ability to allow each explanatory variable to assert qualitatively or quantitatively different influences on different regime choices. This stands in sharp contrast to an ordered-choice model, which assumes (and restricts) that a variable favoring intermediate regimes over fixed regimes must favor flexible regimes over intermediate regimes as well. In other words, the multinomial model allows us to check possibly non-monotonic influence of the regime determinants on the choice of exchange rate regimes.

Let the observed choice of exchange rate regimes be indicated by $j$, with $j = 1$, 2, and 3 for fixed, intermediate, and flexible regimes, respectively. The probability of regime $j$ being adopted by country $i$ in year $t$ is denoted by $p_{it}^{j}$. Potential regime determinants (to be discussed below) are summarized in $x_{i,t}$, but in the model we will actually use $x_{i,t-1}$ to explain the choices in year $t$, since the current values of these variables ($x_{i,t}$) can be influenced by the contemporaneous choice of exchange rate regimes. The coefficients vector

---

[3] See Bhat (1972) for a discussion on the calculation of steady-state distributions.

is denoted by $\beta_j$, which measures the influence of the explanatory variables on the probability of regime $j$ being selected. To be specific,

$$p_{it}^{j} = \frac{\exp(x_{i,t-1}\beta_j)}{\sum_{k=1}^{3}\exp(x_{i,t-1}\beta_k)}.$$

As a standard requirement, the coefficients vector $\beta_j$'s should be normalized properly, and in our case only two vectors among three can be estimated. Therefore, we adopt the following normalization: $\beta_1 \equiv 0$. This means that $\beta_2$ and $\beta_3$ will now measure the relative influence of the explanatory variables on the chances for intermediate and flexible regimes as compared to that for fixed regimes.

If the explanatory variables do not include past regime choices, it is essentially a static model for regime choices. Given high regime persistence discussed before, it is likely that, in addition to the influence of other regime determinants, past regime choices may have their own impact on current regime decisions. Therefore, in a dynamic version of the model, lagged regime choices are also included in the set of regime determinants. We do this by including two regime dummies: $d_{i,t-1}^{j}$, $j =2$ and 3, which takes a value of unity if country $i$ chooses regime $j$ in year $t-1$, and zero otherwise. The dummy for lagged fixed regimes ($j =1$) is omitted to avoid perfect multicollinearity. That is,

$$p_{it}^{j} = \frac{\exp(d_{i,t-1}^{2}\alpha_j + d_{i,t-1}^{3}\gamma_j + x_{i,t-1}\beta_j)}{\sum_{k=1}^{3}\exp(d_{i,t-1}^{2}\alpha_k + d_{i,t-1}^{3}\gamma_k + x_{i,t-1}\beta_k)}.$$

Here, again, proper normalization requires that $\alpha_1 \equiv 0$ and $\gamma_1 \equiv 0$. Both static and dynamic versions of the model are estimated using maximum-likelihood approach based on a pooled panel of 25 countries during the 1990s.

## 3.2   Data and Variables

The dependent variable is a trichotomous indicator based on the eight-regime classification listed in the Appendix. The fixed-rate regimes include currency boards and conventionally fixed-rate regimes, the intermediate regimes cover horizontal bands, crawling pegs, crawling bands, and managed floating regimes, and the flexible-rate regimes include independently floating regimes. This corresponds to the basic classification used in the previous section. The alternative classification reclassifies managed floating regimes as flexible-rate regimes.

The explanatory variables are constructed as proxies for the potential regime determinants suggested by theoretical and empirical works. Detailed explanations on the construction and data sources of the variables are collected in the Appendix. The first group of variables attempt to reflect the considerations raised by the OCA theory. Firstly,

McKinnon (1963) argues that the degree of economic openness and the size of the economy are important determinants of the choice of exchange rate regimes, with small and open economies being better candidates for having fixed exchange rates. Economic openness is captured by the variable OPENNESS, defined as the ratio of total trade to GDP, while economic size is proxied by (the log of) GDP. Secondly, Kenen (1969) argues that countries whose trade is highly concentrated in a limited number of goods should adopt flexible exchange rates, since in this case exchange rate adjustments are almost equivalent to the adjustment of national relative prices and are effective instruments for demand management. But for a country trading mainly with one major partner, fixed-rate regime is again preferred, as it can substantially reduce exchange rate uncertainty faced by domestic exporters and importers. The degree of commodity concentration of trade is measured by the variable COMCON, while that of geographic concentration is proxied by GEOCON. Finally, many empirical studies find that level of economic development is another important regime determinant, although its qualitative influence varies across studies (Savvides, 1990; Edwards, 1998; Rizzo, 1998). This factor is proxied by (the log of) per capita GDP (PCGDP).

The second group of variables are constructed to reflect stabilization considerations and factors related to the risk of currency crises. One such variable is cumulative inflation differentials vis-à-vis a country's main trading partners (CUMINF). Large inflation differentials can indicate persistent problems of weak central bank credibility and large domestic nominal shocks, which raise the value of using an exchange rate anchor for the conduct of monetary policies. Another variable is fiscal budget balances, with large deficits typically signaling an unstable stance of public finance, which makes a fixed exchange rate system at higher stake. This variable is denoted by FISCAL, defined as general government budget balance normalized by GDP, with deficits shown as negative numbers. Also relevant for the sustainability of a fixed exchange rate regime is the sufficiency of international reserves (RESERVE, defined as non-gold international reserves normalized by broad money), since large stock of international reserves can boost the confidence in the local currency and make fixed exchange rate regimes a more viable option (Edwards, 1996; Poirson, 2001).

Finally, we also include a dummy variable for the member countries of the Commonwealth of Independent States (CIS) as a control for group heterogeneity. These countries are the non-Baltic successor countries of the FSU. They started their transition later than the CEE transition economies, and their pace of reform is also slower than the CEE countries.

## 3.3    Empirical Results

We estimate the static and dynamic versions of the multinomial logit model using both the basic and the alternative regime classifications. To save place, however, we will only report results based on the basic classification. The results using the alternative classification are fairly comparable to those reported below. Each version of the model is estimated in three steps. In the first step we only include the OCA fundamentals together with the CIS dummy. In the second step, only stabilization variables and currency crises factors are included (together with the CIS dummy). In the third step all available explanatory variables are used in the estimation. As we have mentioned earlier, we will estimate two sets of coefficients associated with the choice of intermediate and flexible regimes. A positive coefficient means that an increase in the variable will increase the probability for the corresponding regime being selected relative to the probability for a fixed exchange rate regime.

## Results of the Static Model

The empirical results of the static model are presented in Table 4. The first impression is that the CIS countries show a stronger tendency to select intermediate and flexible regimes than their CEE counterparts, as the coefficients for the CIS dummy are usually positive and significant. This is probably due to the fact that these countries are institutionally weaker than the CEE countries and are therefore less able to commit to stable exchange rates. It is also possible that the CEE countries, most of them having an aim of joining the EU, are reluctant to allow their exchange rates to float freely, especially vis-à-vis the euro. Therefore, they are more likely to choose fixed exchange rate regimes than the CIS members. Moreover, for the CIS countries, there is a difference in their attitude toward intermediate and flexible regimes, with intermediate regimes more favored than flexible ones. This can be seen form the fact that the coefficients for the dummy are larger and more significant in $\beta_2$ than in $\beta_3$. This result is mainly due to the fact that the CIS countries have a stronger preference for managed floating regimes, an important component of the intermediate regime group under the basic classification, than for independently floating regimes.

Turning to the OCA fundamentals, we observe first that the influence of trade openness on the choice of exchange rate regimes is mixed. On the one hand, the results show that, if choice options are restricted to either fixed or flexible regimes, then countries with higher degree of economic openness are more likely to adopt fixed regimes, since the coefficients for OPENNESS in $\beta_3$ are negative and significant. This is consistent with the usual prediction of the OCA theory. On the other hand, however, its coefficients in $\beta_2$ are positive (though not significant in all cases), indicating that highly open economies may actually prefer intermediate regimes instead of fixed ones. This is nevertheless consistent with the view that countries are concerned with their competitiveness in their export market, and the more so, that more extensively countries are involved in international trade. As a result, highly open countries may wish to reserve some degree of exchange rate flexibility to help maintain their external competitiveness, and are more likely to choose intermediate regimes instead of truly fixed regimes.

The structure of trade also plays a role in the determination of exchange rate regimes. Countries with concentrated commodity structure of foreign trade tend to choose intermediate or flexible regimes, supporting the view that in this case exchange rate flexibility is a valuable channel for the adjustment of relative prices. The influence of geographic concentration of trade is not as significant as that of commodity concentration. In general, the results hint on the possibility that countries with highly geographically concentrated trade will choose either fixed or flexible regimes; intermediate regimes tend to be the last option that these countries will consider. Going to the fixed corner might be justified by the need to reduce exchange rate risks, while going to the flexible end is probably due to competitiveness considerations.

The results show that economic sizes and the level of economic development have persistently opposite influences on the choice of exchange rate regimes. The negative coefficients for PCGDP in both $\beta_2$ and $\beta_3$ indicate that the more developed a country is, the more likely that a fixed regime is adopted. In particular, the chance for flexible regimes is significantly reduced among rich transition economies. In contrast, the positive and significant coefficients for GDP support the view that larger countries are less willing to give up monetary independence required if fixed regimes are to be adopted, especially in the modern age of high international capital mobility. This result is also consistent with the OCA argument that small economies are better candidates for fixed exchange rate regimes than large economies.

Table 4 Static Multinomial Logit Model

| Variables | Coeff. | t-Ratio | Coeff. | t-Ratio | Coeff. | t-Ratio |
|---|---|---|---|---|---|---|
| $\beta_2$ | | | | | | |
| CONSTANT | 0.834 | 0.285 | 0.843** | 2.221 | -1.649 | -0.304 |
| CIS | 1.829** | 2.391 | 4.797*** | 4.968 | 6.052*** | 3.802 |
| OPENNESS | 0.161 | 0.926 | | | 0.593* | 1.808 |
| GEOCON | -11.577* | -1.848 | | | -13.774 | -1.232 |
| COMCON | 3.207 | 1.295 | | | 9.625** | 2.178 |
| PCGDP | -0.435 | -0.982 | | | -0.203 | -0.273 |
| GDP | 1.508*** | 4.273 | | | 2.048*** | 4.145 |
| FISCAL | | | 19.337*** | 3.081 | 22.896** | 2.583 |
| RESERVE | | | -1.630*** | -3.020 | -1.966*** | -2.926 |
| CUMINF | | | -0.534*** | -2.695 | 0.051 | 0.202 |
| $\beta_3$ | | | | | | |
| CONSTANT | -4.691 | -1.486 | -0.387 | -0.846 | -14.991** | -2.498 |
| CIS | -0.586 | -0.819 | 3.476*** | 3.595 | 1.834 | 1.261 |
| OPENNESS | -1.347*** | -2.662 | | | -1.707** | -2.029 |
| GEOCON | 2.925 | 0.456 | | | 16.344 | 1.399 |
| COMCON | 5.165** | 2.009 | | | 15.210*** | 3.005 |
| PCGDP | -2.173*** | -4.259 | | | -2.319*** | -2.702 |
| GDP | 1.010*** | 2.743 | | | 0.840* | 1.655 |
| FISCAL | | | -3.962 | -0.733 | 6.813 | 1.326 |
| RESERVE | | | -1.456** | -2.357 | -2.138** | -2.543 |
| CUMINF | | | -0.073 | -0.308 | -0.116 | -0.337 |
| Observations | 189 | | 165 | | 164 | |
| Log-likelihood | -151.130 | | -139.019 | | -89.937 | |
| Corr. pred. (%) | 38.6 | | 37.0 | | 42.7 | |

**Note**: *, **, *** denote significance at 10%, 5%, 1% level, respectively.

Among the variables related to stabilization and risks of currency crises, reserve sufficiency is clearly an important regime determinant for transition economies. Its negative and significant coefficients indicate that larger stock of international reserves makes fixed exchange rates more sustainable and fixed regimes more likely to be adopted. The results for the FISCAL variable suggests that countries with large fiscal deficits (negative values) will prefer fixed regimes over intermediate ones, but the preference between fixed and flexible regimes is not clear-cut. This is probably due to the observation that intermediate regimes tend to be more accommodative to fiscal misbehavior than either fixed regimes, where the fiscal authority is subordinated to the paramount objective of keeping the exchange rate stable, or flexible regimes, where any change in the fiscal stance will be immediately reflected in the movement of the exchange rate. The CUMINF variable has in most cases negative coefficients, indicating that countries with larger cumulative inflation differentials vis-à-vis main trading partners tend to choose fixed exchange rate regimes, probably reflecting an attempt to strengthen monetary discipline by resorting to an exchange rate anchor.

Table 5 Dynamic Multinomial Logit Model

| Variables | Coeff. | t-Ratio | Coeff. | t-Ratio | Coeff. | t-Ratio |
|---|---|---|---|---|---|---|
| $\beta_2$ | | | | | | |
| CONSTANT | 2.896 | 0.706 | -1.806** | -2.510 | -3.585 | -0.444 |
| CIS | 1.301 | 1.149 | 6.740*** | 3.547 | 8.422*** | 2.698 |
| LAGINTER | 4.792*** | 4.936 | 6.630*** | 4.591 | 6.002*** | 3.378 |
| LAGFLEX | 3.210*** | 3.433 | 4.225*** | 3.595 | 6.017*** | 2.970 |
| OPENNESS | 0.079 | 0.203 | | | 0.558 | 0.798 |
| GEOCON | -20.126** | -2.200 | | | -13.814 | -0.826 |
| COMCON | 2.648 | 0.784 | | | 3.773 | 0.587 |
| PCGDP | -1.350* | -1.744 | | | -1.215 | -0.872 |
| GDP | 2.033*** | 3.347 | | | 2.728*** | 2.814 |
| FISCAL | | | 25.501*** | 2.718 | 28.071** | 2.343 |
| RESERVE | | | -2.335*** | -2.957 | -2.107 | -1.323 |
| CUMINF | | | -1.021** | -2.389 | -0.883 | -1.506 |
| $\beta_3$ | | | | | | |
| CONSTANT | -2.165 | -0.519 | -2.754*** | -3.253 | -16.959* | -1.920 |
| CIS | -0.150 | -0.146 | 6.788*** | 3.624 | 5.882* | 1.953 |
| LAGINTER | 1.536 | 1.315 | 3.873** | 2.431 | 3.327* | 1.712 |
| LAGFLEX | 3.541*** | 4.473 | 5.637*** | 4.809 | 6.430*** | 3.383 |
| OPENNESS | -1.109* | -1.841 | | | -1.371 | -1.194 |
| GEOCON | -7.233 | -0.817 | | | 11.942 | 0.711 |
| COMCON | 5.336* | 1.679 | | | 12.714* | 1.843 |
| PCGDP | -2.447*** | -3.320 | | | -2.713* | -1.830 |
| GDP | 1.585*** | 2.698 | | | 1.715* | 1.739 |
| FISCAL | | | 9.553 | 1.386 | 13.457* | 1.769 |
| RESERVE | | | -2.330** | -2.213 | -2.338 | -1.364 |
| CUMINF | | | -1.036** | -2.361 | -1.210* | -1.883 |
| Observations | 183 | | 164 | | 163 | |
| Log-likelihood | -89.388 | | -68.417 | | -50.710 | |
| Corr. pred. (%) | 56.3 | | 62.8 | | 58.9 | |

Note: *, **, *** denote significance at 10%, 5%, 1% level, respectively.

## Results of the Dynamic Model

Table 5 reports the results for the dynamic model. The first point to note is that past regime choices do strongly influence current regime decisions. The two regime dummies, LAGINTER and LAGFLEX, always have positive coefficients, and these coefficients are in most cases highly significant. This suggest that, compared to a country with a fixed exchange rate regime in the previous year, countries with intermediate or flexible regimes in last year will be significantly more likely to choose intermediate or flexible regimes this year. And the magnitudes of the coefficients suggest that the influence of being with an intermediate (flexible) regime last year on the probability of choosing the same regime this year is larger than its influence on the probability of choosing a flexible (intermediate) regime this year, although the latter influence is also positive and therefore raises the chance for a flexible (intermediate) regime. These results are consistent with the observed persistency in the choice of exchange rate regimes.

The results for other variables are generally comparable with those reported for the static model. There are few changes in the signs or significance levels of the coefficients across Table 5 and Table 4, indicating that the results reported earlier are generally robust. In terms of the ratio of correct in-sample prediction, the dynamic model performs better than the static model, with the percentage of correct prediction rising from around 40% by the static model to about 60% by the dynamic one.

# 4  Conclusions

This chapter provides an empirical analysis for the evolution and determination of the choice of exchange rate regimes in 25 transition economies in CEE and the FSU during the 1990s. We first apply the IMF's new eight-regime classification scheme to classify exchange rate regimes in our sample countries. We then estimate transition matrices to study the evolution of exchange rate regimes, especially the implications of the "hollowing-out" hypothesis for the choice of exchange rate regimes in transition economies. We finally develop a multinomial logit model to test empirically the influence of various regime determinants on these choices.

The estimated transition matrices show that, while all the exchange rate regimes tend to be persistent over time, fixed regimes are less persistent than intermediate or flexible regimes, mainly due to exits from conventionally fixed pegs. What is more relevant for our analysis is that intermediate regimes remain a viable option among transition economies, which is against the prediction of the "hollowing-out" hypothesis. Therefore, we further test formally three implications of this hypothesis. The results reject all of them at high level of confidence. The analysis based on steady-state regime distributions also suggests that the "hollowing-out" hypothesis is irrelevant for our sample of transition economies.

We estimate both a static and a dynamic version of the multinomial logit model. From the dynamic model we find that past choices of exchange rate regimes have strong influence on current regime choices, consistent with the observed high degree of regime persistency. Both versions of the model provide some support for the relevance of the traditional OCA guidelines for the choice of exchange rate regimes. The results show that small and open economies do prefer fixed exchange rate regimes over flexible regimes, while countries whose trade structures are characterized by high degree of geographical diversification or commodity concentration tend to choose flexible regimes rather than fixed ones. There are evidences, however, that these influences may not be monotonic, since in some cases intermediate regimes are preferred to both fixed and flexible regimes. The variables related to macroeconomic stabilization and the risks of currency crises are also found playing some role in the determination of exchange rate regimes. In general, large fiscal deficits make intermediate regimes and, to a lesser extent, flexible regimes less favorable than fixed regimes, as fixed exchange rates may enforce some form of fiscal discipline in this regard. In a similar vein, large cumulative inflation differentials vis-à-vis trading partners may reflect weak credibility of the monetary authority, so an exchange rate anchor might be called for to help stabilize the economy. Finally, sufficient international reserves can help sustain a fixed exchange rate, so a fixed-rate regime is more likely to be selected when a large stock of international reserves is available.

# Appendix

## Exchange Rate Regimes in Transition Economies

|  | 1990 | 1991 | 1992 | 1993 | 1994 | 1995 | 1996 | 1997 | 1998 | 1999 |
|---|---|---|---|---|---|---|---|---|---|---|
| *EU Accession Candidates: Central and Eastern European Countries* | | | | | | | | | | |
| Bulgaria | 3 | 8 | 8 | 8 | 8 | 8 | 8 | 2 | 2 | 2 |
| Czech Republic | 3 | 3 | 3 | 3 | 3 | 3 | 4 | 7 | 7 | 7 |
| Hungary | 3 | 3 | 3 | 3 | 3 | 6 | 6 | 6 | 6 | 6 |
| Poland | 3 | 5 | 5 | 5 | 5 | 6 | 6 | 6 | 6 | 6 |
| Romania | 3 | 7 | 8 | 8 | 8 | 8 | 8 | 8 | 7 | 7 |
| Slovak Republic | 3 | 3 | 3 | 3 | 3 | 3 | 4 | 4 | 7 | 7 |
| Slovenia | na | (7) | 7 | 7 | 7 | 7 | 7 | 7 | 7 | 7 |
| | | | | | | | | | | |
| *EU Accession Candidates: Baltics* | | | | | | | | | | |
| Estonia | na | na | 2 | 2 | 2 | 2 | 2 | 2 | 2 | 2 |
| Latvia | na | na | (8) | (8) | 3 | 3 | 3 | 3 | 3 | 3 |
| Lithuania | na | na | (8) | (8) | 2 | 2 | 2 | 2 | 2 | 2 |
| | | | | | | | | | | |
| *Other Central and Eastern European Countries* | | | | | | | | | | |
| Albania | 3 | 3 | 8 | 8 | 8 | 8 | 8 | 8 | 8 | 8 |
| Croatia | na | na | 3 | 8 | 4 | 4 | 4 | 4 | 4 | 7 |
| Macedonia | na | na | 8 | 8 | 3 | 3 | 3 | 3 | 3 | 3 |
| | | | | | | | | | | |
| *Commonwealth of Independent States* | | | | | | | | | | |
| Armenia | na | na | (3) | (8) | 8 | 8 | 8 | 8 | 8 | 8 |
| Azerbaijan | na | na | (3) | (3) | 8 | 8 | 8 | 8 | 7 | 7 |
| Belarus | na | na | (3) | (3) | (7) | 7 | 4 | 7 | 7 | 7 |
| Georgia | na | na | (3) | (8) | 7 | 7 | 7 | 3 | 8 | 8 |
| Kazakhstan | na | na | (3) | (8) | 8 | 8 | 8 | 7 | 7 | 8 |
| Kyrgyz Republic | na | na | (3) | (8) | 8 | 7 | 7 | 7 | 7 | 7 |
| Moldova | na | na | (3) | (8) | 8 | 8 | 8 | 8 | 8 | 8 |
| Russia | na | na | (3) | (8) | 8 | 4 | 6 | 6 | 7 | 8 |
| Tajikistan | na | na | na | (3) | (3) | 8 | 8 | 8 | 7 | 7 |
| Turkmenistan | na | na | (3) | (3) | 3 | 7 | 7 | 3 | 3 | 3 |
| Ukraine | na | na | (3) | (8) | 8 | 7 | 7 | 4 | 4 | 7 |
| Uzbekistan | na | na | (3) | (3) | (8) | 7 | 7 | 7 | 7 | 7 |

**Notes**: End-year observations. Codes in parentheses refer to the periods when the newly-introduced national currencies have not yet assumed the status as the sole legal tender. The meanings of the codes are: na=not available, 1=currency union (no separate legal tender), 2=currency board, 3=conventionally fixed pegs, 4=horizontal bands, 5=crawling pegs, 6=crawling bands, 7=managed floating without pre-announced path for the exchange rate, 8=independent floating.

## Explanatory Variables

CIS: Dummy for the member countries of the Commonwealth of Independent States, including Armenia, Azerbaijan, Belarus, Georgia, Kazakhstan, Kyrgyz Republic, Moldova, Russia, Tajikistan, Turkmenistan, Ukraine, and Uzbekistan.

COMCON: Commodity concentration of foreign trade, measured by the Gini-Hirschman coefficient defined below. Commodities are first defined at the one-digit SITC level (0-9) to create ten broad groups and then reclassified into seven main commodity categories. Denote exports of commodity $i$ from country $j$ by $x_{ij}$ and country $j$'s total export by $x_j$, the Gini-Hirschman coefficient for country $j$, $C_j$, is defined as $C_j = \sqrt{\sum_i (x_{ij}/x_j)^2}$. Data on commodity trade are from International Trade Center.

CUMINF: Cumulative differentials in annual consumer price inflation rates vis-à-vis main trading partners. A positive entry denotes a cumulative higher inflation than a weighted average of the main trading partners. The starting year is 1990. The five largest trading partners are involved in the calculation, with weights equal to their respective trade shares. Data source is IMF, *International Financial Statistics* (various issues).

FISCAL: General government budget balance, normalized by GDP. A positive (negative) entry denotes a surplus (deficit). Data source is IMF, *International Financial Statistics* (various issues), and EBRD, *Transition Report* (1999).

GDP: Gross domestic products in current prices, in billions of US dollars and then in logarithms. Data are from IMF, *World Economic Outlook* Database, September 2000.

GEOCON: Geographic concentration of foreign trade, measured by the Gini-Hirschman coefficient denoted by $C_j$ for country $j$. Denote country $j$'s total bilateral trade with country $i$ by $x_{ij}$, and country $j$'s total trade by $x_j$, then $C_j = \sqrt{\sum_i (x_{ij}/x_j)^2}$. Only five largest trade partners are considered for the calculation of this coefficient since they usually account for more than two-thirds of the foreign trade in the countries in question. Data source is IMF, *Direction of Trade Statistics* (various issues).

OPENNESS: Degree of openness to foreign economies, measured by the ratio of total trade volume to GDP. Total trade volume is the sum of goods export (f.o.b.) and goods import (c.i.f.). Trade data are from IMF, *Direction of Trade Statistics* (various issues). GDP data are from IMF, *World Economic Outlook* Database, September 2000.

PCGDP: Per capita GDP, in thousands of US dollars and then in logarithms. Data are from IMF, *World Economic Outlook* Database, September 2000.

RESERVE: Ratio of non-gold international reserves to broad money. Data sources are IMF, *International Financial Statistics* (various issues), *Country Report* (various issues), and EBRD, *Transition Report* (1999).

# References

Berger, H., J.-E. Sturm, and J. de Haan, (2000), "An Empirical Investigation into Exchange Rate Regime Choice and Exchange Rate Volatility," *CESifo Working Paper* No. **263**.

Bhat, U. N., (1972), *Elements of Applied Stochastic Processes* (New York: Wiley).

Boyer, R. S., (1978), "Optimal Foreign Exchange Market Intervention," *Journal of Political Economy*: **1045**--1055.

Dreyer, J. S., (1978), "Determinants of Exchange-Rate Regimes for Currencies of Developing Countries: Some Preliminary Results," *World Development*, Vol. 6 (April), pp. 437--445.

Edwards, S., (1996), "The Determinants of the Choice between Fixed and Flexible Exchange-rate Regimes," *NBER Working Paper* No. **5756**.

Edwards, S., 1998, "Exchange Rate Anchors and Inflation: A Political Economy Approach," in S. Eijffinger and H. Huizinga eds., *Positive Political Economy: Theory and Evidence* (Cambridge: Cambridge University Press).

Eichengreen, B., (1994), *International Monetary Arrangements for the 21st Century* (Washington DC: Brookings Institution).

Fischer, S., (2001), "Exchange Rate Regimes: Is the Bipolar View Correct?" *Journal of Economic Perspectives* (Spring 2001), Vol. 15, No. 2: 3--24.

Fratianni, M., and J. von Hagen, (1992), *The European Monetary System and European Monetary Union* (Boulder and Oxford: Westview Press).

Heller, H. R., (1978), "Determinants of Exchange Rate Practices," *Journal of Money, Credit, and Banking*, Vol. 10 (August): 308--321.

Henderson, D. W., (1979), "Financial Policies in Open Economies," *American Economic Review* **69**(2): 232--39.

International Monetary Fund, (1999), *Exchange Rate Arrangements and Currency Convertibility: Development and Issues* (Washington DC: IMF).

Kenen, P. B., (1969), "The Theory of Optimum Currency Areas: An Eclectic View," in R. Mundell and A. Swoboda, eds., *Monetary Problems of the International Economy* (Chicago: University of Chicago Press).

Masson, P., (2001), "Exchange Rate Regime Transitions," *Journal of Development Economics*, Vol. 64: 571--586.

McKinnon, R., (1963), "Optimum Currency Areas," *American Economic Review* 53 (September): 717--725.

McKinnon, R., (1981), "The Exchange Rate and Macroeconomic Policy: Changing Postwar Perceptions," *Journal of Economic Literature* **19**(2): 531--537.

Melitz, J., (1988), "Monetary Discipline and Cooperation in the ERM: A Synthesis," in F. Giavazzi, S. Micossi, and M. Miller eds., *The European Monetary System* (Cambridge: Cambridge University Press).

Melvin, M., (1985), "The Choice of an Exchange Rate System and Macroeconomic Stability," *Journal of Money, Credit, and Banking*, Vol. 17, No. 4 (November, Part 1): 467--478.

Mundell, R., (1961), "A Theory of Optimal Currency Areas," *American Economic Review* 51 (September): 657--665.

Poirson, H., (2001), "How Do Countries Choose Their Exchange Rate Regime?" IMF Working Paper 01/46.

Rizzo, J.-M., (1998), "The Economic Determinants of the Choice of an Exchange Rate Regime: A Probit Analysis," *Economics Letters* **59** (1998): 283--287.

Savvides, A., (1990), "Real Exchange Rate Variability and the Choice of Exchange Rate Regime by Developing Countries," *Journal of International Money and Finance* **9**: 440--454.

Zhou, J., (2002), *Empirical Studies on Exchange Rate Policies in Transition Economies* (Aachen: Shaker Verlag).

In: International Finance and Monetary Policy
Editor: Gleb P. Severov, pp. 135-156

ISBN: 1-60021-103-8
© 2006 Nova Science Publishers, Inc.

*Chapter 6*

# STAR-GARCH MODELS FOR STOCK MARKET INTERACTIONS IN THE PACIFIC BASIN REGION, JAPAN AND US

### *Giorgio Busetti*

Mps Alternative Investments Sgr, Milan, Italy

### *Matteo Manera*[*]

Department of Statistics, University of Milan-Bicocca, Italy
and Fondazione Eni Enrico Mattei, Milan, Italy

## Abstract

We investigate the financial interactions between countries in the Pacific Basin region (Korea, Singapore, Malaysia, Hong Kong and Taiwan), Japan and US. The originality of the paper is the use of STAR-GARCH models, instead of standard correlation-cointegration techniques. For each country in the Pacific Basin region we find statistically adequate STAR-GARCH models for the series of stock market daily returns, using Nikkei225 and S&P500 as alternative threshold variables. We provide evidence for the leading role of Japan in the period 1988-1990 (pre-Japanese crisis years), whereas our results suggest that the Pacific Basin region countries are more closely linked with US during the period 1995-1999 (post-Japanese crisis years).

**Keywords:** STAR-GARCH models; Stock market integration; Pacific-Basin capital markets; Outliers

**JEL classifications:** C22, C51, C52, F36

---

[*] E-mail address: Matteo.Manera@unimib.it. Corresponding author. Phone: +39-02-6448581, Fax: +39-02-6473312, Department of Statistics – University of Milan-Bicocca – Via Bicocca degli Arcimboldi, 8 – Building U7 – 20126 Milano – Italy

# 1   Introduction

This study analyses the stock market relationships between some Eastern Asian countries using STAR-GARCH models. The idea of investigating the interactions among countries of the so-called Pacific Basin region (namely Korea, Singapore, Malaysia, Hong Kong and Taiwan) is not new in the empirical literature. Several studies (see, among others, Phylatkis, 1999) have supported both the existence of strong interrelations among those countries and the presence of a significant degree of dependence of the whole area on Japan and US. If, on the one hand, it is undisputable that the relationship with Japan is based on geographical as well as historical reasons, on the other hand it is possible to interpret the link with US as an element in favour of the thesis that there exists a global process in developed countries leading to fully integrated economies and financial markets. Moreover, it is important to emphasise that a relevant subset of those studies show that Eastern Asian financial markets are more tightly linked to Japan than to US. Using this idea as the starting point, we have looked for confirmation of the leadership  exerted by the Japanese economy between the end of the 80s and the early 90s and, subsequently, we have tested the hypothesis that the Japanese stock market crisis of 1990-1991 has weakened this role. Until the early 90s, many macroeconomic and financial indicators suggest that Japan has economically dominated the Pacific Basin region. Starting from the deregulation of Hong Kong in 1973 to that of Korea in 1988, there has been a constant increase in the percentage of net capital flows originated in Japan and directed to the Pacific area. Within the same period, the Japanese currency has been widely used in Asian markets, so that some countries, among which is Malaysia, decide to re-denominate part of their debt in terms of the yen. Since mid 1990, not only has the economic expansion of Japan in the Asian area recorded a stop, but also a severe crisis has started. The behaviour of the Nikkei225 index, as shown in Graph 1, is extremely informative on that aspect: in less than ten months, from January to October 1990, the stock index has fallen to its 1986 values.

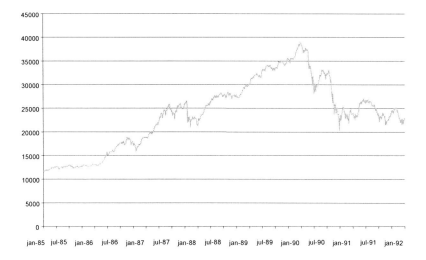

Graph 1. Nikkei225 stock price index (1985-1992)

This study aims at testing the existence of a change of economic leadership in the Pacific Basin region from Japan to US, and the centrality of US as the most important financial market in this area.

The originality of this study rests in the particular use of a class of econometric tools, the so-called STAR and STAR-GARCH models, which have been introduced originally to deal with volatility in financial data, but they are also very useful in developing a concept of relation-integration among markets which is different from the one implied by cointegration or correlation. The fundamental hypothesis of our study is that the influence of the stock market of a leading country on other financial markets does not need to be linear, as correlation and cointegration are implicitly assuming. As Table 1 points out, using the simple concept of correlation of daily returns to describe integration among different stock markets can be unfruitful.

On the contrary, a STAR model offers a different view of the relationships among financial markets, which is based upon an appropriately defined threshold variable. The threshold, through the transition function, the probability that the dependent variable is in one of two, or more, states of the world. For instance, consider the behaviour of an agent who operates on a daily basis in market A. If the agent selects as the threshold variable between two regimes the past returns from the relavant stock index for market B, this means that he acts according to two views of the world represented by the two states of the STAR model and that he chooses to give a larger weight to one or the other regime depending on the levels of past returns from the investments on market B. The degree of influence of market B on market A crucially depends on the choice of the threshold variable. If two or more threshold variables are significant, we select, according to some prespecified criterion, the variable which leads to the most statistically accurate STAR model.

Table 1. Correlation coefficients between daily returns on selected stock market indexes and the thresholds Nikkei225 and S&P500 (1988-1990)

| Threshold | Korea | Hong Kong | Malaysia | Singapore | Taiwan |
|---|---|---|---|---|---|
| Nikkei225 | -0.069 | 0.250 | 0.025 | -0.014 | 0.055 |
| S&P500 | 0.010 | 0.072 | 0.502 | 0.484 | 0.079 |

In order to capture non-linearities with STAR models, sufficiently large samples of data are needed. For this reason we have considered, for each selected country, daily returns on the corresponding stock price indexes during the sub-samples 1988-1990 (pre-crisis period) and 1995-1999 (post-crisis period).

## 2 STAR Models

The idea of using non-linear models to study the behaviour of economic variables is very popular in applied econometrics, and several test statistics have been developed to empirically verify the existence of non-linear processes in many financial time series.

According to the so-called regime-switching models, the time series evolution of many economic variables is characterized by the presence of different states of the world (see, among others, Priestley, 1980, 1988). First and second moments of many time series variables depend upon the regimes and the modalities of transition from a particular state to another. Models where this transition is regulated by an observed variable are termed threshold autoregressive (TAR) or, if the transition from one regime to the other is not abrupt, smooth transition autoregressive (STAR).

## 2.1    Representation of STAR Models

TAR and STAR (see Franses, Teräsvirta and van Dijk, 2002, for a exhaustive survey) are simple autoregressive models whose coefficients depend on a threshold variabile $q$. The simplest case is given by a TAR with two regimes and an autoregressive part of order one:

$$y_t = \begin{cases} \phi_{0,1} + \phi_{1,1} \cdot y_{t-1} + \varepsilon_t & \text{if } q_{t-1} \leq c \\ \phi_{0,2} + \phi_{1,2} \cdot y_{t-1} + \varepsilon_t & \text{if } q_{t-1} > c \end{cases}$$

where $\varepsilon_t$ is a white noise error term with $E(\varepsilon_t | \Omega_{t-1}) = 0$ and $E(\varepsilon^2_t | \Omega_{t-1}) = \sigma^2$. The value $c$, or threshold value, regulates the transition between the two states of the world. If the threshold variable coincides with the lagged dependent variable, the model's name modifies to SETAR (self-exciting TAR).

The major limitation of the TAR model is that the transition between one regime to the other is a sudden jump. This simplistic view has been made more realistic by increasing the number of regimes, or, alternatively, by proposing the STAR model (see Teräsvirta, 1994, among others). STAR has in its simplest version the following specification:

$$y_t = \left( \phi_{0,1} + \phi_{1,1} y_{t-1} \right) \left( 1 - G\left( q_{t-1}; \gamma; c \right) \right) + \left( \phi_{0,2} + \phi_{1,2} y_{t-1} \right) G\left( q_{t-1}; \gamma; c \right) + \varepsilon_t \qquad (1)$$

where $G(.)$ is a probability function which takes values between 0 and 1, and can be interpreted as a weight between the two regimes. $G(.)$ indefinitely increases the number of possible combinations between the states of the world, smoothing the transition between one regime and the other. It is obvious that STAR models introduce non-linearities in the conditional mean.

The most widely used specifications for the function $G(.)$ are exponential (E-STAR) and logistic (L-STAR). The $G(.)$ function for the L-STAR model is:

$$G(q_t, \gamma, c) = (1 + \exp(-\gamma \prod_{i=1}^{n} (q_t - c_i)))^{-1}$$

$$\qquad (2)$$

with $n=1$ in a two-regime model.

The value of $c$ has to lie between the maximum and minimum value of $q_t$, and the smoothness of the model depends on the parameter $\gamma$. The behaviour of the L-STAR model is asymmetric. In the limiting case where $\gamma \to \infty$, $G(.)$ becomes an indicator function $I[q_t > c]$ with $I[A] = 1$ if $A$ is true, and $I[A] = 0$ otherwise. On the contrary, if $\gamma \to 0$, the model is linear with a constant logistic function whose value is 0.5. Classical, non-financial applications of the logistic function involve modelling asymmetries (i.e. recessions and expansions) in economic cycles (see, for example, Teräsvirta, Tjøstheim and Granger, 1994 ).

## 2.2   Hypothesis Testing in STAR Models

The procedure suggested by Teräsvirta (1994) for a correct specification of a STAR model involves first the definition of an appropriate AR($p$) model for the states of the world, then testing for non-linearity.

As far as the specification of the autoregressive order $p$ is concerned, the approach followed in the STAR context is similar to the one of any standard AR model (i.e. partial autocorrelation function of the series, AIC).

On the contrary, there is no standard procedure to identify the threshold variable. The approaches that are more frequently adopted in the empirical literature range from the simple use of some economic intuition to an ex-post informal test based on AIC or BIC, or the choice of the threshold variable that gives rise to the smallest p-value associated with a particular test for non-linearity.

The general structure of any test of non-linearity is to compare the fit of a STAR model with that of a linear model. That is, given a L-STAR model with two regimes

$$y_t = \left( \phi_1 x_t \right)\left( 1 - G(.) \right) + \left( \phi_2 x_t \right) G(.) + \varepsilon_t \tag{3}$$

where $x_t = (1, y_{t-1}, ..., y_{t-p})$, $\phi_i = (\phi_{i,o}, \phi_{i,1}, ..., \phi_{i,p})$, $i=1,2$, linearity implies $H_0$: $\phi_1 = \phi_2$.

Under $H_0$, unfortunately, parameters $\gamma$ and $c$ are unidentified nuisance parameters. Eitrheim and Teräsvirta (1996), Luukkonen, Saikkonnen and Teräsvirta (1998), and Escribano and Jordà (1999) suggest to approximate the $G(.)$ function with a Taylor series. In this way the identification problem is solved and the null hypothesis of linearity can be tested with standard LM-type statistics. Specifically, equation (3) can be re-expressed as:

$$y_t = \left( \phi_1 x_t \right) + \left( \phi_2 - \phi_1 \right) x_t G(.) + \varepsilon_t$$

Provided that $G(.)$ is given by (2), and it is differentiable, it can be approximated around $\gamma=0$, thus obtaining the auxiliary regression:

$$y_t = \beta_0' x_t + \beta_1' x_t s_t + e_t$$

where $\beta_i = (\beta_{i,0}, \beta_{i,1}, ..., \beta_{i,p})$, $e_t = \varepsilon_t + (\phi_2 - \phi_1)' x_t \cdot R_1(q_t; \gamma; c)$, with $R$ indicating the error in the Taylor approximation. In this context, under the null hypothesis $\gamma=0$ we have $\beta_0 \neq 0$ and $\beta_1=0$, where the $\beta$'s are functions of the parameters of the STAR model. Thus the null hypothesis becomes $\beta_1=0$. In the applied literature this test is referred to as the $LM_1$-test, which has a $\chi^2$ asymptotic distribution with $p+1$ degrees of freedom. If one is interested in testing the null hypothesis of linearity against a L-STAR model where $q_t = y_{t-i}$, $0 < i < p+1$, the term $\beta_{1,o} q_t$ must be omitted in order to avoid perfect multicollinearity. It can also be shown that if the two states of the world differ in the value of the constant only, an alternative test should be used. In this case, $G(.)$ has to be approximated up to the third degree, yielding the auxiliary regression:

$$y_t = \beta_0' x_t + \beta_1' x_t q_t + \beta_2' x_t q_t^2 + \beta_3' x_t q_t^3 + e_t \tag{4}$$

The null hypothesis becomes $H_0 \colon \beta_1 = \beta_2 = \beta_3 = 0$. The name for this test is LM$_3$, and it has an asymptotic $\chi^2$ distribution with $3(p+1)$ degrees of freedom. Both test can be calculated using the asymptotic $\chi^2$ version as well as the small-sample $F$ counterpart.

## 2.3   Estimation and Diagnostic Tests in STAR Models

STAR models are typically estimated with Non-linear Least Squares (NLS). NLS is equivalent to Maximum Likelihood or Quasi-Maximum Likelihood, according to whether normality of $\varepsilon_t$ is assumed or not.

If we define $\theta = (\phi_1', \phi_2', \gamma, c)$, then the NLS estimator is:

$$\hat{\theta} = \arg\min_{\phi} Q_T(\theta) = \arg\min_{\phi} \sum_{t=1}^{T}(y_t - F(x_t; \theta))^2$$

where $F(.)$ is the STAR model (4).

Given the regularity condition $E(\varepsilon_t^2) < \infty$ (see Ling and McAleer, 2003), NLS is consistent and asymptotic normal. It is well-known that the choice of appropriate initial conditions play a crucial role in any estimator which uses numerical methods such as Newton-Raphson or Gauss-Newton. The procedure proposed by Leybourne, Newbold and Vougas (1998) notes that the STAR model is linear for given values of $\gamma$ and $c$. Conditional to $\gamma$ and $c$, it is possible to estimate $\phi$ with OLS and obtain $\hat{\phi} = (\hat{\phi}'_1, \hat{\phi}'_2)$, i.e.:

$$\hat{\phi}(\gamma, c) = \left( \sum_{t=1}^{T} x_t(\gamma, c) x_t(\gamma, c)' \right)^{-1} \left( \sum_{t=1}^{T} x_t(\gamma, c) y_t \right)$$

where $x_t(\gamma, c) = (x_t'(1 - G(s_t; \gamma, c)), x_t' G(s_t; \gamma, c))'$.

In this way the minimand function $Q_T$ has a reduced dimension, that is:

$$Q_T(\gamma, c) = \sum_{t=1}^{T}(y_t - \phi(\gamma, c)' x_t(\gamma, c))^2$$

which can now be minimized with respect to $c$ and $\gamma$.

From the empirical viewpoint, it is worth noticing that many studies (see, for instance, Bates and Watts, 1988), point out that estimating $\gamma$ is far from being an easy task. This is mainly due to the fact that a large number of observations in the neighborhood of $c$ is required in order to obtain a reliable estimate of $\gamma$.

In general even reasonable estimates of $\gamma$ come with very high standard errors and $t$-statistics which apparently do not reject the null hypothesis of linearity. In this context, however, the $t$-test is not reliable, for its distribution is not standard. In any case, this problem is mitigated by considering that large variations in $\gamma$ do not have a significant impact on the transition function. The estimation of $c$ is subject to similar problems (see Hansen, 1997), even if a value of $c$ which is not statistically different from zero does not affect the overall validity of the model.

The asymptotic variance/covariance matrix $C$ of $\hat{\theta}$ can be consistently estimated using the robust estimator:

$$A(\theta_0)^{-1} B(\theta_0) A(\theta_0)^{-1}$$

where $A(\theta_0) = \lim_{n \to \infty} E\left[ \partial^2 F_n(\theta) / \partial\theta\partial\theta' \big|_{\theta_0} \right]$, i.e. $A(.)$ is the limit of the Hessian of the objective function,

and $B(\theta_0) = \lim_{n \to \infty} E[n \partial F_n(\theta) / \partial\theta \cdot \partial F_n(\theta) / \partial\theta' \big|_{\theta_0}]$, i.e. $B(.)$ is the limit of the cross-product of the score function.

The most common test for residual autocorrelation in STAR models is based on the auxiliary regression:

$$\hat{\varepsilon}_t = \alpha + \vec{\beta} \cdot \hat{\vec{z}}_t + \sum_{i=1}^{q} \rho_i \cdot \hat{\varepsilon}_{t-i}$$

where $\hat{\varepsilon}_t$ are the residuals under the null of independence of the errors $\varepsilon_t$ and $\hat{\vec{z}}_t = \partial F(x_t; \hat{\theta}) / \partial\theta$, with $F(.)$ being a twice-differentiable function. The analogy with Breusch and Pagan (1980) is clear once we consider that in a linear context the partial derivatives of $F(.)$ with respect to the parameters correspond to the regressors $x_t$. As usual, the null hypothesis is $H_0$: $\rho_i = 0$, and the test in its LM form has an asymptotic $\chi^2$ distribution with $q$ degrees of freedom.

The idea which is behind a test for remaining non-linearity is to detect if a STAR model has captured all the non-linearity which is in the series by evaluating the statistical adequacy of a STAR model with an additional regime (see Eitrheim and Teräsvirta, 1996).

## 2.4    Evaluating the Forecasting Performance of STAR Models

A standard STAR model with $q_t = y_{t-1}$ can be represented as $y_t = F(x_t, \theta) + \varepsilon_t$, where $F(.)$ is defined as in (4), with $x_t = (1, y_{t-1}, ..., y_{t-p})'$. The optimal forecast of $y_{t+h}$ made at time $t$ is $\hat{y}_{t+h|t} = E[y_{t+h} | \Omega_t]$, where $e_{t+h|t} = y_{t+h} - y_{t+h|t}$ is the forecast error. The 1-step ahead forecast is given by $\hat{y}_{t+1|t} = E[y_{t+1} | \Omega_t] = F(x_{t+1}; \theta)$, with $E[\varepsilon_{t+1}|\Omega_t]=0$. In this study we concentrate on static forecasts only. The indicators which are most commonly used to evaluate the forecasting performance of a STAR model are the mean squared error (MSE) and the mean absolute error (MAE):

$$\text{MSE} = \frac{1}{m} \sum_{j=0}^{m-1} (\hat{y}_{T+h+j|T+j} - y_{T+h+j})^2$$

and

$$\text{MAE} = \frac{1}{m} \sum_{j=0}^{m-1} | \hat{y}_{T+h+j|T+j} - y_{T+h+j} |$$

# 3    GARCH Models

ARCH models (Autoregressive Conditional Heteroskedasticity) have been introduced for the first time by Engle (1982) in order to model two phenomena which are typical of many financial time series, namely non-constant conditional variances and volatility clustering.

The simples formulation of a ARCH($r$) model is:

$$\varepsilon_t = \eta_t h_t^{1/2}, \; h_t = \alpha_0 + \alpha_1 \varepsilon_{t-1}^2 + ... + \alpha_r \varepsilon_{t-r}^2$$

where $\alpha_0>0$, $\alpha_i \geq 0$ ($i=1,...r$); $\eta_t$ indicates a white noise error and $h_t$ is the conditional variance of the process. In other terms, if $F_t$ is the $\sigma$-algebra generated by $\{\eta_t, \eta_{t-1},...\}$, then $E(\varepsilon_t^2|F_t) = h_t$.

The first generalization of the ARCH model (GARCH) has been proposed by Bollerslev (1986):

$$\varepsilon_t = \eta_t h_t^{1/2}, \; h_t = \alpha_0 + \sum_{i=1}^{r} \alpha_{i1} \varepsilon_{t-i}^2 + \sum_{i=1}^{s} \beta_i h_{t-i} \tag{5}$$

where $\alpha_0>0$, $\alpha_{i1} \geq 0$ and $\beta_i \geq 0$ ($i=1,...r \backslash s$). The main advantage of this model with respect to the ARCH specification is that the additional term $h_{t-i}$ allows us to reduce the number of parameters in the ARCH component.

The second, more natural generalization is to use a STAR model in the conditional mean of the process and a GARCH specification for the conditional variance (STAR-GARCH models). From an estimation viewpoint, it is easy to deal with STAR-GARCH models since, according to Engle (1982), parameters for the conditional mean and the conditional variance can be estimated seperately, provided that the GARCH specification is symmetric. In this case, given the Hessian for the STAR-GARCH model

$$
H_t(\theta) = \begin{pmatrix} \dfrac{\vartheta^2 l_t(\theta)}{\vartheta\xi\vartheta\xi'} & \dfrac{\vartheta^2 l_t(\theta)}{\vartheta\xi\vartheta\psi'} \\[2mm] \dfrac{\vartheta^2 l_t(\theta)}{\vartheta\psi\vartheta\xi'} & \dfrac{\vartheta^2 l_t(\theta)}{\vartheta\psi\vartheta\psi'} \end{pmatrix} = \begin{pmatrix} H_t^{\xi\xi}(\theta) & H_t^{\xi\psi}(\theta) \\[2mm] H_t^{\xi\psi}(\theta) & H_t^{\psi\psi}(\theta) \end{pmatrix}
$$

where $\theta = (\vec{\xi}, \vec{\psi})$, with $\vec{\xi}$ indicating the vector of parameters in the conditional mean, and $\vec{\psi}$ the vector of parameters of the conditional variance, elements $H^{\xi\psi}$ and $H^{\psi\xi}$ are both zero.

# 4  Outliers in STAR and GARCH Models

## 4.1  Effects of Outliers on STAR Models

Van Dijk, Franses and Lucas (1999) show that LM-type tests tend to reject the null of linearity too often in presence of outliers. Possible solutions to this problem are based on robust estimation techniques which involve different weighting functions. Such techniques can be briefly sketched starting from a simple AR($p$) model $y_t = \phi' x_t + \varepsilon_t$, and modifying the first-order condition $\sum_{t=1}^{T} \omega_r(r_t) \cdot x_t(y_t - \phi' x_t) = 0$, where $r_t$ are the standardized residuals, $r_t \equiv \dfrac{(y_t - \phi' x_t)}{(\sigma_e \omega_x(x_t))}$, with weights $\omega_x(.)$, $\omega_r(.)$ between 0 and 1. The main common characteristic shared by all weighting functions discussed in the literature is to give small weights to values of $\dfrac{(y_t - \phi' x_t)}{\sigma_e}$ that are exceptionally large. For the test LM$_3$, van Dick, Franses and Lucas (1999) suggest to calculate the $R^2$ from regressing the weighted residuals $\hat{\psi}(\hat{r}_t) = \hat{\omega}_r(\hat{r}_t)\hat{r}_t$ on the weighted regressors $\hat{\omega}_x(x_t) \otimes (x_t', x_t's_t, x_t's_t^2, x_t's_t^3)'$. Both weighting functions are obtained from estimating the AR($p$) for $y_t$ under H$_0$. This test has an asymptotic $\chi^2$ distribution with $3(p+1)$ degrees of freedom. Monte Carlo simulations point out that, in the presence of additive as well as innovation outliers, robust tests have more power, and power increases as sample size increases.

Van Dick (1999) analyzes the effects of outliers on the parameters of a STAR model simulating a two-regime logistic specification:

$$y_t = \left(\phi_{0,1} + \phi_{1,1}y_{t-1}\right)\left(1 - G(.)\right) + \left(\phi_{0,2} + \phi_{1,2}y_{t-1}\right)G(.) + \varepsilon_t$$

Estimates of the threshold parameter $c$ do not seem to be particularly affected, provided that the outliers are not numerous enough to justify the existence of a specific regime. This can well happen in presence of many outliers of the same sign. The same is true also for $\gamma$. Conversely, parameters $\phi_{1,i}$, $i=1,2$, are generally biased, as it happens with standard AR($p$) models. Here the magnitude of the bias depends on the specific regime that prevails at the time of the outliers. If, for instance, all outliers fall in just one regime, the bias affecting $\phi_1$ would be noticeable only for that regime.

Several different solutions are available in the literature to reduce the bias in estimating the autoregressive parameters of a STAR model. In this study we consider a simple symmetric trimming algorithm (STA), which is composed by the following steps: i) calculation of the standard deviation of the series over the whole sample; ii) if a single observation is larger than 4 standard deviations, it is trimmed to 4 standard deviations; iii) if an observation is between 3 and 4 standard deviations, it is trimmed to to 3 standard deviations; iv) if an observation is between 2.5 and 3 standard deviations, it is trimmed to 2.5 standard deviations; v) repetition of steps i)-iv) for each obervations in the sample. This procedure has simplicity as its main advantage, but suffers from at least two drawbacks. First, simple STA tends to reduce variability in the series. Second, if different regimes are located far from the mean of the series, simple STA could select as an outlier (and hence exclude from the sample) an observation which instead should be modelled.

## 4.2 Effects of Outliers on GARCH Models

Van Dijk, Franses and Lucas (1999) show that the empirical behaviour of the tests for heteroskedasticity in presence of outliers is very similar to the performance of the tests for linearity in STAR models, that is the null hypothesis is rejected too often. Almost all these tests are based on the residuals of robustly estimated conditional means, once the outliers have been removed and an auxiliary regression of the Breusch-Pagan type is taken into account to check for the presence of linear ARCH effects.

Verhoeven and McAleer (2000), and Chan and McAleer (2001, 2003), among others, point out that the presence of outliers tends to increase $\hat{\alpha}_1$ and to reduce $\hat{\beta}_1$ in the simple GARCH(1,1) model $h_t = \alpha_0 + \alpha_1\varepsilon_{t-1}^2 + \beta_1 h_{t-1}$. Although several procedures are available in the literature to cope with this problem (e.g. Franses and Ghijsels, 1999), the algorithm we use in this study to take into account for outliers is a modification of the simple STA described in Section 4.1, which is motivated by the following considerations: i) irrespective of the selected model, simple STA often produces estimation and forecasting results which are worse than those obtained on the original series; ii) alternative methods to simple STA, such as the Generalized M estimator, heavily depend on the choice of the weighting function (see van Dick, 1999) and are not easy to implement; iii) many estimation procedures which correct for the presence of outlier in GARCH models are based on a priori choices (see the selection of $c$ in Franses and Ghijsels, 1999).

The most important features of our alternative procedure are simplicity (since it is based on the simple STA) and flexibility (the mean of a STAR model is not forced to be constant). Specifically, our modified STA algorithm is formed by the following steps: 1) estimation of a STAR model; 2) residual analysis using a Breusch-Pagan-type test for GARCH effects and estimation of a STAR-GARCH model if appropriate; 3) 1-step ahead forecasts of the conditional mean and variance; 4) application of simple STA, using the 1-step ahead forecast of the mean as the actual mean and the 1-step ahead forecast of the variance as the actual variance; 5) re-estimation of the STAR model on the series corrected for the presence of outliers; 6) overall evaluation of model improvements by comparing the MSE and MAE of the forecasts obtained at steps 3) and 5).

# 5 Empirical Analysis

## 5.1 Data

The first important decision concerns the starting date of the Japanese financial crisis. On the basis of the temporal behaviour of the Nikkei225 stock price index (see Graph 1), which clearly shows a dramatic fall at the beginning of 1990, we set the end of the first period (i.e. pre-crisis) on the 6th june 1990.

The second choice is about the starting date of the pre-crisis period, which is intimately linked to the deregulation characterizing the countries under analysis. As already stated, some countries (e.g. Korea and Taiwan) have deregulated only since 1988, while others (i.e. Hong Kong and Singapore) have started to liberalize their financial markets during the 70s. In order to evaluate different models for different countries on a homogenous basis, we consider the period 5th January 1988 – 6th June 1990 as the maximum common sample.

The second sample (post-crisis) goes from 5th January 1995 to 5th November 1999. The choice of 1995 as the starting date for this period assumes that agents, at the time of implementation of any financial decision, have already incorporated the fall of the Japanese stock price index in their information sets.

We have decided to concentrate our attention on five countries (Korea, Hong Kong, Malaysia, Singapore and Taiwan), since these are the countries which are analyzed by those studies aiming at testing the existence of a strong link between the so-called Pacific Basin region and Japan.

Table 2a. Tests of STAR-type non-linearity (selected countries, 1988-1990)

| Threshold | Hong Kong | Malaysia | Taiwan |
|---|---|---|---|
| Nikkei225 ($F$) | 3.88 (0.01) | 14.31 (0.00) | 1.09 (0.35) |
| S&P500 ($F$) | 3.73 (0.01) | 6.74 (0.00) | 3.26 (0.35) |
| Nikkei225 ($\chi^2$) | 11.65 (0.01) | 42.94 (0.00) | 0.93 (0.43) |
| S&P500 ($\chi^2$) | 11.18 (0.01) | 20.23 (0.00) | 2.78 (0.43) |

**Notes**: The tests reported in this table are based on the $LM_3$ test described in equation (4); $F$ = finite-sample F distribution of $LM_3$; $\chi^2$ = asymptotic $\chi^2$ distribution of $LM_3$; p-values are reported in parentheses.

Table 2b. Tests of STAR-type non-linearity (selected countries, 1995-1999)

| Threshold | Korea | Hong Kong | Singapore |
|---|---|---|---|
| Nikkei225 ($F$) | 1.89 (0.13) | 1.12 (0.00) | 8.75 (0.00) |
| S&P500 ($F$) | 12.11 (0.00) | 1.12 (0.00) | 6.71 (0.00) |
| Nikkei225 ($\chi^2$) | 5.67 (0.13) | 33.69 (0.00) | 26.24 (0.00) |
| S&P500 ($\chi^2$) | 36.34 (0.00) | 33.60 (0.00) | 20.14(0.00) |

**Notes**: see Table 2a.

**Graph 2a.** Stock price index (Korea, 1988-1990)

**Graph 2b.** Daily returns (Korea, 01/01/88-07/06/90)

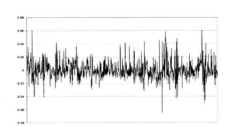

**Graph 2c.** Stock price index (Korea, 1995-1999)

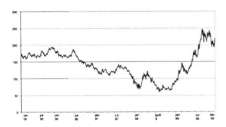

**Graph 2d.** Daily returns (Korea, 06/01/95-03/11/99)

**Graph 3a.** Stock price index (Hong Kong, 1988-1990)

**Graph 3b.** Daily returns (Hong Kong, 05/01/88-07/06/90)

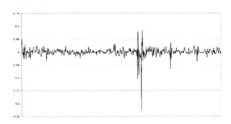

**Graph 3c.** Stock price index (Hong Kong, 1995-1999)

**Graph 3d.** Daily returns (Hong Kong, 06/01/95-03/11/99)

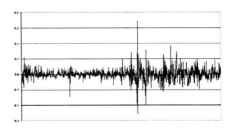

The novelty of our approach is how the potential existence of this link is modelled and tested, that is using STAR and STAR-GARCH models. Moreover, we are also interested in investigating to what extent the financial Japanese crisis has weakened those relationships, and whether US has substituted Japan in its economic leadership in this area.

Our empirical investigation proceeds as follows. First, we check the autocorrelation properties of the original series and determine the order $p$ of the AR model. Second, we test for linearity and explanatory power of alternative threshold variables, that is one-period lagged Japan Nikkei225 and US S&P500 stock price indexes. Third, we estimate a L-STAR model and test for its statistical adequacy using residual based diagnostic tests. Fourth, we test for ARCH effects in STAR residuals. Fifth, we estimate an appropriate STAR-GARCH model (if ARCH effects are present). Sixth, we correct for the presence of outliers using both STA and modified STA algorithms. Seventh, we re-estimate the STAR model and check for estimation improvements using MSE and MAE calculated on the forecasting horizon 8th November 1999 - 28th December 2001. It is worth noticing that the comparison between simple and modified STA is not feasible on the first period. In fact, if it were, the implied forecasting exercise would have been conducted on the Japanese crisis period, in violation of the ceteris paribus condition which is the maintained assumption of our comparative analysis.

## 5.2    Results

Korea has started the process of liberalization in 1988. The Korean stock price index over the first period (Graph 2a) shows a sharp drop in 1990, which is probably due to the Japanese financial crisis. The correlogram of the corresponding series of returns (Graph 2b) suggests an AR model with $p=1$. The estimation of a STAR(1) model reveals that only the Japanese Nikkei225 stock price index is the appropriate threshold variable. The STAR (1) residuals are not autocorrelated, although they exhibit significant ARCH effects, which lead to the estimation of a STAR(1)-GARCH(1) specification (see Table 3a). The adjustment parameter $\gamma$ has a quite high value, which is nevertheless justified in the literature. The first regime is predominant, whereas the second regime has a weight equal to one when the threshold variable takes extreme values (i.e. less than 1%, Graph 7). This is the reason why the weighting function takes the value one more frequently at the end of the sample, that is close to the Japanese crisis. Even in the absence of significant outliers, an application of the simple STA produces a strong bias in the series, since the distinction between the two states of the world disappears. In fact, STA eliminates from the sample all the extreme observations which are responsible for the identification of the second regime. Instead, the application of our modified STA does not alter substantially the estimation results. If we take into consideration the second period (Graphs 2c-2d), it is evident that the Japanese crisis affects both the levels of the index and the volatility of returns. The STAR(1)-GARCH(1) specification which uses the US S&P500 as the threshold variable is preferable on the basis of both the non-linearity test (Table 2b) and in-sample AIC. The presence of strong kurtosis in the residuals is an indicator of outliers. Both procedures, simple STA and modified STA, produce results which are very close to the starting model in terms of MSE and MAE. Table 3b reports the estimated coefficients of the STAR(1)-GARCH(1) model obtained after the application of the simple STA, since this specification is superior in terms of more accurate forecasts and reduced standard errors. With respect to the first sample, the value of $\gamma$ is larger, whereas the standard error for the threshold parameter $c$ is smaller. The transition function indicates the absence of polarization towards a particular state of the world. In summary, in the first period only Nikkei225 can be used as a threshold variable, whereas in the post-crisis period the most statistically adequate threshold is US S&P500. One possible interpretation is that, prior to 1988, the Korean financial market is heavily dependent on Japan, while, after 1995, progresses in world integration have strenghtened the relationships with both Japan and US, attributing the stock market leadership to the latter.

Hong Kong's stock exchange is the most developed within the Pacific Basin region, since it dates back to 1973. A quick inspection to the Hong Kong stock price index during the first period (Graph 3a) reveals the presence of a strong increasing trend, with two marked corrections on july 1989 and july 1990. Obviously, daily returns are characterized by large outliers around the 300th observation (Graph 3b). The correlogram of returns is compatible with an AR(1) model, whereas the tests for non-linearity suggest that both Nikkei225 and S&P500 are statistically adequate threshold variables, with a slight preference for the former (Table 2a). Once estimated, the two STAR(1) behave very differently. In particular, the model with S&P500 as the threshold variable is characterized by very high standard errors even after the use of both simple and modified STA. In the light of these results, the selected model is STAR(1)-GARCH(1) with Nikkei225 as the threshold variable after adjusting the residuals with simple STA (Table 3a, Graph 8). The results obtained in the second period (Graphs 3c-3d) are more controversial. On the one hand, the STAR(1) model with S&P500 as the threshold after applying simple STA is preferable in terms of residual sum of squares and AIC; on the other hand, the STAR(1) model with Nikkei225 as the threshold produces lower MSE and MAE, when both simple and modified STA are used (Tables 2b, 4). Irrespective of the trimming algorithm and the threshold variables, STAR residuals are affected by ARCH effects. To summarize, the empirical results are quite clear in the first period, where the statistically adequate model has Nikkei225 as the threshold. Conversely, in the post-crisis period both threshold variables yield statistically adequate STAR models, although it is not possible to define which is the leading country for Hong Kong.

Table 3a. Estimated STAR-GARCH models (selected countries, 1988-1990)

| Specification | Korea | Hong Kong | Malaysia | Singapore |
|---|---|---|---|---|
| STAR($p$) GARCH($r,s$) | STAR(1) GARCH(1,1) | STAR(1) GARCH(1,1) | STAR(2) GARCH(1,1) | STAR(1) GARCH(1,1) |
| Threshold | Nikkei225 | Nikkei225 | Nikkei225 | Nikkei225 |
| Trimming | Modified STA | Simple STA | Simple STA | Simple STA |
| $\gamma$ | 31.433** | 16.502** | 1427.965 | 13.080** |
| $c$ | -0.016** | 0.004** | -0.009 | -0.009** |
| $\delta_1$ | 0.001 | - | -0.004 | -0.039* |
| $\phi_1$ | -0.731** | -0.160** | -0.476**(-0.322) | -0.512** |
| $\delta_2$ | 5.0E-4 | - | 1.0E-03 | 4.9E-4 |
| $\phi_2$ | 0.088 | 0.192 | 0.087 (0.108) | -0.173* |
| $\alpha_0$ | 3.1E-5* | 2.0E-5** | 8.9E-6** | 9.5E-6** |

| Specification | Korea | Hong Kong | Malaysia | Singapore |
|---|---|---|---|---|
| STAR($p$) GARCH($r,s$) | STAR(1) GARCH(1,1) | STAR(1) GARCH(1,1) | STAR(2) GARCH(1,1) | STAR(1) GARCH(1,1) |
| Threshold | Nikkei225 | Nikkei225 | Nikkei225 | Nikkei225 |
| Trimming | Modified STA | Simple STA | Simple STA | Simple STA |
| $\alpha_1$ | 0.106** | 0.098** | 0.122** | 0.064** |
| $\beta_1$ | 0.707** | 0.774** | 0.791** | 0.810** |
| RSS | 0.085 | 0.140 | 0.064 | 0.054 |
| AIC | -8.675 | -8.156 | -8.929 | -9.113 |

**Notes**: RSS = residual sum of squares; AIC = Akaike information criterion; * (**) = significance at 5% (1%); nE-m = $n10^{-m}$; second-order autocorrelation coefficients for each regime are reported in round brackets.

Table 3b. Estimated STAR-GARCH models (all countries, 1995-1999)

| Specification | Korea | Hong Kong | Malaysia | Singapore | Taiwan |
|---|---|---|---|---|---|
| STAR($p$) GARCH($r,s$) | STAR(1) GARCH(1,1) | STAR(1) GARCH(1) | STAR(1) GARCH(1) | STAR(1) GARCH(1,1) | STAR(1) GARCH(0,0) |
| Threshold | S&P500 | S&P500 | S&P500 | S&P500 | Nikkei225 |
| Trimming | Simple STA | Modified STA | Simple STA | Modified STA | - |
| $\gamma$ | 410.000 | 153.988** | 34.000** | 10.005 | 2857.676 |
| $c$ | -0.018 | -0.016** | -0.006** | -0.027** | 0.012* |
| $\delta_1$ | -7.4E-3 | 0.004** | 0.006** | 0.012 | -0.001** |
| $\phi_1$ | -0.329** | -0.325** | -0.476** | -0.504 | 0.026 |
| $\delta_2$ | 1.3E-4 | - | - | 4.0E-4 | 4.0E-3* |
| $\phi_2$ | 0.133** | 0.108** | 0.220** | 0.238** | -0.086* |
| $\alpha_0$ | 2.0E-6** | 3.2E-6** | 1.8E-6** | 2.1E-7 | - |
| $\alpha_1$ | 0.079** | 0.101** | 0.116** | 0.131** | - |
| $\beta_1$ | 0.919** | 0.891** | 0.887** | 0.865** | - |
| RSS | 0.522 | 0.368 | 0.394 | 0.174 | 0.257 |
| AIC | -7.545 | -7.896 | -7.828 | -8.615 | -8.255 |

**Notes**: see Table 3a.

Malaysia is the country in the Pacific Basin region with the strongest commercial and financial relationships with Japan. This condition is confirmed by the decision of denominating part of Malaysia's debt in tems of the Japanese currency. During the period 1998-1991, the Malaysia stock price index has shown a continuous, upward trend up to march 1990 (Graph 4a). From april 1990 the index records a sharp drop, due to the incoming Japanese financial crisis. The corresponding series of returns shows some important outliers at the beginning and at the end of the sample, while, contrary to the previous cases, the correlogram points out the presence of second-order autocorrelation (Graph 4b). Thus, we have implemented the tests for non-linearity on the STAR(2) specification. In this case, both threshold variables are statistically adequate, but Nikkei225 seems to be preferable on standard goodness of fit considerations (Table 2a). Since the residuals are characterized by ARCH effects and outliers, we have re-estimated the model using the simple STA (Table 3a, Graph 9). The second period (Graph 4c) is characterized by a severe financial crisis in 1998, which affects the series of returns in terms of the number of outliers, excess kurtosis and increased volatility (Graph 4d). The correlogram of this series is compatible with third-order autocorrelation. Using the simple STA, the best model in terms of estimated standard errors and AIC is STAR(1)-GARCH(1,1) with S&P500 as the threshold (Table 3b). Although Malaysia has experienced the strongest economic links with Japan, over the analyzed period our empirical approach seems to suggest a progressive substitution between Japan and US as the most influential country on the Malaysian stock market.

Table 4. Comparison between MSE and MAE of alternative STAR-GARCH models (selected countries, 1995-1999)

| Threshold | Trimming | Hong Kong | | Singapore | |
|---|---|---|---|---|---|
| | | MSE | MAE | MSE | MAE |
| Nikkei225 | - | 0.032 | 1.383 | - | - |
| Nikkei225 | Simple STA | 0.030 | 1.331 | - | - |
| Nikkei225 | Modified STA | 0.029 | 1.330 | - | - |
| S&P500 | - | - | - | 0.024 | 1.168 |
| S&P500 | Simple STA | 0.033 | 1.431 | 0.027 | 1.290 |
| S&P500 | Modified STA | - | - | 0.023 | 1.143 |

Notes: MSE = Mean Squared Error; MAE = Mean Absolute Error; MSE and MAE are calculated on the forecasting horizon 8th november 1999 – 28th december 2001.

The liberalization of Singapore dates back to 1978, which makes this country the second best developed financial market in the region, after Hong Kong. If we concentrate on the first period (Graphs 5a-5b), the Singapore stock price index shows a steady upward trend until the end of 1990, while the corresponding returns are highly volatile and affected by outliers at the beginning of the sample and around the 400th observation. Both threshold variables are statistically adequate, although the lowest p-value of the test for non-linearity is recorded when Nikkei225 is the threshold. In fact, if the STAR(1)-GARCH(1,1) model with Nikkei225 is satisfactory (Table 3a, Graph 10a), the estimation of the corresponding specification after replacing the Japanese stock price index with S&P500 has been problematic, due to difficulties of convergence of the underlying numerical estimation algorithm. The use of the simple STA has contributed to solve this problem only partially. The second period (Graphs 5c-5d) shows the gradual decline of the Singapore stock market. The non-linearity test indicates Nikkei225 as the most appropriate threshold variable (Table 2b). Both thresholds produce STAR(1) model residuals which pass standard diagnostics, whereas the specification with S&P500 has lower residual sum of squares and AIC, but higher parameter standard errors. Due to the massive presence of outliers in the post-crisis period, we have re-estimated both models after applying the simple as well as the modified STA. The model with Nikkei225 increases its forecasting performance in both cases, while the model with S&P500 shows some improvement only after using the modified STA (Table 4). In any case, AIC is favourable to the latter. In the transition function computed on the selected model the second regime is over-represented, whereas the first regime indicates a limiting situation, since the threshold value is around –2% (Graph 10b). The results are in line with the original motivation of this study, that is the presence of a switch, from the first to the second period, between Japan and US in the role of financial leader within the Pacific Basin region.

**Graph 4a.** Stock price index (Malaysia, 1988-1990)

**Graph 4b.** Daily returns (Malaysia, 1988-1990)

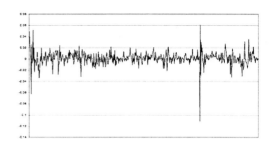

**Graph 4c.** Stock price index (Malaysia, 1995-1999)

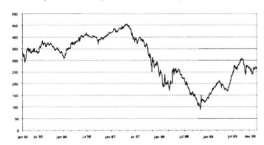

**Graph 4d.** Daily returns (Malaysia, 1995-1999)

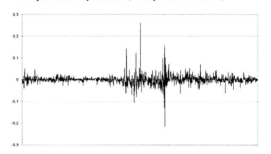

**Graph 5a.** Stock price index (Singapore, 1988-1990)

**Graph 5b.** Daily returns (Singapore, 05/01/88-07/06/90)

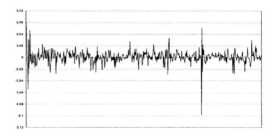

**Graph 5c.** Stock price index (Singapore, 1995-1999)

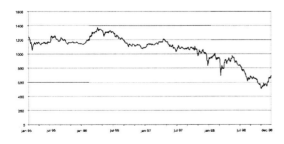

**Graph 5d.** Daily returns (Singapore, 1995-1999)

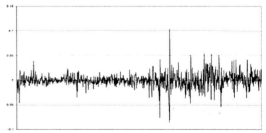

**Graph 6a.** Stock price index (Taiwan, 1988-1990)

**Graph 6b.** Daily returns (Taiwan, 1988-1990)

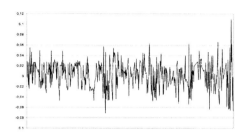

**Graph 6c.** Stock price index (Taiwan, 1995-1999)

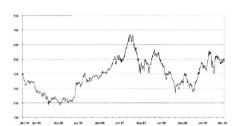

**Graph 6d.** Daily returns (Taiwan, 1995-1999)

**Graph 7.** Transition function of selected STAR model with Nikkei225 (Korea, 1988-1990)

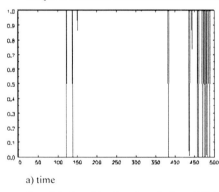

a) time

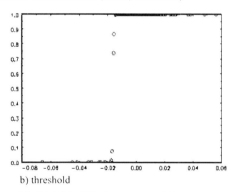

b) threshold

**Graph 8.** Transition function of selected STAR model with Nikkei225 (Hong Kong, 1988-1990)

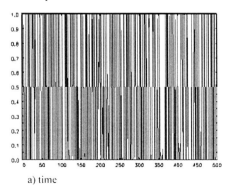

a) time

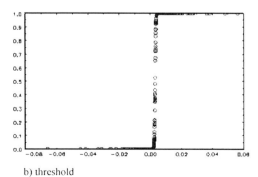

b) threshold

**Graph 9.** Transition function of selected STAR model with Nikkei225 (Malaysia, 1988-1990)

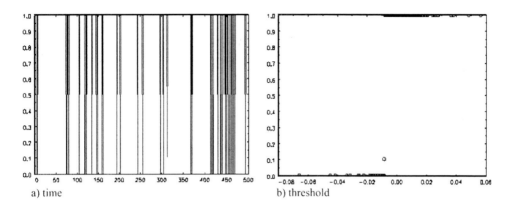

a) time      b) threshold

**Graph 10a.** Transition function of selected STAR model with Nikkei225 (Singapore, 1988-1990)

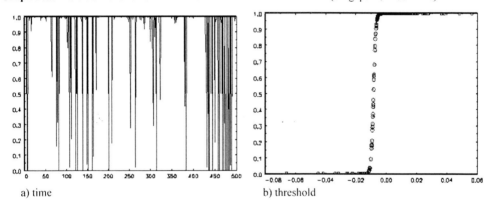

a) time      b) threshold

**Graph 10b.** Transition function of selected STAR model with S&P500 (Singapore, 1995-1999)

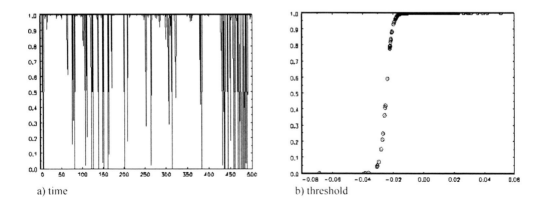

a) time      b) threshold

As Korea and Malaysia, also Taiwan has started to liberalize its financial market since 1988 only. During the first period of analysis (Graph 6a) the stock price index has recorded a strong upward trend up to mid 1990, followed by a steep drop caused by the Japanese financial crisis. With respect to the series of returns, the Taiwan index is almost free from the presence of outliers (Graph 6b). The absence of significant threshold variables in the tests for non-linearity prevents us from estimating any appropriate STAR model (Table 2a). This picture is confirmed in the second period (Graphs 6c-6d); here the threshold variable Nikkei225 appears to be significant in a STAR(1) specification, which is by no means different from a simple AR(1) model according to the values of the estimated coefficients, residual sum of squares and AIC (Table 3b). Undoubtly, among the countries we have analyzed in this study, Taiwan is the biggest exception. If it is not difficult to relate the results obtained on the pre-crisis period to the immaturity of its stock market, the empirical findings of the second sub-sample suggest that Taiwan has built up very strong links with the Japanese financial system and that these relationships, which were unsignificant during the late 80s, have been reinforced by the Japanese crisis.

# 6   Conclusion

The aim of this work is to analyse the financial markets of Korea, Hong Kong, Malaysia, Singapore and Taiwan in order to empirically verify the effects of the Japanese financial crisis of 1990-1991 on the relationships between the Pacific Basin region, on the one hand, and Japan and US, on the other. The econometric investigation has been conducted with statistically adequate STAR and STAR-GARCH models, where Nikkei225 and S&P500 have played the role of threshold variables. The underlying idea is that the Japanese crisis has affected the financial leadership of this country in Eastern Asia in favour of US. The statistical significance of the variable S&P500 in appropriate STAR-GARCH specifications, together with the irrelevance of Nikkei225, is then interpreted as empirical evidence of a strong and progressive process of global integration which looses even the strongest links among the countries of a specific geographical area. At the same time, the switch between Japan and US in the financial leadership over the Pacific Basin region can be read as an indication of openess of the Asian countries towards a unique, global financial market.

The leadership of Japan within the Pacific Basin region is undisputable, at least until the early 90s. Both economic data and our empirical results on the first sub-sample agree to indicate Japan as the main financial market in the area. It is noticeable that Japan is the most important reference not only to the well-developed financial systems, such as Singapore, but also to the newly-liberalized stock markets, such as Korea. Among the five countries under scrutiny, only Taiwan is atypical, since in this case we were unable to find any statistically adequate STAR model. This result can be justified by noting that Taiwan financial market was born in 1988 only, the starting year of our empirical investigation. Possibly, economic and financial dynamics internal to Taiwan have produced greater impacts than any exogenously driven process of integration.

In the first period, it is interesting to point out that S&P500 is statistically adequate as threshold variable in only two cases, namely Singapore and Malaysia. It is relatively easy to justify the influence of the S&P500 index on Singapore stock market, which has been open to the international context since 1978, On the contrary, one possible explanation for the behaviour of the Malaysian stock market is that it has been oriented to integration since the beginning of its liberalization.

In the second period, the significance of S&P500 is evident in all models.

All the analyzed time series are characterized by volatility, excess kurtosis and outliers. Nevertheless, the STAR-GARCH models we have finally selected are statistically robust, and the trimming algorithms we have adopted have proved to be effective. When the comparison has been possible, the modified STA has shown its superiority relative to the simple STA, since the latter suffers from the tendency to bias the series with ample fluctuations in their conditional means.

## Acknowledgments

Paper presented at the $3^{rd}$ International Conference on Financial Engineering and Statistical Finance, held at Hitotsubashi University, Graduate School of International Corporate Strategy, Institute of Statistical Mathematics, Tokyo, 17 March 2003. A special thanks to Damiano Brigo, Umberto Cherubini, Toshiki Honda, Michael McAleer, Fabio Mercurio, Kazuhiko Ohashi and Peter Thomson for their many insightful suggestions. Most computations have been based on modifications of the Gauss programs which complement the book by Franses and van Dijk (2000) and can be downloaded from the following URL: http://www.few.eur.nl/few/people/franses  and  http://www.few.eur.nl/few/people/djvandijk. This study does not necessarily reflect the views of Monte Paschi Alternative Investment.

## References

Bates, D.M. and D.G. Watts (1988), *Nonlinear Regression and Its Applications*, New York, Wiley.

Bollerslev, T. (1986), "Generalized autoregressive conditional heteroskedasticity", *Journal of Econometrics*, **31**, 307-327.

Breusch, T. and A. Pagan (1980), "The LM test and its applications to model specification in econometrics", *Econometrica*, **47**, 1287-1294.

Chan, F. and M. McAleer (2003), "Estimating Smooth Transition Autoregressive models with GARCH errors in presence of extreme observations and outliers", *Applied Financial Economics*, **13**, 581-592.

Chan, F. and M. McAleer (2001), "Evaluating the forecasting performance of Smooth Transition Volatility models", in F. Ghassemi, M. McAleer, L. Oxley and M. Scoccimarro (eds.), *Proceedings of the International Congress on Modelling and Simulation, Volume 3: Socio-economic Systems*, Canberra, Australia, Australian National University, 2001, 1349-1354.

Eitrheim, Ø. and T. Teräsvirta (1996), "Testing the adequacy of smooth transition autoregressive models", *Journal of Econometrics*, **74**, 59-76.

Engle, R. F. (1982), "Autoregressive conditional heteroscedasticity with the estimates of the variance of the United Kingdom inflation", *Econometrica*, **50**, 987-1007.

Escribano, A. and O. Jordà (1999), "Improved testing and specification of Smooth Transition regression models", in R. Rothman (ed.), *Nonlinear Time Series Analysis of Economic and Financial Data*, Boston, Kluver, 289-319.

Franses, P.H., and H. Ghijsels (1999), "Additive outliers, GARCH and forecasting volatility", *International Journal of Forecasting*, **15**, 1-9.

Franses, P.H., T. Teräsvirta and D. van Dijk (2002), "Smooth Transition Autoregressive models: a survey of recent developments", *Econometric Reviews*, **21**, 1-47.

Franses, P.H. and D. van Dijk (2000), *Nonlinear time series models in empirical finance*, Cambridge, Cambridge University Press.

Hansen, B.E. (1997), "Inference in TAR models", *Studies in Nonlinear Dynamics and Econometrics*, **2**, 1-14.

Leybourne, S., P. Newbold and D. Vougas (1998), "Unit roots and smooth transition", *Journal of Time Series Analysis*, **19**, 83-97.

Ling, S. and M. McAleer (2003), "Asymptotic theory for a vector ARMA-GARCH model", *Econometric Theory*, **19**, 280-310.

Luukkonen, R., P. Saikkonnen and T.Teräsvirta (1998), "Testing linearity against Smooth Transition autoregressive models", *Biometrika*, **75**, 491-499;

Phylaktis, K. (1999), "Capital market integration in the Pacific Basin region: an impulse response analysis", *Journal of International Money and Finance*, **18**, 267-287.

Priestley, M.B. (1980), "State-dependent models: a general approach to nonlinear time series analysis", *Journal of Time Series Analysis*, **1**, 47-71.

Priestley, M.B. (1988), *Nonlinear and Nonstationarity Time Series Analysis*, London, Academy Press.

Teräsvirta, T. (1994), "Specification, estimation, and evaluation of smooth transition autoregrssive models", *Journal of the American Statistical Association*, **89**, 208-218.

Teräsvirta, T., D. Tjøstheim and C.W.J. Granger (1994), "Aspects of modelling nonlinear time series", in R.F. Engle and D.L. McFadden (eds.), *Handbook of Econometrics*, **4**, Amsterdam, North-Holland, 2917-2957.

van Dijk, D., P.-H. Franses and A. Lucas (1999), "Testing for smooth transition nonlinearity in the presence of additive outliers", *Journal of Business & Economic Statistics*, **17**, 217-235.

van Dijk, (1999), *Smooth Transition Models: Extensions and Outliers Robust Inference*, Ph.D. thesis.

Verhoeven, P. and M. McAleer (2000), "Modeling outliers and extreme observations for ARMA-GARCH processes", Econometric Society World Congress 2000, *Contributed Paper* n. 1922.

In: International Finance and Monetary Policy        ISBN 1-60021-103-8
Editor: Gleb P. Severov pp. 157-186        © 2006 Nova Science Publishers, Inc.

*Chapter 7*

# NONLINEAR TOOLS FOR ANALYZING AND FORECASTING FINANCIAL TIME SERIES: AN APPLICATION TO US INTEREST RATES

*Nicolas Wesner*
MODEM Université Paris X Nanterre

### Abstract

This article aims to present qualitative and quantitative techniques which stem from the theory of deterministic chaos and to apply them to the study of US interest rates dynamics. The first part of the article provides theoretical backgrounds concerning the detection of nonlinear determinism in a time series and the use of this property for prediction. Methods for estimating the dimension of a time series, visual recurrence analysis, local prediction methods and surrogate data analysis are described. Then, those methods are applied to weekly variations of yields on US 3 month and 1 year Treasury bill and 5 year and 10 year Treasury bonds. Dimension estimation does not provide evidence in favour of low dimensional chaos but visual recurrence analysis permits us to detect several regime changes in the time series. In order to explore the possibility to exploit nonlinearities for prediction, out of sample forecasts from a local predictor are compared with those from a linear model. Finally surrogate data analysis is performed to assess the statistical significance of the results. In particular the method permits us to reject the hypotheses that nonlinear mean predictability is spurious and that it comes from linear dependencies.

## 1 Introduction

Nonlinearity is evoked when a process responds differently to similar impulses. Although it is common practice for economic theory to postulate nonlinear relationships between economic variables (production functions being an example), the concern in nonlinear quantitative methods is not so old. Economists made use of linear tools for a long time but the interest for nonlinear quantitative analysis has rapidly grown the last two decades. In many domains of economic and financial research, numerous publications focus on the way taking nonlinearity into account can help to provide better explanations and better forecasts of observed data. All those works support the view that linear models can only be a poor approximation of economic processes which are naturally nonlinear.

Nonlinear econometric modelling is now well represented by the family of GARCH models whose founder Engle won the recent Nobel prize "for method of analyzing time series with time varying volatility". Engle's model of autoregressive conditional heteroscedasticity (Engle 1982) gave rise to many extensions which allow specific structures such as long memory, asymmetry, threshold effect, regime switches...etc. Although those models were elaborated by and for economists, quantitative methods coming from other sciences have also known a growing interest recently, and that particularly in finance. Those methods are nonlinear and nonparametric that is nonstructural. This departure from the classical framework of GARCH models can be justified by the fact that nonlinearity in higher conditional moments could serve as proxies for neglected nonlinearities in the conditional mean. Authors made use of genetic algorithms (Neely et al. 1997), wavelet decomposition (Aussem et al. 1998) and artificial neural networks (Gençay 1999) for predicting exchange rates and stock prices, and thus for testing for market efficiency. One of the most appealing concept from nonlinear dynamical system theory: deterministic chaos gave also rise to many nonparametric quantitative tools for analyzing and predicting time series. Methods for estimating dynamical invariants characterizing chaotic behavior such as the correlation dimension (Grassberger and Procaccia 1983) which measure the dimension of the system or Lyapunov exponent (Wolf et al. 1985) which measures sensitive dependence on initial conditions were largely applied to macroeconomic and financial time series (Jaditz and Sayers 1993, Brock et al. 1991). So far, there is few or no statistical evidence of actual economic data having been generated by a deterministic mechanism. The problem is that there is no statistical test which has chaos as null hypothesis, so that non-rejection of the null could be claimed to be evidence in favor of chaos. Nevertheless, local prediction methods (Farmer and Sidorowich 1987), initially designed for the prediction of chaotic time series, were applied with some success to stock prices indices and exchange rates data (Lebaron 1992, Fernadez Rodriguez et al. 1999, Fernandez Rodriguez et al. 2003).

This article aims to apply some tools from the theory of deterministic chaos to US interest rates data. Visual recurrence analysis, local prediction methods and surrogate data analysis are applied to weekly data of Treasury bond and Treasury bill yields. The objective is not to determine the true nature of the data generating process but to explore the possibility to exploit nonlinearities to produce reliable forecasts. Section 2 presents some theoretical backgrounds and describes the methods of visual recurrence analysis, local prediction and surrogate data analysis. In section 3 those methods are applied to the data.

## 2   Methodology

Chaotic dynamics take place in many well known physical systems. Few nonlinear deterministic equations can produce a very complex dynamics in some ways similar to random stationary time series. The trajectories of a chaotic system converge to a strange attractor, that is a compact set with a fractal dimension which is different from a fixed point or a limit cycle. The most important point is that the concept of deterministic chaos implies the generic possibility that an apparently random phenomenon is actually generated by a deterministic process and thus concerns all domains of scientific research. In economics, unlike physical sciences, the elementary laws are unknown. Therefore the theoretical assumption of chaos is necessary ad-hoc. However, empirical investigation of economic and financial time series can easily be performed in the framework of chaos theory. Indeed chaos theory has significantly changed the approach of data analysis in providing new tools for distinguishing random time series from deterministic ones. For this purpose, time series are analyzed not only in the time domain but in the phase space too. This geometrical approach, which relies on the reconstruction of the experimental attractor in the phase space (usually by the method of time delays), does not require the knowledge of the equations (if any) which generate the data.

## 2.1    Reconstruction of Dynamics by the Method of Time Delays

Let $s(t)$ $(t = 1, ..., N)$ be a time series that is believed to be generated by an unknown or unobservable deterministic process. Following Brock (1986), $s(t)$ is said to have a smoothly deterministic explanation if there exist a system $\{M, F, h\}$ such as :

$$F : \mathrm{M} \longrightarrow \mathrm{M} \tag{1}$$

$$x(t + 1) = F\left(x\left(t\right)\right)$$

*where F is an unobservable, smooth (i.e. twice differentiable almost everywhere) mapping, M is a d dimensional manifold and $x\left(t\right) \in M$ is the state of the system at time t.*

The observed time series is related to the dynamical system by the measurement function $h$ :

$$h : \mathrm{M} \longrightarrow \mathrm{IR} \tag{2}$$

$$s(t) = h\left(x\left(t\right)\right)$$

where *h is a unobservable smooth mapping,*

State space reconstruction is aimed to recover informations about the unknown system $\{M, F, h\}$ only from the observed time series $s\left(t\right)$. The most common technique used for this purpose is the method of time delays. The basic idea is that the past and future of a time series contain information about unobserved state variables that can be used to define a state at the present time. Concretely, lagged observations of the original time series are used to construct a new series of vectors $y(t)$ called *m-histories*:

$$y(t) = (s(t), s(t - \tau), ..., s(t - \tau(m - 1))) \tag{3}$$

*where m is the embedding dimension and $\tau$ the time delay usually fixed to one.*

Formally this procedure can be written as follows :

$$H : \mathrm{M} \longrightarrow \mathrm{IR}^m \tag{4}$$

$$H\left(x\left(t\right)\right) = \left(s\left(t\right), s\left(t - \tau\right), ..., s\left(t - \tau\left(m - 1\right)\right)\right)$$

*where H is smooth and unobservable.*

The method of time delays introduced by Takens (1981) and Packard (1980) is quite old and was used for a long time by statisticians (Benzécri 1982, 1988). The main contribution made by the authors is the demonstration that it is possible to preserve geometrical invariants such as the eigenvalues of a fixed point, the fractal dimension of an attractor or the Lyapunov exponent of a trajectory. This was shown numerically by Packard and proven mathematically by Takens.

Takens studied the delay reconstruction map $\Phi$ which maps the states of a $d$ dimensional dynamical system into $m$ dimensional delay vectors :

$$\Phi : M \longrightarrow \mathbb{R}^{m^2} \tag{5}$$

$$\Phi(x) = \left[ H(x), H\left(F^{-\tau}(x)\right), ..., H\left(F^{-\tau(m-1)}(x)\right) \right]$$

Takens demonstrated that with $m \geq 2d + 1$, $\Phi$ is generically an embedding, that is a diffeomorphic mapping between a compact set in a finite or infinite dimensional space and a subspace of finite dimension (see Sauer et al. 1992 for a more formal definition of an embedding). The main point is that if $\Phi$ is an embedding then a smooth dynamics $G$, equivalent to the original $F$, is induced on the space of the reconstructed vectors :

$$G(y(t)) = \Phi \circ F \circ \Phi^{-1}(y(t)) \tag{6}$$

$G$ is a diffeomorfism to $F$ and is called topologically conjugate to $F$. That is $G$ conserves the same properties as $F$. Therefore, with $\tau = 1$:

$$G : \mathbb{R}^{m^2} \longrightarrow \mathbb{R}^{m^2} \tag{7}$$

$$y(t+1) = G(y(t))$$

The reconstructed states can be used to estimate $G$, and since $G$ is equivalent to the original dynamics $F$, those can be used to extract informations about the underlying, unknown system.

In order to characterize the nature, deterministic or random, of the underlying dynamical system, and to make nonlinear forecast of the observed time series, traditional methods measure and exploit spatial correlations. Spatial correlation defines correlation between points on an attractor and can be formally measured by the Euclidean distance. This property specific to deterministic time series is actually a property of a continuous mapping : images of close points are close. Indeed, if the system $\{M, F, h\}$ is deterministic, that is if $F : M \longrightarrow M$ is a smooth and single valued mapping, then $F$ is a continuous mapping (see Aleksic 1990). In this case, the distances between the images of the close points are small: for every two points $x(i), x(j) \in M$ whose distance $\| x(i) - x(j) \|$ is smaller than $\varepsilon$ one can find that the distance between their images $\| x(i+1) - x(j+1) \|$ is smaller than some small $\beta$.

Thus, according to the theorem of Takens, if the time series $s(t)$ has a deterministic explanation, then for any pair of points $(y(i), y(j))$, for a small $\alpha > 0$, and for an adequate choice of $m$, there exists a small $\delta > 0$ so that:

$$if \ \| y(i) - y(j) \| < \alpha, then, \| G(y(i)) - G(y(j)) \| < \delta \tag{8}$$

It is important to notice that the condition that the measurement function $h$ be smooth entails that the result of the theorem does not necessarily hold even approximately when the data are contaminated by noise. The term noise refers here to a stochastic process created by a large number of independent sources. There are two ways that noise could enter into the system. The first way is additive or measurement noise, in this case equation (2) writes:

$$h : \mathrm{M} \longrightarrow \mathrm{IR} \tag{9}$$

$$s(t) = h\left(x\left(t\right)\right) + \varepsilon_t$$

Alternatively noise can be "dynamic" when the data generator is subject to random shocks:

$$F : \mathrm{M} \longrightarrow \mathrm{M} \tag{10}$$

$$x(t + 1) = F\left(x\left(t\right)\right) + \varepsilon_t$$

In both cases the Takens embedding theorem fails and we can no longer assume that there exists a deterministic map characterizing the time evolution of $s\left(t\right)$. However, numerical investigations of toy models indicate that reconstruction even from heavily contaminated series can be performed quite successfully. Moreover, the method of time delay is used for a long time by statisticians who never mentioned the concept of determinism. Their works suggest that it should be applied to real world data and thus to noisy time series (Benzécri 1982, 1987, 1988).

## 2.2   Determining the Dimension of a Time Series

The dimension is a measure of the complexity of a dynamical system. Roughly speaking, the dimension can be view as the number of independent quantities needed to specify the state of the system at any given time, that is the number of degrees of freedom of the system. Determining the dimension of a time series is then crucial in the characterization of the underlying system. Indeed, like the Lyapounov exponent which measures sensitive dependence on initial conditions, the dimension is an invariant that can be used to detect low dimensional chaos and thus to discriminate between stochastic and deterministic time series.

Many techniques are available and most of them measure spatial correlations in the phase space. The correlation dimension of Grassberger and Procaccia $D_G$ approximates the Hausdorf dimension of fractal attractors through the method of time delays (Grassberger and Procaccia 1983). According to the theorem by Mane (1981), the optimal or minimum embedding dimension of a time series is related to the fractal dimension $d_f$ of the attractor by $d_f \leq m \leq 2d+1$. The correlation dimension is closely related to the correlation integral $C_m\left(r\right)$ :

$$C_m\left(r\right) = \frac{2}{\left(N - m + 1\right)N} \sum_{i=1}^{N-m+1} \sum_{j=1}^{i-1} \theta\left(r - \left\|y\left(i\right) - y\left(j\right)\right\|\right) \tag{11}$$

*where $\theta$ is the step function $\theta\left(x < 0\right) = 0$, $\theta(x \geq 0) = 1$. According to Brocks (1986), the correlation dimension is independent of the choice of norm.*

$C_m(r)$ measures the probability that two vectors are within $r$ of each other in all their Cartesian coordinates. The estimation of the correlation dimension $D_G$ relies on the scaling property of the correlation integral $C_m(r)$. Indeed, as $r \to 0$:

$$C_m(r) \simeq r^{D_G} \qquad (12)$$

So $D_G$ is estimated by:

$$\frac{d\log(C_m(r))}{d\log(r)} \qquad (13)$$

As a practical matter one investigates the estimated $D_G$ as $m$ increased. In principle, a random process has an infinite correlation dimension, so its estimate increases with the embedding dimension. For a deterministic process, the estimates should reach a finite saturation limit beyond some relatively small $m$.

As argued by many authors, there are quite severe inherent limitations on the Grassberger and Procaccia algorithm. Indeed, Brock (1986) noted that near unit root process may produce spuriously low correlation dimension estimates. Moreover Theiler (1986) point out that data limitations may lead to unreliable inference (see also Smith 1988 and Osborne et al. 1989 for limits of dimension calculation).

The false nearest neighbor approach (Kennel et al. 1992) is perhaps the most popular method for estimating the optimal embedding dimension. According to the authors, although it can be fooled by near unit root process, the method does not strongly depend of the number of observations. It relies on the idea that choosing too low an embedding dimension results in point that are far apart in the original phase space being moved closer together in the reconstruction space. False neighbors are defined as points apparently lying close together due to projection that are separated in higher embedding dimensions.

Nearest neighbors $y(i)$ and $y(j)$ are declared false if:

$$\frac{|s(i+1) - s(j+1)|}{\|y(i) - y(j)\|} > R_{tol} \qquad (14)$$

or if:

$$\frac{\|y(i) - y(j)\|^2 - |s(i+1) - s(j+1)|^2}{R_A^2} > A^2{}_{tol} \qquad (15)$$

where

$$R_A^2 = \frac{1}{N} \sum_{k=1}^{N} [s(k) - \langle s \rangle]^2, \quad \langle s \rangle \; is \; the \; mean \; of \; s(t) \qquad (16)$$

For a deterministic process, the percentage of false nearest neighbors should drop to zero or some acceptable small numbers by increasing the embedding dimension. For the following application as in most studies, $R_{tol}$ is set to 10 and $A_{tol}$ to 2.

There are many other approaches for estimating the optimal embedding dimension of a time series. Most of them are based on the observed continuity of trajectories in the state space (Broomhead et al. 1987, Aleksic 1990, Wayland et al. 1993, Zbilut et al. 1998). In a different way, Sugihara and May (1990) and Casdagli (1992) proposed that deducing the optimal predictive model can help to distinguish between deterministic and noisy time series. More recently, Cao (1997) proposed a modified version of the false nearest neighbor approach for detecting high dimensional chaos, and Wesner (2004) proposed a measure of determinism specially adapted to small sample sets. Notwithstanding the proliferation of such techniques of dimension estimation, the two methods presented above remain undoubtedly the most commonly used in the literature.

## 2.3   Recurrence Plot Analysis

Eckmann et al. (1987) introduced a graphical technique for the representation of erratic time series called recurrence plots. This method evaluates temporal and phase space distance of state vectors and can be used to detect certain form of determinism and nonstationarity. Basically, recurrence plots, also named proximity diagrams, can be view as a graphical representation of the integral of correlation with the exception that temporal correlations can be detected. This approach relies on the method of time delays described previously.

In the simplest case, recurrence plots of a time series of length $N$ are reconstructed from a matrix $(N - m + 1) * (N - m + 1)$, whose $(i, j)$ element contains the distance of the two embedding vectors $y(i)$ and $y(j)$. A threshold distance $r$ is defined and embedding vectors $y(i)$ and $y(j)$ with distances smaller than $r$ are considered as recurrence points. Then, in an $(N - m + 1) * (N - m + 1)$ square, a dot is printed at position $(i, j)$ if the two corresponding vectors are recurrent. By definition, the probability that a recurrence occurs at a randomly selected location $(i, j)$ is equal to correlation integral of the time series $Cm(r)$.

More detailed diagrams can be obtained in defining a color map. The resulting recurrence plot is a color-coded matrix, where each $(i, j)$ entry is calculated as the distance between vectors $y(i)$ and $y(j)$ in the reconstructed series. Then, the distances are mapped to colors from the pre-defined color map and are displayed as colored pixels in their corresponding places. As noted by Kononov (1999), in order to make diagrams more meaningful, it is necessary for the color mapping to be meaningful too. The author proposes to use hot colors (yellow, red, and orange) and cold colors (blue, black) to display small and large distances. In the same way, a "grey palette" can be used: a gradation from the withe, for small distances, to the black for large distances.

Visual inspection of the resulting diagrams gives a qualitative impression about many properties of the time series considered. The main diagonal $y(i) = y(j)$ can be view as the arrow of time (from the lower left to the upper right). Recurrence plots tend to be nearly symmetric with respect to this diagonal because, in general, if $y(i)$ is close to $y(j)$, then $y(j)$ is close to $y(i)$ (nevertheless, the plots are not necessarily symmetric since close points have not necessarily the same nearest neighbors). The overall picture given by the diagrams is not always fully understandable, and the precise meaning of the patterns observed is sometime unknown. Zbilut and al. (1998) propose different parameters for the statistical quantification of recurrence plots but they give little clues on how to interpret these numbers. Nevertheless, recurrence plot can be a useful starting point for the analysis of a time series since many properties can be clearly detected.

The following examples will show the possibilities given by the method. Recurrence plots of five time series were constructed by means of the software from Kononov (1999) "Visual Recurrence Analysis v 4.2" available from http://pweb.netcom.com/~eugenek/download.html. In all cases the diagrams were constructed for $m = 5$, and the palette of colors, displayed on the right of the diagrams, is grey. Thus, recurrence points are represented by white points on the diagrams.

### 2.3.1   White Noise

The first time series is a white noise signal :

$$n(t) = \varepsilon(t) \tag{17}$$

*where $\varepsilon(t)$ is gaussian noise with a zero mean and unit variance: $\varepsilon(t) \rightsquigarrow N(0,1), t = 1, ..., 1000.$*

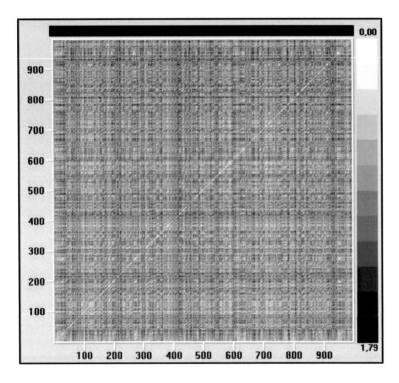

Figure 1: Recurrence plot of white noise time series.

As shown in figure 1, no specific structure can be observed and colors are distributed uniformly over the entire diagram. Indeed, for independent and identically distributed observations, the locations of recurrence are random.

### 2.3.2   Random Walk with Drift

$$b(t) = A + b(t-1) + \varepsilon(t) \tag{18}$$

*where $\varepsilon(t)$ is white noise $\varepsilon(t) \rightsquigarrow N(0,1), t = 1, ..., 2000.$*

As shown in figure 2, recurrence plots of time correlated signals display some regularities near the main diagonal. Those white patterns observed in the diagram are related to the trends in the time series. Indeed, a drift in a process is recognized by the overall reduction of recurrences away from the main diagonal. In the present case, white zones, which indicate that two periods of time display some similarities, are lying on the main diagonal and black or darker areas which describe differences between two periods are away from it.

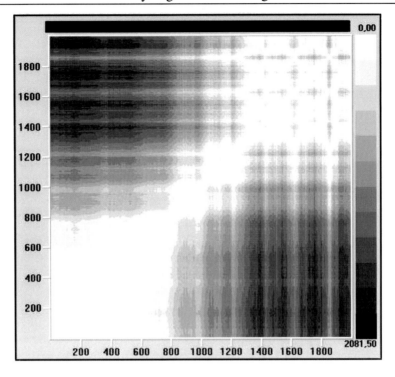

Figure 2: Recurrence plot of a random walk with drift.

### 2.3.3 Chaotic Time Series

Two time series were analyzed: a signal $l(t)$ generated by the chaotic Lorenz system, and a chaotic signal with additive noise $l_b(t)$:

$$\frac{dl}{dt} = -s_1 - s_2, \frac{ds_1}{dt} = l + as_1, \frac{ds_2}{dt} = 0.2 + ls_2 - bs_2, a = 0.22, b = 4.25 \tag{19}$$

$$l_b(t) = l(t) + 0.3\sigma\varepsilon(t) \tag{20}$$

*where $\varepsilon(t)$ is gaussian noise with zero mean and unit variance, $\sigma$ is the variance of the chaotic time series $l(t)$, and $t = 1, ..., 2000$.*

Recurrence plots of chaotic time series are very sensitive to the value of the embedding dimension: for the Lorenz system, the deterministic structure becomes apparent for m superior to 2. Recurrence plots (see figures 3) of the chaotic time series is far more structured than the previous ones. Unlike random walk diagrams, white zones are not only lying on the main diagonal but are dispersed among the entire diagram. Deterministic patterns are revealed by white extended lines parallel to the main diagonal. Indeed, points forming those diagonal segments satisfy the continuity property of the trajectories in the phase space. As shown by Zbilut et al. (1998), the proportion of points forming those segments can be related to a measure of the degree of determinism in the time series. Moreover, the average length of those segments are claimed to be proportional to the shanon entropy and their distance to the main diagonal to the highest Lyapunov exponent of the system (see Cadagli 1997 for the recovering of dynamical invariants from recurrence plots).

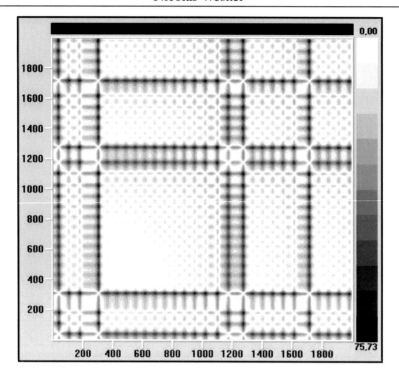

Figure 3: Recurrence plot of a chaotic time series from the Lorenz system.

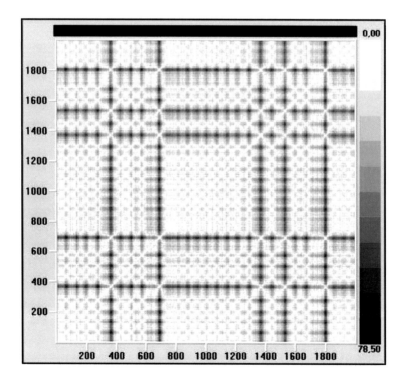

Figure 4: Recurrence plot of a chaotic time series with additive noise (30% noise).

Recurrence plots of the noisy chaotic time series still displays diagonal segments but is less structured than the previous one (see figure 4). Nevertheless even with noise added, deterministic patterns can still be detected.

### 2.3.4  Structural Break

The last signal is characterized by a structural break, the first and last 700 observations are generated by a gaussian noise process and the 600 others are generated by the chaotic process of Lorenz. The mean and variance of gaussian noise are set equal to those of the chaotic time series.

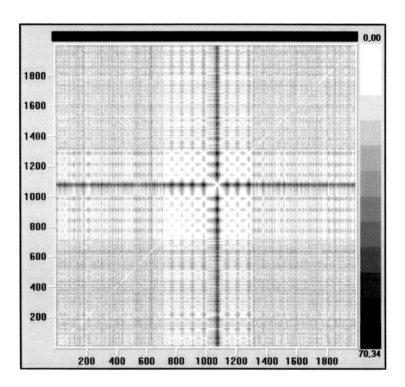

Figure 5: Recurrence plot of a time series displaying a structural break in the middle of the sample set (chaotic transient).

As shown in figure 5, the transition from random to deterministic dynamics is clearly apparent. The broad vertical and horizontal bands passing through and through the diagram describe a structural break. The square formed by the two bands represents a period which displays much more recurrences than the rest of the sample set. This period corresponds precisely to the chaotic observations. Indeed white diagonal segments which represent deterministic patterns can be observed in this square. So this last example shows that the method permits one to locate with accuracy the occurrence of a structural change even if it does not affect the first two moments. Numerical simulations show that the method is also able to detect any regime shift which affects significantly the distribution of observations.

## 2.4   Local Prediction Methods

Local prediction methods rely on the reconstruction of data in the phase space by the method of time delays. The basic idea is to exploit the property of "phase space continuity" by observing the dynamics of near neighbors. In order to construct linear or nonlinear predictors, local prediction methods use close points in the phase space and their images to approximate function $G$ (equation (6)) (see Farmer and Sidorowich 1987 and Casdagli 1989).

### 2.4.1   Nearest Neighbor Predictor

There exists several ways to approximate future trajectories of a time series in the phase space, but the nearest neighbor predictor is the simplest. As shown by Farmer and Sidorowich (1987), this method is particularly efficient for predicting chaotic time series. The forecast of the observation $s(t)$ given by the nearest neighbor method is only based on the nearest neighbor of $y(t-1)$, say $y(t\prime-1)$:

$$y(t\prime-1) = \arg\min\left[\|\,y(u) - y(t-1)\,\| \,/u = m, ..., t-2\right] \tag{21}$$

Prediction of observation $s(t)$ then writes:

$$s^p(t) = s(t') \tag{22}$$

*where $s(t')$ is the first component of $y(t\prime)$ the image of $y(t\prime-1)$.*

### 2.4.2   Locally Constant Predictor

The locally constant predictor is believed to be more suitable in the presence of noisy data because it produces forecasts in averaging past trajectories. The forecast of the observation $s(t)$ given by the locally constant predictor is based on the $k$ nearest neighbors of $y(t-1)$, say $y(t^n-1), n = 1, ..., k$. The $k$ nearest neighbors are chosen so that they minimize:

$$\sum_{n=1}^{k} \|\,y(t^n-1) - y(t-1)\,\|, t^n - 1 \in [m, ..., t-2] \tag{23}$$

Locally constant predictor averages the images of the $k$ nearest neighbors. The forecast of the observation $s(t)$ given by the predictor writes:

$$s^p(t) = \frac{\sum_{n=1}^{k} s(t^n)}{k} \tag{24}$$

*where the $s(t^n), (n = 1, ..., k)$ are first components of $y(t^n), (n = 1, ..., k)$, the images of the $k$ first neighbors of $y(t-1)$.*

### 2.4.3   Locally Linear Predictor

Locally linear approximation of function $G$ makes use of ordinary least square regression. Like the locally constant predictor it is believed to be more efficient than the nearest neighbor approach in the presence of noise. Here again, the forecast of observation $s(t)$ is based on the $k$ nearest neighbors of $y(t-1)$, say $y(t^n-1)$, $n = 1, ..., k$, which are chosen so that they minimize the quantity in equation $(23)$.

Local linear predictor for $s(t)$ is obtained in considering the following regression model:

$$s^p(t) = \hat{a_0}s(t^n-1) + \hat{a_1}s(t^n-2) + ... + \hat{a_{m-1}}s(t^n-m+1) + \hat{a_m} \quad (25)$$

whose coefficients have been fitted by a linear regression of $s(t)$ on $y(t^n-1)$, $n = 1, ..., k$. Therefore, the $\hat{a_i}$ are the value of $a_i$ that minimize:

$$\sum_{n=1}^{k}[s(t) - a_0 s(t^n-1) - a_1 s(t^n-2) - ... - a_{m-1}s(t^n-m+1) - a_m]^2 \quad (26)$$

Many other techniques are available for the approximation of trajectories in the phase space. Actually, locally linear prediction is a special case of the locally weighted regression[1] from Cleveland (1979). Moreover, nonlinear local regression can be performed using quadratic functions, radial basis function, artificial, neural networks or any other nonlinear function (see Casdagli 1989). Although those methods are more complex and much more data and computer expensive than those presented above, their superiority has not been well established for financial time series.

Finally, it is important to notice that local prediction techniques can be viewed as a systematized version of chartism (Elms 1994). Chartism is an old tool from technical analysis which consists in recognizing geometrical figures in the evolution of prices (see Murphy 1999). Reconstructed vectors in the phase space are segments of trajectory and spatial correlations correspond to geometric similarity between two segments. Thus, like chartism, local predictors seek to construct forecasts of future behavior based on matching patterns observed in past behavior. The main difference however is that a local predictor is not a structural model in the sense that figures or charts are not defined a priori but are learned from the data.

## 2.5   Assessing Statistical Significance with Surrogate Data

The method of surrogate data is a form of bootsraping which was introduced by Theiler et al. (1992) for distinguishing between chaotic time series and colored noise. This approach allows to transfer a complex problem such as the demonstration of the existence of deterministic chaos in a time series to the formal statistical framework of hypothesis testing. Statistical hypothesis testing involves two components: a null hypothesis against which observations are tested and a discriminating quantity. The method of surrogate data follows this recipe, but it permits one to treat the two components separately. Thus, the choice of a null hypothesis does not restrict the choice of the discriminating quantity.

Surrogate data is an ensemble of data sets similar to the observed time series, but consistent with the null hypothesis. The discriminating quantity is related to the problem considered. Surrogate data analysis consist in comparing the value of the discriminating quantity

---

[1]Locally weighted map is a linear combination of local linear regressors which are constructed in using points from all regions of the attractor. Weights of local predictors are set in function of the distance between the region of the attractor they cover and the origin of the trajectory to be predicted.

obtained from original data with those obtained from surrogate data. If they are significantly different, the null hypothesis can be rejected. Significance is defined by the difference between the original and the mean surrogate value of the quantity, divided by the standard deviation of the surrogate values. With $Q$ being the discriminating quantity, the standard score for the test is defined as follow:

$$S = \frac{|Q^a - \langle Q^s \rangle|}{\sigma_{Q^s}} \qquad (27)$$

where $Q^a$ is the value of the discriminating quantity obtained for the original data, $\langle Q^s \rangle$ is the mean of the values of $Q$ obtained for the surrogate data $Q^s$ and $\sigma_{Q_s}$ is the standard deviation of the $Q^s$.

The standard score is a dimensionless quantity often called "sigmas" by physicists. Less than 2 sigmas are not statistically significant and 10 sigmas are strongly significant. More than 2 sigmas can conduct to the rejection of the null hypothesis.

## 3   Application to US Interest Rates

The expectation theory of the term structure represents the main theoretical basis for the modelling of interest rates. According to it, market efficiency implies a no arbitrage condition which relates long term interest rate to a product of expected future short rates. With respect to this theory, the dynamics of interest rates have been traditionally modeled as linear stochastic processes (Merton 1973, Campbell and Schiller 1984, Cox et al. 1985). However, many statistical indications for nonlinear dynamics in interest rates have been reported in the literature. For example, Hamilton (1988) finds that a Markov switching model fits US interest rate data better than an autoregressive model. Granger (1993) shows that the US short term interest rate depends in a nonlinear manner on the spread between long and short interest rates. Kozicki (1994) finds asymmetry in the form of differing responses to positive and negative shocks. Finally, several authors find evidence of structural breaks in the mean and the volatility of interest rate changes (Pfann et al.1996, Gray 1996, Ang and Bekaert 2002). Following Barkoulas et al (1997) who find substantial nonlinear mean predictability in the 3 month Treasury bill rate dynamics, the next application investigates the possibility to make reliable predictions of US interest rates in exploiting nonlinear dependencies.

### 3.1   Data

Data under investigation are the weekly 3 month and 1 year US Treasury bill yields and yields on 5 year and 10 year Treasury bonds. The 3 month yields are percentage annual rates obtained from the secondary market and 1, 5 and 10 year are constant maturity rates. The sample period ranges from 1962-01-05 to 2003-10-31, there are 2182 observations.

## 3.2  Preliminary Results

### 3.2.1  Summary Statistics

In order to test for weak stationarity, the Augmented Dickey Fuller (ADF) test was performed for each time series, to levels $I(t)$ and changes $s(t)$ of interest rates:

$$s(t) = I(t) - I(t-1) \tag{28}$$

*where $I(t)$ is the level of interest rate at the date $t$.*

To apply the ADF test to interest rate levels $I(t)$, the following linear regression is estimated (see Fuller 1996):

$$s(t) = a\,I(t-1) + b_1 s(t-1) + \ldots + b_p s(t-p) + 1 + u(t) \tag{29}$$

*where $t = p + 2, \ldots, N$, $p = \frac{5N}{4}$ and $u(t)$ is white noise.*

Under the null hypothesis, $I(t)$ is a unit root process: $H_0 : a = 0$. Under the alternative hypothesis, $I(t)$ is a zero mean stationary process: $H_1 : a < 0$. Thus the test statistics is the t-value of $a$. The same test is performed to the series of yield changes $s(t)$.

As largely reported in the literature, the null hypothesis of unit root process is accepted for interest rate levels and rejected (at the 5% level) for yield changes (results not reported here are available upon request). Those results lead to the conclusion that all yield series are integrated process of order one and that further analysis should be performed to yield changes.

Table 1: Summary statistics for yield changes for the period 1962/01/05-2003/10/31.

|                            | 3 month  | 1 year   | 5 year   | 10 year  |
|----------------------------|----------|----------|----------|----------|
| Mean                       | -0,00082 | -0.00089 | -0.00032 | 0.00011  |
| Median                     | 0        | 0        | 0        | 0        |
| Stand.dev                  | 0.21847  | 0.19798  | 0.15729  | 0.13751  |
| Skewness                   | -0.6292  | -0.9193  | -0.4555  | -0.6371  |
| Kurtosis                   | 19.8148  | 15.7247  | 8.5328   | 7.9473   |
| first order autocorrelation| 0.2697   | 0.3467   | 0.3046   | 0.2856   |

Summary statistics for the weekly variations of 3 month, 1 year, 5 year and 10 year yields are presented in Table 1. The means for all time series are not significantly different from zero and series are negatively skewed and leptokurtic. Moreover, first order autocorrelation coefficients are positive and significant for all time series (higher order coefficients are not).

### 3.2.2  Test for Independence

Brock, Dechert and Scheinkmann (1987) proposed a test for independence based on the correlation integral from Grassberger and Procaccia (1983). The test starts with the idea that under the null hypothesis of independent and identically distributed observations, the correlation integral $C_m(r)$ should verify:

$$C_m(r) \rightarrow (C_1(r))^m \ as \ N \rightarrow \infty \tag{30}$$

*where N is the number of observations.*

The authors show that, under the null hypothesis of i.i.d. observations, the following statistic converges in distribution to a standard normal variable with a unit variance:

$$BDS(m,r) = \frac{C_m(r) - (C_1(r))^m}{V_{r,m,T}\sqrt{N}} \rightarrow N(0,1) \ as \ N \rightarrow \infty \tag{31}$$

*where $V_{r,m,N}$ is an estimate of the standard variation of $[C_m(r) - (C_1(r))^m]$* (see Brock et al. 1996).

Simulation studies have shown that the test has power against a large class of alternatives, including linear or nonlinear and deterministic or stochastic models. Therefore, a rejection of the null hypothesis does not suggest the type of alternative model one should consider. For this application and following Hsieh (1989) the BDS statistic was calculated for $m$ ranging from 1 to 10 and $r$ was set to $\frac{\sigma}{2}$, with $\sigma$ being the standard deviation of the time series.

To avoid rejections of the null hypothesis due to linear correlation, the test was performed to yield changes and to residuals obtained from fitting an AR process to the original time series[2]. For each time series, the number of lags was chosen by the Akaike criterion (23 for the 3 month, 23 for the 1 year, 11 for the 5 year and 19 for the 10 year).

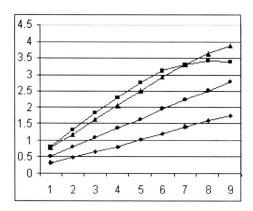

Figure 6: BDS statistic as a function of the embedding dimension, for the 3 month (rhombs), 1 year (rounds), 5 year (triangles) and the 10 year (squares) rates.

As can be shown on figure 6, the null hypothesis of i.i.d. observations is strongly rejected for all original time series and for any value of $m$. Moreover, the null hypothesis is still rejected for the residuals of the linear model (see figure 7). Therefore, those results suggest that linear dependence in mean does not fully account for rejection of the null. All

---

[2]The approach of using residual diagnostics in nonlinearity testing, which was first proposed by Brock (1986), was criticized by Theiler and Eubank (1993) who find that in some cases analyzing a time series after linear residuals are taken may reduce power against chaotic null hypothesis.

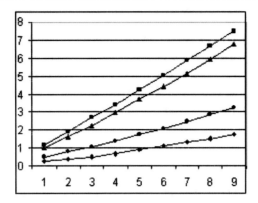

Figure 7: BDS statistic for the residuals of the linear model. Same notations as Figure 1.

of that does not automatically imply the presence of nonlinear dependencies exploitable for conditional mean prediction since dependence of higher order moments as well as any form of instationarity can conduct to this result. Nevertheless, it is undoubtedly a necessary condition for any nonlinear forecasting technique to be useful.

## 3.3   Visual Recurrence Analysis

Recurrence plots of the yield change series were constructed as previously by means of the software from Kononov. First, it appears that the value of the embedding dimension does not clearly affect the appearance of the diagrams. Low dimensional deterministic chaos is therefore not expected to take place. The embedding dimension was set to 5 for the four time series.

A rapid comparison of the four diagrams shows that recurrence plots of long term interest rates are globally more sombre than those of short term rates (see figures 8, 9, 10, 11). That should mean that the dynamics of short term rates are more predictable than the dynamics of long term rates because the former contain more recurrence points. The detail of the diagrams reveals a property common to all series examined. Principally, recurrence plots reveal that the dynamics of yield variations are characterized by a sequence of more or less significant structural changes. Those regime shifts are represented by broad vertical and horizontal bands passing through and through the diagram. The darker the band is, the more unlike is the period, and the width of the band represents the length of the period.

Interestingly the most dramatic regime shift occurs exactly at the same time for the four time series. This regime is represented by two orthogonal dark bands in the middle of the diagrams. This "black period" which is the most singular episode of the sample set begins precisely the 12th October 1979, that is the week the 10 year and 5 year rates passed over the 10% level. This episode ends the 12th November1982 for the 1 year, the 5 year and the 10 year, and the 17th September 1982 for the 3 month. For the 5 and 10 year yields, it is followed by a "grey period", which ends the 20th November 1987. A closer look on the data shows that yield changes present much higher volatility during this "black period" (see table 2). The structural break does not only affect volatility: means and medians are also less close to zero during this regime.

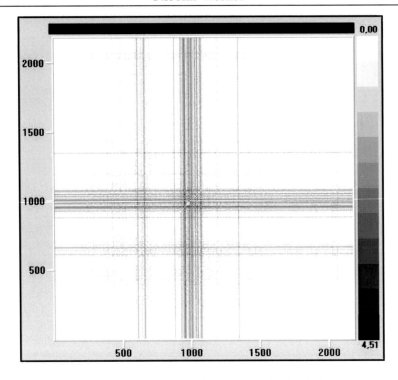

Figure 8: Recurrence plot of the 3 month yield changes.

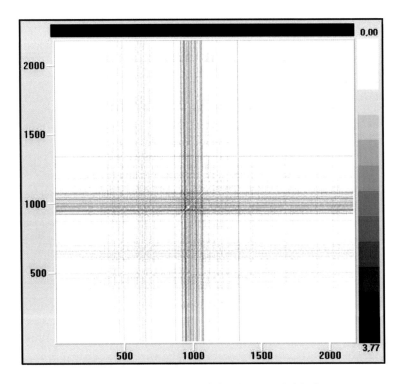

Figure 9: Recurrence plot of the 1 year yield changes.

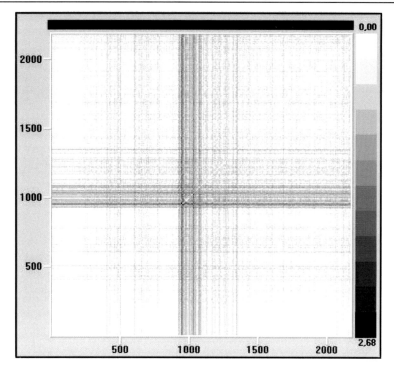

Figure 10: Recurrence plot of the 5 year yield changes.

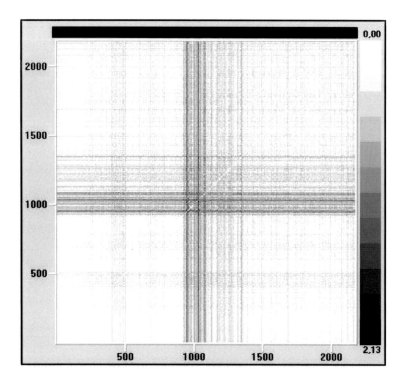

Figure 11: Recurrence plot of the 10 year yield changes.

Table 2: Summary statistics for yield changes during the influential period from 10/12/1979 to 11/12/1982.

|                          | 3 month   | 1 year    | 5 year   | 10 year  |
|--------------------------|-----------|-----------|----------|----------|
| Mean                     | -0.015584 | -0.01189  | 0.00512  | 0.00617  |
| Median                   | -0.025    | 0.03      | 0.02     | 0.045    |
| Standard deviation       | 0.63677   | 0.55203   | 0.38594  | 0.32822  |
| Skewness                 | -0.1461   | -0.4528   | -0.3397  | -0.5795  |
| Kurtosis                 | 0.824     | 0.758     | 0.628    | 0.786    |
| first order autocorrelation | 0.319  | 0.3619    | 0.3285   | 0.31     |

Statistical evidence regarding the presence of regime shifts in the dynamics of US short term interest rates was largely related in the literature (see Hamilton 1988, Das 1993, Naik and Lee 1993, Pfann et al. 1996). According to Pfann et al. (1996) until they reach double digits, interest rates behave like a random walk. At higher levels however they show a mean reverting tendency. The regime shift described above seems to fit this description of the behavior of interest rates. Nevertheless, for the rates studied here, the ending of the regime referred as the black period does not coincide with the fall under the 10% level. Moreover, for the 3 month and 1 year T Bill, the black period begins when the rates reach respectively 11 and 12%. Finally, many other structural changes are observable on the diagrams. Those regimes are shorter and less singular than the "black period" but it appears that they are not related to a particular level of yields. Thus it seems that the level of interest rate is not the only state variable that triggers regime switches. Indeed, there are many economic reasons to believe that interest rates are subject to regime shifts. As has been well documented, the conduct of monetary policy has first order effect on the term structure, and is subject to discrete changes in regime (see Froyen 1996). For example, Caporale and Grier (2000) find that structural breaks in the mean of the US real interest rates are consistent with changes in political regimes and more specifically, changes in party control of the US presidency or either branch of Congress. Finally, through the analysis of Federal Reserve Bank's reaction function for the postwar US economy, Clarida et al. (2000) report a regime shift in the Fed's behavior after Volcker's appointment as the Fed chairman in 1979. All those explanations are not necessarily exclusive and the true nature of those regime changes is beyond the scope of this study.

The main objective here is to explore the possibility to exploit those nonlinearities for prediction. The application of the method of recurrence plot has not produced positive evidence in favor of the presence of a deterministic component in the dynamics of interest rates variations. Nevertheless, it shed light on the occurrence of structural breaks in the dynamics. The presence of structural changes in a time series is a form of nonlinearity that can not be treated by means of linear tools.

## 3.4   Dimension Analysis

The algorithm of Grassberger and Procaccia and the method of false nearest neighbors were applied to the four time series of interest rate variations.

Globally, results are mixed. Dimension correlation estimates do not stabilize at some finite value except for the 10 year yield change (see figure 12). Nevertheless, estimates are relatively low. Otherwise, percentages of false neighbors decrease with $m$ and are relatively low (about 10%) for $m$ superior to four or five (see figure 13).

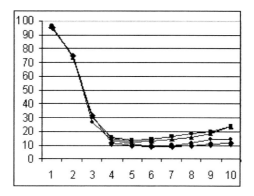

Figure 12: Correlation dimension estimates as a function of the embedding dimension.

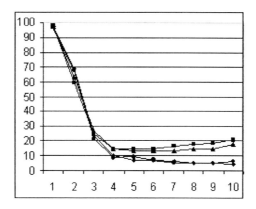

Figure 13: Percentages of false nearest neighbors as a function of the embedding dimension.

Knowing that the time series under investigation are autocorrelated and contain many structural breaks, those results are not surprising. In order to illustrate the potential effect of regime shifts, the both techniques of dimension estimation were applied to the time series from the beginning of the black period the 12th October 1979. As can be seen in figures 14, dimension estimates are higher than those estimated on the full sample and do not stabilize anymore for the 10 year yield changes. Thus those confusing results can not conduct to any conclusion concerning the presence of low dimensional chaos.

Many other techniques of dimension estimation could be used to try to find out the true nature of the time series. The application of those methods to surrogate data could permit us to test against various hypothesis at first glance compatible with the time series analyzed: linearly correlated noise, colored noise with structural break, autoregressive conditional heteroscedasticity process...etc. Nevertheless, in this context of financial time series analysis, the most interesting exercise seems to be the comparison of the forecasting performances

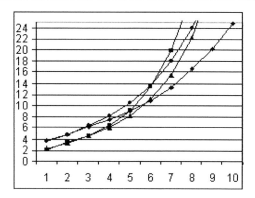

Figure 14: Correlation dimension estimates for observations from October 1979.

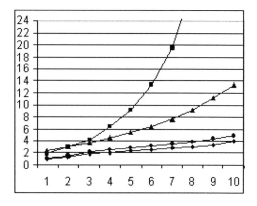

Figure 15: Percentages of false neighbors for observations from October 1979.

of stochastic linear model and nonlinear deterministic predictor.

## 3.5   Prediction

Predictive performances of a local predictor were compared to those by a linear auroregressive model for sign and level forecasts. Out of sample one step ahead forecasts were performed for the last 200 observations of each time series. Thus, in all cases, the learning set contains 1981 observation. The statistical significance of the results was assessed by means of surrogate data analysis. More precisely, the null hypotheses of white noise and linearly correlated noise were tested against the hypothesis of the presence of nonlinearities exploitable for conditional mean prediction.

### 3.5.1   Predictors

A pre testing set of 100 observations was used to select the optimal nonlinear predictor among the three local predictors presented in section 2.4. The optimal embedding dimension was estimated trough the learning set by means of the false nearest neighbors method and predictive performances were measured by means of the root mean square error criterion. As can be seen in table 3, the locally constant predictor outperforms the two other predictors.

Table 3: Optimal embedding dimension m* and root mean square error for the nearest neighbor method NN, the locally linear predictor LL and the locally constant predictor LC (k=20).

|          | m* | NN     | LL     | LC     |
|----------|----|--------|--------|--------|
| 3 month  | 6  | 0.1636 | 0.1077 | 0.0956 |
| 1 year   | 5  | 0.1214 | 0.0948 | 0.0867 |
| 5 years  | 4  | 0.1524 | 0.1088 | 0.1009 |
| 10 years | 5  | 0.136  | 0.1264 | 0.0949 |

The poor results obtained by the nearest neighbors predictor rule out definitively the conjecture that interest rate variations are generated by a strictly deterministic low dimensional process.

The predictive performances of the locally constant predictor were then compared to those by a linear autoregressive process. For each time series, the embedding dimension was estimated on the learning set on the basis of the false nearest neighbors method (estimated optimal values are the same than for the pre testing set). In all cases, the number of lags for the linear model was set to 1 because higher order coefficients were not statistically significant.

### 3.5.2  Measuring Forecast Accuracy

Out of sample forecasts were evaluated for level and sign predictions by means of the normalized mean square error and the percentage of correct directional forecasts. The normalized mean square error $NMSE$ is a quantity defined as the ratio of the mean square error of forecasts from the model tested to the mean square error of the mean predictor. Therefore, a value of $NMSE$ less that one indicates better performance than the mean value predictor.

$$NMSE = \frac{\sum_t \left[ s^P(t) - s(t) \right]^2}{\sum_t \left[ s(t) - \langle s \rangle \right]^2} \tag{32}$$

*where $s^P(t)$ is the forecast of $s(t)$ from the predictor, and $\langle s \rangle$ is the mean of $s(t)$.*

To assess statistical significance to the accuracy of sign predictions, a sign test inspired by the works of Diebold and Mariano (1995) was performed. Under the null hypothesis, the probability to obtain a correct forecast equals the probability to obtain a wrong one just as in a flip coin game. With $s(t)$ the actual variation and $s^P(t)$, the variation predicted, the null hypothesis $H0$ writes:

$$H0 : \Pr ob \left[ s(t).s^P(t) < 0 \right] = \Pr ob \left[ s(t).s^P(t) > 0 \right] \tag{33}$$

Under the null, with $n$ being the number of correct forecasts and $N^F$ the number of observations in the testing set, the statistic $D$ follows a centered normal law $N(0,1)$:

$$D = \frac{\left( n - 0.5 N^F \right)}{\sqrt{0.25 N^F}} \tag{34}$$

### 3.5.3   Surrogate Data Analysis

The method of surrogate data was used in order to assess predictability in the statistical framework of hypothesis testing. For each interest rates series, two sets of thirty surrogate time series were constructed in respect of the two null hypotheses of white noise and linearly correlated noise.

The null hypothesis of white noise means that apparent predictability is actually spurious. Therefore, under the null, the predictor can not produce better forecasts for the original data than for independent observations. In this case, surrogate data were constructed in scrambling the original time series. Thus they conserve the same distribution, but linear and nonlinear dependence, if any, are destroyed.

The hypothesis of linearly correlated noise, or linear predictability hypothesis, means that good predictive performances of a nonlinear model are caused by linear correlation rather than by nonlinear dependencies. In this case, surrogate data were generated by the following linear process:

$$S(t) = \sum_{k=1}^{q} a_k S(t - k) + \sigma \varepsilon(t) \qquad (35)$$

*where $\varepsilon(t)$ is uncorrelated noise with unit variance, and parameters $q$, $a_k$ and $\sigma$ are equivalent to the original time series.*

So surrogate time series conserve the same mean and variance and the same autocorrelation functions than the original series, but nonlinear dependencies if any are removed.

### 3.5.4   Results

**Directional forecasts:**   Directional forecasts produced by linear and nonlinear models are relatively accurate. Except for forecasts of the 10 year yield changes from the linear model, the hypothesis that the probability to obtain a correct forecast equals $\frac{1}{2}$ is rejected in all cases (see table 4). However the superiority of the nonlinear model over the linear model is not striking. For the 3 month yield changes, both methods produce equivalent results and for the 5 year yields, the linear process produce better directional forecast. Therefore, the superiority of the nonlinear model can not be assessed for directional forecasts.

Table 4: percentages of correct directional forecasts for the autoregressive model (AR) and the locally constant predictor (LC). *(**,***) indicates that the null hypothesis that the probability to obtain a correct forecast equals the probability to obtain a wrong one is rejected at 10% (5%, 1% )level.

|      | 3 month | 1 year   | 5 year  | 10 year   |
|------|---------|----------|---------|-----------|
| AR   | 55%*    | 58%**    | 57.5%*  | 52%       |
| LC   | 55%*    | 59.5%*** | 55%*    | 60.5%***  |

Surrogate data analysis leads to the rejection of the hypothesis of spurious predictability in all cases except for forecasts of the 10 year yield changes from the linear model (see table 5). In summary those results indicate that linear correlation can be exploited to make reliable directional forecasts. Nevertheless, one must notice that the null hypothesis of white noise is not always strongly rejected and that less than 3 sigmas should be considered as a weak evidence in favor of the alternatives.

Table 5: Standard scores for the null hypothesis of spurious directional predictability.

|     | 3 month | 1 year | 5 year | 10 year |
|-----|---------|--------|--------|---------|
| AR  | 2.07    | 2.92   | 3.05   | 1.31    |
| LC  | 2.07    | 3.42   | 2.21   | 4.21    |

**Level forecasts:**   According to the normalized mean square error criteria, and except for the 5 year and 10 year yield data, the nonlinear model clearly outperforms the linear model (see table 6). Moreover, except for the forecasts of 5 year rates from the local predictor, both models outperform the mean value predictor.

Table 6: Normalized mean square error.

|     | 3 month | 1 year | 5 year | 10 year |
|-----|---------|--------|--------|---------|
| AR  | 0.9876  | 0.9843 | 0.9695 | 0.9613  |
| LC  | 0.8946  | 0.9396 | 1.0287 | 0.9648  |

Surrogate data analysis leads to the rejection of the hypothesis of spurious predictability in all cases except for forecasts of the 3 month yield changes from the linear model and for the 5 year from the nonlinear predictor (see table 7). Standard scores for the linear model are low (under 3 signmas) wich means that statistical evidence for non spurious linear predictability is weak. The hypothesis of linear predictability, which was tested for forecasts from the locally constant predictor, is also rejected for the 3 month, 1 year and 10 year yields. That means that the relatively accurate level forecasts obtained from the local predictor are not related to the presence of autocorrelation in the time series. Nevertheless, here again standard scores are low, indicating that statistical evidence in favor of nonlinear predictability is not strong, particularly for the 10 year rates.

Table 7: Standard scores for level forecasts.

|                                         | 3 month | 1 year | 5 year | 10 year |
|-----------------------------------------|---------|--------|--------|---------|
| H0: spurious predictability, AR model   | 1.99    | 2.08   | 2.49   | 2.84    |
| H0: spurious predictability, LC model   | 5.23    | 3.71   | -      | 2.72    |
| H0: linear predictability, LC model     | 4.5     | 2.95   | -      | 2.08    |

# 4   Conclusion

The results above enable us to draw some conclusions concerning the properties of US interest rates dynamics. First, as largely reported in the literature, weekly yield changes are positively autocorrelated. Many explanations were proposed: interest rates smoothing (Sack and Wieland 2000), optimal policy inertia (Woodford 1999), the central Bank response to persistent shocks (Rudebusch 2001) and time aggregation (Cowles 1960). All those explanations are certainly not mutually exclusive but the main point here is that this persistence can be exploited to make reliable directional forecasts. Second, as shown by visual recurrence analysis, structural breaks are an important aspect of US interest rates dynamics. This kind of nonlinearity was also noted by many authors and many interpretations were proposed. Finally the main result is that nonlinear mean predictability was found in the 3 month, the 1 year and the 10 year yields data. The superiority of local predictor over linear model was already reported by Barkoulas et al. (1997) for the 3 month Treasury Bill rate. The main contribution of this article is that nonlinear predictability of yield changes is assessed here in the statistical framework of hypothesis testing. Indeed, surrogate data analysis permits us to make sure that predictability is not spurious and that it does not come from linear correlation. In the present case, results of this analysis show that statistical evidence in favor of nonlinear predictability is positive but not strong.

Concerning the dynamics of interest rates, some points remain unclear. Principally, the above results do not permit us to determine the true nature of the data generating process nor the source of nonlinear dependencies. It may be that structural breaks do not fully account for the presence of nonlinearity. This application led to the rejection of the hypotheses of white noise and colored noise but many alternatives are possible: stochastic process with regime shift in mean or in variance, high dimensional chaos, low dimensional chaos mixed with noise...etc. Discriminating among those alternative hypotheses was not the purpose of this work but it can be considered as an interesting area for future research.

More generally, this application has shown the potential of nonlinear tools such as visual recurrence analysis, surrogate data analysis or local predictors. Indeed, it appears that visual recurrence analysis can be a useful tool for detecting and locating structural breaks of any kind. Moreover, local predictor can deal with any sort of nonlinearity and do not require any knowledge of the data generating process. Finally, surrogate data analysis permits us to assess statistical significance to predictive performance evaluation.

# References

[1] Akaike H. (1974) "A new look at the statistical model identification", *IEEE Transactions of Automatic Control* **19**, 716-723.

[2] Aleksic Z., "Estimating the embedding dimension", *Physica D* **52** (1991) 362-368.

[3] Ang A., Bekaert G. (2002) "Regime Switching Interest Rates", *Journal of Financial Economics*, **63**(3), 443-494.

[4] Aussem A., Campbell J., Murtagh F. (1998) "Wavelet-based Feature Extraction and Decomposition Strategies for Financial Forecasting", *Journal of Computational Intelligence in Finance*, March/ April, 5-12.

[5] Barkoulas, Baum C.J., Onochie J. (1997) "A Nonparametric Investigation of the 90 Day T Bill Rate", *Review of Financial Economics*, **6**, 2, 181-198.

[6] Benzécri J.P. (1982) *Histoire et Préhistoire de l'analyse des données,* Paris, Dunod.

[7] Benzécri J.P. ( 1987) "L'analyse des séries chronologiques décalées exemple de l'histoire monétaire de la France de 1910 à 1945 ", *Les Cahiers de L'analyse des Données*, vol.XII n°4, p.291-309.

[8] Benzécri J.P. (1988) *La pratique de l'analyse des données*, *Tome V: Economie*, Paris, Dunod.

[9] Brock W.A. (1986) "Distinguishing Random and Deterministic Systems: Abriged Version", *Journal of Economic Theory* **40**, 168-195.

[10] Brock W.A. Dechert W.D, LeBaron B., Scheinkmann J.A. (1996) "A Test for Independence based on the Correlation Dimension", *Econometric Reviews* **15**, 197-235.

[11] Brock W.A. Hsieh D., LeBaron B.(1991) *Nonlinear Dynamics, Chaos, and Instability: Statistical Theory and Economic Evidence*. MIT Press, Cambridge, MA.

[12] Broomhead D.S., Jones R. and King G.P. (1987) "Topological dimension and local coordinates from time series data", *Physica D* **20**, 563-569.

[13] Campbell J.Y., Shiller R.J. (1984) "A Simple Account of the Behavior of Long-Term Interest Rates", *American Economic Review*, **74**, 44-54.

[14] Caporale T, Grier K.B. (2000) "Political Regime Change and the Real Interest Rate", *Journal of Money Credit and Banking* **31**, 234-247.

[15] Cao L. (1997) "Practical method for determining the minimum embedding dimension of a scalar time series", *Physica D* **110,** 43-50.

[16] Casdagli M.C. (1989) "Nonlinear prediction of chaotic time series", *Physica D* **35** 335-356.

[17] Casdagli M.C. (1992) "Chaos and Deterministic versus Stochastic Nonlinear Modelling", *Journal of the Royal Statistical Society B*, **54**, 303-328.

[18] Casdagli M.C. (1997) "Recurrence plots revisited", *Physica D* **108**, 12-44.

[19] Clarida R, Gali J., Gertler M. (2000) "Monetary policy rules and macroeconomic stability: Evidence and some theory", *Quaterly Journal of Economics*, Vol.115, 145-180.

[20] Cleveland W., Devlin S. (1988) "Locally Weighted Regression", *Journal of American Statistical Association*, **83**, 596-610.

[21]  Cowles A. (1960) "A Revision of Previous Conclusions Regarding Stock Prices Behavior", *Econometrica* **28**, 909-915.

[22]  Cox J.C., Ingersoll J.E., Ross S.A. (1985) "A Theory of the Term Structure of Interest Rates", *Econometrica*, **53**, 385-407.

[23]  Das S.R. (1993) "Mean Rate Shifts and Alternative Models of Interest Rate: Theory and Evidence", *Working Paper Stern School of Business*.

[24]  Eckmann J.P., Oliffson S.Kamphorst and Ruelle D. (1987) "Recurrence plots of dynamical system", *Europhysics Letters* Vol. 4 No. 9, 973-977.

[25]  Elms D. (1994) "Forecasting in Financial Markets ", in *Chaos and Non Linear Model in Economics*, Eds. Creedy&Martin.

[26]  Engle R.F. (1982) "Autoregressive conditional heteroskedasticity with estimates of the variance of united kingdom inflation", *Econometrica*, **50**, 987-1007.

[27]  Farmer J.D. and Sidorowich J.J. (1987) "Predicting chaotic time series", *Physical Review Letters,* vol.59 n°8, 845-848.

[28]  Fernandez-Rodriguez F., Sosvilla-Rivero S., Garça-Artiles M.D. (1999) "Dancing with bulls and bears : Nearest-neighbour forecast for the Nikkei index", *Japan and the World Economy* **11**, 395-413.

[29]  Fernandez Rodriguez F., Sosvilla-Rivero S., Andrada Felix J. (2003) "Nearest Neighbours Predictions in Foreign Exchange Rate Markets", in Shu Heng CHen and Paul Wang (eds.), *Computational Intelligence in Economics and Finance*, Berlin Physica Verlag, 279-375.

[30]  Froyen R.T. (1996) *Macroeconomics*, Prentice-Hall, Inc.

[31]  Fuller W.A. (1996) *Introduction to Statistical Time Series*, (2nd Ed.), Eds. John Willey, New York.

[32]  Gençay R. (1999) "Linear, nonlinear and essential foreign exchange rate prediction with some simple technical trading rules", *Journal of International Economics*, **47**, 97-107.

[33]  Granger C.W.J. (1993) *Modelling Nonlinear Economic Relationships*, Oxford: Oxford University Press.

[34]  Grassberger P. and Procaccia I. (1983) "Chararcterization of strange attractors", *Physical Review Letters* n°50, 189-208.

[35]  Hamilton J. (1988) "Rational Expectations, Econometric Analysis of Changes in Regimes: An Investigation of the Term Structure of Interest Rates", *Journal of Economic Dynamics and Control*, **12**, 385-423.

[36]  Hsieh D. (1989) "Testing for Nonlinear Dependence in Daily Foreign Exchange Rates", *Journal of Business* **62**, 339-369.

[37] Jaditz T. and Sayers C. (1993) "Is chaos generic in economic data?", *International Journal of Bifurcation and Chaos*, **3**(2), 745-755.

[38] Kennel M., Brown R. and Abarbanel H. (1992) "Determining embedding dimension for phase-space reconstruction using a geometrical construction", *Physical Review* **A45** 3403.

[39] Kozicki S. (1994) "A Nonlinear Model of the Term Structure", *Working paper Federal Reserve Board*, Washington DC.

[40] LeBaron B. (1992) "Nonlinear Forecast for the S&P Stock Index", in *Nonlinear Modelling and Forecasting, SFI Studies in the Sciences of Complexity*, Eds. Casdagli Eubank, Vol.XII., 381-393

[41] Mané R. (1981) "On the dimension on the compact invariant sets of certain nonlinear maps", In: Rand D.A., Young L.S. (Eds.), *Dynamical Systems and Turbulence, Lecture notes in mathematics* 898, Springer Berlin, 522-557.

[42] Merton R.C. (1973) "Theory of Rational Option Pricing", *Bell Journal of Economics and Management Science*, **4**, 141-183.

[43] Murphy J.J. (1999) *Technical Analysis of the Financial Markets: A Comprehensive Guide to Trading Methods and Applications*, Prentice Hall Press.

[44] Naik V., Lee M.H. (1993) "The Yield Curve and Bond Option Prices with discrete Shifts in Economic Regimes", *Working Paper, University of British Columbia.*

[45] Neely C.J., Weller P.A.and Ditmar R.D. (1997) "Is technical analysis in foreign exchange markets profitable? A genetic programming approach", *Journal of Financial and Quantitative Analysis*, **32**, 405-426.

[46] Osborne A.R. and Provenzale A (1989) "Finite correlation dimension for stochastic systems with power-laws spectra", *Physica D***35** , 357-381.

[47] Pfann G.A., Schotman P.C. and Tschernig R. (1996) "Nonlinear Interest Rate Dynamics and Implications for the Term Structure", *Journal of Econometrics* **74**, 149-176.

[48] Rudebush G. (2001) "Term Structure Evidence on Interest Rate Smoothing and Monetary Policy Inertia", *Working Paper Federal Reserve Bank of San Fransisco*, No. 2001-02.

[49] Sack B., Wieland V. (2000) "Interest Rate Smoothing and Optimal Monetary Policy: A Review of Recent Empirical Evidence", *Journal of Economics and Business*, **58**, 205-228.

[50] Sauer T., Yorke J.A., Casdagli M. (1992) "Embodology", *Journal of Statistical Physics* **65**(3/4), 193-215.

[51] Smith L.A. (1988) "Intrinsic limits of dimension calculations", *Physics Letters A*, **133**, 283-288.

[52] Sugihara G. and May R. (1990) "Nonlinear Forecasting as a Way of Distinguishing Chaos from Measurement Error in Time Series", *Nature* **344**, 734-741.

[53] Takens F. (1981) "Detecting strange attractors in fluid turbulence", In Rand D.A., Young L.S. (Eds.) *Dynamical System and Turbulence, Lecture notes in mathematics*, Springer Verlag, Berlin 366-381.

[54] Theiler J. (1986) "Spurious dimension from correlation algorithm applied to time series data", *Physical Review* **A34** 2427-2432.

[55] Theiler J. Galdrikian B., Longtin A., Eubank S., Farmer J.D. (1992) "Using Surrogate Data to Detect Nonlinearity in Time Series", *Nonlinear Modelling and Forecasting, SFI Studies in the Sciences of Complexity*, Eds. Casdagli Eubank, Vol.XII., 163-188.

[56] Theiler J., Eubank S., (1993) "Don't bleach chaotic data", *Chaos*, **3**, 771-782.

[57] Wayland R., Bromley D., Pickett D. and Passamante A. (1993) "Recognizing determinism in a time series", *Physical Review Letters* vol.70 n°5, 580-587.

[58] Wesner N. (2004) "Searching for chaos on low frequency", *Economics Bulletin*, vol.3(1), 1-8.

[59] Woodford M. (1999) "Optimal Monetary Policy Inertia", *NBER Working Paper*, No.**7264**.

[60] Wolf A., Swift J.B., Swinney H.L. and Vastano J.A. (1985) "Determining Lyapunov exponents from a time series", *Physica D* **16** 285-317.

[61] Zbilut J.P., Giuliani A. and Webber C.L. (1998) "Recurrence quantification analysis and principal components in the detection of short complex signal", *Physics Letters* **A 237** 131.

In: International Finance and Monetary Policy                    ISBN: 1-60021-103-8
Editor: Gleb P. Severov, pp. 187-208                    © 2006 Nova Science Publishers, Inc.

*Chapter 8*

# THE MACROECONOMY AND THE YIELD CURVE: THE SEARCH FOR A UNIFIED APPROACH

## *Zeno Rotondi*[1]

Capitalia and University of Ferrara

## Abstract

This work focuses on the recent literature - started by the seminal article of Ang and Piazzesi (2003) - aimed at developing macro-finance models that combine finance specifications of the term structure of interest rates with standard macroeconomic aggregate relationships for output and inflation. We review the alternative models proposed in this new literature and discuss their main features. An alternative analysis based on the theory of cointegrated vector autoregressive models is developed and tested with the data available for the US.

## 1   Introduction

In the finance literature there exist two alternative approaches for modeling the yield curve: the equilibrium approach and the no-arbitrage approach. The no-arbitrage approach focuses on perfectly fitting the term structure at a point in time in order to ensure that no arbitrage opportunities exist. While, the equilibrium approach focuses on modeling the dynamics of the instantaneous rate typically using affine models.

Prominent contributions in the no-arbitrage approach include Hull and White (1990) and Heath, Jarrow and Morton (1992), while the equilibrium approach is exemplified by the contributions of Vasicek (1977), Cox, Ingersoll and Ross (1985). There exist in the literature also affine no-arbitrage models that are extremely popular, as Duffie and Kan (1996), Litterman and Scheinkman (1991), Dai and Singleton (2000).[2]

---

[1] The opinions expressed herein are the author's only and they should not be attributed under any circumstance to Capitalia Banking Group.
[2] See Piazzesi (2003) for a recent review of affine term structure models.

Both approaches have found that almost all movements in the yield curve can be captured by a framework in which yields are linear functions of few unobservable or latent factors. But these models offer little insight into the nature of the underlying factors, although they provide a relatively good description of the forces that drive movements in interest rates. For example, Litterman and Scheinkman (1991) label their factors "level", "slope" and "curvature", but this terminology reflects the effect the factors have on the yield curve rather than the identification of the economic sources of the shocks.[3]

Starting from the nineties there has been an attempt at making yield curve factors more interpretable. Rudebusch (1995) and Balduzzi, Bertola and Foresi (1997) have proposed term structure models with central bank's target rate as a factor. More recently Ang and Piazzesi (2003), followed by several others, have introduced term structure models with economic factors.

In the next sections we review briefly the latter generation of models in order to examine the main features of this new literature on macroeconomics and the term structure of interest rates. For exposition reason we follow an order that is not chronological. Moreover, the present review of the literature does not pretend to be exhaustive, but mainly functional to our empirical analysis.

In the last part of this chapter, we develop an alternative analysis based on the theory of cointegrated vector autoregressive models and we test it with the data available for the US. The approach followed in the empirical analysis is based on the literature on cointegration analysis of the yield curve as exemplified by Anderson, Granger and Hall (1992).[4] As argued by Diebold and Li (2003), the empirical literature that models yields as a cointegrated system with one common stochastic trend - the short rate - and stationary spreads relative to the short rate is more similar in spirit to the equilibrium approach for modeling the yield curve.[5]

# 2 The new Literature on the Macroeconomy and the Yield Curve

## 2.1 Inclusion of Macro Variables in Finance Specifications of the Yield Curve

The model of Diebold, Rudebusch and Aruoba (2004) provides a simple way of adding macroeconomic variables in a finance specification of the yield curve. The building block of their framework is the representation of the yield curve by means of cross-section of yields at any point in time proposed by Nelson and Siegel (1987):

---

[3] This terminology of the three main factors underlying the dynamics of the yield curve is now become standard, but for instance Dai and Singleton (2000) have called them "level", "slope" and "butterfly".

[4] Anderson, Granger and Hall (1992) consider US yields. See also Balbo and Rotondi (2002) for a more recent analysis of this data.

[5] This similarity has been emphasized also by Anderson, Granger and Hall (1992, p.119): *"The assertion that the same common variable underlies the time series behaviour of each yield to maturity is not new to the literature on the term structure. Cox, Ingersoll and Ross (1985) build a continuous tie general equilibrium model of real yields to maturity in which the instantaneous interest rate is common to all yields."*

$$y(\tau) = \beta_1 + \beta_2 \left( \frac{1 - e^{-\lambda\tau}}{\lambda\tau} \right) + \beta_3 \left( \frac{1 - e^{-\lambda\tau}}{\lambda\tau} - e^{-\lambda\tau} \right),$$

(1)

where $\beta_1, \beta_2, \beta_3$ and $\lambda$ are parameters, while $\tau$ denotes maturity.

As shown by Diebold and Li (2003), if we introduce time varying $\beta_1, \beta_2, \beta_3$ the Nelson-Siegel representation can be interpreted in terms of time-varying level, slope and curvature factors multiplying the factor loadings. Formally the measurement equation is given by

$$y(\tau) = f_{1,t} + f_{2,t} \left( \frac{1 - e^{-\lambda\tau}}{\lambda\tau} \right) + f_{3,t} \left( \frac{1 - e^{-\lambda\tau}}{\lambda\tau} - e^{-\lambda\tau} \right) + \varepsilon_t(\tau),$$

(2)

where $f_{1,t}, f_{2,t}, f_{3,t}$ correspond to the latent factors, respectively level, slope and curvature.

They make several assumptions. First they assume an unconstrained factor dynamics with the transition equation represented by the following VAR(1)

$$\left( f_{k,t} - \mu_k \right) = \sum_{j=1}^{3} A_{k,j} \left( f_{j,t-1} - \mu_j \right) + \eta_{k,t},$$

(3)

with k=1,2,3.

Moreover they assume absence of link between factor loadings and factor dynamics. The white noise transition and measurement disturbances are orthogonal.

The addition of the macroeconomy in their framework is straightforward. Considering three additional macro variables, manufacturing capacity utilization (CU), the Federal Funds rate (FFR) and the inflation rate (INFL) , equation (3) can be rewritten as

$$\left( f_{k,t} - \mu_k \right) = \sum_{j=1}^{6} A_{k,j} \left( f_{j,t-1} - \mu_j \right) + \eta_{k,t},$$

(4)

with k=1,...6.

Finally, in their empirical analysis they compute optimal yield predictions by means of Kalman filter over the sample 1972-2000 of monthly data.

Their main findings are the following. First consider the impulse-response functions analysis. The response of macro variables to yield curve factors shows that a shock to the level factor increases CU, FFR and INFL. The response of yield-curve factors to macro variables shows that: a shock to INFL increases the level factor; a shock to CU and FFR increases the slope factor.

The variance decomposition analysis shows that macro variables explain yields: CU explains yields at 60 lags (25-35%); FFR explains yields most at 12 lags (31-63%). Also yield-curve factors explain macro variables: the level factor explains 20% of FFR, but only at 60 lags.

## 2.2   No-arbitrage Constraint

The previous model does not consider the no-arbitrage constraint, but Ang and Piazzesi (2003) show that it is useful in predicting yields and Ang, Piazzesi and Wei (2004) show that it is also useful in predicting GDP growth.

In Ang and Piazzesi (2003) macro factors (principal components of observables) and latent factors follow independent vector autoregressive process. The short rate depends on both macro and latent factors and the no-arbitrage restriction is imposed. Moreover they impose the restriction that inflation and output are independent of the policy interest rate. Formally the model is a special case of discrete-time versions of the affine class due to Duffie and Kan (1996). The sample considered in the estimation is 1952-2000, with monthly data.

Their findings are the following. Shocks to inflation affect positively all yields, with the impact decreasing with horizon. Shocks to real activity affect positively all yields, with a maximum impact at 10-20 lags. Responses from restricted VAR are much stronger than responses from unrestricted VAR. Inflation factor explains substantial fractions of yield variability, up to 70%; while real-activity factor explains only small fractions of yield variability, up to 15%. Macro factors explain mainly movements at the short and middle end of the yield curve, while unobservable factors still account for most of the movements at the long end,of the yield curve.

In their alternative analysis, Ang, Piazzesi and Wei (2004) examine the predictive power of the yield curve concerning GDP growth. Here they consider three factors: two yield factors (level and slope) and real GDP growth. The short rate depends on all three factors and there is again the no-arbitrage constraint. The data are quarterly and the sample is 1964-2001.

They use three methods to determine whether the above factors help forecast GDP growth. The first is regressing future economic growth on the factors, without modelling the factors themselves. The second is modelling factors with an unrestricted VAR and using the prediction from it to forecast future GDP growth. The third is similar to the second one, but arbitrage-free restriction is imposed.

They find that the predictive power of the spread increases with term spread. Increases of the term spread impact positively GDP growth, especially in the short-run and more for the VAR model than for OLS regression. Increases of the short rate impact negatively GDP growth, more so for VAR model than for OLS regression. Finally, contrary to previous findings, they show that the short rate has more predictive power than any other term spread.[6]

---

[6] The term spread has been successful at predicting recessions with discrete choice models (see Estrella and Mishkin 1998), it is also an important variable in the construction of Stock and Watson's (1989) leading business cycle indicator index. However, Stock and Watson (2003) show that the presence of parameter instability may weaken the leading indicator property of the term spread. For a theoretical justification for the leading indicator property of the term spread see Rendu de Lint and Stolin (2003).

## 2.3    Macro Variables Dependence on the Policy Interest Rate

Hördahl, Tristani and Vestin (2004), following Ang and Piazzesi (2003), introduce macroeconomic variables into the standard affine term structure framework based on latent factor. The main innovation is that they remove the assumption of inflation and output independent of the policy interest rate imposed in Ang and Piazzesi (2003). This is achieved by setting a macroeconomic model with both forward- and backward-looking expectations, rather than employing a bivariate VAR of inflation and output.[7] After solving, bond yields are linearly related to macroeconomic fundamentals. Again the arbitrage-free condition is imposed in the model. The data used in the estimation are German monthly data for the sample period 1975-1998.

By using the complete macro-finance model they are able to show several interesting results. The inflation target for Germany is found to have declined from 4% in 1975 to around 1% in 1998. Shocks to the inflation target lead to a gradual increase in inflation and output and push up the middle portion of the yield curve more than the short or long end of the curve. Moreover, monetary policy shocks tend to reduce output with little impact on prices and cause the yield curve to flatten, although this latter effect dissipates after four to five years.

Moreover, they test if their model is capable of replicating the empirical failure of the Expectations Hypothesis, as exemplified in Campbell and Shiller (1991).[8] Dai and Singleton (2002) have shown that affine models based on unobservable factors can be very successful in accounting for the empirical failure of the Expectations Hypothesis. Following the analysis of Dai and Singleton, Hördahl, Tristani and Vestin show that out-of-sample forecasting performance is comparable to the best available affine term structure models, apart from long-term yields. They argue that the latter limitations of the model appears to play a crucial role in the tests of the Expectations Hypothesis, which present a limited degree of success.

## 2.4    Monetary Policy Regime Shifts

Rudebusch and Wu (2003) use an affine no-arbitrage model in which the yield curve depends on few latent factors, level and slope, and two macro factors, inflation and output gap (capacity utilization). They allow for a bi-directional feedback between the term structure factors and macro variables. Latent factors are affected by macro variables through inflation targeting and monetary policy inertia.

The sample used is 1988-2000 of monthly data. Such a short sample is motivated by the following argument. The relationships among yields may have been relatively stable during the post-war period, as it is implicitly assumed by most empirical analyses based on finance specifications of the term structure of interest rates. But most of the empirical evidence suggests that the relationship between interest rates and macroeconomic variables may have changed during the post-war period. This latter result is a consequence of monetary policy

---

[7] The macroeconomic model is a variant of Rudebusch and Svensson (1999) and Rudebusch (2002).

[8] Recently Favero (2001) and Carriero, Favero and Kaminska (2004) have questioned the findings of Campbell and Shiller (1987, 1991). In particular they show that empirical rejections of the Expectations Theory may be caused by improper modelling of expectations.

regime shifts which imply changes in central banks reaction functions for setting monetary policy.[9]

In the finance section of their model the short-term interest rate is defined as the sum of two latent term structure factors

$$r_t = k + f_{1,t} + f_{2,t},$$

(5)

where $k$ is a constant and $f_{1,t}, f_{2,t}$ correspond to the latent factors, respectively level and slope. This is similar to the standard affine no-arbitrage term structure framework. The new ingredient is represented by the dynamics of these latent factors, defined as

$$f_{1,t} = \rho_1 f_{1,t-1} + (1 - \rho_1)\pi_t + \upsilon_{1,t},$$

(6)

$$f_{2,t} = \rho_2 f_{2,t-1} + (1 - \rho_2)[\alpha y_t + \beta(\pi_t - f_{1,t})] + \upsilon_{2,t}$$

(7)

$$v_{2,t} = \theta v_{2,t-1} + u_{2,t},$$

(8)

where $\pi_t$ is the inflation rate and $y_t$ is the output gap. As argued by Rudebusch and Wu, equation (6) is a "useful but imperfect approximation" of the relationship between movements in the level factor and movements in the perceived inflation target of the central bank. Equations (7) and (8) represent a partial adjustment dynamic specification for the slope factor, which reflects the specifications used in the literature started by Taylor (1993) to model central banks behaviour in setting the policy interest rate. The complete macro-finance model is obtained by combining equations (6)-(8) with a small standard New Keynesian macroeconomic model of inflation and output.[10]

The main findings of their empirical analysis are the following. Both inflation and output shocks impact (positively) more the slope than the level factor. Both inflation and output respond positively (negatively) to the level (slope) shocks. Inflation and output explain little of the variation in yields at long horizons, up to 7%. The level explains 82% of the variation in inflation, while the slope explains 69% of the variation in output.

## 2.5   Discussion

After the review made of this new literature on macro-finance modelling of the term structure of interest rates it is interesting to individuate the issues that still deserve some attention in future research.

---

[9] For an historical analysis of the Taylor's rule and the Fed see Judd and Rudebusch (1998), Orphanides (2001,2003a,2003b), Clarida, Galì and Gertler (2000).

[10] Again the macroeconomic model is a variant of Rudebusch and Svensson (1999) and Rudebusch (2002).

An important issue is the presence of non-linear relationships between interest rates, ignored in the above literature. There exists empirical evidence on non-linear responses of long rates to the short rate. The findings based on threshold models in Enders and Granger (1998) and Enders and Siklos (2001) are supportive of asymmetry in the adjustment toward equilibrium in the relationship between short- and long-term interest rates. Clements and Galvão (2002), also based on threshold models, show that the results of tests on the implications of the Expectations Hypothesis depend on the size and sign of the spread. In particular the long maturity spread is successful in predicting future changes of the short rate only when it is high.

The importance of non-linearities between interest rates is supported also by the theory. For instance, Ellingsen and Söderstrom (2001) provide a closed-form expression for the yield curve where long and short rates depend on inflation and output shocks as well on the preferences of the monetary authority. When the short rate moves because of inflation and output shocks, long rates move in the same direction. However, when the short rate moves because of changes in preferences – i.e. changes in the weights assigned to the objectives in the central bank's loss function – long rates move in the opposite direction.

Other issues concerning the new literature are the importance of regime breaks and non-stationarities. As shown by Ang, Piazzesi and Wei (2004) the term spread positively predicts GDP growth only during the 1971-1989 period. The importance of taking into account the existence of regime breaks for the term structure of interest rates is well documented by the Markov-switching models used in the literature for testing the Expectations Hypothesis under regime shifts. As shown, for example, by Sola and Driffill (1994) the restrictions of the Expectations Theory are not rejected in the Markov-switching approach.[11]

Moreover focusing on a small sample with a stable regime, like that chosen for instance by Rudebusch and Wu (2003), may imply biased estimates of autoregressive coefficients.

Finally, in most of the models considered structural parameters are identified by using inflation and capacity utilization in the data set, but usually these variables display unit or near unit roots.

# 3   Empirical Analysis

In the next sections we develop an alternative analysis based on the theory of cointegrated vector autoregressive models and test it with the data available for the US. Our analysis represents a further attempt at developing a framework for analyzing the yield curve integrated with macro factors. The main innovation compared to the previous literature is that our analysis explicitly addresses the problem of non stationarity of financial and macroeconomic time series.

---

[11] See Driffill, Kenc and Sola (2004) for a comparison of the predictive power of several parameterization of the switching CIR (Cox, Ingersoll and Ross (1985)) process for the short term interest rate.

## 3.1   Cointegration Analysis of the Yield Curve

Campbell and Shiller (1987) and Engle and Granger (1987) are the first who have tested for and found cointegration between the yield on a long-term bond and that on a short-term bond. While Anderson, Granger and Hall (1992), Shea (1992) have found that the term structure is well modelled as a cointegrated system.

In a cointegrated system of the yield curve it is also possible to test the Expectations Hypothesis. Let $X_t$ be a vector of $s$ interest rate series of different maturity regarded as a set of integrated $I(1)$ processes

$$X_t^{'} = (R_t^{(1)},...., R_t^{(s)}) . \qquad (9)$$

The multivariate vector error correction model (VECM) for $X_t$ is

$$\Delta X_t = \Gamma_1 \cdot \Delta X_{t-1} +...+ \Gamma_{k-1} \cdot \Delta X_{t-k+1} + \Pi \cdot X_{t-k} + u_t \qquad (10)$$

where $\Gamma_i = - (I-A_1...-A_i)$, $i=1,....,k-1$, $\Pi = - (I-A_1...-A_k)$; $u_t$ is a multivariate gaussian error term and $\Delta$ is the the first difference operator. It can be shown that $\Pi = \alpha\beta'$, where $\alpha$ represents the speed of adjustment to disequilibrium, while $\beta$ is a matrix of long-run coefficients such that the term $\beta'z_{t-k}$ embedded in (10) represents up to $s-1$ cointegrating vectors.

Let's consider the following relationship between long-term nominal interest rate $R_t$ and short-term nominal interest rate $r_t$ (one-period bond)

$$R_t^{(m)} = \left(1 - k_m\right)\sum_{\tau=t}^{\infty} k_m^{\tau-t} E_t r_t + \theta_t^{(m)};$$

$$k_m \equiv \frac{D_m}{1 + D_m};$$
$$\qquad (11)$$

where $m(>1)$ and $D_m$ are respectively the maturity and the duration of the long-term bond, while $\theta$ is a term premium which may account for risk considerations or investors' preferences about liquidity. In (11) we have used the property that any finite maturity bond can be approximated by an infinite maturity consol bond provided the (geometric) weights ensure that the duration of the consol is equal to the duration of the finite maturity bond.[12]

The Pure Expectations Hypothesis asserts that in (11) the term premium is zero, while an other version of the Expectations Hypothesis claims that the term premium is constant over time and across maturities. According to the Liquidity Preference Hypothesis the term premium increases with the time period to maturity $m$, but is constant over time. Finally,

---

[12] See Shiller, Campbell and Schoenholtz (1983) for the proof. In the linear approximation given by expression (11) it is assumed that the duration of the long-term bond is constant and equal to $D$.

According to the Time Varying Risk Hypothesis the term premium depends on the maturity $m$ and varies over time.[13]

Expression (11) can be rewritten as

$$R_t^{(m)} = \left(1 - k_m\right)r_t + k_m E_t R_{t+1}^m + \theta_t^{(m)}.$$

(12)

Now, by rearranging (12), we can formulate three alternative specifications of the relationship between the long-term interest rate and the short-term interest rate that can be tested by means of cointegration analysis. The first is the following

$$R_t^{(m)} - r_t = \frac{k_m}{1 - k_m} E_t \Delta R_{t+1}^{(m)} + \frac{\theta_t^{(m)}}{1 - k_m},$$

(13)

where we have subtracted $k_m R_t^{(m)}$ from both sides of (12). If we assume that the term premium and the first difference of the long-term rate are stationary, then expression (13) implies that: (i) $\Pi$ has rank $s$-$1$, i.e. there exist $s$-$1$ linearly independent cointegrating vectors, where $s$ is the number of yields; (ii) any spread between long-term and short-term rates must be stationary. Hence, the model predicts that any of the $s$-$1$ yield series $R_t^{(m)}$ is cointegrated with the one-period yield $r_t$, so that the spreads appear to be components of the term structure's cointegrating vectors.

To analyse the validity of such hypotheses one can employ the tests developed by Johansen (1988) (the *maximal eigenvalue* test, or *λ-max* test, and the *trace* test) to select the dimension of the cointegration space, which in the present case should be of rank $s$-$1$, and the related maximum likelihood procedures to test the validity of the spread restrictions imposed on the cointegrating relationships.

Alternatively, we may use the following specification, derived from (13) by subtracting the analogous expression for the yield with maturity $n$:

$$R_t^{(m)} - R_t^{(n)} = \frac{k_m}{1 - k_m} E_t \Delta R_{t+1}^{(m)} - \frac{k_n}{1 - k_n} E_t \Delta R_{t+1}^{(n)} + \left( \frac{\theta_t^{(m)}}{1 - k_m} - \frac{\theta_t^{(n)}}{1 - k_n} \right),$$

(14)

where $n<m$. The testing procedure for expression (14) is analogous to that of expression (13). Here the model predicts that any of the $s$-$1$ yield series $R_t^{(m)}$ is cointegrated with a given yield $R_t^{(n)}$, so that the spreads appear to be components of the term structure's cointegrating vectors.

In the case when the term premia are not stationary we can use the following expression

---

[13] The are other two theories of the term structure, which however are not relevant for the purposes of our empirical analysis: Market Segmentation Hypothesis and Preferred Habitat Theory.

$$R_t^{(m)} - R_t^{(n)} - \left[(1 - k_m) - (1 - k_n)\right]r_t =$$

$$+ k_n\left(E_t R_{t+1}^{(n)} - E_{t-1}R_t^{(n)}\right) - k_m\left(E_t R_{t+1}^{(m)} - E_{t-1}R_t^{(m)}\right) + \left(\Delta\theta_t^{(m)} - \Delta\theta_t^{(n)}\right)$$

$$+ \left\{R_{t-1}^{(m)} - R_{t-1}^{(n)} - \left[(1 - k_m) - (1 - k_n)\right]r_{t-1}\right\}. \tag{15}$$

Expression (15) is obtained by taking the first difference of expression (12) and subtracting the analogous expression for the yield with maturity $n$. In (15) it is assumed that the terms within brackets in the right-hand side are all stationary.[14] Now, the new model predicts that any of the $s$-2 yield series $R_t^{(m)}$ is cointegrated with a given yield $R_t^{(n)}$ and the one-period yield $r_t$.

In general the duration is an increasing function of a bond's maturity, but this is not always true.[15] This implies that the sign of the term $\left[(1 - k_m) - (1 - k_n)\right]$ in (15) is uncertain. Nevertheless, given the definition of $k$, if $D_m > D_n$ the term above is negative.

## 3.2    Empirical Evidence Based on the Alternative Specifications of the Expectations Hypothesis

In the existing literature on cointegration and the yield curve the Expectations Hypothesis has been tested only by using specifications (13) and (14) and it has been almost invariably rejected. In table 1 we have reported the main findings. As it is possible to see the results seem to suggest that the interest rates at different maturities are typically cointegrated, usually with one cointegrating vector. As one may expect, the cointegration becomes weaker in the cases where the range of yields included in the analysis comprises the long end of the yield curve together with short end. The rationale for this can be found in the fact that cointegration and correlation go together in the yield curve, and we often find strongest cointegration at the short end were correlations are highest.

However cointegration between yields, with the presence of a single common trend, is only a necessary condition for the Expectations Hypothesis. The sufficient condition is represented by the validity of the restrictions on the cointegrating vectors implied by specifications (13)-(15). Unfortunately, those restrictions are typically rejected, or accepted only in restricted subsamples and for a small subset of yields. Thus, these findings suggest only limited support for the Expectations Hypothesis. One possible explanation for this conclusion is that the rejection on larger samples may be caused by problems associated with monetary regime shifts. In other words, the acceptance of the restrictions during small subsamples could be due to the stationarity of risk or liquidity premia of yields in presence of

---

[14] The assumption that the term within $\{\ \}$ in the right-hand side of (15) is stationary is implied by the existence of cointegration in the left-hand side of expression (15). In a sense this is tautological, just as tautological are the assumptions of stationarity for the term premia made in the left-hand side of expressions (14) and (13).

[15] See for instance Benninga (1997).

a stable monetary regime. This conclusion seems to be supported, for instance, by the evidence in Anderson, Granger and Hall (1992).

Table 1 – Findings of the empirical literature on cointegration and the yield curve for US monthly interest rates

| Authors | Interest rates | Common stochastic trend | Spread restriction |
|---|---|---|---|
| Anderson, Granger and Hall (1992) | ■ 11 rates: 1-m through 11-m;<br>■ 1970:3 – 1988:12;<br>■ zero-coupon yields derived from Treasury Bills. | 1 | Rejected |
| | ■ 4 rates: 1-m through 4-m;<br>■ 1970:3 – 1979:9;<br>■ zero-coupon yields derived from Treasury Bills. | 1 | Fail to reject |
| Shea (1992) | ■ 4 rates: 1-m, 3-y, 5-y, 10-y;<br>■ 1952:1 – 1978:12;<br>■ zero-coupon yields derived from Treasury Bills, Notes and Bonds. | 1 | Fail to reject |
| Zhang (1993) | ■ 19 rates: 1-m through 30-y;<br>■ 1964:2 – 1986:12;<br>■ zero-coupon yields derived from Treasury Bills, Notes and Bonds. | 3 | NA |
| | ■ 12 rates: 1-m through 12-m;<br>■ 1964:2 – 1986:12;<br>■ zero-coupon yields derived from Treasury Bills, Notes and Bonds. | 1 | NA |
| Engsted and Tanggaard (1994) | ■ 4 rates: 1-m, 2-m, 4-m, 12-m;<br>■ 1952:1 – 1979:9;<br>■ zero-coupon yields derived from Treasury Bills, Notes and Bonds. | 1 | Fail to reject |
| | ■ 4 rates: 1-m, 2-y, 5-y, 10-y;<br>■ 1952:1 – 1979:9;<br>■ zero-coupon yields derived from Treasury Bills, Notes and Bonds. | 1 | Fail to reject |
| Balbo and Rotondi (2002) | ■ 8 rates: 1-m, 3-m, 6-m, 12-m, 3-y, 5-y, 7-y, 10-y;<br>■ 1989:1 – 2002:10;<br>■ zero-coupon yields bootstrapped from swap rates. | 1 | Rejected |
| | ■ 8 rates: 1-m, 3-m, 6-m, 12-m, 3-y, 5-y, 7-y, 10-y;<br>■ 1992:1 – 2001:2;<br>■ zero-coupon yields bootstrapped from swap rates. | 1 | Fail to reject |

# 4   New Findings

## 4.1   Considering Only Yields

In the present empirical analysis we will focus on specification (13). We have used a large sample of monthly (end-of-month) zero-coupon constant maturity government bond yields for US, ranging from 1952:01 to 2003:11.[16] For the estimation the sample period is the same of Ang and Piazzesi (2003), from 1952:06 to 2000:12. But as our data end in 2003:11, we will use the data not used in the estimation for conducting an out-of-sample forecasting experiment on alternative models.

**Figure 1 - Monthly Zero-Coupon Bond Yields**
*Sample period: 1952:1 - 2003:11*

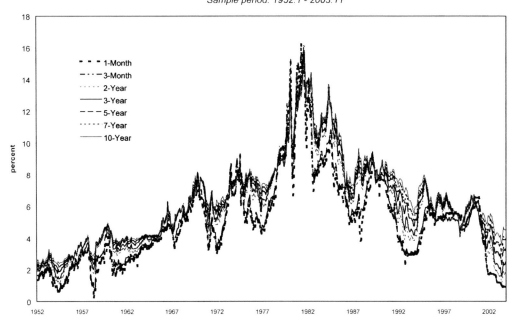

Maturities are one month, three months, two years, three years, five years, seven years and ten years. In figure 1 are plotted all the yields considered.

Augmented Dickey-Fuller unit root test statistics were computed for each of the seven yields. For the sample 1952:06 - 2000:12 the test statistics show no evidence against the null hypothesis that there is a unit root in yields level, but the data clearly reject the null hypothesis that there is a unit root in the first differences.[17] Hence we can conclude, in line with the previous literature, that over the sample considered each yield is a $I(1)$ process.

Subsequently we have tested that the yields are cointegrated with $(s-1)$ cointegrating vectors, with $s=7$. The results obtained from Johansen and Juselius likelihood based

---

[16] The data used here are the same of Fornari and Luisi (2004). We thank Fabio Fornari for having kindly provided the data on US yields used in their work. Notice that in their sample data from 1952 to 1991 are taken from McCulloch and Kwon (1993), which calculated monthly observations by means of a cubic spline method; while data from 1992 to 2003 are estimated using the BIS/DBS smoothing spline method used at the Bank for International Settlements (BIS). An exception is the one-month yield, which is the one-month T-Bill yield taken from FRED II database.

[17] Details of this analysis can be provided by the author on request.

procedures are reported in table 1.[18] Both the λ-*max* and *trace* statistics accept the restriction that the rank of the cointegrating space is not more than six, but rejects the hypothesis that the rank is not more than five. Thus, the necessary condition of the theory under investigation is supported by the data.

Let's see if also the sufficient condition of the theory holds. Conditional on there being six cointegrating vectors, the null hypothesis is that six linearly independent spreads between the one-month yield and the remaining six yields comprise a basis for the cointegration space. As it is possible to see from table 2, contrary to previous empirical evidence, the null hypothesis is not rejected. This is surprising given the large sample and relative large number of yields considered here. A standard finding of the previous literature is that the theory holds only for small subsamples due to the presence of changes in monetary regimes. While according to our findings the confirmation of the theory is more related to the consideration of a very large sample. In fact the one considered here is by far the largest considered in the literature on the yield curve and cointegration analysis.

Table 1 – Hypothesis Tests to Determine the Cointegration Rank for the Set of Yields Considered for the Sample 1952:06 – 2000:12

| Null Hypothesis About Rank $r$ | λ-max Test Statistic | 5% Critical Value | Trace Test Statistic | 5% Critical Value |
|---|---|---|---|---|
| $r \leq 6$ | 3.84 | 9.24 | 3.84 | 9.24 |
| $r \leq 5$ | 17.37 | 15.67 | 21.21 | 19.96 |

**Note**: The critical values are from Osterwald-Lenum (1992), which differ slightly from those reported in Johansen and Juselius (1990).

Table 2 – Test that the Spread Vectors are Cointegrating for the Sample 1952:06 – 2000:12

| Restrictions with $r_t$ = 1-month yield | Rank | LR Test Statistic | DF | Probability |
|---|---|---|---|---|
| **Expression (13)** | $r = 6$ | 8.66 | 6 | 0.19 |
| **Expressions (13) and (16)** | $r = 7$ | 18.15 | 12 | 0.11 |

**Note**: The test is conditional on the rank of the cointegration space being $r$, and the LR test statistic has a Chi-squared distribution with DF degrees of freedom.

## 4.2 Introducing Macro Factors in the Framework

Let's introduce macro factors into the analysis. In figure 2 are plotted the monthly inflation and output gap series considered in the present analysis. This data are taken from FRED II, of the Federal Reserve Bank of St. Louis. The output gap is measured by the percent deviation of log industrial production from a trend. We have used the deviation of output from its long-run level as measured by a quadratic trend estimated by means of recursive least squares.

---

[18] The lag order selected is four, the same chosen for the case when macro factors are included in the yields dataset. The cointegration rank test is performed under the assumption of an intercept in the cointegrating equations, without deterministic trend.

Augmented Dickey-Fuller unit root test statistics were computed for two macro factors. For the sample 1952:06 - 2000:12 the test statistics show no evidence against the null hypothesis that there is a unit root in the level, but the data clearly reject the null hypothesis that there is a unit root in the first differences.[19]

Subsequently we have tested that yields are cointegrated with macro factors. The results obtained from Johansen and Juselius likelihood based procedures are reported in table 3.[20] The *trace* statistic accepts the restriction that the rank of the cointegrating space is not more than seven at the five percent critical value, while the λ-*max* statistic indicates at most five cointegrating vectors. Thus, the necessary condition of the theory under investigation – i.e. that the rank of the cointegrating space is greater or equal to six - is partially supported by the data. According to the *trace* statistic beyond six yield spreads one cointegrating vector is left. We interpret the latter as a "long-run" Taylor (1993) rule, i.e. an interest rate rule which specifies the central bank's response to current inflation and output gap. Our choice is similar in the spirit to that followed by Ang and Piazzesi (2003), where the short rate dynamics is modelled as a version of the Taylor rule with the errors being unobserved latent factors orthogonal to macro factors.[21]

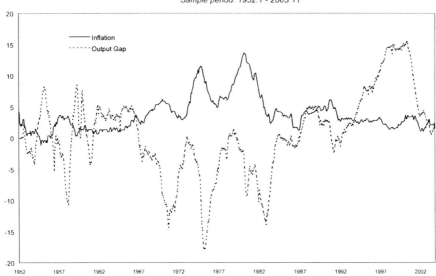

**Figure 2 - Monthly Data for Macro Factors**
*Sample period: 1952:1 - 2003:11*

In Ang and Piazzesi and our analysis it is assumed for simplicity that during the sample period the Taylor rule relationship is stable. But this is not true as the estimated coefficients are highly sensitive to the sample period selected due to the presence of regime shifts.

---

[19] Again, details of this analysis can be provided by the author on request.

[20] The lag order selected is four and it was chosen according the Akaike Information Criterion. The cointegration rank test is performed under the assumption of an intercept in the cointegrating equations, without deterministic trend.

[21] See also Ang, Dong and Piazzesi (2004) for an analysis of "no-arbitrage" Taylor rules, where they extend the analysis on backward-looking policy rules developed in Ang and Piazesi (2003) to forward-looking policy rules.

The empirical literature on monetary policy rules supports the existence of regime shifts in the behavior the Fed. For a review on historical monetary policy rules of the Fed see for instance Orphanides (2003a), (2003b), (2001), Romer and Romer (2002), Judd and Rudebusch (1998), Clarida, Galì, Gertler (2000). Rudebusch (2003) discusses the implications of these shifts in the behavior of the central bank for the assessment of the Lucas critique. Moreover there exist also attempts towards estimating time-varying Taylor rules (see for example Jalil (2004)).

In our analysis the introduction of macro factors implies that beyond the restrictions on the cointegrating vectors given by (13) we have also the additional restriction that

$$r_t = \phi + \phi_\pi \pi_t + \phi_y y_t, \tag{16}$$

where $r_t$, $\pi_t$ and $y_t$ are respectively the one-month yield, inflation and output gap.

Let's see if the sufficient condition of the theory holds also when a long-run Taylor rule is included. Conditional on there being seven cointegrating vectors, the null hypothesis is that six linearly independent spreads between the one-month yield and the remaining six yields together with a long-run Taylor rule for the one-month yield comprise a basis for the cointegration space. As it is possible to see from table 2, the null hypothesis is not rejected.

Table 3 – Hypothesis Tests to Determine the Cointegration Rank for the Set of Yields and Macro Factors Considered for the Sample 1952:06 – 2000:12

| Null Hypothesis About Rank r | λ-max Test Statistic | 5% Critical Value | Trace Test Statistic | 5% Critical Value |
|---|---|---|---|---|
| $r \leq 7$ | 12.94 | 15.67 | 17.03 | 19.96 |
| $r \leq 6$ | 19.88 | 22.00 | 36.91 | 34.91 |
| $r \leq 5$ | 26.05 | 28.14 | 62.97 | 53.12 |
| $r \leq 4$ | 42.04 | 34.40 | 105.01 | 76.07 |

**Note:** The critical values are from Osterwald-Lenum (1992), which differ slightly from those reported in Johansen and Juselius (1990).

Table 4 – Long-Run Taylor Rule for the One Month Yield for the Sample 1952:06 – 2000:12

| Coefficients of equation (16) | Ang and Piazzesi (2003) | Cointegrating Vector |
|---|---|---|
| $\phi$ | 0.43 (0.01) | 0.10 (0.66) |
| $\phi_\pi$ | 0.15 (0.01) | 1.29 (0.10) |
| $\phi_y$ | 0.01 (0.01) | 0.44 (0.04) |

**Note:** Standard errors in parentheses. We have checked to see whether the restrictions (12) and (16) identify all cointegrating vectors for each possible rank. The identification condition is checked numerically by the rank of the appropriate Jacobian matrix. Asymptotic standard errors for the estimated cointegrating parameters are reported only if the restrictions identify the cointegrating vectors. See Boswijk (1995) for the technical details. The estimation approach of Ang and Piazzesi (2003) is ordinary least squares (OLS) based on the specification of the latent factors as orthogonal to the macro factors. They use the restrictions from no-arbitrage to separately identify the individual latent factors.

In table 4 it is possible to compare Ang and Piazzesi estimates of the Taylor rule's coefficients with those obtained in the present analysis. In both cases the coefficients on inflation and real activity are significant and positive. The main difference is that in the case of Ang and Piazzesi the coefficient on inflation is less than one. This is a disappointing feature, as Henderson and McKibbin (1993) and Clarida, Galì and Gertler (2000) show that for the coefficient of inflation is required a value greater than one for stability in macroeconomic models with these types of policy rules.

**Figure 3 - Response of 1-Month Yield to Generalized One Standard Deviation Innovations**

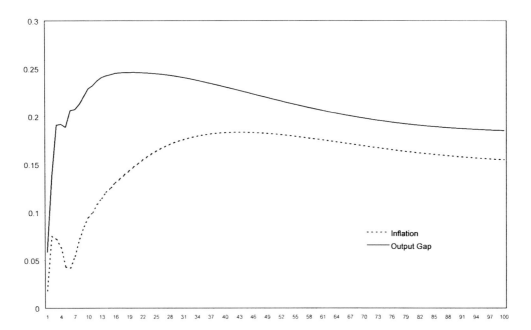

## 4.3    Impulse Responses

In figures 3,4 and 5 we have reported impulse responses of one month, two years and ten years yields from the model with macro factors. The dotted line corresponds to the impulse responses to inflation while the continuous line to those associated to output gap.

The analysis followed is a generalized impulse response analysis for cointegrated vector autoregressive (VAR) models, based on Pesaran and Shin (1998) methodology. The main advantage of this approach is that it constructs an orthogonal set of innovations that does not depend on the VAR ordering.

Figure 4 - Response of 2-Year Yield to Generalized One Standard Deviation Innovations

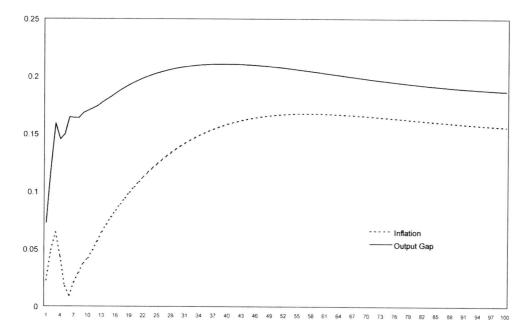

From the figures it is possible to see that shocks to inflation and output gap initially increase yields. The response of the one month yield to output gap shocks is hump-shaped with hump occurring after sixteen months, with an increase of around 25 basis points. Moreover, during the first year the responses to output gap shocks are larger for the one month yield compared to the other yields, and for the two year yield compared to the ten year yield. A similar pattern is observable for the responses to inflation shocks, but these responses are always smaller that those corresponding to output gap shocks.

## 4.4    Predictive Power of Alternative Models

The error correction models estimated by full information maximum likelihood (FIML) for the alternative set of data (yields with or without macro factors) have been used to obtain 35 one-step ahead forecasts over the period 2001:01 – 2003:11.

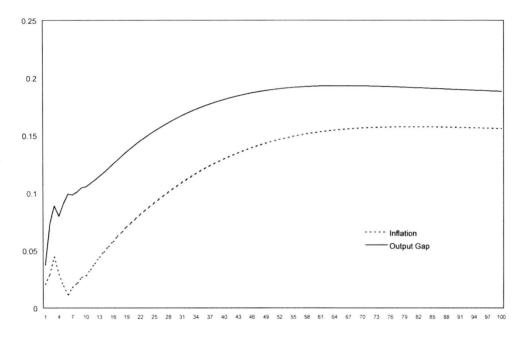

Figure 5 - Response of 10-Year Yield to Generalized One Standard Deviation Innovations

In table 5 we can compare the predictive accuracy of the two alternative models. According to this forecasts the error correction model with the macro factors has lower root mean squared error (RMSE), mean absolute error (MAE) and mean absolute percentage error (MAPE) for all the considered yields. In particular, for the RMSE the improvement in forecast deriving from the inclusion of macro factors ranges between a 3-9 percent reduction.

Table 5 – Summary Statistics for One-Step Ahead Forecast Errors for the Sample 2001:01 – 2003:11

| Yields in Level | Mean | Standard Deviation | Root Mean Squared Error | | Mean Absolute Error | | Mean Absolute Percentage Error | |
|---|---|---|---|---|---|---|---|---|
| | | | Only Yields | With Macro Factors | Only Yields | With Macro Factors | Only Yields | With Macro Factors |
| **1-Month** | 2.16 | 1.42 | 0.31 | 0.30 | 0.23 | 0.22 | 12.16 | 11.55 |
| **3-Month** | 2.08 | 1.25 | 0.32 | 0.31 | 0.25 | 0.24 | 13.40 | 12.61 |
| **2-Year** | 2.74 | 1.08 | 0.40 | 0.37 | 0.36 | 0.32 | 14.95 | 13.23 |
| **3-Year** | 3.20 | 1.01 | 0.38 | 0.35 | 0.34 | 0.30 | 11.92 | 10.44 |
| **5-Year** | 3.86 | 0.83 | 0.34 | 0.31 | 0.29 | 0.27 | 8.30 | 7.38 |
| **7-Year** | 4.32 | 0.67 | 0.30 | 0.28 | 0.26 | 0.23 | 6.21 | 5.57 |
| **10-Year** | 4.80 | 0.57 | 0.27 | 0.25 | 0.22 | 0.21 | 4.79 | 4.48 |

**Note**: One-step ahead forecast errors are obtained from the restricted vector error correction model (VECM) estimated with full information maximum likelihood (FIML) for the alternative set of variables.

# 5 Concluding Observations

In the first part of this chapter we have reviewed the new literature aimed at developing macro-finance models that combine finance specifications of the term structure of interest rates with standard macroeconomic aggregate relationships for output and inflation. After presenting the alternative models we have discussed the main features of this new literature - started by the seminal article of Ang and Piazzesi (2003). In the second part we have developed an alternative analysis based on the theory of cointegrated vector autoregressive models and tested it with the data available for the United States. The main finding of our empirical analysis are the following. In the model with only yields we show that, contrary to the standard finding of the related literature, the restrictions implied by the Expectations Hypothesis are satisfied. While in the model with yields and macro factors either the cointegration analysis, either the predictive accuracy statistics confirm the importance of macro factors in explaining the dynamics of the yield curve.

# References

Anderson, H. M., C. W. J. Granger and A. D. Hall (1992), "A Cointegration Analysis of Treasury Bill Yields", *Review of Economics and Statistics*, **8**, 116-26.

Ang, A., S. Dong and M. Piazzesi (2004), "No-Arbitrage Taylor Rules", mimeo University of Chicago.

Ang, A. and M. Piazzesi (2003), "A No-Arbitrage Vector Autoregression of Term Structure Dynamics with Macroeconomic and Latent Variables", *Journal of Monetary Economics*, **50**, 745-87.

Ang, A., M. Piazzesi and M. Wei (2004), „What Does the Yiled Curve Tell us about GDP Growth?", mimeo University of Chicago. *Forthcoming Journal of Econometrics*.

Balbo, A. and Z. Rotondi (2002), "The Term Structure of Interest Rates and the Expectations Hypothesis: New Evidence Based on Swap Interest Rates", paper presented at the XI International "Tor Vergata" Conference on Banking and Finance, Roma.

Balduzzi, P., G. Bertola and S. Foresi (1997), "A Model of Target Changes and the Term Structure of Interest Rates", **39**, 223-49.

Benninga, S. (1980). *Financial Modeling.* The MIT Press.

Boswijk, H. Peter (1995). "Identifiability of Cointegrated Systems," Technical Report, Tinbergen Institute.

Campbell, J. Y. and R. J. Shiller (1987), "Cointegration and Tests of Present value Models", Journal of Political Economy, **95**, 1062-88.

Campbell, J. Y. and R. J. Shiller (1991), "Yield Spreads and Interest Rates Movements: A Bird's Eye View", *Review of Economic Studies*, **58**, 495-514.

Carriero, A., C. Favero, I. Kaminska (2004), "Financial Factors, Macroeconomic Information and the Expectations Theory of the Term Structure of interest Rates*", CEPR Discussion Papers*, no. **4301**.

Clarida, R., Galì, J., Gertler, M., (2000), "Monetary Policy Rules and Macroeconomic Stability: Evidence and Some Theory", *Quarterly Journal of Economics*, **115**, 147-180.

Clements, M. and A.B. Galvao (2003), "Testing the Expectations Theory of the Term Structure of Interest Rates in Threshold Models", *Macroeconomic Dynamics,* **7**, 567-85.

Cox, J. C., J. E. Ingersoll and S. A. Ross (1985), "A Theory of the Term Structure of Interest Rates", *Econometrica*, **53**, 385-407.

Dai, Q. and K. J. Singleton, (2000), "Specification Analysis of Affine Term Structure Models", *Journal of Finance*, **55**, 385-407.

Dai, Q. and K. J. Singleton, (2002), "Expectations Puzzles, Time-Varying Risk Premia, and Affine Models of the Term Structure", *Journal of Financial Economics*, **63**, 415-441.

Diebold, F. and C. Li (2003), "Forecasting the Term Structure of Government Bond Yields", *NBER Working Papers*, no. **10048**.

Diebold, F., Rudebusch, G. and B. Aruoba (2004), "The Macroeconomy and the Yield Curve: A Dynamic Latent Factor Approach", *NBER Working Papers*, no. **10616**.

Driffill, J. and M. Sola (1994), "Testing the Structure of Interest Rates Using a Stationary Vector Autoregression with Regime Switching", *Journal of Economic Dynamics and Control*, **18**, 601-29.

Driffill, J., T. Kenk, M. Sola and F. Spagnolo (2004), "On Model Selection and Markov Switching: An Empirical Examination of Term Structure Models with Regime Shifts", *CEPR Discussion Papers*, no. **4165**.

Duffie, D. and R. Kan, (1996), "A Yield-Factor Model of Interest Rates", *Mathematical Finance*, **6**, 379-406.

Ellingsen, T. and U. Söderström (2001), "Monetary Policy and Market Interest Rates", *American Economic Review*, **91**, 1594-1607.

Enders, W. and C. Granger (1998), "Unit-Root Tests and Asymmetric Adjustment with an Example Using the Term Structure of Interest Rates", *Journal of Business and Economic Statistics*, **16**, 304-11.

Enders, W. and P. Siklos (2001), "Cointegration and Threshold Adjustment", *Journal of Business and Economic Statistics*, **19**, 166-76.

Engle, R. and C. Granger (1987), "Co-Integration and Error Correction: Representation, Estimation and Testing", *Econometrica*, **55**, 251-77.

Engsted, T. and C. Tanggaard (1994), "Cointegration and the US Term Structure", *Journal of Banking and Finance*, **18**, 167-81.

Estrella, A. and F. Mishkin (1998), "Predicting US Recessions: Financial Variables as Leading Indicators", *Review of Economics and Statistics*, **80**, 45-61.

Favero, C. (2001), "Does Macroeconomics Help Understand the Term Structure of Interest Rates?", *CEPR Discussion Papers*, no. **2849**.

Fornari, F. and M. Luisi (2004), "Cross Country Behavior of Affine Term Structure Models", mimeo Bank for International Settlements. Paper presented at the International Conference on Forecasting Financial Markets, June 2004, Paris.

Heat, D., R. Jarrow and A. Morton, (1992), "Bond Pricing and the Term Structure of Interest Rates: A New Methodology for Contingent Claims Valuation", *Econometrica*, **60**, 77-105.

Henderson, D., W. McKibbin, (1993), "A Comparison of Some Basic Monetary Policy Regimes for Open Economies: Implications of Different Degrees of Instrument Adjustment and Wage Persistence", *Carnegie-Rochester Conference Series on Public Policy*, **39**, 221-317.

Hördahl, P., O. Tristani and D. Vestin (2004), "A Joint Econometric Model of Macroeconomic and Term Structure Dynamics", *ECB Working Papers*, no. **405**. Forthcoming Journal Econometrics.

Hull, J. and A. White, (1990), "Pricing Interest-Rate-Derivative Securities", *Review of Financial Studies*, **3**, 573-92.

Litterman, R. and J. Scheinkman, (1991), "Common Factors Affecting Bond Returns", *Journal of Fixed Income*, **1**, 54-61.

Jalil, M. (2004), "Monetary Policy in Retrospective: A Taylor Rule Inspired Exercise", mimeo University of California, San Diego.

Johansen, S. (1988), "Statistical Analysis of Cointegration Vectors", *Journal of Economic Dynamics and Control*, **12**, 231-54.

Johansen, S. and K. Juselius (1990), "Maximum Likelihood Estimation and Inference on Cointegration - with Applications to the Demand for Money", *Oxford Bulletin of Economics and Statistics*, **52**, 169-210.

Judd, J., G., Rudebusch (1998), "Taylor's Rule and the Fed: 1970-1997", Federal Reserve Bank of San Francisco Economic Review, n. 3.

McCulloch, J.H., H.C. Kwon, (1993), "U.S. Term Structure Data: 1947-1991", Ohio State University, mimeo.

Nelson, C.R., and A.F. Siegel (1987), "Parsimonious Modeling of Yield Curves", *Journal of Business*, **60**, 473-489.

Orphanides, A. (2001), "Monetary Policy Rules, Macroeconomic Stability and Inflation: A View from the Trenches", Board of Governors of the Federal Reserve System, *Finance and Economics Discussion Series*, n. **62**. (Forthcoming in Journal of Money, Credit, and banking).

Orphanides, A. (2003a), "The Quest for Prosperity Without Inflation", *Journal of Monetary Economics*, **50**, 633-663.

Orphanides, A. (2003b), "Historical Monetary Policy Analysis and the Taylor Rule", *Journal of Monetary Policy*, **50**, 983-1022.

Osterwald-Lenum, M. (1992), "A Note with Quantiles of the Asymptotic Distribution of the Maximum-Likelihood Cointegration Rank Test Statistics", *Oxford Bulletin of Economics and Statistics*, **54**, 461-472.

Pesaran, H., Y. Shin, (1998), "Generalised Impulse Response Analysis in Linear Multivariate Models", *Economics Letters*, 58, 17-29.

Piazzesi, M., (2003), Affine Term Structure Models, in: Y. Ait-Sahalia and L.P. Hansen (eds.), *Handbook of Financial Econometrics*, forthcoming.

Rendu de Lint, C. and D. Stolin (2003), "The Predictive Power of the Yield Curve: A Theoretical Assessment", *Journal of Monetary Economics*, **50**, 1603-22.

Romer, C., D., Romer (2002), "A rehabilitation of Monetary Policy in the 1950's", American Economic Review, *Papers and Proceedings*, **92**, 121-127.

Rudebusch, G. (1995), "Federal Reserve Interest Targeting, Rational Expectations, and the Term Structure", *Journal of monetary Economics*, **35**, 245-74.

Rudebusch, G. (2002), "Assessing Nominal Income Rules for Monetary Policy with Model and Data Uncertainty", *Economic Journal*, **112**, 402-32.

Rudebusch, G. (2003), "Assessing the Lucas Critique in Monetary Policy Models", Forthcoming in Journal of Money, Credit and Banking.

Rudebusch, G. and L.E.O. Svensson (1999), "Policy Rules for Inflation Targeting", in: J. Taylor (ed.), *Monetary Policy Rules*, University of Chicago Press.

Rudebusch, G. and T. Wu (2003), "A Macro-Finance Model of the Term Structure, Monetary Policy, and the Economy", mimeo Federal Reserve Bank of San Francisco.

Shea, G. S. (1992), "Benchmarking the Expectations Hypothesis of the Interest-Rate Term Structure: An Analysis of Cointegration Vectors", *Journal of Business and Economics Statistics*, **10**, 347-66.

Shiller, R. J., J. Y. Campbell and K. L. Schoenholtz (1983), "Forward Rates and Future Policy: Interpreting the Term Structure of Interest Rates", *Brookings Papers on Economic Activity*, **1**, 173-217.

Stock, J. H. and M. W. Watson (1989), "New Indexes of Coincident and Leading Economic Indicators", in "NBER Macroeconomic Annual: 1989", 351-94, Cambridge, MIT Press.

Stock, J. H. and M. W. Watson (2003), "Forecasting Output and Inflation: The Role of Asset Prices", *Journal of Economic Literature*, **41**, 788-829.

Taylor, J., (1993), "Discretion Versus Policy Rules in Practice", *Carnegie-Rochester Conference Series on Public Policy*, **39**, 195-214.

Vasicek, O. (1977), "An Equilibrium Characterization of the Term Structure", *Journal of Financial Economics*, **5,** 177-88.

Zhang, H. (1993), "Treasury Yields Curves and Cointegration", *Applied Economics*, **25**, 361-367.

In: International Finance and Monetary Policy        ISBN: 1-60021-103-8
Editor: Gleb P. Severov, pp. 209-228        © 2006 Nova Science Publishers, Inc.

Chapter 9

# THE EFFECT OF GOVERNMENT OWNERSHIP ON BANK PROFITABILITY AND RISK: THE SPANISH EXPERIMENT

## *Ana Isabel Fernández, Ana Rosa Fonseca* and *Francisco González*
University of Oviedo, Madrid. España.

## Abstract

This paper analyzes the effects on Spanish savings banks' performance and risk when they shed their mutual structure to become government-owned banks. Such a situation arose in 1985 when Spain's central government allowed regional parliaments to modify savings bank ownership regulations. Regional regulations increased government participation at the expense of depositors' ownership. This regulatory change constitutes a natural experiment to study the consequences of government ownership on bank behavior. The results of our study suggest that enhanced government ownership leads to an increase in risk. This is particularly marked amongst those savings banks that most increased the weight of local and regional governments on their governance bodies. However, no variation in savings bank performance has occurred. The net result, therefore, is an increase in performance-adjusted risk.

**JEL Classification:** G21, G32

**Keywords:** savings banks, government ownership, regulation, performance, risk

## 1   Introduction

This study analyzes the effects on performance and risk-taking that are brought about by increased local and regional government ownership of Spanish savings banks. In Spain, this situation dates back to 1985 and the coming into force of the so-called LORCA law (*Ley de*

* Financial support provided by the Spanish Science and Technology Ministry and FEDER, Project SEC 2002-04765 is gratefully acknowledged. Fonseca would also like to acknowledge the financial support provided by Herrero Bank Foundation

*regulación de normas básicas sobre órganos rectores de las cajas de ahorros*), which laid down the legal framework for savings banks' governance bodies and established the percentage representation of depositors, employees and public administrations alike in savings bank ownership. Regional regulations subsequently modified savings banks' governance, increasing the presence of local and regional governments, basically to the detriment of depositors' representatives. This legislative change constitutes a *de facto* experiment whereby the consequences on performance and risk-taking when savings banks lose their mutual structure to become government-owned banks can be analyzed.

Unlike stock-owned banks, whose governance bodies are made up of a representation of stockholders, the composition of savings banks' governance bodies is established by law and as such is an exogenous variable. One of the potential backlashes of such exogeneity might be to prevent governance bodies from adapting to the optimum requirements of a competitive market, and systematic differences may exist between the levels of efficiency and risk of differently organized thrift institutions (Demsetz and Lehn, 1985). This paper hopes to contribute to the extensive literature that analyzes the effect of organizational form on bank efficiency and risk-taking by considering a novel facet in the field, the shift from a mutual structure to becoming a government-owned bank.

Most of the literature has focused on comparing the efficiency and risk-taking of stock-owned and mutual banks, as these are the two prevailing organizational forms in the United States[1]. Despite the ubiquity of government-owned banks in a raft of countries, as highlighted by La Porta et al (2002), fewer studies have analyzed the impact of state ownership on financial institutions. This is a gap in the scope of research made even more surprising by the fact that savings banks' governance is a key issue in a number of European countries, where debate rages on the question of whether such state-run institutions should be converted into stock-owned banks. Whilst in Belgium, Denmark, Great Britain, Holland, Ireland, Italy and Sweden savings banks have become stock-owned companies, in other countries such as Germany, Austria, Greece, Portugal, Switzerland and Spain there are savings banks that are partially owned by the state or by local and regional governments. Within this latter group of countries there is open debate nowadays on savings banks' ownership. Opinions range from extremes advocating conversion into stock-owned thrift institutions to more moderate proposals that defend current structure whilst calling for some modification of the percentage representation of each collective in savings bank governance. International organizations have added their weight to the debate. The International Monetary Fund (IMF), for example, in its 1999 report, and the organization for Economic Cooperation and Development (OECD) in its report on Spain for the year 2000, both include among its recommendations a consideration of a possible shift in Spanish savings banks' organizational form towards the stock-owned thrift institution.

---

[1] For a comparative analysis of the efficiency of mutal banks and stock-owned banks, see among others, Altumbas et al., 2001; Blair and Placone, 1988, Cebenoyan et al. 1993; Daniels and Sfiridis, 2001; Mester, 1991,1993; O'Hara, 1981; Valnek, 1999; Verbrugge and Golstein, 1981 and Verbrugge and Jahera, 1981. For an analysis of the differences in risk between mutual al and stock-owned banks see, among others, Hadaway and Hadaway, 1984; Masulis, 1987; Cordell et al., 1993; Esty ,1997a, 1997b; Karels and McClatchey, 1999; Lamm-Tennant and Starks, 1993; O'Hara, 1981; Scharand and Unal, 1998 and Verbrugge and Goldstein, 1981).

The relatively few papers that analyze the impact of state ownership on banks' efficiency have yet to come up with conclusive results[2]. La Porta et al. (2002) analyze data from government–owned banks in 92 countries, concluding that the presence of the state "politicizes" the resource allocation process within financial institutions, since it allows governments to finance investments that may well be politically desirable but are nevertheless inefficient from an economic stance. Sapienza (1999) also concludes that Italian state-owned banks pursue political objectives in their lending policy. Barth et al. (2001) use data on government ownership from Bankscope to report that enhanced government ownership of banks is generally associated with less efficient and less well-developed financial systems. Verbrugge et al. (1999) analyze 65 bank privatizations in 25 countries and document a limited improvement in bank profitability, operating efficiency, and non-interest revenue after privatization. As for Spanish savings banks, Melle and Maroto (1999) not only highlight a positive relationship between public administrations' representation on boards of directors and the percentage of loans savings banks give the public sector but also point out that this enhanced lending to the public sector induces a negative effect on savings banks' performance. However, such findings are supported by neither Grifell-Tatjé and Novell (1997) nor Lozano (1998), who claim that government-owned savings banks and stock-owned banks in Spain have similar levels of productive efficiency.

In contrast to studies suggesting the greater efficiency of stock-owned banks, Altunbas et al. (2001) conclude that government-owned German savings banks are more efficient than their respective private counterparts. As for Belgium, Tulkens (1993) also concludes that public banks' branches are relatively more efficient than those of private banks.

The dearth of studies on the impact of government ownership on banking efficiency is even more exacerbated as far as its influence on financial intermediaries' risk taking incentives are concerned, as we know of no studies in this field. This paper therefore hopes to fill a knowledge gap by describing not only the impact of government ownership on savings banks' incentives to take risks but also by analyzing performance change when government ownership replaces a mutual structure. To this end, we use a different approach to the one used in previous studies in that we analyze savings banks' performance change and risk-taking after their governance bodies have been modified by regulations increasing government ownership.

The paper is structured as follows: section 2 presents the characteristics of Spanish savings banks' ownership and the legislative changes introduced since 1985. Section 3 discusses our hypotheses as to the effects of more government ownership on savings bank performance and risk. Section 4 and 5 present the methodology and discuss the empirical results. Finally, section 6 presents the paper's conclusions.

---

[2] However, there exist in the industrial sector abundant evidence showing that public firms are less efficient than their private counterparts. Boardman and Vining (1989) provide a summary table with the empirical evidence on the relative efficiency of public and private firms.

## 2 The Regulation and Governance of Spanish Savings Banks

There are three types of banks in Spain's banking sector: commercial stock-owned banks, savings banks and credit cooperatives. All three types of banks compete under equal conditions in the loan, deposit and financial service markets and their accounting practices, external reporting and credit-risk management standards are also the same to all practical intents and purposes.

In terms of economic importance, commercial and savings banks hold the lion's share of the Spanish market. Thus, Spanish stock banks accounted for 61.46% of the banking system's total balance sheet during the 1984-2000 period, with savings banks chalking up 35.24% and cooperatives holding a mere 3.30%. Table 1 gives percentages of total assets, deposits and loans for each type of bank as part of Spain's banking system, and also gives the number of offices and employees that they have.

Savings banks were initially created in 1835 in Spain as non-profit making organizations. They had a clearly defined social commitment and instead of paying dividends, benefits were allocated to social and cultural activities. Furthermore, they were involved in a different business to commercial stock-owned banks. Differences extended to both geography and client-type, as savings banks basically ran their business each within their particular region, catering for families and small and medium-sized businesses. On the contrary, stock banks were oriented to the national market and industrial firms were more important clients. Two further hallmarks of savings banks were the higher percentage of loans granted to the public sector and the higher percentage of mortgage loans to total private loans. These differences are rooted in state legislation, which banned savings banks from operating beyond their geographic boundaries and obliged them to direct part of their activities towards families. These limitations were withdrawn, however, in 1977, and since 1989 stock banks and savings banks have been subject to the same operative regulations. Nevertheless, despite there no longer being legal differences relating to how each type of bank may operate, time has only moderated their hallmarks, as each continues to operate in the markets where it had its largest market share.

At present, the only regulatory difference between stock and savings banks in Spain relates to ownership. The greatest idiosyncrasy of the Spanish savings bank is its peculiar ownership structure, which falls neither into the category of stock-based institutions, nor that of mutuals. Their basic governance mechanisms are the General Assembly and the Board of Directors, made up of representatives from four groups whose percentage representation is established by law.

Table 1 Importance of each type of bank ownership in Spain

| | 1984 | 1985 | 1986 | 1987 | 1988 | 1989 | 1990 | 1991 | 1992 | 1993 | 1994 | 1995 | 1996 | 1997 | 1998 | 1999 | 2000 | Mean |
|---|---|---|---|---|---|---|---|---|---|---|---|---|---|---|---|---|---|---|
| **Savings Banks** | | | | | | | | | | | | | | | | | | |
| % total assets | 30.14 | 32.11 | 34.28 | 34.82 | 37.29 | 38.66 | 38.42 | 36.51 | 35.43 | 32.50 | 33.37 | 33.62 | 34.72 | 35.02 | 36.48 | 37.26 | 38.41 | 35.24 |
| % total deposits | 35.36 | 39.12 | 42.86 | 43.49 | 45.25 | 45.74 | 45.30 | 45.48 | 46.98 | 18.31 | 19.75 | 49.47 | 51.70 | 51.71 | 50.73 | 51.31 | 51.22 | 42.57 |
| % total loans | 26.33 | 26.55 | 28.28 | 30.40 | 32.58 | 34.07 | 34.41 | 33.13 | 35.51 | 37.78 | 38.09 | 38.65 | 39.02 | 40.06 | 41.50 | 42.17 | 43.26 | 35.40 |
| N. branches | 10,440 | 10,797 | 11,061 | 11,754 | 12,252 | 13,168 | 13,720 | 14,031 | 14,291 | 14,485 | 14,880 | 15,214 | 16,094 | 16,636 | 17,582 | 18,119 | 19,268 | 14,341 |
| N. employees | 69,438 | 71,042 | 72,707 | 74,530 | 78,023 | 83,026 | 84,609 | 83,359 | 82,900 | 82,710 | 83,758 | 84,336 | 87,370 | 90,153 | 93,812 | 97,276 | 101,718 | 83,574 |
| **Stocks Banks** | | | | | | | | | | | | | | | | | | |
| % total assets | 66.73 | 64.48 | 62.21 | 61.74 | 59.43 | 58.28 | 58.48 | 60.26 | 61.60 | 64.62 | 63.60 | 63.14 | 61.85 | 61.47 | 59.89 | 59.12 | 57.92 | 61.46 |
| % total deposits | 60.38 | 56.07 | 52.15 | 51.31 | 49.62 | 49.29 | 49.78 | 49.49 | 47.89 | 46.35 | 44.62 | 44.64 | 41.82 | 41.33 | 43.28 | 42.43 | 42.46 | 47.82 |
| % total loans | 70.27 | 69.93 | 68.18 | 66.10 | 64.40 | 62.97 | 62.54 | 63.76 | 61.10 | 58.82 | 58.14 | 57.22 | 56.60 | 55.29 | 53.74 | 52.90 | 51.80 | 60.81 |
| N. branches | 16,412 | 16,606 | 16,518 | 16,498 | 16,691 | 16,677 | 16,917 | 17,824 | 18,058 | 17,636 | 17,557 | 17,842 | 17,674 | 17,530 | 17,450 | 17,140 | 15,811 | 17,108 |
| N. employees | 164,330 | 161,621 | 157,805 | 155,334 | 154,696 | 155,658 | 157,010 | 161,987 | 159,281 | 152,845 | 151,174 | 148,946 | 142,827 | 139,198 | 135,164 | 127,889 | 122,374 | 126,361 |
| **Credit Cooperatives** | | | | | | | | | | | | | | | | | | |
| % total assets | 3.13 | 3.41 | 3.51 | 3.44 | 3.28 | 3.06 | 3.10 | 3.23 | 2.98 | 2.88 | 3.03 | 3.24 | 3.42 | 3.52 | 3.64 | 3.62 | 3.67 | 3.30 |
| % total deposit | 4.26 | 4.81 | 4.99 | 5.20 | 5.13 | 4.97 | 4.91 | 5.04 | 5.13 | 5.34 | 5.63 | 5.89 | 6.48 | 6.96 | 5.99 | 6.26 | 6.32 | 5.49 |
| % total loans | 3.40 | 3.52 | 3.54 | 3.50 | 3.02 | 2.96 | 3.05 | 3.11 | 3.40 | 3.40 | 3.78 | 4.13 | 4.37 | 4.65 | 4.76 | 4.92 | 4.94 | 3.79 |
| N. branches | 3,315 | 3,350 | 3,382 | 3,248 | 3,029 | 2,890 | 2,919 | 3,018 | 3,080 | 3,072 | 3,107 | 3,195 | 3,311 | 3,468 | 3,607 | 3,697 | 3,888 | 2,883 |
| N. employees | 10,896 | 10,823 | 10,225 | 10,153 | 9,674 | 9,592 | 9,968 | 10,643 | 11,016 | 11,225 | 11,195 | 11,626 | 12,024 | 12,804 | 13,286 | 13,855 | 14,495 | 10,794 |

Table 1 reports total assets, deposits and loans for each type of bank as a percentage of the whole Spanish system for the 1984-2000 period. The number of branches and employees is also shown.

In 1985, the 31/1985 national law, or LORCA law, unified what until then had been a gamut of differing statute-regulated governance systems established in different Spanish savings banks by establishing the following percentage governance representation: 1) 40% local and regional governments, 2) 44% depositors, 3) 11% founders and 4) 5% employees. Since in some cases the founding members also happened to be local and regional governments, the final percentage of public administrations in savings banks' General Assemblies and on Boards of Directors can be as high as 51%. In this way, the LORCA law unified the disparity in Spanish savings bank governance, which had previously been established differently depending on each savings bank's statutes[1]. With a structure whereby ownership lies with depositors, employees and governments, savings banks may be described as hybrids of mutual, cooperative and a government-owned banks.

Table 2 Participation of depositors, employees and regional and local governments in the ownership of savings banks

| | | EMPLOYEES | DEPOSITORS | LOCAL AND REGIONAL GOVERNMENTS | FOUNDERS | OTHER INSTITUTIONS | TOTAL LOCAL AND REGIONAL GOVERNMENTS |
|---|---|---|---|---|---|---|---|
| NATIONAL LAW 31/1985 | | 5 | 44 | 40 | 11 | | |
| REGION | YEAR REGIONAL LAW PUBLICATION | | | | | | |
| ANDALUCIA | 1986 | 5 | 44 | 40 | 11 | | 57.78 |
| ARAGÓN | 1991 | 7 | 41 | 42 | 10 | | 42 |
| ASTURIAS | 1988 | 5 | 20 | 40 | 35 | | 75 |
| BALEARES | 1989 | 5 | 39 | 34 | 16 | 6 | 45 |
| CANARIAS | 1990 | 5 | 26 | 44 | 10 | 15 | 59.95 |
| CANTABRIA | 1990 | 5 | 22 | 38 | 10 | 25 | 66 |
| CATALUÑA | 1985 | 5-10 | 30-40 | 15-25 | 25-35 | | 30.93 |
| CASTILLA LA MANCHA | 1997 | 7 | 22 | 40 | 10 | 21 | 70.05 |
| CASTILLA LEÓN | 1990 | 5-10 | 35-40 | 25-35 | 5-10 | 5-30 | 42.08 |
| EXTREMADURA | 1994 | 5 | 44 | 40 | 11 | | 41.1 |
| GALICIA | 1985 | 5-15 | 30-40 | 15-25 | 25-35 | | 31.9 |
| MADRID | 1992 | 8 | 28 | 32 | 20 | 12 | 55 |
| MURCIA | 1988 | 7 | 30 | 33 | 30 | | 63 |
| NAVARRA | 1987 | 5 | 44 | 40 | 11 | | 58.3 |
| PAÍS VASCO | 1991 | 5 | 41 | 32 | 22 | | 53.3 |
| LA RIOJA | 1988 | 5 | 31 | 31 | 33 | | 64.4 |
| VALENCIA | 1990 | 11 | 28 | 28 | 5 | 28 | 57.7 |

This Table presents the participation percentage that employees, depositors and regional and local governments have in the General Assembly and Board of Directors of the savings banks as established in 1985 by Law 3/81 and in each of the regional laws passed later. The last column shows the total government ownership after adding the ownership governments have directly by law to the one they have being savings bank's founders.

However, the LORCA law also empowered Regional Parliaments to modify these representation percentages. These post-LORCA regulations, which are summarized in Table

---

[1]Although dispersion would demand an individual analysis of each savings bank, it is nevertheless possible to indicate that savings banks' structure before 1985 was basically mutual since depositors had ownership percentages of over 50% in most savings banks, and in some cases these reached 83%.

2, have tended to increase the presence of local and regional governments on the governance bodies of savings banks at the expense of depositors. They also returned minor levels of representation to a range of "other institutions" whose pre-LORCA representation has been annulled by the new law[2]. According to regional regulations, the group with the greatest representation is public administrations. Whereas depositors' representation stands at an average of 33%, local and regional government participation ranges between a minimum 30.93% and a maximum 75%, depending on whether the public administrations are also founders or members of other institutions. The final column in Table 2 presents the total percentage that public administrations have on average in savings banks' ownership, including additional percentages assigned to local or regional bodies by dint of them doubling as savings bank founders. The new percentages established for depositors by regional laws imply an average fall of 11% with respect to the percentage LORCA established for depositors, whilst the maximum percentage public administrations can reach rises from 51% to 75%. The employees' percentage has remained generally stable at 5% and has increased only in four regions to percentages ranging between 10% and 15%.

In short, regional regulations have triggered a decrease in the mutual character of Spanish savings banks, coupled with an increase in state ownership. This process of partial conversion of mutual banks into state banks is atypical and different from the conversion processes analyzed so far in the literature, namely, the conversion in the USA of mutual banks into stock-owned banks[3] and the privatization process of public firms in a number of countries around the world[4].

The latest change in ownership regulations of Spanish savings banks was in 2002, when a "Financing Law" came into force that capped public administration participation in savings banks' governing bodies at 50%. This meant modifying the structure of the General Assemblies of savings banks in 12 of the 17 self-governing regions of Spain.

# 3 Changes in Savings Banks' Ownership and Banks' Performance and Risk

Firm's property rights theory suggests that state and mutual enterprises should perform less efficiently and less profitably than private enterprises (Boardman and Vining, 1989). The reason suggested is straightforward: a lack of capital market discipline weakens owners' control over management, leaving it freer to pursue its own interests and giving it fewer incentives to be efficient.

However, the increase in political control brought on by the inception of regional laws fail to affect the non-existent discipline exerted by the capital market on savings banks' managers, merely substituting depositors' control for political control. Therefore, in order to predict the effects of the change, not only must the percentage representation of each group – public administrations, employees and depositors – be analyzed but also the incentives of

---

[2] These "other organizations" to whom regional government regulations again give a minority presence on governance bodies of savings banks vary from one region to the next depending on the different charitable and cultural associations and organizations in each region.

[3] See, among others, Hadaway and Hadaway (1984), Masulis (1987), Cordell et al. (1993), Esty (1997a, 1997b) and Schrand and Unal (1998).

[4] Megginson and Netter (2001) carry out a survey of empirical studies on privatization.

each of them to monitor and supervise managers' decisions. The partial guarantee of deposits and the dispersion of the depositor group have been used as arguments to justify high management discretionality in mutual banks, as the depositors lack the incentives to monitor bank managers (O'Hara, 1981; Rasmunsen, 1988; Dewatripont and Tirole, 1993a, 1993b). Coverage of deposit insurance in Spain is limited to 20,000 euros per depositor. However, history would suggest that the partial guarantee of the deposit insurance is "de facto" an implicitly total guarantee, as historically the banking systems has always guaranteed 100% of the deposits of insolvent banks. The supervisory authority's reaction is based upon the belief that when a bank is "*too big to fail*" the social backlash caused by there not being total coverage is enormous.

As has been pointed out, there is little incentive for depositors to monitor bank managers. Nor do the structure and characteristics of depositor groups encourage such control and follow-up. Firstly, the representation system is random and disregards the amount deposited by each depositor. Nor can a market system be instigated whereby voting rights can be negotiated freely, as delegating votes is not allowed. Under such circumstances, depositors are unlikely to give the necessary consideration to decisions on issues relevant to their interests. On the one hand, a depositor who is really interested in playing a role in the bank's management may be deprived of the opportunity by the random nature of the electoral process. On the other hand, those who are elected may lack the incentive to invest resources in obtaining information about the bank because third parties cannot be prevented from benefiting form the efforts that they make. In short, the considerable dispersion of a large number of depositors, the random nature of the election of representatives process, and the high percentage participation of local and regional governments all suggest that depositors have little influence on decision taking in savings banks and that much is left to the discretion of bank managers.

However, enhanced state ownership of savings banks at the expense of depositors entails lowering the weight of management objectives and increasing political ones. Both La Porta et al. (2002) and Sapienza (1999) show that one of the spin-offs of politicizing decision-taking in government-owned banks is the pursuit of politically attractive but financially unprofitable projects. Most financial economist see political influence over depositary institutions' credit allocation as the major reason for the financial crisis of many countries in Latin America and Southeast Asia (Kaufman, 1999). It seems to be the case that politization in decision-taking has a negative effect on performance, which adds to the capital market's lack of discipline which already characterized the mutual structure.

Unlike the consequences on bank performance, there are arguments that suggest both a positive and a negative effect on banks' risk-taking after the introduction of greater political control.

On the one hand, the fact that public administrations are major clients of savings banks may increase the ex-ante bank risk-taking incentives by allowing them to substitute losses from failed risky investment with subsidies (Barth et al. 2001). Furthermore, the subsidies option also encourages the politization of decision taking and the tendency to undertake politically desirable but financially risky projects. In this case, the final result would be an increase in savings banks' risk-taking.

On the other hand, political interest in maintaining savings banks as an instrument by which to fulfill political objectives, as shown by La Porta et al. (2002) and Sapienza (1999), may lead to risk limitation with the joint aims of guaranteeing the continuity of the institution and avoiding a crisis in the savings bank. In other words, politicians may have incentives to limit savings bank risk up to a level that guarantees their solvency so that they do not lose an instrument that may be difficult to substitute. The threat of losing a political instrument would thereby have the effect of discouraging risk, just as the loss of high charter value does for stock-owned banks in regulated environments, as Keeley (1990) was first to point out.

Since political participation in savings banks' decision-taking could favor both higher and lower risk levels, the effect regulatory changes that increase state participation may have on savings banks' risk level is an empirical question. Analysis of post-legislation savings bank risk variation will highlight which of the two hypotheses prevails.

Even though regional government regulations basically consisted of increasing the presence of public administrations in savings banks to the detriment of depositors, they also led to a rise from 5% to 15% employee ownership in four regions of Spain, which means that savings banks share some of the hallmarks of cooperatives. Jensen and Meckling (1979) point out that employee participation in company ownership may lead to penchants for investment projects that recoup investment in a period that is equal to or less than the time the employee will remain in the organization, just as it may also provoke rejection of profitable projects that provide cash flows beyond the term of employment. Moreover, there are other incentives to take decisions that will have negative impacts on savings banks' profits, such as setting extremely lucrative salaries and other perks. As far as risk is concerned, employees will clearly be inclined towards low-risk investments that will not endanger job stability or salary levels. As is also the case with managers, employees have much of their wealth tied up with the organization they work for, and are therefore more loath to take risks than other stakeholders who can diversify their risk to a greater extent. The logic of these arguments leads to the prediction that greater employee ownership of savings banks should bring about a reduction in both profits and risk.

# 4 Empirical Analysis

In order to test the effect that different participation of public administrations, employees and depositors has on savings banks' operative behavior, we compare bank performance and risk before and after the introduction of the above-mentioned regional regulations.

Information on the composition of savings banks' governance bodies was obtained from their annual reports and, failing this, was requested from the thrift institution itself by mail. Savings banks that had been involved in mergers were excluded from the analysis so that other co-existing factors could be isolated[5] . This yielded relevant information on 30 savings banks for between 1984 and 1999, 24 of whose boards of directors underwent some change as a result of the new law.

Since savings banks have no market value, it is impossible to use market value-based performance and risk measures. We therefore use two different measures of return on assets to measure performance. Earnings are measured after (ROA1) and before (ROA2) depreciation and provisions for loan losses reserves. The use of these two measures is

---

[5] Mergers in Spanish savings banks were rife during the period of analysis. In 1984 there were 77 savings banks in Spain, whereas at the end of 1999 numbers had dropped to 50. This merger process was especially intense at the beginning of the 1990s. In 1990, 17 savings banks dissolved and two were absorbed, creating 7 new entities and in 1991, 9 entities dissolved and one was absorbed to create two new savings banks.

intended to isolate the impact of possible profit smoothing that can be caused by managerial discretionality regarding the allowances for depreciation and loan losses provisions[6].

Following Esty (1997a), Williams (1999) and Cebenoyan et al. (1995,1999) we use the time series profit variability, defined as the standard deviation of the two measures of return on assets (RISK1 and RISK2), respectively, as a measure of risk. To analyze the change in the ROA-adjusted risk we use the coefficient of variation, where the standard deviation of the return on assets is divided by the average return on assets over the same period (CV=RISK/ROA).

Change in savings banks' performance and risk-taking is analyzed by comparing the ROA, RISK and CV during the four-year periods before and after the introduction of the regional regulations that modified the composition of the savings banks' governance bodies in the respective region. The year when the regional law was enforced is omitted in the analysis to better separate the possible effect of the law on savings bank performance and risk. Our analysis covers the period 1984-1999, since in our sample of savings banks the first change in ownership following regional regulations occurred in 1988 and the last in 1995.

Differences observed over the pre- and post-regulation periods may be due to economic factors that affect the sector which are unrelated to modifications to savings banks' governance. In order to overcome this problem, the ROA, the standard deviation of ROA and the coefficient of variation for each savings bank in the four preceding and ensuing years are adjusted by dividing each variable by the respective median of the six savings banks that did not change their ownership or governance bodies between 1984 y 1999[7]. The three performance, risk and risk-adjusted measures are the following:

$$AROA_{it} = \frac{ROA_{it}}{NCROA_t} \tag{1}$$

$$ARISK_{it} = \frac{RISK_{it}}{NCRISK_t} \tag{2}$$

$$ACV_{it} = \frac{CV_{it}}{NCCV_t} \tag{3}$$

where $AROA_{it}$, $ARISK_{it}$ and $ACV_{it}$ are, respectively, the adjusted return on assets, the adjusted risk and the adjusted coefficient of variation of savings bank i in period t. $NCROA_t$, $NCRISK_t$ and $NCCV_t$, are, respectively, the median of the return on assets, risk and coefficient of variation of the six savings banks that did not experience any variation in their governance bodies through out 1984 and 1999[8]. All these variables are estimated for the pre-

---

[6] Beatty et al. (1995) and Scholes et al. (1990), among others, have offered evidence of income smoothing in commercial banks.

[7] The six savings banks that did not change their board of directors belong to three different self-governing regions: Andalucía, Castilla La Mancha and Navarra.

[8] Besides the estimations in this paper, we also analyzed a different period – three years before and after the passing of the regional regulation. The risk adjustment of the six savings banks that did not change their governance

regulatory change period and for the post-regulatory change period.

A descriptive analysis of each performance and risk measure, together with the percentages of public administrations (GOVERN), depositors (DEP) and employees (EMP) owning savings banks during the period of four years before and four years after the change in the ownership, is shown in Table 3.

Table 3 Descriptive statistics

| VARIABLES | BEFORE REGIONAL LEGISLATION | | | | | AFTER REGIONAL LEGISLATION | | | | |
|---|---|---|---|---|---|---|---|---|---|---|
| | Mean | Median | Standard deviation | Maximun | Mínimum | Mean | Median | Standard deviation | Máximum | Mínimum |
| GOVERN | 25.875 | 28.000 | 22.357 | 68.00 | 0.00 | 42.667 | 41.500 | 16.523 | 75.00 | 20.00 |
| EMP | 6.208 | 5.000 | 4.393 | 25.00 | 3.00 | 8.500 | 8.000 | 3.612 | 18.00 | 5.00 |
| DEP | 56.791 | 54.500 | 16.699 | 83.00 | 22.00 | 37.292 | 40.000 | 6.670 | 45.00 | 20.00 |
| LN(AT) | 12.080 | 12.164 | 1.285 | 15.05 | 8.46 | 12.665 | 12.719 | 1.306 | 15.80 | 9.13 |
| AROA1 | 0.858 | 0.863 | 0.141 | 1.20 | 0.59 | 0.874 | 0.854 | 0.132 | 1.21 | 0.61 |
| AROA2 | 0.781 | 0.784 | 0.308 | 1.36 | 0.25 | 0.884 | 0.809 | 0.298 | 1.55 | 0.41 |
| ARISK1 | 1.076 | 0.944 | 0.604 | 2.25 | 0.20 | 0.794 | 0.561 | 0.718 | 2.88 | 0.06 |
| ARISK2 | 1.165 | 0.996 | 0.719 | 2.61 | 0.09 | 1.082 | 0.878 | 0.775 | 3.53 | 0.12 |
| ACV1 | 1.347 | 1.133 | 0.696 | 2.71 | 0.32 | 1.206 | 1.080 | 0.745 | 3.30 | 0.17 |
| ACV2 | 1.640 | 1.637 | 0.928 | 3.14 | 0.15 | 0.994 | 0.664 | 1.063 | 3.94 | 0.08 |
| # observations | 24 | | | | | 24 | | | | |

This table presents the descriptive statistical tests of the percentages of governments (GOVERN), employees (EMP) and depositors (DEP) in savings banks' ownership as well as the adjusted return on assets (AROA), the adjusted standard deviation of the return of assets (ARISK) and the adjusted coefficient of variation (ACV) of Spanish savings banks during the period of four years before and four years after the passing of the regional regulation.

# 5   Results

## 5.1   Mean Differences

Change in savings banks' risk levels after the increase of government ownership is initially measured through the mean differences between the period of four years before and four years after regional regulation enforcement. Three statistical tests were used to analyze the statistical significance of the change. Together with the parametric mean difference test, we used two other non-parametric tests: the Wilcoxon signed rank test and the sign test. The non-parametric tests do not require any assumptions about the distribution of the variables analyzed and are more adequate in the case of reduced sample sizes[9]. The Wilcoxon signed rank test analyzes whether the sum of ranks of the positive differences differs significantly from the sum of ranks of the negative differences. The sign test, which compares the number of differences that are positive with the number of differences that are negative, is a less powerful test than Wilcoxon's since it does not take into account the magnitude of the differences.

---

bodies was undertaken by differences instead of by quotient. The results were basically the same and for this reason are not reported in the paper.

[9] The Shapiro-Wilk normality test has shown that all the variables meet the normality condition. The statistical test t of means is therefore justified.

The differences in AROA, ARISK, ACV and the ownership percentages of each collective between the preceding and the ensuing period are shown in Table 4.

Table 4 Mean differences

| VARIABLES | Mean difference | | Test t | Wilcoxon test | | Sign test | | |
|---|---|---|---|---|---|---|---|---|
| | Post value previous-value | Shapiro-Wilk test | | Sum positive ranks | Sum negative ranks | Value Z | Positive differences | Negative differences |
| GOVERN | 16.792 | 0.923*** | 6.74*** | 1.50 | 274.50 | -4.159*** | 1 | 22*** |
| EMP | 2.292 | 0.852*** | 1.76* | 31.00 | 140.00 | -2.376** | 3 | 15*** |
| IMPOSIT | -19.500 | 0.947*** | -6.39*** | 8.00 | 292.00 | -4.059*** | 22*** | 2 |
| LN(AT) | 0.575 | 0.964*** | 9.35*** | 0.00 | 300.00 | -4.286*** | 0 | 24*** |
| AROA1 | 0.0156 | 0.944*** | 0.917 | 190.00 | 110.00 | -1.143 | 16 | 8 |
| AROA2 | 0.1029 | 0.944*** | 1.411 | 197.00 | 103.00 | -1.343 | 15 | 9 |
| ARISK1 | -0.014 | 0.959*** | -0.09 | 143.00 | 157.00 | -0.200 | 12 | 12 |
| ARISK2 | -0.370 | 0.972*** | -1.89* | 91.00 | 209.00 | -1.69* | 8 | 16 |
| ACV1 | -0.142 | 0.977*** | -0.71 | 190.00 | 110.00 | -1.143 | 15 | 9 |
| ACV2 | -0.646 | 0.955*** | -3.02*** | 242.00 | 58.00 | -2.629*** | 17* | 7 |

* Significantly different from zero at the 10% level
** Significantly different from zero at the 5% level
*** Significantly different from zero at the 1% level

This table shows the mean difference between the period of four years before and after the modification of savings banks' ownership introduced by the regional regulation together with the values of the parametric statistical test of mean difference and the non-parametric Wilcoxon and sign tests. GOVERN is the percentage of government ownership, EMP is the percentage of employees' ownership and DEP is the percentage of depositors' ownership. AROA1 and AROA2 are the adjusted return on assets before and after, respectively, depreciation and provisions for loan losses reserves. ARISK1 and ARISK2 are the adjusted standard deviation of two previous measures of return on assets. Finally, ACV1 and ACV2 are the adjusted coefficient of variation, defined from the two measures of performance and risk previously indicated.

All three tests indicate that changes in the composition of the savings banks' governance bodies are statistically significant. There is a 16.8% average increase in local and regional governments' and a 2.3% increase in employees' participation at the expense of a 19.5% drop in depositors' representation by 19.5%. Analysis of the change in savings banks' size, measured through the natural logarithm of total assets, points to it increasing over both periods of time.

The results of the three tests are similar when we analyze performance and risk changes. The return on assets of the savings banks that increased government ownership did not undergo any statistically significant variation between the period preceding and following the change in ownership. However, the reduction in the standard deviation of the return on assets before depreciation and provisions for loan loss reserves (ARISK2) is statistically significant. This risk reduction is also statistically significant after adjusting for performance, as shown by the change in the coefficient of variation (ACV2).

## 5.2 Regression Analysis

As Healy et al. (1992) point out, changes in savings banks' performance and risk between the periods preceding and following ownership change may also be due to continuity in the savings bank's trend rather than to the effect of the change in the percentage representation of each of the collectives involved in the savings banks' governance bodies. The benchmark for post-change performance and post-change risk thus depend on their relation with those of the previous period. If there were no relation between preceding and ensuing values, the appropriate benchmark for performance and risk in the latter period would be zero and the analysis of mean difference previously carried out would offer an adequate measure of the change in both variables. Alternatively, the appropriate benchmark would be the performance (risk) in the preceding period if the savings bank that before the modification in the regional legislation has levels of performance (risk) higher or lower than those of the savings banks that do not vary the composition of their board of directors is likely to realize the same result after the regulatory change in the ownership. In order to correct this problem, the abnormal variation of ROA, RISK and CV is obtained from the intercepts of three regressions in which the adjusted values in the post-change period are used as dependent variables, and the adjusted values of ROA, RISK and CV in the preceding period as independent variables. The OLS-estimated regressions were the following:

$$AROA_{i, post} = \alpha_0 + \alpha_1 AROA_{i, pre} + \alpha_2 CSIZE_i + \sum \alpha_t Y_{it} + \varepsilon_i \tag{4}$$

$$ARISK_{i, post} = \beta_0 + \beta_1 ARISK_{i, pre} + \beta_2 CSIZE_i + \sum \beta_t Y_{it} + \omega_i \tag{5}$$

$$ACV_{i, post} = \delta_0 + \delta_1 ACV_{i, pre} + \delta_2 CSIZE_i + \sum \delta_t Y_{it} + \xi_i \tag{6}$$

where $AROA_{i,post}$, $ARISK_{i,post}$, $ACV_{i,post}$ are, the return on assets, risk and the coefficient of variation of savings bank i during the four-year period after the year when the regional legislation related to savings bank $i$ was introduced, divided by the median of each equivalent variable for the six savings banks that do not modify their ownership. $AROA_{i,pre}$, $ARISK_{i,pre}$, $ACV_{i,pre}$ are, the return on assets, risk and the coefficient of variation of savings bank $i$ for the four-year period prior to the introduction of regional legislation adjusted by the median of the 6 savings banks.

The value of coefficients $\alpha_1$, $\beta_1$ y $\gamma_1$ would capture any correlation between the levels of performance, risk and performance-adjusted risk of the preceding and ensuing periods, so that ($\alpha_1 AROA_{pre,i}$, $\beta_1 ARISK_{pre,i}$ and $\gamma_1 ACV_{pre,i}$) measure the effect of pre-regulation changes, respectively, in performance, risk and performance-adjusted risk during the post-regulation period. The intercept of each regression ($\alpha_0$, $\beta_0$, $\gamma_0$) would be, respectively, our measure of abnormal savings banks' performance, risk and performance-adjusted risk originated by ownership change.

Pre- and post-regulation changes in size, ($CSIZE_i$), - as measured by the natural logarithm of total assets - are also controlled for in these regressions. Mean difference analysis had revealed an increase in savings banks' size after regional legislation had been enacted, thus expanding financial intermediaries' opportunities for diversification and potentially reducing risk levels. Thus, changes in savings bank size must be controlled for before any risk differences can be attributed to ownership change. Finally, since regional legislations were enforced in different years for each region, a set of time dummies is introduced for each year in which regional regulations were passed ($Y_{88}$, $Y_{89}$, $Y_{90}$, $Y_{91}$, $Y_{92}$, $Y_{93}$, $Y_{95}$). Thus, $Y_{it}$ takes the value 1 if savings bank ownership modifications occurred in the year t and takes the value zero otherwise. These variables are intended to control possible time effects derived from the fact that changes in regional regulations occurred in different years. The dummy for 1988 is omitted from the estimations.

The results of these regressions for the 24 savings banks that modified the composition of their governance bodies are shown in Table 5.

Table 5 Regressions of change in risk

| | $AROA1_{post,i}$ | $AROA2_{post,i}$ | $ARISK1_{post,i}$ | $ARISK2_{post,i}$ | $ACV1_{post,i}$ | $ACV2_{post,i}$ |
|---|---|---|---|---|---|---|
| | (1) | (2) | (3) | (4) | (5) | (6) |
| INTERCEPT | 0.295 | 1.111*** | 2.715*** | 2.478* | 2,77** | 1,56 |
| | (1.22) | (3.28) | (3.39) | (2.04) | (2,52) | (1,18) |
| $AROA1_{pre,i}$ | 0.838*** | | | | | |
| | (5.02) | | | | | |
| $AROA2_{pre,i}$ | | 0.399** | | | | |
| | | (2.72) | | | | |
| $ARISK1_{pre,i}$ | | | 0.064 | | | |
| | | | (0.31) | | | |
| $ARISK2_{pre,i}$ | | | | 0.167 | | |
| | | | | (0.65) | | |
| $ACV1_{pre,i}$ | | | | | -0,09 | |
| | | | | | (-0,39) | |
| $ACV2_{pre,i}$ | | | | | | 0,45** |
| | | | | | | (2,40) |
| $CSIZE_i$ | -0.014 | -0.112 | -2.919** | -4.23*** | -2,86** | -4,08** |
| | (-0.007) | (-0.26) | (-2.61) | (-3.07) | (-2,02) | (-2,50) |
| D89 | -0.130 | -0.509* | 0.876 | 0.441 | 1,34 | 0,59 |
| | (-1.26) | (-1.86) | (1.05) | (0.50) | (1,48) | (0,59) |
| D90 | -0.155* | -0.748*** | 0.364 | 0.116 | 0,42 | 0,70 |
| | (-1.84) | (-3.37) | (0.60) | (0.15) | (0,55) | (0,84) |
| D91 | -0.150* | -0.540** | -0.362 | 0.494 | -0,20 | 1,07 |
| | (-1.91) | (2.73) | (-0.66) | (0.64) | (-0,28) | (1,42) |
| D92 | -0.093 | -0.206 | 0.247 | 0.835 | 0,68 | 0,92 |
| | (-1.08) | (-0.97) | (0.44) | (1.08) | (0,99) | (1,22) |
| D93 | -0.284** | -0.993*** | -0.771 | 1.653* | -0,56 | 4,24*** |
| | (-2.74) | (3.60) | (-0.99) | (1.82) | (-0,63) | (4,22) |
| D95 | -0.147 | -0.523* | -0.368 | 0.108 | -0,13 | 0,88 |
| | (-1.37) | (-1.90) | (-0.51) | (0.10) | (-0,15) | (0,82) |
| # observations | 24 | 24 | 24 | 24 | 24 | 24 |
| Adjusted $R^2$ | 69.94 | 58.75 | 39.12 | 26.78 | 28,96% | 56,49% |
| F | 7.69*** | 5.09*** | 2.85** | 2.05* | 2,17* | 4,73*** |

* Significantly different from zero at the 10% level
** Significantly different from zero at the 5% level
*** Significantly different from zero at the 1% level

This table shows the OLS estimations of the equations [4], [5] and [6]. The dependent variables are the adjusted return on assets (AROA1post,i; AROA2post,i), the adjusted standard deviation of the return on assets (ARISKpost,i: ARISKpost,i) and the adjusted coefficient of variation (ACV1post,i; ACVpost,i) in the period of four years after the change in the regional legislation. Each of the variables is adjusted by quotient by the respective measure in the six savings banks that do not change their governance structure. As independent variables we introduce in each of the regressions the same dependent variable but measured in the period of four years previous to the change in the board of directors. As control variables we introduce the change in the natural logarithm of total assets that each of the savings bank experiences between the previous period and the posterior period (CSIZE) and a set of dummy variables corresponding to each of the years when a change in the regional legislation has occurred, which take the value 1 if the modification of the savings banks' ownership has taken place in the year t and take the value 0 otherwise. In the estimations the dummy corresponding to the year 1998 is omitted. The values of the t-student test are shown in brackets.

The intercepts of regressions (3) and (4) shown in Table 5 indicate an increase in the standard deviation of both measures of return on assets after controlling for size change and the correlation between pre-and post-regulation change. This increase in volatility goes hand in hand with an increase in the return on assets before depreciation and provisions for loan losses reserves (column 2) but not with the return on assets after depreciation and provisions for loan losses reserves (column 1). The increase in risk but not in performance after depreciation and provisions for loan losses reserves causes the coefficient of variation to also experience a statistically significant increase when performance is measured after depreciation and provisions for loan losses reserves (column 5). Size change has a negative coefficient in the regressions of the standard deviation of return on assets and the coefficient of variation. This latter result is consistent with the diminishing effect of risk that has traditionally been associated with size when size increases the diversification opportunities for thrifts. Thus, the reduction in savings banks' risk that the mean difference analysis highlighted might be motivated more by the increase in size, than by the change in the savings banks' ownership, since an increase rather than a reduction in savings banks' risk is observed together with an increase in government ownership when we correct for size and for the correlation between pre-and post legal change in the regression analysis.

Two additional explanatory variables – each savings bank's change in government ownership ($CGOVERN_i$) and change in employees' ownership ($CEMP_i$) triggered by regional changes in the law – are also included in the equations for a more in-depth analysis of the impact of ownership change on performance and risk. The squares of these two variables ($CGOVERNQ_i$ and $CEMPQ_i$) are also applied, so as to capture potential non-linear effects, while the change in depositor ownership is omitted to avoid correlation problems. The new estimated models therefore stand as follows:

$$AROA_{i,\,post} = \phi_0 + \phi_1 AROA_{i,\,pre} + \phi_2\,CSIZE_i + \phi_3\,CGOVERN_i + \phi_4\,CGOVERNQ_i + \phi_5\,CEMP_i + \phi_6\,CEMPQ_i + \sum \phi_t\,Y_{it} + \tau_i \quad (1)$$

$$ARISK_{i,\,post} = \varphi_0 + \varphi_1\,ARISK_{i,\,pre} + \varphi_2\,CSIZE_i + \varphi_3\,CGOVERN + \varphi_4\,CGOVERNQ + \varphi_5\,CEMP_i + \varphi_6\,CEMPQ + \sum \varphi_t\,Y_{it} + \psi_i \quad (2)$$

$$ACV_{i,\,post} = \gamma_0 + \gamma_1\,ACVA_{i,\,pre} + \gamma_2\,CSIZE_i + \gamma_3\,CGOVERN + \gamma_4\,CGOVERNQ + \gamma_5\,CEMP_i + \gamma_6\,CEMPQ + \sum \gamma_t\,Y_{it} + \upsilon_i \quad (3)$$

Results of the estimations for each of the performance and risk measures are shown in Table 6.

Table 6 Change in board of directors and risk

| | $AROA1_{post,i}$ | $AROA2_{post,i}$ | $ARISK1_{post,i}$ | $ARISK2_{post,i}$ | $ACV1_{post,i}$ | $ACV2_{post,i}$ |
|---|---|---|---|---|---|---|
| | (1) | (2) | (3) | (4) | (5) | (6) |
| $\alpha_0$ | 0.585 | 0.683 | 1.321 | 2.205 | 0,77 | 2,18 |
| | (1.59) | (1.15) | (1.26) | (1.43) | (0,51) | (1,10) |
| $AROA1_{pre,i}$ | 0.750*** | | | | | |
| | (3.87) | | | | | |
| $AROA2_{pre,i}$ | | 0.553*** | | | | |
| | | (3.79) | | | | |
| $ARISK1_{pre,i}$ | | | -0.143 | | | |
| | | | (-0.99) | | | |
| $ARISK2_{pre,i}$ | | | | -0.033 | | |
| | | | | (-0.16) | | |
| $ACV1_{pre,i}$ | | | | | -0,22 | |
| | | | | | (-1,30) | |
| $ACV2_{pre,i}$ | | | | | | 0,20 |
| | | | | | | (1,11) |
| $CGOVERN_i$ | -0.003 | -0.012* | -0.017 | -0.027 | -0,01 | -0,03 |
| | (-1.05) | (-2.06) | (-1.60) | (-1.75) | (-0,68) | (-1,73) |
| $CGOVERNQ_i$ | 0.00003 | 0.0001 | 0.0008*** | 0.0009*** | 0,001*** | 0,001** |
| | (0.51) | (1.41) | (4.40) | (3.41) | (3,21) | (2,79) |
| $CEMP_i$ | -0.014 | 0.003 | 0.139 | -0.042 | 0,20 | -0,07 |
| | (-0.74) | (0.07) | (1.72) | (-0.36) | (1,79) | (-0,46) |
| $CEMPQ_i$ | 0.0007 | -0.0008 | -0.004 | 0.802 | -0,008 | 0,004 |
| | (0.70) | (-0.38) | (-1,12) | (0.38) | (-1,31) | (0,53) |
| $CSIZE_i$ | -0.014 | 0.002 | -1.56* | -2.71** | -1,38 | -2,85* |
| | (-0.07) | (0.007) | (-2.01) | (-2.42) | (-1,24) | (-1,93) |
| D89 | -0.35 | -0.464 | -0.427 | -2.062 | 0,24 | -2,66 |
| | (-1.24) | (-0.78) | (-0.38) | (-1.28) | (0,15) | (-1,27) |
| D90 | -0.355 | 0.468 | 0.747 | -0.585 | 1,23 | -0,74 |
| | (-1.33) | (-0.79) | (0.67) | (-0.37) | (0,78) | (-0,35) |
| D91 | -0.320 | -0.193 | -0.032 | -0.029 | 0,44 | 0,05 |
| | (-1.34) | (0.37) | (-0.03) | (-0.02) | (0,32) | (0,03) |
| D92 | -0.28 | 0.141 | 0.144 | -0.127 | 0,89 | -0,51 |
| | (-1.1) | (0.26) | (0.14) | (-0.09) | (0,63) | (-0,27) |
| D93 | -0.492* | -0.773 | 0.179 | 1.366 | 0,83 | 3,37 |
| | (-1.91) | (-1.35) | (0.16) | (0.89) | (0,55) | (1,67) |
| D95 | 0.287 | -0.098 | -1.636 | -1.774 | -1,34 | -1,66 |
| | (-1.09) | (-0.17) | (-1.59) | (-1.14) | (-0,90) | (-0,85) |
| Turning point of $CGOVERN_i$ | | | 9.78% | 14.14% | 5.84% | 16.28% |
| # observations | 24 | 24 | 24 | 24 | 24 | 24 |
| Ajusted $R^2$ | 67.33 | 67.93 | 75.43 | 59.39 | 63,49% | 68,73% |
| F | 4.95*** | 5.06*** | 6.89*** | 3.80** | 4,33** | 5,21*** |

\* Significantly different from zero at the 10% level
\*\* Significantly different from zero at the 5% level
\*\*\* Significantly different from zero at the 1% level

This table shows the OLS estimations of the equations [7], [8] and [9]. The dependent variables are the adjusted return on assets (AROA1post,i; AROA2post,i), the adjusted standard deviation of the return on assets (ARISKpost,i: ARISKpost,i) and the adjusted coefficient of variation (ACV1post,i; ACVpost,i) in the period of four years after the change in the regional legislation. Each of the variables is adjusted by quotient by the respective measure in the six savings banks that do not change their governance structure. As independent variables we introduce in each of the regressions the same dependent variable but measured in the period of four years previous to the change in the ownership. CGOVERN and CEMP are, respectively, the variation in the government ownership and the employees' ownership. These two variables are also introduced square (CGOVERNQ and CEMPQ). As control variables we introduced the change in the natural logarithm of total assets that experiences each of the savings banks between the previous period and the posterior period (CTA) and a set of dummy variables corresponding to each of the years when a change in the regional legislation has occurred, which take the value 1 if the modification of the composition of the board of directors of the savings bank i has taken place in the year t and take the value 0 otherwise. In the estimations the dummy corresponding to the year 1998 is omitted. The values of the t-student test are shown in brackets.

The negative coefficient of CGOVERN in regression (2) highlights that savings banks that most increased their government ownership were those that least increased their return on assets before depreciation and provisions for loan losses reserves. Again, we do not observe any relation between ownership change and the return on assets after depreciation and provisions for loan losses reserves in regression (1). In contrast, the positive sign of CGOVERNQ in regressions (3) and (4) indicates that the rise in the standard deviation of both measures of return on assets was greater for those savings banks that most increased government ownership after the introduction of regional regulation. Far from this positive relation between change in government ownership and change in the standard deviation of return on assets being observed for every type of change in government ownership, it is only observed, in fact, for changes in ownership of above 9.78% or 14.14%, depending on the measure of the return on assets used.

Furthermore, the positive relation between risk and government ownership holds when we adjust risk by performance in columns (5) and (6). For changes in government ownership higher than 5.84% and 16.28%, in the case of ACV1 and ACV2 respectively, there is a positive relation between the change in the risk adjusted by performance and the variation in government ownership of savings banks. This positive relationship is not consistent with the argument that politicians tend to limit savings banks' risk to a level that guarantees their solvency if faced with the threat of losing a useful instrument to reach political goals. On the contrary, the relation found between variation in risk and variation in government ownership suggests a positive influence of political presence on savings banks' risk levels, irrespective of whether it is performance adjusted or not. This result is consistent with the fact that the objective of reaching political goals in decision-taking may not coincide with the objective of economic efficiency and may in fact increase the thrifts' risk. Similarly, the result is also consistent with the options public administrations enjoy of transferring funds to savings banks through the commercial relationship they maintain with them, and of compensating losses provoked by politically-motivated decisions with fund transfers.

Unlike the results for the shift towards government ownership, we do not observe a significant relation between the change in employees' ownership and the level of post-legislative performance and risk.

# 6 Conclusions

Although there are both mutual and government-owned banking institutions, possible differences in performance and risk between them have yet to be analyzed. This paper provides some evidence on this issue by analyzing Spanish savings banks' change in performance and risk after regional regulations increased political control of decision-taking at the expense of reducing depositors' ownership.

Although mean difference analysis initially seems to indicate that there has been some reduction in savings banks' risk in the four years after the change in ownership with respect to the four years before that change, regression analysis reveals that an increase in savings banks' risk level occurs when the correlation between pre- and post-legislative change and the change in the thrifts' size are controlled. The analysis of mean differences fails to observe significant variations of savings banks' performance after the ownership whereas the regression analysis reveals an increase in the return on assets before depreciation and provisions for loan losses reserves; this increase is in any case smaller, the larger the increase in government ownership.

The smaller performance increase compared to risk increase observed in Spanish savings banks subject to increased government ownership leads to an increase in performance-adjusted risk, i.e. in the coefficient of variation. Furthermore, we observe that the coefficient of variation rises in line with enhanced government ownership for increases in political presence higher than 5.84% and 16.28%, depending on whether performance is measured after or before depreciation and provisions for loan losses reserves. In short, results obtained suggest a positive influence of public administrations on savings banks' risk level but not on their performance. These findings are consistent with results of studies carried out in other countries indicating that the pursuit of political objectives in decision-taking may facilitate more risky investments, and that the option of fund transfer that is a spin-off of the commercial relationship between savings banks and regional governments may also facilitate this type of heightened risk.

# References

Altunbas, Y., Evans, L. and Molyneux, F. (2001). Bank ownership and efficiency. *Journal of Money, Credit and Banking* **33**, 926-954.

Barth, J. R., Caprio G. Jr. and Levine R. (2001). Banking systems around the globe:do regulations and ownership affect performance and stability?. Frederic S. Mishkin, Editor: *Prudential supervision: What works and what doesn't*, University of Chicago Press.

Beatty, A., Chamberlain, S.L. and Magliolo, J. (1995). Managing financial reports of commercial banks: the influence of taxes, regulatory capital and earnings. *Journal of Accounting Research* **33**, 231-261.

Blair, D. and Placone D. (1988). Expense preference behavior, agency cost, and firm organization. *Journal of Economics and Business* **40**, 1-15.

Boardman, A. and Vining A. (1989). Ownership and performance in competitive environments: a comparison of the performance of private, mixed and state-owned enterprises. *Journal of Law and Economics* **32**, 1-33.

Cebenoyan, A.S., Cooperman, E.S. and Hudgins, S. (1993). The relative efficiency of stock versus mutual savings and loans: a stochastic cost frontier approach. *Journal of Financial Services Research* **7**, 151-170.

Cebenoyan, A.S., Cooperman, E.S. and Register, CH.A. (1995). Deregulation, reregulation, equity ownership and S&L risk-taking. *Financial Management* **24**, 63-76.

Cebenoyan, A.S., Cooperman, E.S. and Register, CH.A. (1999). Ownership structure, charter value and risk-taking behavior for thrifts. *Financial Management* **28**, 43-60-

Cordell, L.R., Macdonald, G.D. and Wohar M.E., (1993). Corporate ownership and the thrift crisis. *Journal of Law and Economics* **36**, 719-756.

Daniels, K.N. and Sfiridis, J.M. (2001). The relative cost efficiency of stock versus mutal thrifts: does organizational form matter?. Paper presented at *2001* FMA Annual Meeting, Toronto.

Dewatripont, M. and Tirole J. (1993a). Efficient governance structure: implications for banking regulation. Mayer, C., Vives X., Eds., *Capital Markets and Finacial Intermediation*. Cambridge University Press, 12-35.

Dewatripont, M. and Tirole J. (1993b). *The prudential regulation of banks*. Editions Payot, Lausanne.

Demsetz, H. and Lehn K. (1985). The structure of corporate ownership: causes and consequences. *Journal of Political Economy* **93**, 1155-1177.

Esty, B.C. (1997a). Organizational form and risk taking in the savings and loan industry. *Journal of Financial Economics* **44**, 25-55.

Esty, B.C. (1997b). A case study of organizational form and risk shifting in the saving and loan industry. *Journal of Financial Economics* **44**, 57-76.

Grifell- Tatjé, E. and Lovell C. (1997). The sources of productivity change in Spanish banking. *European Journal of Operational Research* **98**, 364-380.

Hadaway, B.L. and Hadaway S.C. (1984). Implications of savings and loan conversions in a deregulated world. *Journal of Bank Research* **15**, 44-55.

Hansmann, H. (1988). Ownership of the firm. *Journal of Law, Economics and Organization* **4**, 267-303.

Healy, P.M., Palepu K.G. and Ruback R.S. (1992). Does corporate performance improve after mergers?. *Journal of Financial Economics* **31**, 135-175.

Jensen, M.C. and Meckling, E.H. (1979). Rights and production functions:an application to labor-managed firms and codetermination. *Journal of Business* **52**, 469-506.

Karels G.V. and Mclatchey C. (1999). Deposit Insurance and risk-taking behavior in the credit union industry. *Journal of Banking and Finance* **23**, 105-134.

Kaufman, G.G. (1999). Helping to prevent banking crisis: Taking the "State" out of State banks. *Review of Pacific Basin Financial Markets and Policies* **2**, 83-98.

Keeley, M. C. (1990). Deposit Insurance, risk, and market power in banking. *The American Economic Review* **80**, 1183-1200.

La Porta, R., Lopez-de-Silanes F. and Shleifer A. (2002). Government ownership of banks. *Journal of Finance* **57**, 265-301.

Lamm-Tennant, J. and Starks L.T. (1993). Stocks vs. mutual ownership structures: the risk implications. *Journal of Business* **66**, 29-46.

Lozano, A. (1998). Efficiency and technical change for Spanish banks. *Applied Financial Economics* **8**, 289-300.

Masulis, R.W. (1987). Changes in ownership structure: Conversions of mutual saving and loans to stock charter. *Journal of Financial Economics* **18**, 29-59.

Megginson, W.L. and Netter J.M. (2001). From state to market: a survey of empirical studies on privatization. *Journal of Economic Literature* **39**, 321-389.

Melle, M. and Maroto J.A. (1999). Una aplicación del gobierno de empresas: incidencia de las Administraciones Públicas en las decisiones asignativas de las cajas de ahorros españolas. *Revista Europea de Dirección y Economía de la Empresa* **8**, 9-40.

Mester, L. (1991). Agency costs among saving and loans. *Journal of Financial Intermediation* **1**, 257-278

Mester, L.J. (1993). Efficiency in the saving and loan industry. *Journal of Banking and Finance* **17**, 267-288.

O'Hara, M. (1981). Property rights and the financial firm. *Journal of Law and Economics* **29**, 317-332.

O'Hara, M. and Shaw, W. (1990). Deposit insurance and wealth effects: the value of being "too big to fail". *Journal of Finance* **45**, 1587-1600.

Rasmusen, E. (1988). Mutual banks and stock banks. *Journal of Law and Economics* **31**, 395-421.

Sapienza, P. (1999). What do state-owned firms maximize? Evidence from the Italian Banks. Northwestern University Mimeo.

Scholes, M.S., Wilson, G.P. and Wolfson, M.A. (1990). Tax planning, regulatory capital planning and financial reporting strategy for commercial banks. *The Review of Financial Studies* **3**, 625-650.

Schrand C. and Unal H. (1998). Hedging and coordinated risk management: Evidence from thrift conversions. *Journal of Finance* **53**, 979-1013.

Shleifer, A. (1998). State versus private ownership. *Journal of Economic Perspectives* **12**, 133-150.

Tulkens, H. (1993). On FDH efficiency analysis: some methodological issues and applications to retail banking, courts and urban transit. *Journal of Productivity Analysis* **4**, 183-210.

Valnek, T. (1999). The comparative performance of mutual building societies and stock retail banks. *Journal of Banking and Finance* **23**, 925-938.

Verbrugge, J.A., Megginson W.L. and Owens W.L. (1999). State ownership and the financial performance of privatized banks: an empirical analysis. Paper presented at the World Bank /Federal Reserve bank of Dallas Conference on Banking Privatization, Washington, D.C..

Verbrugge, J.A. and Goldstein S.G. (1981). Risk return and managerial objetives: some evidence from the saving and loan industry. *Journal of Financial Research* **4**, 45-58.

Verbrugge, J.A. and Jahera J.S. (1981). Expense preference behavior in the savings and loan industry. *Journal of Money, Credit and Banking* **13**, 405-476.

Williams, Z.D. (1999). CEO control and project selection: Evidence from mutual thrift conversions. Working paper, Haas School of Business, University of California, Berkeley.

In: International Finance and Monetary Policy
Editor: Gleb P. Severov, pp. 229-260

ISBN: 1-60021-103-8

**Chapter 10**

# LIQUIDITY CONSEQUENCES
# OF LOCKUP EXPIRATIONS

## *Charles Cao*[*]*, Laura Casares Field and Gordon Hanka*

Department of Finance, Smeal College of Business, Penn State University,
609 BAB 1, University Park, PA, 16802

## Abstract

A principal purpose of an IPO is to gain access to a liquid market. However, post-IPO liquidity may be impaired by the information asymmetry between outsiders and the firm's founders and early investors. Consequently most IPOs feature "lockups" that prohibit insider share sales for six months. In this paper we present the first detailed analysis of the liquidity consequences of lockups, by examining liquidity changes around the expirations of 1,497 IPO lockups in the period 1995-1999. We find substantial increases in market depth as measured by quote depth, average trade size, and number of trades. As predicted by asymmetric information models, we find a statistically significant increase in trading costs as measured by effective bid-ask spreads. However, this effect has small magnitude and dissipates within a week. We find no material increase in the asymmetric information component of the spread, nor do we find other expected signatures of information asymmetry. Overall, these data show that a large body of well informed, block-holding insider traders can enter a market from which they had previously been absent, and substantially change trading volume and share price, without reducing market depth or causing more than a small, temporary widening of bid-ask spreads. A practical implication is that market liquidity probably cannot be enhanced by strengthening the current legal restrictions on trading by insiders, even in young, growth firms with potentially high information asymmetry.

# 1  Introduction

Insider trading is now legally restricted in the U.S. and most other Western countries (Bhattacharya and Daouk (2001)).[1]  These restrictions are justified partly by the hypothesis

---

[*] E-mail address: charles@loki.smeal.psu.edu.  Thanks to Wilson Kong for excellent research assistance.  This paper has benefited from the comments of Ian Domowitz, Heather Hulburt, Michelle Lowry, Harold Mulherin, Chris Muscarella, Dennis Sheehan, and the participants of the Penn State Finance workshop

that insiders are "informed traders" who will impair market liquidity by creating a lemons problem that deters other investors from trading. This prediction flows from any of several popular microstructure models, including Copeland and Galai (1983), Glosten and Milgrom (1985), Kyle (1985), and Leland (1992).

The problem of insider trading is likely to be particularly acute in the period immediately following the firm's Initial Public Offer (IPO). Newly public firms tend to be young, high-growth firms with limited historical data. In most cases a majority of the shares are owned by founders and early investors who have a particularly sharp information advantage. Thus, asymmetric information costs could be severe, potentially defeating the IPO's purpose of creating a liquid market for the firm's shares. To mitigate this problem, the insiders of IPO firms typically submit to a "lockup", foreswearing any share sales for some fixed period, typically six months. From the insiders' perspective, the lockup is a tradeoff, sacrificing short-term liquidity in the hope of building a deeper, more liquid market in which the insiders can ultimately realize a higher value for their shares. To date, we do not know if this tradeoff is optimal.

In this paper we provide additional information on IPOs and lockups, and on the more general problem of insider trading, by presenting the first comprehensive examination of the changes in market liquidity when lockups expire and allow insider traders to enter the market en masse. We take as a starting point the recent papers that document significant post-expiration changes in share price and trading volume, including Bradley, Bradford, Roten and Ha-Chin (2001), Brav and Gompers (2000), Ofek and Richardson (2000), and especially Field and Hanka (2001).

Like most of the recent papers on lockup expirations, Field and Hanka (2001) focus on changes in price and volume, but they also note in passing that there is little change in the closing, quoted, bid-ask spread. This result is somewhat puzzling, as a lockup expiration should sharply increase the information asymmetry between market participants. Perhaps this result indicates that information asymmetry affects quote depth rather than affecting the spread. Alternatively, closing quotes may be a poor measure of spreads, as market makers know that they are not obliged to trade at their closing quote. Indeed, the quoted spread is typically not offered by any single market maker, but is rather a composite of the bid and ask from two different market makers that are each quoting wider spreads. It is also possible that lockup expirations increase the asymmetric information component of the spread, but that this increase is masked by a reduction in the fixed-cost component, due to the post-expiration increase in trading volume.

We investigate further by examining a sample of 1,497 lockup expirations in the period 1995-1999. We use TAQ data to examine intraday quote depth and effective spreads. We find that, for a few days immediately around the expiration, effective bid-ask spreads do, in fact, widen by 3-4 percent, or about 0.12 percent of share price. This widening is statistically significant, but is closed within a week. This modest increase in spreads is consistent with a temporary increase in information asymmetry, but has plausible alternative explanations, such as a temporary increase in trading urgency that reduces the price-elasticity of demand for

---

[1] In the U.S., trading on the basis of "material, non-public information" is banned under Rule 10b-5 of the Securities Exchange Act of 1934. Section 16 of the Act bans short selling by "Insiders" (officers, directors, and ten percent blockholders); allows the firm to recover any profits that insiders make on positions held for less than six months (the short-swing rule) and requires insiders to disclose their trades on Form 4 no later than the 10th day of the following month.

transactions.  When we search for evidence of permanently increased information asymmetry, by comparing the thirty trading days before the expiration to the thirty days after the expiration, we find no clear increase in spreads, and the spread changes that we do observe seem to be driven largely by price changes.  In multivariate tests that control for share price, volatility, and trading activity, we find no abnormal changes in spreads.   When we decompose the spread into adverse selection and fixed-cost components, we find that the adverse-selection component does not change after lockup expiration, though the fixed-cost component declines by about half a penny, consistent with the argument that an increase in the tradable float will reduce per-trade costs by allowing the market maker to amortize his fixed costs over a larger number of trades.

While the post-expiration increase in spreads is small and temporary, we find large and persistent increases in market depth.  Average quote depth in the thirty day period after lockup expiration is twenty percent higher than in the thirty days prior to the lockup expiration, and this increase is not explained by concurrent changes in price, volatility, or trading activity.  Other measures of market depth also increase substantially.  The average number of trades per day increases by 32 percent, and average trade size increases by 18 percent.  The effective spread for large block trades does not materially change.  Bacidore (1997) and Harris (2000) suggest that changes in net market liquidity can be measured by changes in the ratio of the quoted depth to the quoted spread.  In our sample, the depth-to-spread ratio increases by an average of 27 percent after the lockup expiration.

If insiders sell some of their shares after lockup expiration, the number of tradable shares will increase, and the resulting liquidity benefits may mask any increase in asymmetric information costs.  However, multivariate controls for trading volume do not change the univariate result that lockup expirations result in increased quote depth without materially changing spreads.  As a further test we identify a subsample of firms in which the major pre-IPO shareholders (officers, directors, and five percent blockholders) do not sell any of their shares during our event window.  Since these shareholders collectively own an average of 84% (median=93%) of the locked-up shares, this subsample of firms should experience only modest increases in the number of tradable shares.  In this subsample we find the same result: a substantial increase in quote depth but no clear change in spreads.

Since our data give little evidence that lockup expirations produce gross liquidity impairment, we test for more specific signatures of information asymmetry.  A lockup prohibits insider sales, but it does not prohibit insider purchases, so we expect the expiration of the lockup to affect bid-side quote depth more than it affects ask-side quote depth.  However, the data show no such asymmetry.  We do find a predicted negative relation between spread changes and trading activity, but we do not find a predicted inverted-U shaped relation between spread changes and trade size.

Overall, these results indicate that a large body of well informed, block-holding insider traders can enter a market and substantially change trading volume and share price, without reducing market depth or causing more than a small, temporary widening of bid-ask spreads.  Perhaps the simplest explanation for this result is that, even under relatively extreme conditions, expected losses to insider traders are minor compared with the other costs of making a market, and hence have little effect on liquidity.  A practical implication is that market liquidity probably cannot be improved by strengthening the current legal restrictions on insider trading, either with stricter laws or by adopting voluntary constraints.

The paper is organized as follows. The next section presents an overview of lockup agreements. Section 0 surveys some of the related literature. Section 0 describes our data and methods. Section 0 presents univariate tests for the predicted gross liquidity impairment after lockup expirations. Section 0 presents multivariate and subsample tests to determine whether the predicted liquidity impairment is being masked by confounding factors. Section 0 presents detailed tests for more subtle evidence of asymmetric information costs. Section 0 concludes.

## Lockups

Nearly all IPOs have lockups. The only common exceptions are events such as mutual-to-stock conversions, in which there are no pre-IPO shares to lock up. Typically, two thirds of the outstanding shares are locked up, and more than 80 percent of the locked-up shares are owned by officers, directors, and five percent blockholders. In recent years, more than ninety percent of lockup agreements have a term of six months. When the lockup expires, insiders are suddenly freed to sell their shares, subject to the constraint that no individual insider may sell more than the equivalent of a week's total trading volume.[2]

Theoretically, we expect lockup expirations to result in both liquidity-motivated and information-motivated insider trades. We expect liquidity-motivated trades because the founders and early investors may have a large fraction of their personal wealth tied up in the firm. We also expect that the lockup expiration will present insiders with a strong temptation to trade based on their superior information about the firm's prospects, as it is their first opportunity to sell shares without advance disclosure, and hence it is their first opportunity to act on their private beliefs about the firm's true value without bearing the cost of price changes caused by the revelation of those beliefs. Furthermore, in the period immediately after a lockup expiration, it will be uniquely difficult to prosecute insiders for illegal, information-based selling, as an information-motivated insider seller cannot easily be distinguished from the liquidity-motivated insiders who are likely to be selling at the same time.

Empirically, lockup expirations have large and obvious effects. Average trading volume doubles in a single day and is permanently increased by 40-60 percent, while share price drops significantly (Bradley, Bradford, Roten, Ha-Chin (2001), Brav and Gompers (2000), Ofek and Richardson (2000)). In the six months between the IPO and lockup expiration, fewer than 10 percent of firms disclose insider sales, but 17 percent of firms disclose insider share sales within a week of the lockup expiration, and among these firms the abnormal price drop at the expiration is twice as large (Field and Hanka (2001)). For comparison, in a typical one-year period, about half of the exchange listed firms in the U.S. will report some insider trading (Lakonishok and Lee (2000)).

Lockup expirations have several nice attributes that permit clean empirical tests. The expiration event is visually obvious in time series plots of volume and price, so there is little

---

[2] Under Rule 144 of the Securities Act of 1933, all shares issued outside of a registered offer, including shares held since before the IPO, are "Restricted shares". Rule 144 requires that such shares be held at least a year before sale (two years if prior to Feb. 1997); requires sales to be disclosed on Form 144; and limits the total quarterly sales by any individual to the greater of the average weekly trading volume or one percent of the total shares outstanding.

ambiguity about the relevant event date. The lockup period is largely standardized at 180 days following the IPO, so the timing of the expiration is relatively exogenous for any given firm, and does not systematically coincide with other events like earnings announcements. The lockup applies only to insider sales and not to purchases, so the lockup expiration should have a distinctive, asymmetric effect on bid-side and ask-side depth. Finally, since lockup expirations are common and affect only one firm at a time, we can construct a sample of many hundreds of independent events.

The details of lockup expirations correspond reasonably well with the assumptions of standard, asymmetric information models of market liquidity. For example, the locked-up insiders seem likely candidates for the "informed traders" postulated by most models. Since the locked-up insiders almost always include the founders and early investors in the firm, they certainly possess detailed inside information, and their informational advantage could be especially sharp in the young, growth firms that constitute the bulk of our sample. More formally, in most models a trader is "informed" if and only if his trades tend to foreshadow subsequent price changes. By this definition there is considerable empirical evidence that insider trades are, on average, informed.[3] More specifically, the insiders who trade after lockup expirations seem to be informed, as their trades (as subsequently disclosed to the SEC) are associated with economically and statistically significant drops in share price (Field and Hanka (2001)).

Another crucial assumption is that the market maker is averse to trading losses. For Nasdaq firms (the bulk of the sample), the dominant market maker is usually the underwriting firm, which may have objectives other than maximizing trading profits (Michaely and Wolmack (1999), Ellis, Michaely and O'Hara (2000a)). However, by the time of the lockup expiration (six months after the IPO) it is reasonable to assume that market makers are averse to trading losses, as more than half of trading volume is handled by market makers who are not affiliated with the underwriter, and even the underwriter-affiliated market makers typically cease their price support activities and begin to earn positive trading profits within a month of the IPO (Aggarwal (2000), Ellis, Michaely and O'Hara (2000a)).

Finally, even though lockup expirations are predictable well in advance, we do not expect them to affect market liquidity until the actual expiration day, unlike gross price changes which (in an efficient market) we expect to occur in advance. The predicted reduction in market liquidity is caused by the probability that the next trade will be executed against an informed insider, not by the possibility that insiders may enter the market on some future date, so we may reasonably expect to observe a discrete reduction in liquidity on the day that insiders are expected to enter the market.

---

[3] Evidence that insider trades are profitable and/or foreshadow future events can be found in Damodaran and Liu (1993), Halpern (1974), Mandelker (1974), Jaffe (1974), Finnerty (1976), Baesel and Stein (1979), Keown and Pinkerton (1981), Penman (1982, 1985), Elliot, Morse and Richardson (1984), Seyhun (1988 and 1992), Hirschey (1989), Lin and Howe (1990), John and Lang (1991), Seyhun and Bradley (1997), Noe (1999), and Lakonishok and Lee (2000). Evidence that disclosures of large insider trades can move the stock price is found in Givoly and Palmon (1985). Counterexamples include Meulbroek (2000) who finds no price declines on days with sales by insiders of Internet firms, and Eckbo and Smith (2000), who find that Swedish insiders did not earn abnormal profits during a period of lax enforcement of insider trading laws .

# Related Literature

Standard models predict that informed trading will impair market liquidity, by forcing market makers to widen the spread and reduce quote depth in order to protect themselves against the adverse price changes that follow informed trades (Copeland and Galai (1983), Glosten and Milgrom (1985), Kyle (1985), Leland (1992)). However, despite the substantial welfare and policy implications of this issue, empirical research is sparse and only emerging, and many questions remain unanswered. For example, are the liquidity consequences of informed trading large enough to justify state intervention? Would liquidity be enhanced by stronger insider trading laws? Does insider trading affect liquidity at all times, or only around times of high perceived information asymmetry? Is trading by designated insiders (i.e., officers, directors and blockholders) more harmful than that of analysts and other informed parties? To date, the answers to these questions are unknown.

Direct empirical measurements of the liquidity consequences of insider trading are rare, and they tend not to find the predicted liquidity impairment. Cornell and Sirri (1992) examine insider trading around Anheuser Busch's tender offer for Campbell Taggart, using ex post court records to identify insider trades, and conclude that trading volume and liquidity increased when insiders were active. The most comprehensive empirical test of the liquidity consequences of insider trading is found in Bettis, Cole and Lemmon (2000). They examine a sample of 284 firms whose internal policies restrict insider trading, and find that effective spreads increase by about two basis points (or 0.02 percent of share price) during "trading windows" when insiders are allowed to trade. By comparison, after lockup expirations we find temporary spread increases of approximately 14 basis points, although we find no long-term spread changes.

Other tests for a relation between information asymmetry and liquidity have focused on earnings announcements, hypothesizing that information asymmetry will be unusually high just before and perhaps just after the announcement, because some traders will have advance knowledge of earnings or will better understand their implications. Venkatesh and Chiang (1986) examine earnings and dividend announcements, and find that spreads widen only around unusual earnings announcements, those that are separated from a previous announcement by more than ten days but less than thirty days. Lee, Mucklow and Ready (1993) use intraday data and find evidence that spreads widen around earnings announcements, especially in the minutes immediately prior to the announcement, but they express doubt about whether the resulting increase in trading costs is economically significant.

The issue addressed in this study, liquidity, is one component of a broader debate on the merits of insider trading. A good overview of this debate can be found in Leland (1992). Some researchers argue that insider trading can be an efficient way to compensate managers for creating new wealth (Manne (1966), Bebchuk and Fershtman (1994), Noe (1997)). However, managers might actually destroy wealth in order to maximize their trading profits (Hirshleifer (1974), Bagnoli and Khanna (1992)). Insider trading may also accelerate price discovery, leading to more efficient allocation of resources (Bernhardt, Hollifield and Hughson (1995), Baiman and Verrecchia (1996)). However, Fishman and Hagerty (1992) argue that insider trading could actually make prices less informative, by reducing outsiders' incentive to gather information. The prospect of trading against insiders may make outsiders less willing to invest in new firms (Manove (1989)), though Leland (1992) argues the reverse.

# Data and Methods

## Data

Our initial sample is all IPOs in the Securities Data Corporation (SDC) New Issues database, in the period 1995-1999. For a firm to be included in the sample, we require the firm to have at least 3 months of TAQ data available both prior to and after the expiration day. Thus, the earliest expiration day for our sample firm is April, 1995 and the latest expiration date is June 31, 1999. (We have TAQ data though Sep. 1999.) We exclude carveouts, stocks with issue price below $5, REIT's, ADR's, unit offers, and firms that conduct a seasoned equity offer before the lockup expires (seasoned offer dates are also from SDC). These exclusions leave a potential sample of 1,534 firms. For each firm, we obtain a complete record of trades and quotes for the period from 30 days before the lockup expiration to 30 days after, from the TAQ database distributed by the NYSE. After excluding 37 firms that have fewer than ten days with valid TAQ data in either the pre- or post-expiration windows, we have a final sample of 1,497 firms. For the TAQ data, we apply standard screens to eliminate trades and quotes flagged as opening, non-standard delivery trades, as well as all Best Bid/Offer (BBO) ineligible quotes. BBO-ineligible quotes are closing quotations, trading halts, pre-opening indications, and non-firm quotations. Our results are qualitatively unchanged if we apply more stringent screens for minimum share price or trading activity.

Table 1: Summary statistics for sample firms

| Year of Lockup Expiration | Number of Firms | Issue Value ($Millions) | Lockup Period (Days) | Percent of Total Shares Sold in IPO | Percent with Venture Financing |
|---|---|---|---|---|---|
| 1995 | 165 | 63 [31] | 210 [180] | 35% [33] | 39% |
| 1996 | 495 | 72 [42] | 188 [180] | 33% [33] | 47% |
| 1997 | 406 | 60 [33] | 196 [180] | 33% [30] | 36% |
| 1998 | 356 | 78 [39] | 198 [180] | 39% [33] | 28% |
| 1999 | 75 | 208 [49] | 218 [180] | 39% [33] | 24% |
| All Years | 1,497 | 76 | 196 | 35% | 38% |

The sample is 1,497 U.S. lockup expirations in the period April, 1995 through June, 1999. Reported below are the sample means and medians (in brackets.)

Table 1 presents summary statistics for the sample firms, by year of the lockup expiration. The typical IPO offers one third of the total outstanding shares, leaving two thirds of the shares in the hands of pre-IPO shareholders, almost all of which will be locked up. Most lockups are for 180 days, but the mean lockup period is somewhat longer, at 196 days. As measured by the offer price, the typical IPO firm has a total equity value of $76 million. All years 1995-1999 are represented in the sample, but the first and last years have fewer firms due to our mid-year sample cutoffs. The characteristics of the sample firms do not change dramatically from year to year, except for a steady decline in the proportion of firms with venture capital financing, and an increase in the mean firm value in 1999. This increase is due to a few large IPOs. The decline in the percentage of firms with venture financing may be due to the "hot" IPO market, which probably increased the number of IPOs from lower-quality firms that could not attract venture financing.

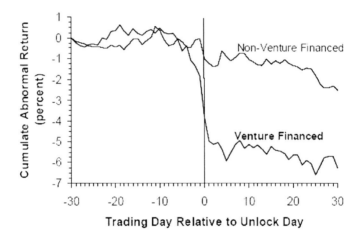

Figure 1 shows the time series of total trading volume and cumulative abnormal returns (relative to the CRSP value-weighted index return) around the lockup expiration. Previous research has shown that abnormal returns and trading volume around lockup expirations depends strongly on whether the firm is venture financed, so we show results separately for venture- and non-venture financed firms.[4] In our sample, 570 firms (38 percent) are venture financed, so the results for the full sample are roughly intermediate between those of the venture- and non-venture financed subsamples. The figures show a large increase in trading volume and concurrent decline in share price immediately around the lockup expiration, especially among venture financed firms. These effects are larger than those shown in previous papers (e.g., Bradley, Bradford, Roten, and Ha-Chin (2001), Brav and Gompers (2000), Field and Hanka (2001), and Ofek and Richardson (2000)) because the effects have grown larger over time. This result confirms that lockup expirations are meaningful events that are not rendered moot by early lockup releases or by executive hedging instrument such as collars or exchange funds. Bettis, Bizjak, and Lemmon (1999) examine executive hedging

---

[4] Data on the presence of venture financing are obtained from SDC.

instruments, and Field and Hanka (2001) find that only a few percent of lockup agreements are released early.

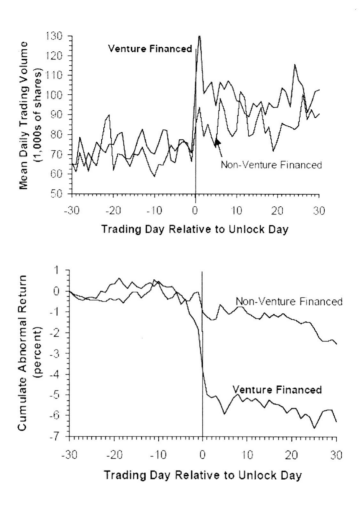

Figure 1: Volume and abnormal returns around the lockup expiration.

Cumulative abnormal returns are measured relative to the return on the CRSP value-weighted index, and are based on closing quote midpoints. The sample is 1,497 U.S. lockup expirations in the period April, 1995 through June, 1999. Data are from TAQ.

For our purposes, one of the attractive features of lockup expirations is that they are relatively exogenous events, not systematically timed to coincide with confounding events like earnings announcements. To verify this claim, we obtained the dates of all earnings announcements for our sample firms in the period around the lockup expiration. Earnings announcements are obtained from First Call (for years 1995-1997) or from the Dow Jones news retrieval service (for years 1998 and 1999). When we plot the frequency of earnings announcements around the lockup expiration (results available on request) the only obvious pattern is a seven calendar day (five trading day) seasonal. Lockup expirations tend to be on

Mondays, while earnings announcements are most common on Tuesday. This seasonal pattern is not materially distorted around the lockup expiration, so lockup expirations do not seem to mark periods of unusually high or low incidence of earnings announcements. We also replicate our main tests in the subsamples with and without earnings announcements in either the twenty or sixty windows surrounding the lockup expiration, and find no qualitative change in the results.

## Methods

### Measuring the Bid-Ask Spread

We compute several measures of bid-ask spreads. The quoted spread is defined as the difference between the bid and ask, while the relative quoted spread is defined as the quoted spread divided by the midpoint of the quoted bid and ask. While quoted spreads are informative, a better measure of execution costs is given by the effective spread, defined as twice the absolute difference between the transaction price and the midpoint of the prevailing quoted spread. Most of our tests will focus on the relative effective spread (the effective spread expressed as a percentage of the quote midpoint) which we judge to be the best single measure of trading costs.

For each firm, we compute the daily average spread for each day in the pre-expiration and post-expiration windows, take the mean of the thirty daily averages, then compute the percentage difference between the means in the pre- and post-expiration windows. Our univariate tests measure the cross-sectional mean and median of these 1,497 firm-level percentage changes. Formally, each firm's spreads are computed as

$$\text{Quoted Spread} = \frac{1}{N_D} \sum_{d=1}^{N_D} \left( \frac{1}{N_{Q,d}} \sum_{q=1}^{N_{Q,d}} \left( A_{q,d} - B_{q,d} \right) \right) \tag{1}$$

$$\text{Relative Quoted Spread} = \frac{1}{N_D} \sum_{d=1}^{N_D} \left( \frac{1}{N_{Q,d}} \sum_{q=1}^{N_{Q,d}} \left( \frac{A_{q,d} - B_{q,d}}{M_{q,d}} \right) \right) \cdot 100\% \tag{2}$$

$$\text{Effective Spread} = \frac{1}{N_D} \sum_{d=1}^{N_D} \left( \frac{1}{N_{T,d}} \sum_{t=1}^{N_{T,d}} 2 \left| P_{t,d} - M_{t,d} \right| \right) \tag{3}$$

$$\text{Relative Effective Spread} = \frac{1}{N_D} \sum_{d=1}^{N_D} \left( \frac{1}{N_{T,d}} \sum_{t=1}^{N_{T,d}} 2 \frac{\left| P_{t,d} - M_{t,d} \right|}{M_{t,d}} \right) \cdot 100\% \tag{4}$$

where $N_D$ is the number of days in the event window (usually 30). $N_{Q,d}$ is the number of quote updates on day $d$, and $N_{T,d}$ is the number of transactions on day $d$. $A_{q,d}$, $B_{q,d}$, and $M_{q,d}$ are the ask, bid, and midpoint respectively, for quote update $q$ on day $d$. $P_{t,d}$, $A_{t,d}$, $B_{t,d}$, $M_{t,d}$ are the transaction price and the prevailing ask, bid, and midpoint, respectively, for transaction $t$

on date $d$. While most of our results are presented for the event window [-30,+30], we also conducted our tests with the window [-60,+60] and obtained qualitatively similar results.

**Measuring Market Depth and Trading Activity**

We compute several measures of market depth and trading activity. Ask depth is defined as the number of shares offered for sale at the ask price. Bid depth is defined similarly, and the average of the bid and ask depth is referred to as quote depth. Average shares per transaction, average number of daily transactions, and average daily volume are defined in the obvious manner. The depth-to-spread ratio, a measure of net improvement in liquidity, is defined as the sum of the bid and ask depth divided by the quoted relative spread. These measures are averaged over firms, days, and quote updates in the same manner as spreads are averaged.

During our sample period, market-wide spreads and quote depths were trending downward, due presumably to the NASDAQ odd-eighth's quote controversy. However, the effect of this trend is small during our short sample window, so we do not control for it.

# Univariate Tests for Liquidity Impairment after Lockup Expirations

## Changes in Bid-Ask Spreads after Lockup Expirations

Figure 2 shows the time series of daily mean effective spreads for the 61-day event window centered on the lockup expiration. The upper panel shows effective spreads measured in pennies per share; the lower panel shows relative effective spreads measured as a percentage of share price. Results are shown separately for venture- and non-venture financed firms; the results for the whole sample are intermediate between these two subsamples. The upper panel shows that, after the lockup expiration, the effective spread narrows markedly in venture financed firms, but does not change much in non-venture finance firms. The drop in the spread among venture financed firms parallels the drop in their share price, so the lower panel shows no obvious change in the relative effective spread for either venture- or non-venture financed firms.

Table 2 presents the time series of daily "abnormal" relative effective spreads for the period immediately around the lockup expiration. The tabulated values give the percentage deviations from the pre-expiration mean, which is measured in the period [-30,-6]. The result shows that relative effective spreads widen by 3-4 percent in the period [-2,+5], but then return to their pre-expiration levels. The temporary widening has small magnitude, but is statistically significant.

Tabulated values represent the percentage deviation from the mean relative effective spread for the period [-30,-6]. Formally, on each day $T$, the tabulated value of the relative effective spread $Y_T$ is calculated as:

$$Y_T = \left( \frac{S_T}{\frac{1}{25} \sum_{t=-30}^{-6} S_t} - 1 \right) \cdot 100\%$$

where $S_t$ is the relative effective spread on day $t$, and day 0 is the lockup expiration day. The sample is 1,497 U.S. lockup expirations in the period April, 1995 through June, 1999.

Table 2: Daily Abnormal Spreads

| Day | Abnormal Relative Effective Spread | t-stat |
|---|---|---|
| -10 | -0.5% | [-0.6] |
| -9 | -0.4 | [-0.4] |
| -8 | 1.3 | [ 1.4] |
| -7 | 0.8 | [ 0.9] |
| -6 | 1.0 | [ 1.0] |
| -5 | 1.9 | [ 1.9] |
| -4 | 1.2 | [ 1.2] |
| -3 | 1.3 | [ 1.4] |
| -2 | 3.1* | [ 3.0] |
| -1 | 4.3* | [ 4.2] |
| 0 | 3.5* | [ 3.4] |
| 1 | 3.9* | [ 2.6] |
| 2 | 2.0 | [ 1.8] |
| 3 | 4.3* | [ 2.3] |
| 4 | 2.6* | [ 2.4] |
| 5 | 3.2* | [ 2.6] |
| 6 | 0.2 | [ 0.2] |
| 7 | 1.9 | [ 1.5] |
| 8 | 0.5 | [ 0.4] |
| 9 | 0.9 | [ 0.8] |
| 10 | 1.0 | [ 0.8] |

*Indicates significance at the 5% level (two-tailed test).

Table 3: Tests for Persistent Univariate Changes in Bid-Ask Spreads

| Variable | | All Firms (n=1,497) | | | Venture-Backed (n=570) | | | Non-Venture Backed (n=927) | | | P-value for t-test of difference in % change for venture vs. non-venture |
|---|---|---|---|---|---|---|---|---|---|---|---|
| | | Before | After | % Change | Before | After | % Change | Before | After | % Change | |
| **Quoted Spread** | *Mean* | 43.8 | 43.4 | -0.1 | 46.8 | 45.0 | -3.1* | 42.0 | 42.4 | 1.8 | 0.00 |
| | *(S.E.)* | (0.5) | (0.6) | (0.6) | (0.9) | (1.0) | (0.9) | (0.6) | (0.7) | (1.2) | |
| | *Median* | 38.9 | 38.5 | -1.2 | 43.8 | 40.3 | -5.1* | 37.0 | 37.9 | -0.6 | |
| | *% Positive* | | | 44% | | | 38% | | | 49% | |
| **Effective Spread** | *Mean* | 32.7 | 31.9 | -1.1 | 37.0 | 34.5 | -5.3* | 30.1 | 30.2 | 1.4 | 0.00 |
| | *(S.E.)* | (0.5) | (0.5) | (0.6) | (0.8) | (0.8) | (1.0) | (0.6) | (0.6) | (0.8) | |
| | *Median* | 28.8 | 27.3 | -2.6 | 33.9 | 30.5 | -7.7* | 26.0 | 25.6 | -1.1 | |
| | *% Positive* | | | 42% | | | 34% | | | 47% | |
| **Relative Quoted Spread** | *Mean* | 3.6 | 3.7 | 3.4* | 3.6 | 3.7 | 3.4* | 3.6 | 3.6 | 3.2* | 0.85 |
| | *(S.E.)* | (0.1) | (0.1) | (0.7) | (0.1) | (0.1) | (1.2) | (0.1) | (0.1) | (0.9) | |
| | *Median* | 3.0 | 3.0 | -1.0 | 3.3 | 3.1 | -0.0 | 2.9 | 2.9 | -1.8 | |
| | *% Positive* | | | 47% | | | 50% | | | 46% | |
| **Relative Effective Spread** | *Mean* | 2.7 | 2.7 | 1.9* | 2.8 | 2.9 | 0.7 | 2.6 | 2.6 | 2.7* | 0.16 |
| | *(S.E.)* | (0.1) | (0.2) | (0.7) | (0.1) | (0.1) | (1.1) | (0.1) | (0.1) | (1.1) | |
| | *Median* | 2.3 | 2.3 | -2.6 | 2.6 | 2.4 | -2.9 | 2.1 | 2.1 | -2.4 | |
| | *% Positive* | | | 46% | | | 44% | | | 47% | |

*Indicates significance at the 5% level using two-tailed t-test (for mean) or signed rank test (for median).

Summary measures of bid-ask spreads for the 30-day periods before and after the IPO lockup expiration day. Spreads are measures in pennies per share; relative spreads are measured as a percentage of the quote midpoint. The quoted spread is the difference between the ask and bid quotes. The effective spread is calculated as $2\times|P_t - M_t|$, where $P_t$ is the transaction price at time $t$ and $M_t$ is the midpoint of the bid and ask quotes in effect at time $t$. The sample is 1,497 U.S. lockup expirations in the period April, 1995 through June, 1999. Reported statistics are based on the distributions of the 1,497 firm-level means and changes. Standard errors (S.E.) are in parentheses. Intraday data are from the TAQ database.

Table 4: The Effect of Lockup Expiration on Market Depth

| Variable | | All Firms (n=1,497) | | | Venture-Backed (n=570) | | | Non-Venture Backed (n=927) | | | P-value for difference in % change for venture vs. non-venture |
|---|---|---|---|---|---|---|---|---|---|---|---|
| | | Before | After | % Change | Before | After | % Change | Before | After | % Change | |
| **Quote Depth** | Mean | 796 | 867 | 22* | 704 | 785 | 23* | 844 | 918 | 21* | 0.57 |
| | (S.E.) | (19) | (19) | (2) | (15) | (16) | (2) | (28) | (29) | (2) | |
| | Median | 745 | 792 | 4* | 692 | 755 | 6* | 762 | 808 | 3* | |
| | % Positive | | | 57% | | | 59% | | | 56% | |
| **Depth-to- Spread Ratio** | Mean | 704 | 810 | 27* | 562 | 666 | 30* | 794 | 898 | 26* | 0.38 |
| | (S.E.) | (26) | (30) | (2) | (18) | (24) | (3) | (40) | (48) | (3) | |
| | Median | 510 | 556 | 10* | 480 | 536 | 12* | 534 | 582 | 9* | |
| | % Positive | | | 60% | | | 63% | | | 58% | |
| **Effective Spreads on Trades of 10,000 Shares or More** | Mean | 1.2 | 1.2 | 3.9 | 1.5 | 1.5 | 7.6 | 1.1 | 1.1 | 1.7 | 0.27 |
| | (S.E.) | (0.1) | (0.1) | (2.5) | (0.1) | (0.1) | (4.6) | (0.1) | (0.1) | (2.9) | |
| | Median | 1.0 | 1.0 | -2.8 | 1.3 | 1.2 | -0.9 | 0.9 | 0.9 | -5.2 | |
| | % Positive | | | 46% | | | 49% | | | 45% | |
| **Number of Daily Trades** | Mean | 59 | 73 | 32* | 65 | 74 | 47* | 55 | 72 | 23* | 0.00 |
| | (S.E.) | (5) | (9) | (3) | (8) | (7) | (5) | (7) | (14) | (3) | |
| | Median | 22 | 24 | 8* | 24 | 30 | 16* | 20 | 20 | -4 | |
| | % Positive | | | 52% | | | 61% | | | 48% | |
| **Trade Size (Shares)** | Mean | 1,717 | 1,827 | 18* | 1,708 | 1,982 | 28* | 1,722 | 1,731 | 12* | 0.00 |
| | (S.E.) | (28) | (28) | (2) | (38) | (49) | (3) | (39) | (34) | (2) | |
| | Median | 1,438 | 1,560 | 5* | 1,493 | 1,690 | 10* | 1,418 | 1,433 | -0 | |
| | % Positive | | | 57% | | | 68% | | | 50% | |
| **Daily Volume (Shares)** | Mean | 70,105 | 90,171 | 58* | 72,160 | 99,644 | 86* | 68,842 | 84,346 | 41* | 0.00 |
| | (S.E.) | (3,214) | (4,980) | (4) | (4,362) | (5,568) | (7) | (4,445) | (7,271) | (4) | |
| | Median | 37,663 | 43,890 | 14* | 42,373 | 61,495 | 41* | 34,180 | 34,013 | 1 | |
| | % Positive | | | 57% | | | 68% | | | 50% | |

*Indicates significance at the 5% level using two-tailed t-test (for mean) or signed rank test (for median).
Summary statistics for market depth and trading activity during the 30-day periods before and after the IPO lockup expiration day. The "% Change" column is based on the distribution of percentage changes. Standard errors (S.E.) are in parentheses. Quote Depth is the average of the bid and ask depth. The Depth-to-Spread Ratio is (Bid Depth + Ask Depth) / (Relative Quoted Spread). The sample is 1,497 U.S. lockup expirations in the period April, 1995 through June, 1999. Reported statistics are based on the distributions of the 1,497 firm-level means and changes. Because of the scarcity of block trades, the sample size for the block trade spread results is only 263 firms, of which 98 are venture-financed.

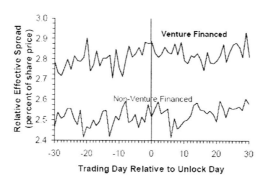

Figure 2: Average effective spreads around the lockup expiration.

Effective spreads are measures in pennies per share; relative effective spreads are measured as a percentage of the quote midpoint. The effective spread is calculated as $2 \times |P_t - M_t|$, where $P_t$ is the transaction price at time $t$ and $M_t$ is the midpoint of the bid and ask quotes in effect at time $t$. The sample is 1,497 U.S. lockup expirations in the period April, 1995 through June, 1999. Data are from TAQ.

Table 3 presents formal tests for a persistent change in spreads, by comparing several measures of spreads for the thirty day periods before and after the lockup expiration. Results are shown for the whole sample and for the subsamples of firms with and without venture financing. In addition to effective spreads, results are also shown for quoted spreads. The results are consistent with the inferences drawn from Figure 2. The only significant changes in absolute spreads are in the venture-finance subsample, which shows a decline of 3-8 percent, depending on the definition of the spread and the measure of central tendency. These spread declines mirror the price declines, which are also largely confined to the venture financed subsample. The simultaneous declines in absolute spreads and share prices results in small, ambiguously-signed changes in relative spreads. The mean change in the relative effective spread is +1.9 percent, but the median change has the opposite sign, at -2.6 percent. Relative quoted spreads show similar, ambiguously-signed changes. The disagreement between the signs of the mean and median indicates that spread changes are skewed, with a majority of firms enjoying narrower spreads after the lockup expiration, while a few firms see spread increases of a somewhat larger magnitude. A detailed examination of the data (not reported) indicates that this skewness is pervasive, and is not driven by just a few extreme observations.

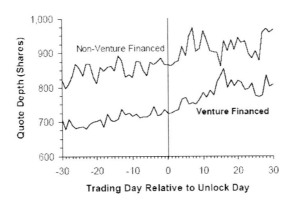

Figure 3: Average quote depth around the lockup expiration.

Quote depth is the average of the bid-side and ask-side depth, which are the minimum number of shares that the market maker guarantees to transact at the quoted price. The sample is 1,497 U.S. lockup expirations in the period April, 1995 through June, 1999. Data are from TAQ.

As robustness checks, we repeated our tests using a [-60,+60] event window, with qualitatively similar results. Also, we expect the results may depend on the exchange mechanism. Our sample is dominated by NASDAQ firms, with only 223 (15%) being traded on NYSE. In unreported tests we find no significant long-term spread changes in either the NYSE or NASDAQ subsamples.

Overall, after lockup expiration we observe a statistically significant, but small and temporary widening in bid-ask spreads. The magnitude of the change is 3-4 percent of the pre-expiration spread, and it lasts about a week.

## Changes in Market Depth after Lockup Expirations

Trading costs depend not only on bid-ask spreads, but also on market depth, roughly defined as the ability to trade large numbers of shares without seriously affecting price. Market depth is typically measured by trading activity (number and size of trades), by quote depth (the number of shares that the market maker guarantees to transact without changing the price), and by the effective spreads on block trades of 10,000 shares or more. The total cost of trading is sometimes summarized by the depth-to-spread ratio, which is the quoted depth divided by the quoted spread (Bacidore (1997), Harris (2000)). Here we test for post-expiration changes in these measures of market depth.

Table 4 presents summary measures of the pre- to post-expiration changes in quote depth, depth-to-spread ratio, effective spreads on block trades, daily number of trades, and average trade size. Results are presented for the whole sample, as well as for the venture- and non-venture financed subsamples. Comparing the thirty day periods before and after lockup expiration, the mean change in quote depth is +22 percent (median = four percent), and the mean change in the depth-to-spread ratio is +27% (median = 10 percent). Thus, we find substantial increases in quote depth after lockup expirations. A daily time series of abnormal quote depth (presented later) reveals no evidence of short-term reductions.

The changes in the effective spreads on block trades (the third row of Table 4) have the same ambiguous sign as we observed previously for the spreads on all trade sizes. The mean change in the effective spread is positive, but the median change is negative. Both the mean and median change have small magnitude, less than four percent of the pre-expiration spread, and neither is statistically significant.

Consistent with the increase in total trading volume (row 6), both the number of daily trades (row 4) and the average trade size (row 5) increase significantly after lockup expirations, especially among venture-financed firms. On average, number of trades per day increases by 32%, and average trade size increases 18%. The median changes have the same sign but smaller magnitude, and all of the mean and median changes are significantly different from zero. The changes in trading activity in the venture-financed subsample are roughly double those in the non-venture financed subsample.

Overall, our results show that trading volume and quote depth deepen by 20% or more after lockup expiration. Net trading costs, as measured by the depth-to-spread ratio, decline sharply, but the effective spreads for block trades do not change very much. These results do not support the hypothesis that market depth is impaired by the presence of insider traders.

## Tests for Hidden Liquidity Impairments

Our univariate tests reveal only a small and temporary increase in spreads, and a large and persistent increase in market depth. Thus, we find no large or persistent impairment of market liquidity after lockup expirations. One potential explanation for this result is that the liquidity consequences of increased information asymmetry are masked by other consequences of lockup expirations. Here we present several tests for liquidity impairment that might be masked by confounding effects, especially changes in share price, trading activity, and the number of tradable shares. The following subsections present, in turn, multivariate regression tests, spread decomposition tests, and tests for a subsample of firms in which the number of tradable shares does not increase because insiders do not sell.

Table 5: Percent Changes in Spreads and Quote Depth by Post-Expiration Price Change

|  |  | Price Falls (n=796) | Price Rises (n=701) |
|---|---|---|---|
| **Relative Effective Spread** | *Mean* | 12.2* | -10.1* |
|  | *(S.E.)* | (1.1) | (0.7) |
|  | *Median* | 6.4* | -12.4* |
|  | *% Positive* | 62% | 23% |
| **Quote Depth** | *Mean* | 24.6* | 17.8* |
|  | *(S.E.)* | (2.6) | (2.0) |
|  | *Median* | 6.0* | 1.8* |
|  | *% Positive* | 60% | 55% |

*Indicates significance at the 5% level using two-tailed t-test (for mean) or signed rank test (for median)
Reported statistics are based on the distribution of percentage changes between the pre- and post-expiration windows, [-30,-1] and [+1,+30]. "Price Falls" and "Price Rises" are based on the average share price over the pre- and post-expiration windows. The relative effective spread is calculated as $(2 \times | P_t - M_t |) / M_t$, where $P_t$ is the transaction price at time t and $M_t$ is the midpoint of the bid and ask quotes in effect at time t. Quote depth is the average of the bid and ask depth, the number of shares the market maker

guarantees to transact at the quoted price. Standard errors (S.E.) are in parentheses. The sample is 1,497 U.S. lockup expirations in the period April, 1995 through June, 1999. Intraday data are from the TAQ database.

## Multivariate Regression Tests

Spreads and quote depth are functions of share price, trading activity, trade size, and volatility, all of which are likely to change when the lockup expires. Price changes, in particular, seem to be important in our sample. The relative spread is known to be a declining function of share price, due to minimum tick size and other factors (Harris (1994)). Since share prices tend to fall after lockup expiration, we also expect to observe some widening of the relative spread. Table 5 shows spread changes for subsamples based on whether the average share price rises or falls between the pre- and post-expiration periods. The results show that, if the share price falls after the lockup expiration, the relative effective spread tends to widen, by an average of 12 percent (median = six percent). If the share price rises after the lockup expiration, the relative effective spread tends to narrow, by an average of 10 percent (median = 12 percent). These effects are highly statistically significant, and price changes have substantial power to predict whether the spread will widen or narrow after the lockup expiration. For example, Table 5 shows that the relative effective spread narrows in 77 percent of the 701 firms whose price rises after the lockup expiration. In unreported tests, we find that the relative effective spread narrows in 90 percent of the 185 firms whose price rises more than twenty percent, and the relative effective spread widens in 77 percent of the 192 firms whose price drops more than 20 percent.

To test for abnormal changes in spreads and quote depth, we estimate regression models of the relative effective spread and quote depth as functions of share price, volatility, and trading activity. The sample for this test includes two observations per firm: one observation for the pre-expiration period and another for the post-expiration period. A dummy variable indicates whether the observation occurs in the pre- or post-expiration period, and the coefficient on this dummy is our primary test statistic. The dependent variables are the thirty-day means of either the relative effective spread or quote depth, as presented in the earlier tables. The explanatory variables are volatility and the thirty day means of closing share prices, daily number of trades, daily average trade size, and daily volume. We measure volatility by the standard deviation of the thirty daily returns, calculated from closing midpoints. Formally, we estimate models of the form:

$$
\begin{bmatrix} Y[-30,-1]_{i=1} \\ ; \\ ; \\ Y[-30,-1]_{i=1,497} \\ Y[+1,+30]_{i=1} \\ ; \\ ; \\ Y[+1,+30]_{i=1,497} \end{bmatrix} = \alpha + \beta_1 \begin{bmatrix} 0 \\ ; \\ ; \\ 0 \\ 1 \\ ; \\ ; \\ 1 \end{bmatrix} + \beta_2 \cdot Price + \beta_3 \cdot Volatility + \beta_4 \cdot Trade\ Activity + \varepsilon \tag{5}
$$

where $i$ indexes the 1,497 firms in the sample, $Y$ is the thirty-day mean of either the relative effective spread or the quote depth (average of the bid depth and the ask depth) as presented in the earlier tables, and "Trade Activity" is either total volume, or number of trades and average trade size. In the spread model we control for the reciprocal of price, rather than price, as the dependent variable has price in its denominator.

Table 6 presents the coefficient estimates. The coefficients on the control variables are sensible and in most cases highly significant. The relative effective spread is negatively related to share price, daily volume, and daily number of trades, and is positively related to volatility and average trade size. Quote depth is negatively related to share price and volatility, and is positively related to daily volume, daily number of trades, and average trade size. Our primary test statistic is the dummy coefficient, $\beta_1$, which indicates whether the post-expiration period experiences a change in spreads or quote depth that is not explained by changes in the other variables. In the spreads model, the bulk of the explanatory power (39 percent of a maximum 43 percent) comes from the control for price changes, and the coefficient on the post-expiration dummy variable is not statistically significant in any specification. In the quote depth model, the dummy coefficient has positive sign and is always statistically significant. Thus we find no evidence for abnormal changes in spreads after controlling for price changes, but we do find significant increases in quote depth that are not explained by the concurrent changes in price, volatility, or trading activity. These results give no indication of abnormal liquidity impairment that might be attributed to asymmetric information.

Table 6: Regression analysis of relative effective spreads and quote depth.

**Panel A: Dependent Variable is Relative Effective Spread (in percentage points)**

| Model: | 1 | 2 | 3 | 4 |
|---|---|---|---|---|
| Intercept [$t$-stat] | 1.5 [34.5] | 2.1 [31.9] | 1.6 [28.2] | 1.3 [17.7] |
| **Dummy for post-expiration period** | **-0.05 [-0.9]** | **0.09 [1.5]** | **0.01 [0.1]** | **-0.05 [-0.9]** |
| 1 / Price | 11.5 [44.4] | | 10.7 [40.0] | 11.1 [40.9] |
| Volatility | | 20.6 [15.0] | 5.7 [4.9] | 4.3 [3.6] |
| Volume (in 100,000) | | -0.4 [-18.5] | -0.2 [-13.7] | |
| Number of daily trades (in 1,000) | | | | -0.7 [-7.4] |
| Trade size (in 10,000) | | | | 1.1 [5.2] |
| Adjusted $R^2$ | 0.39 | 0.13 | 0.43 | 0.41 |

**Panel B: Dependent Variable is Quote Depth (average of bid and ask depth, in 100's)**

| Model: | 1 | 2 | 3 | 4 |
|---|---|---|---|---|
| Intercept | 8.4 [34.8] | 8.3 [32.6] | 9.8 [31.7] | 8.2 [20.0] |
| **Dummy for post-expiration period** | **0.71 [2.9]** | **0.53 [2.2]** | **0.46 [2.0]** | **0.60 [2.4]** |
| Price | -0.03 [2.62] | | -0.09 [-8.3] | -0.05 [-4.2] |
| Volatility | | -26.1 [4.9] | -32.2 [-6.1] | -13.5 [-2.4] |
| Volume (in 100,000) | | 8.6 [11.0] | 11.8 [13.6] | |
| Number of daily trades (in 1,000) | | | | 2.3 [3.9] |
| Trade size (in 10,000) | | | | 5.8 [5.7] |
| Adjusted $R^2$ | 0.01 | 0.04 | 0.06 | 0.02 |

This table reports coefficient estimates from a cross sectional OLS model of the effective spread or quote depth, as a function of share price, trading volume, and volatility.   The dependant variable is the mean relative effective spread or mean quote depth, as defined in the text.   Price is the mean of the thirty closing midpoints.  Volume is the mean of the thirty daily trading volumes.  Number of Daily Trades and Average Trade Size are the means of the thirty daily averages; Volatility is the standard deviation of the thirty daily returns, computed from the closing midpoint.  The sample contains two observations per firm; one observation for the pre-expiration period [-30,-1], and another for the post-expiration period [1,30], with a dummy variable taking a value of 1 in the post-expiration period.  $T$ statistics are given in brackets.    The sample has 2,994 observations, corresponding to 1,497 U.S. lockup expirations in the period April, 1995 through June, 1999.

## Changes in the Asymmetric Information Component of the Spread

Bid-ask spreads are thought to be composed of two elements: the "asymmetric information" component, which compensates the market maker for expected losses to informed traders, and the remainder or "fixed cost" component, which compensates the market maker for the other costs of making a market.  The fixed cost component of the spread may fall after lockup expiration, as the increase in trading activity will allow the market maker to amortize his fixed costs over a larger number of trades.  This effect should have been captured in our multivariate regression model, but as an additional test we apply a standard decomposition of the spread into an asymmetric information component, $\theta$, and a fixed-cost component, $\phi$, using the decomposition model described in Madhaven, Richardson and Roomans (1997). Formally, intraday price changes are assumed to follow:

$$ p_t - p_{t-1} = (\phi + \theta)x_t - \varphi x_{t-1} + \varepsilon_t + \xi_t + \xi_{t-1} \tag{6} $$

where $p_t$ is the share price at time $t$, and $x_t$ is a trade-direction indicator that takes a value of 1 if the trade is buyer-initiated, -1 if the trade is seller-initiated, and 0 if the trade is a cross. The indicator variable is obtained using the inference procedure suggested by Lee and Ready (1991).[1] The term $\varepsilon$ reflects the innovations in beliefs about share value, and $\xi$ reflects errors caused by price discreteness.  For each firm, parameter estimates are obtained from the pooled intraday price changes from all the days in the event window, excluding the price changes from the close to the subsequent open.   For a detailed description of this decomposition, and of our GMM estimation procedure, see Madhaven, Richardson and Roomans (1997).

---

[1] The trade is assumed to be seller initiated if the price is below the spread midpoint, buyer-initiated if the price is above the midpoint, and a cross if the trade is at the midpoint.  Ellis, Michaely, and O'Hara (2000b) find that this procedure works well for Nasdaq stocks.  We also try an alternative inference procedure suggested by Ellis *et al*, and find qualitatively similar results.

Table 7: GMM Estimates of the Spread Components

|  | Period 1: [-30, -1] | Period 2: [1, 30] | Period 3: [1, 10] |
|---|---|---|---|
| θ = Asymmetric information cost per share (cents) | 2.40 (0.04) | 2.41 (0.07) | 2.45 (0.05) |
| φ = Fixed cost per share (cents) | 12.0 (0.2) | 11.6 (0.2) | 11.4 (0.2) |
| Implied Spread (cents) | 28.9 (0.4) | 28.0 (0.5) | 27.6 (0.5) |
| Proportion of asymmetric information cost (%) | 21.7 (0.5) | 21.7 (0.5) | 22.6 (0.5) |

This table reports cross-sectional averages of the estimated parameters of the Modhavan, Richardson and Roomans (1997) model. $\theta$ is the asymmetric information cost per share, $\phi$ is the fixed cost per share. The implied spread is the difference between implied bid and ask prices and is given by $2(\phi+\theta)$. $\theta/(\phi+\theta)$ is the proportion of asymmetric information cost relative to the implied spread. Standard errors are given in parentheses; all coefficients are statistically significant. The sample is 1,497 U.S. lockup expirations in the period April, 1995 through June, 1999. Day zero is the lockup expiration day.

Table 7 summarizes the GMM parameter estimates for the thirty day periods before and after lockup expiration. The table presents the cross-sectional means and standard errors of the firm-level parameter estimates $\theta$ and $\phi$ for the pre- and post-expiration periods. Also presented are the implied total round trip trading cost, $2(\theta+\phi)$, and the proportion of trading costs due to asymmetric information. The coefficients are reasonable in the sense that they are similar to those reported elsewhere, e.g., in Glosten and Harris (1988) and Madhaven, Richardson and Roomans (1997). The main result is that the asymmetric information component, $\theta$, does not change after the lockup expires. In the post-expiration period, the mean value of $\theta$ is 2.41 cents per share, virtually identical to the 2.40 cents in the pre-expiration period. The difference is not statistically significant. The fixed cost component, $\phi$, declines from 12.03 cents to 11.57 cents, a statistically insignificant reduction of 0.46 cents per share. Thus, we find no increase in the asymmetric information component that could be attributed to the presence of insider traders, though we do find the decline in the fixed cost component that one would expect, given the observed increase in trading activity.

The time series of abnormal effective spreads (see Table 2) suggests that the short-term effects of the lockup expiration are larger than the long-term effects. To test whether there is a significant short-term increase in asymmetric information costs, we also estimate the model in the period [+1,+10]. The results, reported in Table 7, show a slightly increased asymmetric information component and slightly reduced fixed-cost component, consistent with the changes one would predict from simultaneous increases in insider trading and total trading volume. However, once again the change in the asymmetric information components between the pre- and post-expiration periods has small magnitude and is not statistically significant.

## Results in a Subsample of Firms where the Tradable Float Does not Increase

The lockup expiration marks not only the arrival of new insider traders, but also the arrival of their newly-tradable shares. Any shares sold by insiders will increase the publicly tradable float, and the subsequent re-trading of these new shares could create long-term liquidity benefits that obscure the long-term costs of increased asymmetric information. Such effects should have been captured by the controls for trading activity in our multivariate model, or by our spread decomposition model, but as a robustness check we replicate our tests in a subsample where there is little or no increase in the number of tradable shares because insiders do not sell. We reason that the hypothesized liquidity impairment is caused not by actual insider sales (which are largely unobservable until after the fact) but rather by the ex ante possibility that insiders *might* sell. However, any liquidity improvements due to an increase in the number of tradable shares will be caused only by actual insider sales. Thus, if we examine a subsample with no insider selling, we should observe the costs of *potential* insider selling, unobscured by any benefits from *actual* insider selling.

Unfortunately, SEC insider trade disclosures are not reliable enough to yield a convincing determination that no insider selling occurred in a particular period, so we must use a less efficient method. We compare the share ownership disclosed in the IPO prospectus with that disclosed in the first proxy statement after the lockup expiration. When the two documents indicate no reduction in the holdings of the pre-IPO shareholders, we conclude that no significant insider sales occurred in our event window.

A weakness of this test is that the prospectus and the proxy do not itemize all shareholdings, only those of officers, directors, and five percent blockholders. On average we are able to account for 84% of the total locked-up shares (median=93%), but we cannot be certain that some or all of the remaining shares are not sold after the lockup expiration.[2] Since this test is very labor intensive, we limit our attention to a relatively small subsample. We restrict the sample to the firms whose IPOs occurred after May, 1996, the first date for which we can obtain prospectus data. We sort the sample by the year of the IPO, and then randomly select 25 percent of the firms in each year. This yields a subsample of 246 firms, of which we could obtain usable data for 216. (Our selection criteria is based on the year of the IPO, rather than the year of lockup expiration, so the sample size that is slightly smaller than one would infer from the year-by-year sample sizes in Table 1.)

Table 8: Percent changes in spreads and market depth for firms with no insider sales.

|  |  | % change |
| --- | --- | --- |
| **Relative Effective Spread** | Mean | 4.2 |
|  | (S.E.) | (2.6) |
|  | Median | -1.9 |
|  | % Positive | 47% |

---

[2] It is conceivable that our method will miss an increase in the public float due to incentive shares that are received by insiders after the IPO and then sold at lockup expiration. However, such an event would be unusual. Incentive shares typically do not vest for at least a year (thus post-IPO incentive shares usually cannot be sold at lockup expiration) and we know of no reason for insiders to time their sale of such shares to coincide with the lockup expiration.

| | | % change |
|---|---|---|
| **Quote Depth** | Mean | 31.1* |
| | (S.E.) | (6.6) |
| | Median | 15.6* |
| | % Positive | 69% |
| **Number of Daily Trades** | Mean | 11.4 |
| | (S.E.) | (6.7) |
| | Median | -6.4 |
| | % Positive | 44% |
| **Trade Size (Shares)** | Mean | 13.7 |
| | (S.E.) | (7.5) |
| | Median | 2.6 |
| | % Positive | 52% |
| **Daily Share Volume** | Mean | 29.4* |
| | (S.E.) | (10.4) |
| | Median | -2.7 |
| | % Positive | 46% |

*Indicates significance at the 5% level using t-test (for mean) or signed rank test (for median).

Percentage changes in spreads, quote depth, and trading activity between the 30-day periods before and after the IPO lockup expiration day. Reported statistics are based on the distribution of firm-level percentage changes. Quote depth is the average of bid-side and ask-side depth. The sample is 128 U.S. firms in which insiders retained more than 99.5% of their shares until at least the first proxy date after the expiration event window. Data are from TAQ.

We find that, in 113 firms (52%), pre-IPO shareholders did not sell any of their shares, and in another 15 firms (7 percent), their share sales amounted to less than 0.5 percent of the shares outstanding. Thus, in 128 firms (59 percent) insiders hang on to virtually all of their shares until at least the first proxy date after the expiration window, typically about a year after the IPO. We find it somewhat surprising that only 41 percent of firms report substantial insider sales, though this result is consistent with Field and Hanka's (2001) finding that 17 percent of firms disclose insider share sales immediately after the lockup expiration.

Table 8 presents the pre- to post-expiration changes in several measures of the market depth and bid-ask spreads for the subsample of 128 firms in which we found little or no insider sales. Despite the relatively small sample, the statistical power of the tests is sufficient to reach some order-of-magnitude conclusions. The pre- to post-expiration changes in bid-ask spreads show the same ambiguous pattern that was observed in the full sample, with positive mean but negative median. The changes in quote depth have substantially positive mean and median, roughly similar to the quote depth increases we observe in the whole sample. For all the measures of trading activity, the mean change is positive but the median change is small or negative, indicating that changes in trading activity are skewed.

Overall these results indicate that, compared with our broader sample, firms with little or no insider selling experience roughly the same post-expiration changes in spreads and depth as we observe in the broader sample. These results confirm that the conclusions we draw from the broader sample are not driven by the increase in the tradable float due to insider sales.

## Tests for More Subtle Evidence of Asymmetric Information Costs

Our tests have revealed that lockup expirations produce only small and temporary changes in spreads, and no reduction of market depth. The temporary increase in spreads may be caused by temporarily increased information asymmetry, but also has plausible alternative explanations. For example, if insiders are particularly eager to sell, then market makers may temporarily widen the spread as compensation for the effort of locating additional buyers, or for taking more shares into their own inventory, or because the demand for their services is temporarily less price-elastic. To search for persuasive evidence of an increase in asymmetric information costs, here we present tests for several "signatures" of asymmetric information. The following tests search for evidence of asymmetric information in the differences between bid-side and ask-side quote depth, in the cross-sectional relation between spread changes and trade size, and in the cross-sectional relation between spread changes and pre-expiration trading activity.

### Asymmetry in the Changes in Bid-Side and Ask-Side Quote Depth

Lockups prevent insider share sales, but not insider purchases. Consequently, the expiration of the lockup will increase the probability that any given share seller is an informed insider, but should not have a large effect on the probability that a share buyer is an informed insider. Market makers who are concerned about trading against insiders should, ceteris paribus, reduce their bid-side quote depth after the lockup expiration, but will not necessarily reduce their ask-side depth. Thus, we predict an asymmetric change in quote depth after the lockup expiration, with the bid-side depth declining more (or increasing less) than the ask-side depth.

Tabulated values represent the deviation from the mean for the period [-30,-6]. Formally, on day $T$, the tabulated value is calculated as:

$$\left( \frac{x_T}{\frac{1}{25} \sum_{i=-30}^{-6} x_i} - 1 \right) \cdot 100\%$$

where $x$ is the market depth measure listed in the column headings, and day zero is the lockup expiration. The sample is 1,497 U.S. lockup expirations in the period April, 1995 through June, 1999.

Table 9:  Daily Abnormal Bid and Ask Quote Depth

| Day | Abnormal Ask Size | t-stat | Abnormal Bid Size | t-stat |
|---|---|---|---|---|
| -10 | 2.0 | [1.7] | 0.0 | [ 0.01] |
| -9 | 7.2* | [4.5] | 2.3 | [ 1.8] |
| -8 | 3.9* | [3.0] | 1.0 | [ 0.8] |
| -7 | 2.4 | [1.8] | -0.1 | [-0.1] |
| -6 | 2.1 | [1.6] | 1.7 | [ 1.3] |
| -5 | 7.1* | [3.6] | 5.8* | [ 3.6] |
| -4 | 9.4* | [4.5] | 7.9* | [ 4.9] |
| -3 | 8.2* | [4.0] | 7.0* | [ 4.2] |
| -2 | 7.7* | [4.1] | 6.7* | [ 4.0] |
| -1 | 8.9* | [3.5] | 8.9* | [ 3.6] |
| 0 | 7.7* | [4.7] | 8.5* | [ 4.2] |
| 1 | 8.1* | [4.5] | 10.7* | [ 5.3] |
| 2 | 10.8* | [5.8] | 13.4* | [ 6.3] |
| 3 | 13.4* | [6.0] | 14.9* | [ 4.1] |
| 4 | 17.8* | [6.4] | 15.4* | [ 5.8] |
| 5 | 17.9* | [8.3] | 18.1* | [ 4.4] |
| 6 | 18.4* | [8.0] | 21.7* | [ 5.2] |
| 7 | 19.6* | [7.0] | 27.8* | [ 2.8] |
| 8 | 17.2* | [6.5] | 24.9* | [ 2.6] |
| 9 | 19.0* | [8.5] | 18.4* | [ 6.0] |
| 10 | 27.6* | [8.4] | 18.6* | [ 7.68] |

*Indicates significance at the 5% level (two-tailed test).

Table 9 presents the daily time series of abnormal bid-side and ask-side quote depth. The tabulated values represent the percentage deviation from the mean in the pre-expiration period [-30,-6]. The results show steadily increasing quote depth, beginning a week before the lockup expiration and continuing throughout the event window. The results show no evidence that bid-side depth declines relative to ask-side depth. In fact, in the days immediately around the lockup expirations, the abnormal bid depth is actually larger than the abnormal ask depth. Of the eight days in the period [-2,+5], only two show larger abnormal ask depth, while five show larger abnormal bid depth.

Table 10: Test for Persistent Asymmetric Changes in Bid and Ask Quote Depth

| | | Before | After | % Change |
|---|---|---|---|---|
| **Ask-Side** | *Mean* | 795 | 875 | 22* |
| **Quote Depth** | *(S.E.)* | (15) | (17) | (2) |
| | *Median* | 742 | 799 | 4* |
| | *% Positive* | | | 57% |
| **Bid-Side** | *Mean* | 797 | 859 | 21* |
| **Quote Depth** | *(S.E.)* | (23) | (21) | (2) |
| | *Median* | 749 | 785 | 4* |
| | *% Positive* | | | 58% |

% level using two-tailed t-test (for mean) or signed rank test (for median).

Summary statistics for percentage changes in bid and ask quote depth between the 30-day periods before and after the IPO lockup expiration day. Quote depth is the number of shares the market maker guarantees to transact at the bid or ask price. The sample is 1,497 U.S. lockup expirations in the period April, 1995 through June, 1999. Reported statistics are based on the distributions of the 1,497 firm-level means and changes.

Table 10 tests for longer term effects by presenting summary measures of the percentage changes in bid-side and ask-side quote depth between the thirty day periods before and after the lockup expiration. Again, the results do not show the predicted asymmetry. The mean changes in bid-side and ask-side depth are nearly identical, at 21 and 22 percent, respectively. The difference is not statistically significant. The median changes are the same, at four percent, and the percent positive changes are similar, at 57 and 58 percent, respectively.

Thus, we do not find the asymmetry between bid-side and ask-side depth changes that we would expect if quote depth is a declining function of the probability of trading against an insider. If anything, the short-term changes in quote depth seem to imply the reverse.

## The Relation between Spread Changes and Trade Size

Asymmetric information may be a bigger problem for some trades than for others. We hypothesize that informed traders will want to trade enough shares to make a meaningful profit, but will not trade in such large blocks as to call attention to themselves. Consistent with this hypothesis, Barclay and Warner (1993) find that most price movements are driven by medium sized trades. Thus we predict that, if spread increases after lockup expiration are driven by asymmetric information, then spread increases should be largest for medium-sized trades, perhaps in the range from 1,000-10,000 shares.

Table 11 shows pre- to post-expiration changes in relative effective spreads for various classes of trade size. The results are not as predicted, as the spreads on medium-sized trades (1,000-5,000 shares or 5,000-10,000 shares) actually decline relative to those on smaller or larger trades. The most pronounced difference is a median eight percent decline in the spreads on trades of 5,000-10,000 shares. Thus, the relation between trade size and spread changes does not support the hypothesis that asymmetric information widens the bid-ask spread after lockup expirations.

Table 11: Changes in the Relative Effective Spreads by Trade-Size Category

| Trade Size | | Before | After | % Change |
|---|---|---|---|---|
| **100-500 (shares)** | *Mean* | 2.8% | 2.8% | 2.1%* |
| | *(S.E.)* | (0.1) | (0.1) | (0.8) |
| | *Median* | 2.5 | 2.4 | -2.7 |
| | *% Positive* | | | 45% |
| **501-1,000** | *Mean* | 2.5 | 2.5 | 2.4* |
| | *(S.E.)* | (0.1) | (0.1) | (0.1) |
| | *Median* | 2.1 | 2.0 | -2.9 |
| | *% Positive* | | | 46% |

| Trade Size | | Before | After | % Change |
|---|---|---|---|---|
| **1,001-5,000** | *Mean* | 2.4 | 2.4 | 2.1* |
| | *(S.E.)* | (0.1) | (0.1) | (0.8) |
| | *Median* | 2.0 | 2.0 | -3.5 |
| | *% Positive* | | | 46% |
| **5,001-10,000** | *Mean* | 1.6 | 1.5 | 1.7 |
| | *(S.E.)* | (0.1) | (0.1) | (1.6) |
| | *Median* | 1.3 | 1.2 | -7.9* |
| | *% Positive* | | | 41% |
| **> 10,000** | *Mean* | 1.3 | 1.2 | 3.9 |
| | *(S.E.)* | (0.1) | (0.1) | (2.5) |
| | *Median* | 1.0 | 1.0 | -2.8 |
| | *% Positive* | | | 46% |

*Indicates significance at the 5% level, using two-tailed t-test (for mean) or signed rank test (for median).

The relative effective spread is calculated as $(2 \times | P_t - M_t |) / M_t$, where $P_t$ is the transaction price at time $t$ and $M_t$ is the midpoint of the bid and ask quotes in effect at time $t$. The "% Change" column is based on the distribution of percentage changes. Standard errors (*S.E.*) are in parentheses. The sample is 1,497 U.S. lockup expirations in the period April, 1995 through June, 1999. Reported statistics are based on the distribution of the firm-level means and changes.

## The Relation between Spread Changes and Trading Activity

Expected asymmetric information costs should be an increasing function of the probability of trading against an insider, which depends in turn on the volume of trading by outsiders. This implies that the firms with lower trading volume before the lockup expiration should tend to experience larger spread increases after the lockup expiration, since they will tend to experience larger increases in the probability of trading against an insider. A weakness of this test is that the same prediction follows from some of the alternative hypotheses. For example, we expect the same effect if spread changes are driven by the effort required to locate buyers for the insiders' shares, or by a reduction in the price-elasticity of demand for trades, since the arrival of a large block of insider sellers will have a relatively larger effect in a thin market.

Table 12: Changes in Relative Effective Spreads by Pre-Expiration Trading Frequency

| | *N Trades < 14*<br>*499 firms* | *14 ≤ N Trades < 35*<br>*499 firms* | *N Trades ≥ 35*<br>*499 firms* |
|---|---|---|---|
| *Mean* | 4.5* | 2.1 | -0.8 |
| *(S. E.)* | (1.3) | (1.3) | (1.2) |
| *Median* | -0.91 | -3.0* | -3.2* |
| *% Positive* | 48% | 44% | 43% |

*Indicates significance at the 5% level using two-tailed t-test (for mean) or signed rank test (for median).

Summary measures of the percentage changes in the relative effective spread from [-30,-1] to [1,30]. (Day 0 is the lockup expiration.) Firms are partitioned into three equal-sized groups based on average daily number of trades in the period [-30,-1]. Reported statistics are based on the distribution of firm-level percentage changes. Standard errors (*S.E.*) are in parentheses. The sample is 1,497 U.S. lockup expirations in the period April, 1995 through June, 1999.

Table 12 shows changes in relative effective spreads as a function of pre-expiration trading activity. The sample is partitioned into three equal size subsamples based on the respective average daily number of trades in the [-30,-1] window. The results are as predicted, showing a strong negative relation between pre-expiration trade activity and post-expiration spread changes. The mean change in the spread is +4.5 percent for firms in the lowest third of pre-expiration trading activity, +2.1 percent for firms in the middle third of trade activity, and -0.8 percent for firms in the highest third of trading activity. The corresponding median spread changes are -0.9 percent, -3.0 percent, and -3.2 percent. The differences between the various trade activity categories are statistically significant. The same pattern is observed in the venture-financed and non-venture financed subsamples, though the pattern is somewhat more pronounced among the venture-financed firms (results not reported).

Overall, of the three signs of increased information asymmetry that we test for, we find only one, a negative relation between spread changes and pre-expiration trading activity. We do not find the predicted asymmetry between bid-side and ask-side depth changes, nor do we find the predicted inverted-U shaped relation between trade size and effective spread changes.

## Conclusions

We examine liquidity changes around the expirations of 1,497 IPO lockup agreements in the period 1995-1999. These events mark the sudden release of a near-total prohibition on insider selling, and represent the first occasion in which an extremely well informed group of insiders – the founders and early investors in a firm – can profit from their inside knowledge by selling their shares without first revealing their intention to do so. Since lockup expirations typically occur in high-growth firms with a limited public history, the information asymmetry between insiders and outsiders is potentially severe. Furthermore, in the period immediately after the lockup expiration it will be uniquely difficult to detect and prosecute insider selling on the basis of material non-public information, as information-motivated insider traders can hide amongst the liquidity-motivated insider traders.

Empirically, lockup expirations represent a material change in market conditions, as evidenced by a permanent 40-60 percent increase in average trading volume. Consistent with the assumptions of asymmetric information models, lockup expirations are also followed by significant abnormal price changes that are correlated with insider share sales. Consequently, standard microstructure models predict a decline in market liquidity, as market makers widen the spread and reduce their quote depth in order to protect themselves against the adverse price changes associated with insider trades. Consistent with this prediction, when we compare the periods before and after lockup expirations we find a statistically significant increase in the effective bid-ask spread. However, the magnitude and duration of this effect are small. Relative effective spreads widen by 3-4 percent, or about 0.12 percent of share price, for about a week. Any longer-term changes in spreads are small, however, and seem to be driven primarily by changes in share price. Meanwhile, we observe a 20 percent increase in quote depth that is not explained by the concurrent changes in price, volatility, or trading activity. More detailed tests reveal no increase in the adverse selection component of the spread, and no evidence of increased asymmetric information costs that are masked by the benefits of increased trading volume.

The simplest interpretation of this result is that expected losses to insider traders are small relative to the other costs of making a market, and hence have little effect on spreads and quote depth. A practical implication of this result is that liquidity probably cannot be improved by strengthening the current legal restrictions on insider trading, or by supplementing them with self-imposed constraints. More broadly, since our sample includes a class of insiders that one would expect to be exceptionally well informed, in young firms with potentially severe information asymmetry, and in a time period when insider trades are clearly moving share prices, the fact that we observe no material liquidity impairment casts doubt on the hypothesis that liquidity is substantially affected by information asymmetry.

Future research might further investigate the impact of insider trading on market liquidity. Under current laws, the insiders in our sample are free to trade on the basis of their general opinions about the firm's quality and prospects, but they may be reluctant to trade on the basis of their specific knowledge of impending events that might trigger large price changes and subsequent SEC investigation (Muelbroek (1992)). Future research could test whether this distinction is important, by examining the liquidity changes around lockup expirations or other significant events in countries and time periods in which insider trading is not regulated.

# References

Aggarwal, Reena, 2000, Stabilization activities by underwriters after initial public offerings, *Journal of Finance* **55**, 1075-1103.

Allen, Franklin and Douglas Gale, 1992, Stock Price Manipulation, *Review of Financial Studies* **5**, 503-529.

Baesel, Jerome, and Garry Stein, 1979, The Value of Information: Inferences from the Profitability of Insider Trading, *Journal of Financial and Quantitative Analysis* **14**, 553-571.

Bagnoli, Mark, and Naveen Khanna, 1992, Insider Trading in Financial Signaling Models, *Journal of Finance* **47**, 1905-1934.

Baiman, Stanley and Robert Verrecchia, 1996, The relation among capital markets, financial disclosure, production efficiency, and insider trading, *Journal of Accounting Research* **34**, 1-22.

Bacidore, Jeffrey, 1997, The impact of decimalization on market quality: An empirical Investigation of the Toronto Stock Exchange, *Journal of Financial Intermediation* **6**, 92-190.

Barclay, Michael and Jerold Warner, 1993, Stealth trading and volatility: Which trades move prices?, *Journal of Financial Economics* **34**, 281-305.

Utpal Bhattacharya, and Hazem Daouk, 2001, The World Price of Insider Trading", Forthcoming in The Journal of Finance

Bebchuk, Lucian Arye, and Chaim Fershtman, 1994, Insider Trading and the Managerial Choice among Risky Projects, *Journal of Financial and Quantitative Analysis* **29**, 1-14.

Bebchuk, Lucian Arye and Christine Jolls, 1999, Managerial Value Diversion and Shareholder Wealth, Journal of Law, *Economics, and Organization* **15**, 487-502.

Bernhardt, Dan, Burton Hollifield, and Eric Hughson, 1995, Investment and Insider Trading, *Review of Financial Studies* **8**, 501-543.

Bettis, J. Carr, John M. Bizjak, and Michael L. Lemmon, 1999, Insider trading in derivative securities: An empirical examination of the use of zero-cost collars and equity swaps by corporate investors, unpublished working paper, Arizona State University.

Bettis, J. Carr, Jeffrey Coles, and Michael Lemmon, 2000, Corporate policies restricting trading by insiders, *Journal of Financial Economics* **57**, 191-220.

Bradley, Daniel, Bradford Jordan, Ivan Roten, and Ha-Chin Yi, 2001, Venture capital and IPO lockup expiration: An empirical analysis, forthcoming in Journal of Financial Research.

Brav, Alon and Paul Gompers, 2000, Insider trading subsequent to initial public offerings: Evidence from expirations of lock-up provisions, working paper, Harvard University.

Copeland, Thomas, and Dan Galai, 1983, Information effects on the bid/ask spread, *Journal of Finance* **38**, 1457-1469.

Cornell, Bradford, and Erik Sirri, 1992, The Reaction of Investors and Stock Prices to Insider Trading, *Journal of Finance* **47**, 1031-1059.

Damodaran, Aswath, and Crocker Liu, 1993, Insider Trading as a Signal of Private Information, *Review of Financial Studies* **6**, 79-119.

Eckbo, Espen, and David Smith, 2000, The Conditional Performance of Insider Trades, *Journal of Finance* **53**, 467-498.

Elliot, John, Dale Morse, and Gordon Richardson, 1984, The Association between Insider Trading and Information Announcements, *Rand Journal of Economics* **15**, 521-536.

Ellis, Katrina, Roni Michaely, and Maureen O'Hara, 2000a, When the underwriter is the market maker: An examination of trading in the IPO aftermarket, *Journal of Finance* **55**, 1039-1074.

Ellis, Katrina, Roni Michaely, and Maureen O'Hara, 2000b, The accuracy of trade classification rules: Evidence from Nasdaq, working paper, Cornell University.

Field, Laura Casares and Gordon Hanka, 2001, The Expiration of IPO Share Lockups, forthcoming in the Journal of Finance

Finnerty, Joseph, 1976, Insiders and Market Efficiency, *Journal of Finance* **21**, pages 1141-1148.

Fishman, Michael, and Kathleen Hagerty, 1992, Insider Trading and the Efficiency of Stock Prices, *Rand Journal of Economics* **23**, 106-122.

Givoly, Dan, and Dan Palmon, 1985, Insider Trading and the Exploitation of Inside Information: Some Empirical Evidence, *Journal of Business*; **58**, 69-87.

Glosten, Lawrence, and Lawrence Harris, 1988, Estimating the components of the bid/ask spread, *Journal of Financial Economics* **21**, 123-142.

Glosten, Lawrence and Paul Milgrom, 1985, Bid, ask and transaction prices in a specialist market with heterogeneously informed traders, *Journal of Financial Economics* **14**, 71-100.

Halpern, Paul, 1974, Empirical Estimates of the Amount and Distribution of Gains to Companies in Mergers, *Journal of Business* **47**, 410-428.

Harris, Lawrence, 1994, Minimum price variations, discrete bid-ask spreads, and quotation sizes, *Review of Financial Studies* **7**, 149-178.

Harris, Lawrence, 2001, Does a large minimum price variation encourage order exposure? Working paper, University of Southern California.

Hirschey, Mark, and Janis K.Zaima, 1989, Insider Trading, Ownership Structure, and the Market Assessment of Corporate Sell Offs, *Journal of Finance* **44**, 971-980.

Hirshleifer, Jack, 1974, The Private and Social Value of Information and the Reward to Inventive Activity, *American Economic Review* **61**, 561-574.

Jaffe, Jeffrey, 1974, Special Information and Insider Trading, *Journal of Business* **47**, 410-428.

John, Kose, and Larry Lang, 1991, Insider Trading around Dividend Announcements: Theory and Evidence, *Journal of Finance* **46**, 1361-89.

Keown, Arthur, and John Pinkerton, 1981, Merger Announcements and Insider Trading Activity: An Empirical Investigation, *Journal of Finance* **36**, 855-869.

Kyle, Albert, 1985, Continuous auctions and insider trading, *Econometrica* **53**, 1315-1335.

Lakonishok, Josef, and Inmoo Lee, 2001, Are insiders' trades informative? Forthcoming in the Review of Financial Studies

Lee, Charles, and Mark Ready, 1991, Inferring Trade Direction from Intraday Data, *Journal of Finance* **46**, 733-746.

Lee, Charles, Belinda Mucklow, and Mark Ready, 1993, Spreads, depths, and the impact of earnings information: An intraday analysis, *Review of Financial Studies* **6**, 345-374.

Leland, Hayne, 1992, Insider Trading: Should It Be Prohibited?, *Journal of Political Economy* **100**, 859-87.

Lin, Ji Chai and John Howe, 1990, Insider Trading in the OTC Market, *Journal of Finance* **45**, 1273-1284.

Madhavan, Ananth, Mathew Richardson, and Matthew Roomans, 1997, Why Do Security Prices Change? A Transaction-Level Analysis of NYSE Stocks, *Review of Financial Studies* **10**, 1035-64.

Mandelker, G., 1974, Risk and Return: The Case of Merging Firms, *Journal of Financial Economics* **1**, 303-335.

Manne, H.G., 1966, *Insider Trading and the Stock Market*. New York (1966).

Manove, Michael, 1989, The Harm from Insider Trading and Informed Speculation, Quarterly Journal of Economics 104, 823-845.

Meulbroek, Lisa, 1992, An Empirical Analysis of Illegal Insider Trading, *Journal of Finance* **47**, 1661-1699.

Meulbroek, Lisa, 2001, Does risk matter? Corporate insider transactions in internet-based firms, Working paper, Harvard University.

Michaely, Roni and Kent Wolmack, 1999, Conflict of interest and the credibility of underwriter analyst recommendations, *Review of Financial Studies* **12,** 653-686.

Noe, Christopher, 1999, Voluntary Disclosures and Insider Transactions, *Journal of Accounting and Economics* **27**, 305-326

Noe, Thomas, 1997, Insider Trading and the Problem of Corporate Agency, *Journal of Law, Economics, and Organization* **13**, 287-318.

Ofek, Eli and Matthew Richardson, 2001, The IPO lock-up period: Implications for market efficiency and downward sloping demand curves, Working paper, New York University.

Penman, Stephen, 1982, Insider Trading and the Dissemination of Firms' Forecast Information, *Journal of Business* **55**, 479-503.

Penman, Stephen, 1985, A Comparison of the Information Content of Insider Trading and Management Earnings Forecasts, *Journal of Financial and Quantitative Analysis* **20**, 1-17.

Seyhun, Nejat, 1988, The Information Content of Aggregate Insider Trading, *Journal of Business* **61**, 1-24.

Seyhun, Nejat, 1992, Why Does Aggregate Insider Trading Predict Future Stock Returns? *Quarterly Journal of Economics* **107**, 1303-1331.

Seyhun, Nejat, and Michael Bradley, 1997, Corporate Bankruptcy and Insider Trading, *Journal of Business* **70**, 189-216.

Venkatesh, P. and R. Chiang, 1986, Information asymmetry and the dealer's bid-ask spread: A case study of earnings and dividend announcements, *Journal of Finance* **41**, 1089-1102.

# INDEX

## A

acceptance, 196
access, x, 88, 92, 97, 229
accounting, 191, 212
accumulation, 30, 31, 32, 84, 95, 108
accuracy, 167, 179, 258
achievement, 5
actual output, 94
adjustable peg, 62, 64
adjustment, 23, 66, 84, 103, 107, 125, 126, 147, 192, 193, 194, 218
affect, vii, 6, 7, 9, 11, 15, 24, 64, 76, 141, 167, 173, 190, 215, 218, 226, 231, 233, 234
Afghanistan, 36
Africa, 30, 33, 36, 56, 58, 88, 114, 115
age, 127
agent, vii, 1, 2, 4, 23, 137
aggregate demand, 11, 12, 66, 118
aggregate supply, 12
aggregates, 91
aggregation, 182
agriculture, 31, 90, 114
Albania, 36, 130
Algeria, 36, 63
algorithm, vii, 29, 30, 34, 35, 36, 37, 53, 54, 115, 144, 145, 148, 150, 162, 176, 186
alternative, ix, 21, 24, 64, 67, 91, 98, 101, 102, 106, 109, 111, 112, 113, 120, 121, 123, 124, 125, 135, 140, 144, 145, 147, 150, 171, 172, 182, 187, 188, 190, 193, 195, 198, 203, 204, 205, 230, 248, 252, 255
alternatives, 4, 7, 16, 172, 181, 182
alters, 107
ambiguity, 10, 233
Angola, 36
arbitrage, 170, 187, 190, 191, 192, 200, 201
Argentina, 36, 62, 64, 65, 66, 82, 83
argument, 5, 6, 10, 74, 127, 191, 225, 231
Armenia, 36, 130, 131
arrow of time, 163
Asia, 154
Asian countries, 136, 154
Asian crisis, 62, 65, 82
assessment, 201
assets, 80, 88, 212, 213, 217, 218, 219, 220, 221, 222, 223, 224, 225, 226
assignment, 107
association, 5, 113
assumptions, 2, 3, 15, 16, 21, 189, 196, 219, 233, 256
asymmetric information, x, 7, 229, 230, 232, 233, 248, 249, 250, 252, 254, 255, 256, 257
asymmetry, x, 158, 170, 193, 229, 230, 231, 234, 245, 252, 254, 256, 257, 260
attacks, 65, 67
attention, 13, 90, 91, 108, 118, 145, 192, 250, 254
attractiveness, 62, 113, 114
Australia, 36, 63, 155
Austria, 36, 210
authority, 11, 13, 15, 63, 64, 68, 69, 98, 99, 128, 130, 193, 216
averaging, 168
Azerbaijan, 36, 130, 131

## B

backlash, 216
Bahrain, 36
bail, 66, 68
balance of payments, 69, 107
balance sheet, 67, 82, 90, 95, 98, 114, 212
Bangladesh, 36
bank ownership, 209, 210, 213, 222
banking, 66, 70, 71, 88, 207, 211, 212, 216, 226, 227, 228

banks, ix, 66, 70, 88, 107, 209, 210, 211, 212, 214, 215, 216, 217, 223, 226, 227, 228
Barbados, 36
bargaining, 5, 6, 7, 8, 9, 10, 11, 12, 13, 14, 15, 16, 17, 18, 21, 22
barriers, viii, 30, 31, 32, 33, 35, 52, 53, 69
barter, 94
basis points, 203, 234
behavior, viii, x, 2, 3, 8, 13, 47, 62, 87, 91, 98, 100, 101, 114, 158, 169, 176, 201, 209, 217, 226, 227, 228
Belarus, 36, 130, 131
bias, 15, 16, 72, 80, 88, 102, 144, 147, 155
BIS, 198
blocks, 254
body, x, 9, 91, 229, 231
Bolivia, 36, 64
bond market, 108
bonds, ix, 66, 80, 91, 92, 93, 97, 98, 107, 157, 170
borrowing, 68, 69, 84, 88, 97, 99
Brazil, 36, 59, 62, 63, 82, 84
broad money, 125, 131
budget surplus, 81
building societies, 228
Bulgaria, 36, 130
bureaucracy, 69
Burkina Faso, 36
business cycle, 4, 23, 190

## C

calibration, 100
Cambodia, 36
Cameroon, 36
Canada, 36, 63
candidates, 4, 5, 7, 125, 127, 233
capital account, 65, 69
capital accumulation, 30, 31
capital controls, 64, 65
capital flows, 62, 65, 66, 67, 90, 91, 118, 136
capital inflow, 66, 67, 68, 70, 100, 103, 108
capital markets, 62, 65, 82, 135, 257
capital mobility, 62, 65, 67, 82, 90, 107, 108, 120, 127
capital outflow, 108
Caribbean, 36
case study, 227, 260
cash flow, 217
causality, 7, 23, 39, 72, 75, 76, 77
CEE, 118, 125, 126, 129
central bank, vii, viii, 3, 4, 11, 13, 14, 15, 16, 17, 19, 23, 24, 61, 64, 87, 88, 90, 91, 95, 97, 98, 99, 102,

107, 108, 113, 114, 118, 120, 125, 188, 192, 193, 200, 201
Chad, 36
channels, 6, 41
chaos, ix, 157, 158, 159, 161, 162, 169, 173, 177, 182, 185, 186
Chile, 36, 63
China, 36, 37, 40, 117
classes, 5, 33, 53, 254
classification, ix, 36, 63, 88, 89, 117, 119, 120, 121, 123, 124, 125, 126, 129, 258
clients, 212, 216
closed economy, 11
clustering, vii, 29, 30, 34, 35, 36, 37, 38, 40, 45, 46, 142
clusters, vii, 29, 30, 33, 34, 35, 36, 52, 53
coefficient of variation, 218, 219, 220, 221, 222, 223, 225, 226
collaboration, 10
collateral, 66
collective bargaining, 11
Colombia, 36, 63
commercial bank, 70, 218, 226, 228
commitment, 62, 66, 68, 69, 90, 91, 98, 212
commodity, viii, 87, 90, 91, 93, 100, 101, 102, 106, 108, 109, 110, 112, 113, 114, 125, 126, 129, 131
Commonwealth of Independent States, 125, 130, 131
compensation, 252
competition, 2, 6, 8, 26, 53
competitiveness, 65, 66, 79, 126
complement, viii, 61, 155
complexity, 20, 24, 161
components, 100, 168, 169, 186, 190, 195, 231, 249, 258
composition, 36, 65, 210, 217, 218, 220, 221, 222, 225
concentration, 125, 126, 129, 131
conceptualization, 31
conditional mean, 138, 143, 144, 145, 155, 173, 178
conduct, viii, 61, 62, 63, 64, 68, 82, 118, 125, 170, 173, 176, 177, 235
confidence, 70, 71, 72, 73, 74, 75, 76, 78, 79, 125
confidence interval, 72, 74, 76, 78, 79
configuration, 53
conflict, 5, 6
confusion, 13
conjecture, 179
consensus, 9, 10, 62, 70
consolidation, 66
construction, 124, 190
consumption, 70, 91, 92, 93, 94, 96, 100, 101, 103, 107, 109, 112, 113

context, vii, 1, 2, 7, 8, 9, 10, 20, 24, 32, 107, 139, 141, 154, 177

continuity, 39, 162, 165, 168, 216, 220

control, 11, 14, 20, 65, 71, 125, 176, 215, 216, 222, 223, 225, 226, 228, 231, 239, 247

convergence, vii, viii, 4, 29, 30, 31, 32, 33, 34, 35, 36, 37, 38, 39, 40, 41, 42, 44, 45, 46, 47, 50, 51, 52, 53, 55, 150

conversion, 210, 215

correlation, 41, 100, 135, 137, 158, 160, 161, 162, 163, 171, 172, 177, 180, 182, 185, 186, 196, 221, 223, 226

corruption, 7

Costa Rica, 64

costs, x, 23, 64, 65, 67, 83, 228, 229, 230, 231, 232, 234, 238, 244, 245, 248, 249, 250, 252, 255, 257

coverage, 35, 216

covering, 30

crawling peg, 64, 65, 70, 90, 124, 130

credibility, 63, 64, 65, 66, 68, 69, 70, 71, 84, 118, 125, 130, 259

credit, 98, 99, 102, 212, 216, 227

creditors, 81

critical value, 199, 200, 201

Croatia, 130

CTA, 225

currency, viii, ix, 61, 62, 63, 64, 65, 66, 67, 68, 69, 70, 73, 78, 80, 82, 84, 88, 89, 91, 92, 93, 97, 98, 100, 101, 103, 107, 108, 113, 117, 118, 119, 124, 125, 127, 129, 130, 136, 149

current account, 64, 70, 79, 80, 82, 95, 96, 104, 105, 107, 114

current account deficit, 64, 70, 79, 80, 82

current prices, 131

cycles, 54, 139

Cyprus, 36

Czech Republic, 36, 130

**D**

data analysis, ix, 157, 158, 159, 169, 178, 180, 181, 182

data set, 169, 193

database, 198, 235, 241, 246

debt, 64, 65, 66, 67, 68, 80, 81, 82, 84, 88, 90, 95, 136, 149

debt service, 88

decisions, 5, 10, 124, 128, 216, 217, 225

decomposition, 158, 189, 245, 248, 250

decreasing returns, 30, 31

deficit, 97, 98, 100, 107, 131

definition, 10, 21, 32, 33, 46, 53, 139, 160, 163, 196, 233, 243

delivery, 235

demand, 9, 10, 11, 12, 15, 63, 64, 68, 70, 73, 90, 93, 94, 97, 103, 118, 125, 214, 252, 259

demand curve, 259

Denmark, 6, 10, 36, 210

dependent variable, 35, 124, 137, 138, 221, 223, 225, 246, 247

deposits, 80, 98, 212, 213, 216

depreciation, 66, 67, 68, 70, 77, 79, 80, 88, 92, 102, 103, 104, 105, 217, 218, 220, 223, 225, 226

deregulation, 136, 145

derivatives, 141

desire, viii, 15, 87, 89, 101

destruction, 31

detection, ix, 157, 186

determinism, ix, 157, 161, 163, 165, 186

devaluation, viii, 61, 65

developed countries, vii, 5, 7, 29, 31, 33, 34, 36, 52, 136

developed nations, 64

deviation, 72, 109, 170, 176, 199, 219, 239, 252, 253

differentiation, 16

diffusion, 31

dimensionality, 108

discipline, 65, 67, 128, 130, 215, 216

disclosure, 232, 257

disequilibrium, viii, 20, 87, 88, 194

disinflation, 23, 70, 71

dispersion, 38, 214, 216

disposable income, 109

disposition, 113

distortions, 67

distribution, 2, 4, 5, 6, 31, 33, 34, 36, 41, 42, 47, 52, 56, 84, 122, 123, 139, 140, 141, 143, 145, 167, 172, 180, 199, 219, 242, 245, 251, 255, 256

distribution of income, 36, 41, 52

divergence, vii, viii, 29, 30, 31, 32, 33, 34, 35, 39, 41, 42, 44, 45, 46, 47, 51, 52, 53

diversification, 129, 221, 223

diversity, 119

dollarization, 62, 63, 65, 66, 67, 68, 69, 83, 118

domain, 19, 159

domestic credit, 99, 102, 107, 108

domestic demand, 66

domestic economy, 7, 67, 91

domestic markets, 69

Dominican Republic, 36

duration, 14, 194, 196, 256

**E**

earnings, 110, 226, 233, 234, 237, 238, 259, 260

East Asia, 36

Eastern Europe, 118, 130
economic crisis, 9
economic development, 69, 125, 126
economic efficiency, 225
economic growth, viii, 29, 30, 31, 32, 34, 39, 40, 44,
    53, 54, 56, 61, 190
economic indicator, 44
economic institutions, 33
economic performance, 4, 18, 19, 20, 21, 22, 24, 26,
    33, 62
economic policy, 3, 9
economic problem, 64
economic theory, 2, 6, 157
economics, vii, 53, 85, 115, 158
Ecuador, 36, 64
effective exchange rate, 79
Egypt, 36
El Salvador, 36, 64
elasticity, 12, 15, 91, 100, 108, 230, 255
elasticity of demand, 230, 255
election, 4, 13, 216
emergence, 6, 9, 68
emerging markets, 61, 66, 68, 69, 83
employees, 8, 210, 212, 213, 214, 215, 217, 219,
    220, 223, 225
employment, 1, 3, 4, 8, 9, 10, 11, 14, 15, 16, 17, 18,
    21, 94, 217
entrepreneurs, 66
entropy, 42, 165
equality, 18, 46, 47, 50
equilibrium, viii, 2, 14, 15, 29, 33, 46, 64, 65, 87, 89,
    99, 103, 187, 188, 193
equity, 227, 235, 236, 258
erosion, 70
estimating, ix, 141, 143, 144, 154, 157, 158, 162,
    201
Estonia, 36, 130
EU, 126, 130
Euro, 64
Europe, 25, 26, 27, 36
European Monetary System, 132
European Union, 68, 70
evidence, ix, 2, 4, 6, 8, 10, 30, 31, 33, 34, 39, 41, 42,
    46, 52, 64, 66, 68, 77, 82, 83, 85, 100, 109, 120,
    121, 122, 135, 154, 157, 158, 170, 176, 181, 182,
    191, 193, 197, 198, 199, 200, 211, 218, 226, 228,
    231, 232, 233, 234, 244, 247, 252, 253, 257
evolution, vii, ix, 29, 36, 42, 83, 117, 118, 119, 120,
    129, 137, 161, 169
exchange controls, 88
exchange rate, viii, ix, 61, 62, 63, 64, 65, 66, 67, 68,
    69, 70, 71, 72, 73, 74, 75, 76, 77, 78, 79, 80, 82,
    83, 84, 85, 87, 88, 89, 90, 91, 92, 94, 97, 98, 99,

102, 103, 104, 105, 106, 107, 108, 109, 112, 113,
    114, 115, 117, 118, 119, 120, 121, 122, 123, 125,
    126, 127, 128, 129, 130, 158
exchange rate policy, 72, 83, 114, 119
exchange rate target, 63, 64, 98
exclusion, 40
execution, 238
exercise, 5, 108, 147, 177
expectation, 2, 11, 170
export-led growth, 69
exports, 66, 90, 94, 109, 131
exposure, 88, 259
expression, 35, 193, 194, 195, 196
external financing, 67, 82
external shocks, 65, 67, 69, 90, 91, 96, 109
externalities, 9, 31

# F

failure, 191
family, 42, 158
fear, 62, 64, 88, 107, 114
feedback, 72, 75, 90, 191
Fiji, 36
finance, vii, ix, 66, 80, 82, 187, 188, 191, 192, 205,
    211, 239, 243
financial crisis, 66, 82, 145, 147, 149, 153, 154, 216
financial fragility, 68, 84
financial institutions, 66, 68, 210, 211
financial intermediaries, 211, 221
financial markets, 68, 70, 71, 114, 120, 136, 137,
    145, 154
financial stability, 69
financial support, 209
financial system, 154, 211
financing, 66, 88, 89, 97, 98, 100, 107, 108, 109,
    236, 243
Finland, 36
firms, x, 5, 6, 7, 8, 11, 88, 94, 211, 212, 215, 227,
    228, 229, 230, 231, 232, 233, 234, 235, 236, 237,
    239, 242, 243, 244, 245, 246, 247, 250, 251, 252,
    255, 256, 257, 259
fiscal deficit, 89, 95, 96, 99, 108, 127, 129
fiscal policy, 81, 97
fixed costs, 231, 248
fixed exchange rates, 64, 65, 68, 84, 90, 125, 130
flexibility, viii, 6, 9, 10, 62, 87, 88, 95, 102, 126, 145
flight, 80
float, 62, 63, 67, 69, 71, 72, 75, 77, 79, 80, 82, 83,
    85, 88, 90, 91, 101, 102, 103, 104, 105, 106, 107,
    108, 109, 110, 111, 112, 113, 126, 231, 250, 252
floating exchange rates, viii, 61, 85, 87, 89, 114
fluctuations, 62, 63, 90, 102, 107, 155

fluid, 186
FMA, 227
focusing, 193
forecasting, 142, 144, 147, 150, 155, 173, 177, 191, 198
foreign aid, 95, 101
foreign capital flows, 80
foreign exchange, viii, 61, 62, 67, 69, 71, 72, 73, 74, 77, 78, 80, 82, 87, 88, 90, 98, 99, 101, 102, 103, 106, 107, 108, 109, 110, 119, 184, 185
foreign exchange market, viii, 61, 62, 72, 77, 82, 102, 103, 107, 185
foreign investment, vii
fractal dimension, 158, 160, 161
France, 5, 6, 7, 9, 36, 183
freedom, 5, 122, 139, 140, 141, 143, 161, 199
full employment, 16, 21
fund transfers, 225

**G**

GDP, 9, 35, 79, 81, 94, 99, 100, 102, 104, 105, 109, 114, 125, 127, 128, 131, 190, 193, 205
generalization, 99, 142, 143
generation, 188
geography, 32, 53, 212
Georgia, 36, 130, 131
Germany, 7, 9, 36, 117, 191, 210
globalization, 62, 82
GNP, 80, 81
goals, 65, 225
gold, 125, 131
goods and services, 101
governance, x, 209, 210, 211, 212, 214, 215, 217, 218, 220, 221, 222, 223, 225, 227
government, viii, ix, x, 4, 5, 6, 7, 9, 10, 11, 12, 13, 14, 15, 16, 17, 19, 20, 21, 24, 62, 65, 68, 70, 71, 80, 81, 82, 87, 90, 91, 92, 95, 96, 97, 98, 99, 101, 107, 108, 112, 113, 125, 131, 198, 209, 211, 214, 215, 217, 219, 220, 223, 225, 226
government budget, 131
government securities, 95, 107, 108
grants, 100, 108
Great Britain, 210
Greece, 6, 10, 210
grouping, 109
groups, vii, viii, 1, 2, 29, 30, 32, 33, 34, 35, 36, 37, 38, 39, 40, 41, 42, 44, 45, 46, 47, 50, 51, 52, 53, 100, 131, 212, 216, 255
growth, vii, viii, x, 4, 7, 29, 30, 31, 32, 33, 34, 35, 36, 37, 38, 39, 41, 42, 44, 45, 46, 47, 51, 52, 53, 54, 55, 56, 57, 59, 61, 62, 63, 66, 69, 81, 84, 99, 102, 104, 105, 107, 108, 115, 190, 193, 229, 230, 233, 256
growth rate, vii, 29, 35, 37, 44, 45, 46, 47, 51, 52, 54, 55, 81, 104, 105, 108
Guatemala, 36
guidance, 118
guidelines, ix, 117, 118, 129
Guinea, 36
Guyana, 36

**H**

hands, 236
hard currency, 118
harmful effects, 62
health, 31, 35, 39, 40
hedging, 67, 236
heterogeneity, 125
heteroscedasticity, 155, 158, 177
heteroskedasticity, 40, 144, 155, 184
hip, 8
Honda, 155
Honduras, 36
Hong Kong, ix, 30, 36, 135, 136, 137, 145, 146, 148, 149, 150, 154
household sector, 92, 93, 95
human capital, 31, 32, 53, 56
human development, viii, 30, 34, 35, 39
Hungary, 130
hypothesis, ix, 3, 15, 30, 33, 44, 45, 46, 47, 52, 117, 118, 119, 120, 121, 122, 123, 129, 136, 137, 169, 171, 177, 178, 180, 181, 182, 198, 199, 200, 229, 245, 254, 257
hypothesis test, 169, 180, 182

**I**

ideas, 31
identification, 139, 147, 182, 188, 201
identification problem, 139
identity, 96
ideology, 6
IMF, ix, 57, 63, 70, 71, 81, 82, 83, 84, 89, 114, 115, 117, 119, 120, 129, 131, 132, 210
imitation, 39
implementation, 31, 32, 68, 69, 145
imports, 66, 70, 88, 91, 92, 113
in transition, 35, 119, 120, 121, 122, 123, 129
incentives, 10, 68, 211, 215, 216, 217
incidence, 237
inclusion, 41, 47, 204

income, vii, viii, 4, 6, 7, 9, 10, 29, 30, 31, 32, 33, 34,
    35, 36, 37, 38, 39, 40, 41, 42, 44, 45, 46, 47, 48,
    50, 51, 52, 53, 54, 55, 56, 57, 81, 87, 88, 89, 90,
    92, 97, 100, 101, 107, 113, 114, 218
income distribution, 4, 6, 30, 41
income inequality, vii, 29, 33, 42, 56
income smoothing, 218
income tax, 9
income transfers, 101
independence, 11, 88, 127, 141, 171
independent variable, 221, 223, 225
India, 36, 37
indication, 154, 247
indicators, 8, 22, 35, 119, 136, 142
indices, 79, 158
Indonesia, 36
industrial relations, 3, 8, 10, 22, 24
industrialized countries, 34
industry, 6, 8, 9, 79, 82, 227, 228
inelastic, 97
inequality, vii, 17, 29, 31, 42, 52, 53, 54
inertia, 182, 191
inferences, 243
infinite, 160, 162, 194
inflation, viii, ix, 1, 3, 4, 7, 8, 10, 11, 14, 15, 16, 17,
    18, 20, 21, 23, 24, 61, 62, 63, 64, 65, 68, 69, 70,
    71, 80, 82, 83, 84, 87, 88, 89, 90, 91, 92, 96, 97,
    98, 99, 100, 103, 104, 105, 107, 108, 109, 112,
    113, 114, 115, 118, 125, 128, 130, 131, 155, 184,
    187, 189, 190, 191, 192, 193, 199, 200, 201, 202,
    203, 205
inflation target, 63, 68, 69, 71, 80, 83, 90, 97, 98,
    113, 115, 191, 192
influence, 6, 7, 9, 11, 13, 20, 21, 22, 24, 73, 74, 76,
    77, 102, 118, 123, 124, 125, 126, 128, 129, 137,
    154, 211, 216, 225, 226
infrastructure, 68
initiation, 66
innovation, viii, 30, 31, 32, 33, 35, 110, 143, 191,
    193
input, 31
insight, 188
inspiration, 1
instability, 8, 21, 22, 88, 90, 190
institutional change, 62
institutions, vii, 2, 3, 5, 26, 33, 53, 64, 68, 210, 212,
    215, 216, 226
instruments, 2, 69, 97, 98, 125, 236
insurance, 91, 100, 102, 109, 112, 113, 216, 228
integration, 62, 65, 67, 69, 82, 135, 137, 148, 154,
    156
intent, 71
interaction, 2, 11, 20, 22, 72

interactions, ix, 2, 10, 24, 135, 136
Inter-American Development Bank, 58
interest, vii, viii, ix, 2, 7, 10, 61, 63, 67, 69, 70, 71,
    72, 73, 74, 75, 76, 77, 78, 79, 80, 81, 82, 84, 90,
    91, 92, 95, 98, 99, 103, 104, 105, 108, 109, 112,
    113, 114, 157, 158, 170, 171, 173, 176, 179, 180,
    182, 187, 188, 190, 191, 192, 193, 194, 195, 196,
    197, 200, 205, 211, 216, 259
interest groups, 2, 10
interest rates, viii, ix, 61, 63, 67, 70, 71, 72, 78, 80,
    82, 84, 90, 112, 114, 158, 170, 173, 176, 180, 182,
    187, 191, 192, 193, 196, 197
International Monetary Fund, 119, 132, 210
international trade, vii, 126
internet, 259
interpretation, viii, 6, 13, 20, 21, 24, 39, 87, 89, 148,
    257
interrelations, 2, 3, 7, 25, 136
intervention, viii, 63, 69, 77, 87, 88, 90, 91, 98, 99,
    101, 102, 103, 106, 107, 108, 109, 113, 114, 119
intuition, 139
invariants, 158, 160, 165
investment, 216, 217
investors, x, 66, 67, 68, 70, 194, 229, 230, 232, 233,
    256, 258
IPO, x, 229, 230, 231, 232, 233, 235, 236, 241, 242,
    250, 251, 254, 256, 258, 259
Iran, 36
Iraq, 36
Ireland, 9, 210
Israel, 64
Italy, 5, 7, 9, 36, 135, 210

## J

Jamaica, 36
Japan, ix, 25, 36, 63, 135, 136, 137, 145, 147, 148,
    149, 150, 154, 184
jobs, 6
Jordan, 36, 258
justification, 4, 190

## K

Kazakhstan, 130, 131
Keynesian, 115, 192
knowledge, 31, 53, 159, 182, 211, 234, 256
Korea, ix, 30, 36, 135, 136, 137, 145, 146, 147, 148,
    149, 153, 154
Kuwait, 36

**L**

labor, vii, 1, 3, 4, 5, 6, 7, 8, 9, 10, 11, 12, 20, 21, 22, 24, 26, 65, 90, 227, 250
labor force, 90
labor markets, vii, 1, 4, 6, 26
labor movements, 7
language, 53
Laos, 36
Latin America, 30, 34, 36, 37, 58, 63, 83, 84, 216
Latvia, 36, 130
laws, 159, 185, 214, 215, 231, 233, 234, 257
lead, vii, 1, 7, 22, 24, 31, 39, 46, 53, 62, 65, 67, 69, 82, 122, 147, 162, 171, 191, 216, 217
leadership, 5, 136, 137, 147, 148, 154
learning, 90, 178, 179
Lebanon, 36
legislation, 4, 6, 9, 10, 212, 217, 221, 223, 225
lending, 66, 68, 81, 211
liability, 63, 65, 66, 67, 69
liberalization, 69, 147, 150, 154
Liberia, 36
life expectancy, 30, 33, 34, 35, 36, 37, 38, 39, 40, 41, 42, 44, 45, 46, 47, 51, 52, 54
likelihood, 75, 76, 118, 121, 122, 124, 127, 128, 195, 198, 200, 203, 204
limitation, 2, 138, 216
linear dependence, 172
linear model, ix, 99, 137, 139, 157, 158, 172, 173, 178, 179, 180, 181, 182
links, 6, 7, 150, 154
liquidity, x, 70, 91, 94, 97, 108, 194, 196, 229, 230, 231, 232, 233, 234, 239, 245, 247, 250, 256, 257
Lithuania, 36, 130
loans, 211, 212, 213, 227, 228
local government, 65, 214
location, 41, 163
long run, 30, 63, 102, 120
lying, 34, 53, 119, 162, 164, 165

**M**

Macedonia, 130
macroeconomic management, 114
macroeconomic models, 202
macroeconomic policies, 63
macroeconomic policy, 4
macroeconomics, 188
Malaysia, ix, 36, 64, 65, 135, 136, 137, 145, 148, 149, 150, 153, 154
management, vii, 1, 2, 3, 11, 22, 23, 62, 83, 98, 118, 125, 215, 216

manufacturing, 9, 31, 79, 82, 189
mapping, 159, 160, 163
market, vii, ix, x, 3, 4, 6, 8, 9, 10, 11, 12, 17, 20, 22, 24, 29, 33, 34, 40, 52, 53, 61, 62, 63, 64, 65, 66, 67, 68, 69, 70, 71, 72, 76, 80, 82, 83, 88, 89, 90, 95, 96, 98, 99, 102, 103, 108, 113, 118, 126, 135, 136, 137, 148, 150, 153, 154, 156, 158, 170, 210, 212, 215, 216, 217, 227, 228, 229, 230, 231, 233, 234, 236, 239, 242, 244, 245, 248, 250, 251, 252, 254, 255, 256, 257, 258, 259
market discipline, 215
market economy, 67, 68
market failure, 33, 53
market share, 212
market structure, 4, 8, 20, 24
markets, 19, 53, 66, 67, 68, 70, 80, 103, 136, 137, 212
Marx, 5
mass, 123
mathematics, 185, 186
matrix, 54, 96, 120, 121, 122, 123, 141, 163, 194, 201
Mauritania, 36
Mauritius, 36
meanings, 130
measurement, 159, 161, 189
measures, 6, 10, 12, 42, 65, 67, 124, 158, 161, 162, 217, 218, 220, 223, 225, 231, 238, 239, 241, 243, 244, 251, 252, 254, 255
median, 4, 218, 221, 231, 238, 241, 242, 243, 244, 245, 246, 250, 251, 252, 253, 254, 255, 256
mediation, 11
membership, 5, 13, 36, 41
memory, 158
mergers, 217, 227
methodological individualism, 6
methodology, 42, 120, 123, 202, 211
Mexico, 29, 36, 57, 77, 83
microeconomic theory, 8
microstructure, 230, 256
microstructure models, 230, 256
middle class, 4
Middle East, 36, 37
minimum price, 259
minority, 215
mobility, 58, 67
model specification, 155
modeling, 46, 52, 187, 188
models, viii, ix, x, 2, 4, 6, 15, 29, 31, 32, 33, 34, 41, 42, 44, 54, 115, 135, 136, 137, 138, 140, 141, 142, 143, 144, 145, 147, 148, 149, 150, 154, 155, 156, 158, 161, 180, 181, 187, 188, 190, 191, 193, 198, 202, 203, 204, 205, 223, 229, 233, 234, 246, 256

modules, 123
Moldova, 130, 131
monetary aggregates, 71, 88
monetary policy, vii, 1, 2, 3, 7, 11, 16, 23, 24, 62, 63,
    64, 65, 67, 68, 69, 83, 90, 91, 96, 98, 113, 114,
    115, 118, 119, 176, 191, 201
monetary policy instruments, 90, 113
monetary policy targets, 2
monetary union, 64, 88, 120
money, 9, 11, 12, 13, 68, 70, 88, 93, 97, 98, 101,
    102, 104, 105, 106, 107, 108, 114
money supply, 11, 12, 13
Mongolia, 36
monopolistic competition, 8
monopoly, 11, 16
Montenegro, 36
moral hazard, 59, 66, 68
Morocco, 36
mortality, 41
motivation, 150
movement, 128
mutual banks, 210, 215, 216
Myanmar, 36

OECD, 4, 8, 21, 22, 25, 26, 27, 31, 46, 210
oil, 34, 38, 70
open economy, 66
open market operations, 98
openness, 65, 69, 125, 126, 131
operator, 11, 194
opportunity costs, 15, 93, 94
optimization, 2, 115
organization, 7, 10, 210, 217, 226
organizations, 10, 210, 212, 215
orientation, 7, 15
originality, ix, 135, 137
outliers, 143, 144, 145, 147, 148, 149, 150, 154, 155,
    156
output, viii, ix, 11, 12, 14, 15, 16, 23, 31, 61, 62, 63,
    65, 66, 67, 69, 90, 94, 98, 99, 100, 104, 105, 107,
    109, 113, 187, 190, 191, 192, 193, 199, 200, 201,
    202, 203, 205
output gap, 100, 191, 192, 199, 200, 201, 202, 203
ownership, x, 209, 210, 211, 212, 214, 215, 216,
    217, 218, 219, 220, 221, 223, 225, 226, 227, 228,
    250
ownership structure, 212, 227, 228

## N

Nash equilibrium, 14
needs, 3, 10, 19, 64, 67, 68, 82
negative externality, 8
negative relation, 47, 231, 256
negotiation, 8, 9, 10, 11
Nepal, 36
Netherlands, 9, 27, 36
neural network, 158, 169
neural networks, 158, 169
Nicaragua, 36
Nigeria, 36
noise, 12, 35, 138, 142, 161, 164, 165, 166, 167, 168,
    169, 171, 177, 178, 180, 181, 182, 189
nonlinear dynamics, 170
North Africa, 36, 37
North America, 9
Norway, 36
novelty, 147
null hypothesis, 139, 140, 141, 144, 158, 169, 170,
    171, 172, 179, 180, 181, 199, 200, 201

## O

observations, 89, 103, 120, 130, 141, 147, 155, 156,
    159, 162, 164, 167, 169, 170, 172, 178, 179, 180,
    198, 219, 222, 224, 243, 246, 248

## P

Pacific, ix, 36, 135, 136, 137, 139, 141, 143, 145,
    147, 148, 149, 150, 151, 153, 154, 155, 156, 227
Pakistan, 36
Panama, 36, 64
parameter, 13, 16, 94, 98, 102, 104, 105, 106, 109,
    138, 144, 147, 148, 150, 190, 248, 249
parameter estimates, 248, 249
Pareto, vii, 1
partition, 36, 53
partnership, 10
per capita income, 30, 35, 40
permit, 177, 182, 232
perspective, 9, 31, 114, 230
Peru, 36
phase diagram, 38, 39
Philippines, 36
Phillips curve, 3, 23, 96, 115
physical sciences, 159
planning, 228
PNA, 94
Poland, 36, 130
polarization, 148
policy choice, 32, 97
policy makers, 69, 80, 118
policy reform, 9, 10
political ideologies, 3, 4
political instability, 70, 118

political participation, 217
political parties, 4, 5, 7, 21, 23, 24
politics, 5, 6
poor, viii, 8, 29, 33, 53, 100, 107, 158, 179, 230
population, 37, 47
portfolio, 89, 90, 91, 94, 98, 103, 107, 114
portfolios, 107
Portugal, 9, 36, 210
positive correlation, 74, 78, 80
positive relation, 211, 225
positive relationship, 211, 225
poverty, 53
poverty alleviation, 53
power, 5, 6, 7, 8, 9, 11, 12, 13, 14, 16, 17, 18, 19, 21,
   143, 147, 172, 185, 190, 193, 227, 246, 247, 251
predictability, ix, 157, 170, 180, 181, 182
prediction, ix, 20, 126, 129, 157, 158, 168, 169, 173,
   176, 178, 183, 184, 190, 217, 230, 255, 256
predictive accuracy, 204, 205
predictors, 168, 169, 178, 179, 182
preference, 3, 4, 7, 14, 16, 18, 19, 22, 65, 100, 126,
   127, 148, 226, 228
presidency, 176
pressure, 5, 80, 103
prevention, 83
price changes, 231, 233, 234, 247, 248, 256
price index, 92
price mechanism, 69
prices, 8, 34, 63, 64, 67, 68, 69, 70, 80, 89, 90, 94,
   99, 100, 102, 103, 104, 105, 106, 107, 108, 109,
   110, 112, 113, 114, 169, 191, 234, 243, 246, 249,
   257, 258
principle, 6, 98, 162
private banks, 211
private enterprises, 215
private ownership, 228
private sector, 2, 66, 68, 88, 98, 101, 108
privatization, 70, 211, 215, 228
probability, 4, 32, 120, 121, 123, 124, 126, 129, 137,
   138, 162, 163, 179, 180, 233, 252, 254, 255
production, 6, 12, 33, 53, 157, 199, 227, 257
production function, 157, 227
productive efficiency, 211
productivity, 31, 32, 79, 80, 82, 94, 227
productivity growth, 79
profitability, 211
profits, 217, 230, 233, 234
program, viii, 54, 61, 65, 66, 69, 70, 71, 81, 115
programming, 88, 185
proliferation, 163
property rights, 215
proposition, 16

public administration, 210, 211, 214, 215, 216, 217,
   219, 225, 226
public debt, 70, 78, 80
public employment, 11
public expenditures, 81
public finance, 125
public investment, 9
public sector, 10, 66, 69, 80, 88, 95, 113, 114, 211
Puerto Rico, 36
purchasing power, 35
purchasing power parity, 35
P-value, 51, 241, 242

## Q

quantitative technique, ix, 157

## R

rainfall, 100
random walk, 165, 176
range, 62, 63, 75, 76, 139, 196, 210, 215, 254
real wage, 8, 10, 11, 12, 15, 16
reality, 85, 90, 119
recall, 47
recession, 23, 90, 103, 109
recognition, 30, 53
reconcile, viii, 87, 89, 103
reconstruction, 159, 160, 161, 162, 168, 185
recurrence, ix, 157, 158, 163, 164, 165, 173, 176,
   182
redistribution, 10, 68
reduction, 13, 19, 88, 89, 97, 103, 107, 112, 164,
   204, 217, 220, 223, 226, 230, 233, 249, 250, 252,
   255
reforms, 4, 6, 32, 66, 69, 70, 81
regression, vii, 29, 34, 40, 41, 42, 44, 45, 46, 51, 52,
   139, 140, 141, 144, 155, 168, 169, 171, 190, 221,
   223, 225, 226, 245, 246, 248
regression analysis, 223, 226
regulation, 209, 218, 219, 220, 221, 223, 225, 227
regulations, x, 209, 210, 211, 212, 214, 215, 217,
   218, 221, 222, 226
rehabilitation, 207
rejection, 122, 158, 170, 172, 180, 181, 182, 196,
   217
relationship, 6, 7, 8, 12, 19, 21, 22, 24, 35, 36, 40,
   45, 114, 136, 191, 192, 193, 194, 195, 200, 225,
   226
relationships, ix, 2, 3, 4, 7, 20, 22, 23, 34, 136, 137,
   147, 148, 149, 154, 157, 187, 191, 193, 195, 205
relative prices, 94, 101, 125, 126

relaxation, 115
relevance, ix, 9, 20, 90, 117, 120, 121, 129
Republicans, 3, 4
reserves, 70, 95, 98, 101, 102, 103, 104, 105, 107, 112, 119, 125, 127, 130, 131, 217, 220, 223, 225, 226
residuals, 141, 143, 144, 147, 148, 149, 150, 172, 173
resolution, 84, 115
resource allocation, 211
resources, 53, 216, 234
retail, 228
retrieval, 237
returns, ix, 37, 90, 135, 137, 147, 148, 149, 150, 153, 236, 237, 246, 248
revenue, 96, 97, 114, 211
rights, 216, 228
risk, ix, x, 4, 66, 67, 68, 70, 80, 82, 125, 194, 196, 209, 210, 211, 212, 216, 217, 218, 219, 220, 221, 222, 223, 224, 225, 226, 227, 228, 259
risk management, 212, 228
risk-taking, 209, 210, 216, 218, 227
robustness, 113, 244, 250
Romania, 36, 130
Russia, 62, 82, 130, 131
Rwanda, 36

## S

safety, 9
sales, x, 90, 98, 108, 229, 230, 231, 232, 233, 250, 251, 252, 256
sample, vii, ix, 29, 33, 35, 36, 40, 41, 47, 53, 54, 72, 75, 77, 120, 122, 129, 140, 143, 144, 145, 147, 149, 150, 154, 157, 163, 167, 170, 173, 177, 178, 179, 189, 190, 191, 193, 198, 199, 200, 218, 219, 230, 231, 233, 234, 235, 236, 237, 239, 241, 242, 243, 244, 246, 247, 248, 249, 250, 251, 252, 254, 255, 256, 257
sample mean, 235
satisfaction, 11
saturation, 162
Saudi Arabia, 36
savings, ix, x, 209, 210, 211, 212, 214, 215, 216, 217, 218, 219, 220, 221, 222, 223, 225, 226, 227, 228
savings banks, ix, x, 209, 210, 211, 212, 214, 215, 216, 217, 218, 219, 220, 221, 222, 223, 225, 226
scaling, 85, 162
scarcity, 242
school, 5
scores, 181
search, 231, 252

securities, 90, 258
security, 5, 9
self, 68, 138, 215, 218, 257
sensitivity, 30, 63, 114
Serbia, 36
series, viii, ix, 29, 30, 31, 32, 33, 71, 114, 135, 139, 141, 144, 145, 147, 149, 150, 153, 155, 158, 159, 161, 162, 163, 171, 172, 173, 180, 194, 195, 196, 199
services, 91, 94, 97, 108, 252
shape, 22, 23
shareholders, 231, 236, 250, 251
shares, 6, 100, 131, 230, 231, 232, 236, 239, 244, 245, 250, 251, 252, 254, 255, 256
shock, 12, 22, 72, 73, 74, 75, 76, 77, 78, 79, 81, 90, 102, 104, 105, 106, 107, 109, 110, 111, 112, 113, 189
short run, 66, 67
short-term interest rate, 192, 195
Sierra Leone, 36
sign, 11, 41, 45, 74, 178, 179, 193, 196, 219, 220, 225, 245, 247
signals, 80, 164
significance level, 75, 76, 129
similarity, 118, 169, 188
simulation, viii, 31, 87, 91, 115
Singapore, ix, 30, 36, 135, 136, 137, 145, 146, 148, 149, 150, 154
single market, 230
skewness, 243
smoothing, 107, 112, 138, 182, 198, 218
smoothness, 138
social class, 5
social group, vii, 1
social relations, 6, 12
social relationships, 12
social welfare, 2
software, 163, 173
solvency, 217, 225
Somalia, 36
South Asia, 36, 37
Southeast Asia, 216
Soviet Union, 118
Spain, ix, 36, 209, 210, 211, 212, 213, 215, 216, 217
specific knowledge, 257
speed, 194
spin, 216, 226
Sri Lanka, 36
stability, 53, 63, 66, 69, 118, 183, 202, 217, 226
stabilization, viii, ix, 61, 63, 65, 66, 67, 68, 69, 70, 71, 117, 118, 125, 127, 129
stages, 32, 71, 94
stakeholders, 217

standard deviation, 40, 45, 74, 78, 103, 106, 108, 110, 111, 112, 144, 172, 218, 219, 220, 222, 223, 224, 225, 246, 248
standard error, 141, 147, 148, 150, 201, 249
standards, viii, 87, 88, 212
state enterprises, 66
state intervention, 234
state-owned banks, 70
statistics, 34, 40, 53, 139, 141, 171, 176, 199, 205, 219, 235, 236, 241, 242, 245, 248, 251, 254, 255
steady-state growth, 33, 45, 47, 52, 99
stochastic model, 99, 172
stochastic processes, 170
stock, ix, 66, 67, 70, 80, 85, 112, 125, 127, 130, 135, 136, 137, 145, 147, 148, 149, 150, 153, 154, 158, 210, 211, 212, 215, 217, 227, 228, 233
stock exchange, 148
stock markets, 85, 137, 154
stock price, 136, 137, 145, 147, 148, 149, 150, 153, 158, 233
stock-owned banks, 210, 211, 212, 215, 217
strategies, 2, 6
strength, 8, 21
stress, 63, 67
stretching, 100
structural changes, 173, 176
structural reforms, 71
substitutes, 91
substitution, 16, 68, 85, 89, 91, 100, 107, 108, 113, 150
substitution effect, 91
Sudan, 36
superiority, 107, 113, 155, 169, 180, 182
supervision, 226
supply, 2, 15, 63, 66, 90, 94, 97, 100, 107, 114
supply shock, 15, 90, 100, 114
surplus, 81, 95, 107, 131
sustainability, 65, 80, 83, 125
Sweden, 36, 210
switching, 90, 103, 109, 137, 170, 193
Switzerland, 36, 210
symmetry, 53
systems, 10, 11, 21, 24, 61, 62, 63, 65, 88, 158, 185, 214, 216, 226

**T**

Taiwan, ix, 36, 135, 136, 137, 145, 149, 153, 154
Tajikistan, 36, 130, 131
Tanzania, viii, 36, 87, 90, 91, 99, 107, 108, 114
targets, 6, 14, 15, 70, 91, 98, 103
tax base, 66, 88
tax rates, 9

taxation, 11, 12, 97
technical assistance, 100
technical change, 227
technological change, 30, 31, 52
technology, 12, 31, 32, 33, 53, 54
test statistic, 122, 137, 171, 198, 199, 200, 246, 247
Thailand, 36
theoretical assumptions, 3
theory, vii, ix, 1, 2, 4, 6, 32, 33, 34, 54, 56, 84, 118, 156, 157, 158, 159, 170, 187, 188, 193, 199, 200, 201, 205, 215
threat, 217, 225
threats, 9
threshold, ix, 31, 135, 137, 138, 139, 144, 147, 148, 149, 150, 154, 158, 163, 193
thresholds, 137, 150
thrifts, 223, 225, 226, 227
time, ix, 3, 5, 8, 9, 12, 13, 22, 23, 35, 40, 41, 44, 45, 54, 62, 65, 66, 72, 74, 78, 90, 97, 98, 99, 102, 107, 108, 114, 120, 129, 137, 142, 144, 145, 154, 155, 156, 157, 158, 159, 160, 161, 162, 163, 164, 165, 166, 167, 168, 169, 171, 172, 173, 176, 177, 178, 179, 180, 181, 182, 183, 184, 186, 187, 188, 189, 190, 193, 194, 195, 201, 212, 217, 218, 220, 221, 222, 232, 233, 236, 239, 241, 243, 244, 245, 248, 249, 250, 253, 255, 257
time periods, 257
time series, ix, 137, 142, 155, 156, 157, 158, 159, 160, 161, 162, 163, 164, 165, 166, 167, 168, 169, 171, 172, 173, 176, 177, 178, 179, 180, 181, 183, 184, 186, 188, 193, 218, 232, 236, 239, 244, 249, 253
timing, 65, 233
Togo, 36
total factor productivity, 31
trade, x, 4, 63, 67, 69, 70, 79, 90, 91, 94, 96, 107, 125, 126, 129, 131, 229, 230, 231, 232, 233, 234, 242, 244, 245, 246, 247, 248, 250, 252, 254, 256, 257, 258
trade costs, 231
trade-off, 63
trading, x, 125, 128, 130, 131, 184, 229, 230, 231, 232, 233, 234, 235, 236, 237, 238, 239, 242, 244, 245, 246, 247, 248, 249, 250, 251, 252, 254, 255, 256, 257, 258, 259
trading partners, 125, 128, 130, 131
trajectory, 33, 44, 160, 169
transactions, 68, 108, 120, 231, 238, 239, 259
transformation, 5, 100
transition, ix, 32, 38, 39, 67, 69, 88, 117, 118, 120, 121, 122, 123, 125, 127, 129, 137, 138, 141, 148, 150, 155, 156, 167, 189

transition economies, ix, 67, 117, 118, 120, 122, 125, 127, 129

transitions, viii, 29, 32, 33, 35, 53, 122

transmission, 41

trend, 41, 42, 47, 51, 88, 114, 148, 149, 150, 153, 188, 196, 197, 199, 200, 221, 239

triggers, 176

Trinidad and Tobago, 36

turbulence, 186

Turkey, viii, 36, 61, 62, 63, 65, 66, 67, 68, 69, 70, 71, 73, 74, 75, 77, 78, 79, 80, 81, 82, 83, 84, 85

Turkmenistan, 36, 130, 131

# U

Ukraine, 36, 130, 131

uncertainty, 4, 125

unemployment, 3, 4, 7, 12, 15, 16, 17, 22, 23

unemployment rate, 23

unionism, 5, 6, 9

unions, vii, 1, 3, 4, 5, 6, 7, 8, 9, 10, 11, 12, 13, 14, 15, 16, 17, 18, 21, 24, 62

United Kingdom, 36, 63, 155

United Nations, 58

United States, 3, 4, 36, 56, 63, 205

Uruguay, 36

Uzbekistan, 130, 131

# V

validity, 141, 195, 196

values, 2, 14, 51, 94, 95, 96, 97, 98, 99, 100, 102, 106, 109, 114, 123, 127, 136, 138, 140, 143, 145, 147, 154, 170, 179, 220, 221, 223, 225, 239, 252, 253

variability, 91, 144

variable, 14, 20, 54, 72, 75, 77, 80, 123, 125, 126, 127, 128, 137, 138, 139, 147, 148, 150, 154, 172, 176, 188, 190, 210, 218, 221, 246, 247, 248

variables, ix, 2, 3, 22, 24, 35, 44, 54, 55, 72, 73, 74, 75, 76, 77, 78, 79, 91, 97, 99, 100, 103, 108, 110, 112, 113, 114, 115, 117, 118, 123, 124, 125, 127, 129, 135, 137, 138, 147, 148, 149, 150, 154, 157, 159, 188, 189, 190, 191, 193, 204, 218, 219, 221, 222, 223, 224, 225, 246, 247

variance, 33, 35, 42, 52, 141, 142, 143, 145, 155, 164, 165, 167, 172, 180, 182, 184, 189

variation, x, 23, 31, 172, 179, 192, 209, 217, 218, 220, 221, 223, 225, 226, 259

vector, ix, 54, 96, 100, 122, 123, 124, 143, 156, 187, 188, 190, 193, 194, 196, 200, 202, 204, 205

velocity, 12

Venezuela, 36

venture capital, 236

Vietnam, 36

volatility, viii, 22, 61, 62, 63, 64, 68, 69, 71, 72, 73, 74, 75, 76, 77, 78, 79, 82, 84, 85, 90, 94, 101, 103, 107, 108, 109, 112, 113, 114, 137, 142, 147, 150, 155, 158, 170, 173, 223, 231, 246, 247, 248, 256, 257

voters, 4

voting, 216

# W

wages, 6, 7, 8, 9, 11, 13, 66, 79

war, 191

wavelet, 158

weakness, 250, 255

wealth, 6, 37, 67, 92, 217, 228, 232, 234

wealth effects, 67, 228

welfare, 18, 107, 234

Western countries, 229

Western Europe, 26

words, 18, 23, 80, 108, 123, 196, 217

work, 8, 9, 35, 41, 83, 100, 113, 114, 154, 182, 187, 198, 217

workers, 4, 5, 6, 7, 8, 9, 11, 14, 18, 24

working hours, 9

World Bank, 35, 70, 83, 115

writing, 10

# Y

Yemen, 36

yield, 4, 92, 95, 148, 171, 172, 173, 174, 175, 176, 177, 180, 181, 182, 187, 188, 189, 190, 191, 193, 194, 195, 196, 197, 198, 199, 200, 201, 203, 205, 250

Yugoslavia, 36

# Z

Zimbabwe, 36, 88